T5-CFU-633

ATLANTIC STUDIES ON SOCIETY IN CHANGE

NO. 99

THE "JEWISH QUESTION" IN EUROPE
The Case of Hungary

Tamás Ungvári

Social Science Monographs, Boulder, Colorado
Atlantic Research and Publications, Inc.
Highland Lakes, New Jersey

Distributed by Columbia University Press, New York
2000

EAST EUROPEAN MONOGRAPHS, NO. DLVI

The publication of this volume was made possible by grants from
Soros Alapítvány [Soros Foundation], Budapest

Translated by Tamás Ungvári, Nóra Arató and Judit Zinner

ISBN 0-88033-454-1
Library of Congress Control Number 00-131493

Printed in the United States of America

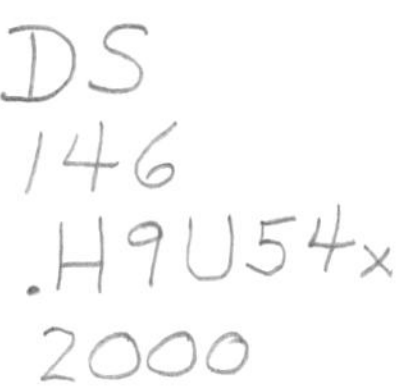

Table of Contents

Table of Contents....v
Preface to the Series and Acknowledgments....vii
Introduction....1
"From Ahasuerus to Shylock"
On the European History of the "Jewish Question. 9
The Liberal Pact of Assimilation....61
The "Jewish Question"
in the Shadow of the Trianon Peace Treaty....91
The Tragedy of the Pariah-Parvenu:
The Case of Szomory....147
The Lost Childhood:
Hungarian-Jewish Symbiosis....167
The Martyr and the Wandering Jew
Compensating Mechanisms Taboos, and Amnesia....185
Strategies of Assimilation....209
The Assimilated Jew and his Talents....231
Jewish Assimilation in Hungary and its Discontent....259
The New Face of Cultural Anti-Semitism....277
Biographies of Key Personalities....317
Selected Bibliography....337
Name Index....349
Geographical Index....357
Volumes Published in "Atlantic Studies on Society in Change"..359

Preface to the Series and Acknowledgments

The present volume is a component of a series that, when completed, will constitute a comprehensive survey of the many aspects of East Central European society.

The books in this series deal with peoples whose homelands lie between the Germans to the west, the Russians, Ukrainians and Belorussians to the east and north, and the Mediterranean and Adriatic seas to the south. They constitute a particular civilization, one that is at once an integral part of Europe, yet substantially different from the West. The area is characterized by a rich diversity of languages, religions and governments. The study of this complex area demands a multidisciplinary approach, and, accordingly, our contributors to the series represent several academic disciplines. They have been drawn from universities and other scholarly institutions in the United States and Western Europe, as well as East and Central Europe. The author of the present volume is a prominent Hungarian expert of his theme.

The editors of course, take full responsibility for ensuring the comprehensiveness, cohesion, internal balance, and scholarly quality of the series we have launched. We cheerfully accept this responsibility and intend this work to be neither justification nor condemnation of the policies, attitudes, and activities of any person involved. At the same time, because the contributors represent so many different disciplines, interpretations, and schools of thought, our policy in this, as in the past and future volumes, is to present their contributions without major modifications.

We would like to thank Professor Nathan Kravetz for his editorial work.

Ms. Andrea T. Kulcsár gave extensive help in arranging, refining, type-setting of the text, and preparing the appendices. I wish to express our gratitude to her.

Budapest, January 1, 2000

Béla K. Király
Editor in Chief

Introduction

The drama in which Jewish assimilation and later its reversal dissimilation, played their parts had many acts, the separate scenes of which would read liberalism, the emergence of the radical right, the rise of nationalism, and finally the Holocaust. The Jewish-Hungarian symbiosis has had its golden age of magisterial productions as well as its declining, resurging, and renascent periods. It played in a special milieu of the Austro-Hungarian Dual Monarchy, on the edge of Europe, in an empire in which there was no common language or shared national feeling. Here the Jewish presence had a special dynamic. Assimilation meant a process of social integration of a group of disenfranchised people who by gaining rights became the promoters of modernity. To be a Jew at the end of nineteenth century was to participate in a belated process of the Enlightenment. The Jew demonstrated what energies social mobility could conjure up, how members of a religious community strove for integration, taking up the "despised" functions of commerce and business.

The social ideal of this society was and remained the nobility. The more they lost real power, the more they occupied a virtual horizon of ideals. The attachment to dated concepts of social roles remained, and enforced the code of conduct in a certain Quixotism. The Jew appropriated functions left on the periphery. The deep irony of the historical development was that these "functions" were enterprise, intellectual curiosity, the advancement of learning and the emulation of "Western" concepts and goals.

The advanced placement of the Jews in East-Central Europe was due to the backwardness of the region. The Jew as an inspiring force of modernity was sooner or later recognized by the ruling elite who conceived emancipation and assimilation as a necessary compromise as if subletting functions to a group they were not willing to incorporate.

Granting the rights to this group as citizens was part of the Enlightenment project. Its primary mover was not the economic necessity to create uniformity in the nation state but to enhance communication and commerce. Ideas preceded reality in this case. As Max Nordau, one of the founding fathers of Zionism, suggested, emancipation was riding the horses of the French Revolution. Concepts of equality in citizens' rights were eminently applicable in states where demographic shifts decided the fates of nations. In the special case of Hungary the mobilizing force of nationalism was the politics of language. In the multi-ethnic Hapsburg empire being in the linguistic majority was to hold the entry ticket to political and national power. In the case of Hungary: their language was spoken by a minority in the Empire and they aspired to be a leading force in the region among Serbs and Croatians, Ruthenians and Rumanians. The incorporation of the Jews tilted the balance for Hungarians. The price of their assimilation was acculturation: to accept the language of the host nation.

Jews were eminently keeping their part of the pact. They identified themselves with the Hungarian cause, they participated on the Hungarian side in the revolt against Austria in 1848, and they took their fair share to promote the truce with Austria in the famous *Ausgleich* (Compromise) in 1867 establishing the dual Monarchy that made Hungary the second, quasi-independent part of the Empire.

The story of the emancipated Hungarian Jews did not differ very much from those who were incorporated in other nation-states. Except that the presence of Jews in public life was noted by the "host community" with condescension, irony, sometimes open hostility. The role the Jews played in modernizing the country blurred the frontlines. Was it the process of urbanization and industrialization against which exasperation mounted and thus by metonimic transference a group of people were resented who seemed to be easily identified with the course of events?

From the mid-nineteenth century the economic betterment of Hungary went equally with the conspicuous rise of Jews to prominence in the economy. It was only in 1840 that Jews in Hungary were allowed to settle in cities. At the end of the century the anti-Semitic mayor of Vienna called Budapest, capital of Hungary "Judapest," the city of Jews. How much of this was reality or a matter of perception is debatable. In the public theater the "Jewish Question" pulsated with drama, violent and passive, with vibrant battles, struggles, polemics, victories, and submissions. The "plot" of the drama of Gentile-Jewish relations in Hungary until 1919 showed similarities to the process of assimilation in other countries, especially in Germany. There were certain peculiarities to Hungarian Jewish history, but to claim uniqueness would be stretching the argument too far. The uniqueness unfolded in the twenty years history of independent Hungary, seceded from Austria, in becoming a sovereign state.

In the aftermath of the First World War the territory of Greater Hungary was severely truncated in the peace treaties. A large number of ethnic Hungarians became subjects of neighboring Czechoslovakia, Yugoslavia, Romania. The demographic shift transformed the fabric of a formerly multi-ethnic country. The only identifiable minority, or social group in Hungary that could be defined as alien were the Jews. The Jews who were disenfranchised from the moment when independent Hungary was born.

The assimilation of the Jews heretofore deemed the most successful in Europe was suddenly terminated by the first European legislation aimed against an ethnic-religious community, the so-called *numerus clausus* severely regulating the admission of students of Jewish extraction the admission to higher education.

One should not underestimate the symbolism of this legislation. It was directed against the learning of the Jew, the people of the book. Contemporary sources already had the full perception of the spiritual dimension of the law. It was challenged at international forums like the League of Nations. It was modified in 1927, and the enforcement of the legislature was as sloppy as were the bureaucracies in eastern European countries.

The damage inflicted upon the Jewish community was irreversible. It conjured up again the image of a pariah-people and revoked the silent pact of assimilation. The situation was aggravated by the fact that for Hungary the great war ended in the rule of the Republic of Councils, the communist off-shoot of the Bolshevik Revolution in Russia.

This was, however, the longest-lasting communist enterprise in Europe at the end of the war. The legitimization of independent Hungary came from defeating the chimera of communism, a venture identified in the ideology of counter-revolution as "Jewish rule."

Seventeen of the thirty commissars of the communist experiment were of Jewish extraction. In the eyes of their detractors this fact was unassailable proof of all the anti-Semitic fantasies about the world conspiracy of Jews, of their assumed radical temper, cosmopolitanism, and footlessness. The bloodthirsty "Lenin-boys" were accused just short of ritual murder.

The Bolshevik revolution shattered the Jewish community in Hungary as much as did the openly anti-Semitic counter-revolution. Defense strategies were worked out, a majority of them in vain. The "Jewish Question" dominated the discourse in Hungary between the two world wars, more hopelessly so than in Germany or in the successor-states of the Austro-Hungarian Monarchy.

My book deals with the uniqueness of the "Jewish Question" in Hungary. Comparing it to the European history of the "question," there is here a distinct chapter of a nation-state, with a large number of Jews in Europe, which was dealing in a paradigmatic way with an ethnic-religious minority first admitted then disenfranchised.

Sixty-nine percent of the Hungarian Jewish population perished in the Holocaust. It was, however, no miracle that in today's Europe the largest Jewish community is the Hungarian. My book addresses the reason by outlining the special position of Jews in the Hapsburg empire, describing the acculturation of the Jews and the barriers to their integration, and demonstrating the decline of the relationship when Hungary entered the period of the Second World War and then became a part of the Soviet orbit. The rise and fall of the Hungarian Jew is closely tied to the cultural history of the "host" nation, but the Jewish drama had its independent acts of tragedy and comedy, satire and farce, laced with the stirrings and passions of hate, love, fear, imprisonment, exile, and death.

Out of this complex drama the resilience of the Hungarian Jew transpires. The root of this strength came from many sources. Hungary was at the crossroads of Jewish migration in the Habsburg Empire. In the nineteenth century it granted a charter to factions of the denomination, to the orthodox as well as to the reformed one. The linguistic isolation of the "Magyar" gave rise to a special culture of an "imaginary community" comprising descendents of diverse ethnicity unified by the special position of the language. In the commitment of building a modern Hungary a fair share was taken by the Jews, and the solution to the "Jewish Question" during the Second World War emerged as a suicidal action that ruined the economy and the mental balance of the country. The specter of having a Hungary without their Jews haunted some of the best gentiles.

The survival of a substantial number of Hungarian Jews due to their own resilience, heroism, and suffering was also partly due to certain historical facts: among the European nations the Hungarian Jewish Holocaust was the latest, owing to the hesitance in the implementation of the anti-Jewish legislation in the ruling elite. The wavering attitude of Admiral Horthy in giving in to German demands of the "final solution" testifies also to importance of the Jewish presence. To some sane minds Hungary was unimaginable without the cultural energy of the Jews.

This book is a testimony of the Jewish presence, a comprised guide to the efforts of assimilation, acculturation, integration or separation. To the reader with a certain knowledge of the East-Central European scene the names and events of the story will be familiar. There was no need for a glossary to the Hungarian edition of a more detailed version of this study that just recently appeared with the Publishing House of the Academy of Sciences. Here an appendix is needed to identify the historical actors, those glittering, powerful, and eventually diminishing movers among the dramatic personae. I trust that the chapters will reveal the arguments around the "Jewish Question" that were debated in the streets of Budapest, in the universities, in newspapers and journals, the names of which are so hard to pronounce for the English-speaking reader.

I hope that with the help of footnotes and appendices the text itself will intimate the grandeur of the drama of Hungarian Jews, illuminate the variety of commitments in their ranks, reveal the characters of their enemies, clarify their motivations and express the vulnerability of the "defendants" of the "Jewish Question."

A debt of personal order is due here to the editor of the book, Professor Nathan Kravetz, who scrutinized the manuscript with the sharp eye of a scholar and writer. My gratitude is extended to the Rosenthal Institute of Holocaust Studies of the City University of New York for the grant of the O. & J. Winter fellowship and personally to Professor Randolph L. Braham. It was the encouragement and trust of Professor Béla K. Király that made this book possible with the help of Andrea Tevely.

This work was written partly in Hungarian translated by faithful hands and partly in English by the author. Locations of labor varied, and attachments were flashed over the oceans so becoming to *Atlantic Research and Publications* to which I am proud to serve as vice-president.

The year 2000, Budapest-Los Angeles.

"From Ahasuerus to Shylock"
On the European History of the "Jewish Question"

Emancipation and Political System

The Jewish question is an historical concept used to describe the situation of Jews in European societies changing as each country's social image and social interpretation of the "Jew" changes. The idea became a "question" during the time of the emancipation and social integration of the Jews. Prior to emancipation there had not existed a "Jewish question" because political powers dealt with the issue of Jewish migration or settlement without turning it into a "question." At the time of emancipation, various debates about the "question" arose with alternative responses considered: Would the Jews be truly emancipated or would they be forced back into a pariah status?[1]

The term "Jewish question" has always had embedded in it a connotation of a "contrary opinion." Protestors against integration struggled with a number of religious, social, moral, and political arguments against the naturalization and emancipation of the "eternal Jew" in the face of the momentum of the Enlightenment. It was in the 1820s that the Jews became a "question," raised mostly by those demanding complete assimilation. It was debatable whether the Jews were a hidden political nation retaining its cultural autonomy by means of religious isolation and debatable whether its expulsion could be an alternative to its total integration.[2]

An anonymous German author posed the choice in the following way: either we profit from the full admission of Jews into society or we decide to drive them out.[3] Then he proceeded to modify his view slightly by saying that expulsion would not conform to the politics of the time and, therefore, it was more reasonable to fully admit the Jews into society according to the principles of the current political system.

Solving the Jewish Question via the political system inspired the Prussian government official, Christian Wilhelm von Dohm's pamphlet "On Improving the Civil Rights of the Jews" which argued for emancipation and which attracted attention all over Europe.[4] The original text mentioned *bürgerliche verbesserung,* that is civic improvement. Dohm discussed with the Jewish religious reformer Mendelssohn his own petition to clarify the Jews' situation in Alsace-Lorraine. Both in its origin and in spirit, the petition retained the contractual character of Jewish emancipation, based on mutual understanding.[5]

The contract was undeclared and informal, and understandably so. The state offered emancipation while the law secured its terms. In this way, the "question" was referred to the sphere of the civil society, an uncontrolled area of group dynamics and informal bargains. The "civic" nature of emancipation aimed at establishing the individual's freedom of movement.

In Dohm's view emancipation of the Jews was the state's task.[6] So far, European governments had been unable to decrease the friction among the religious communities and unable to generate patriotic feelings in the masses in order to destroy religious prejudices. Therefore, in the spirit of Enlightenment Dohm offered a program to the nation-state: in order to establish a proper government, the adjustment of seemingly mutually exclusive principles was needed.[7] Dohm daringly declared that a Jew was first a human being and then a Jew. This was a new anthropology of the political system, inferring civil equality from universal natural laws.[8]

In the processes of the European Enlightenment, social and legal emancipation became the touchstone of development for the new nation-state. Emancipation surpassed the older politics of tolerance as represented by the Austrian Joseph II.[9] The world of faculties, orders, guilds, and bodies was being reformed by the standardizing effort of the modern state, where—as Dohm stated—religious differences were being overshadowed by the central government's interests.

Emancipation served the mutual interests of groups in society and assumed, although unstated, a contractual character. Obviously, the agreement could be offered by the state because it held a position of power while the Jewish communities were captives of both the ghettos and their own traditions. Thus, the decision to be made on choosing between nation or religion was forced onto them by the emancipation project. The Jewry considered themselves a traditional nation whose religion was "constitutive" of its identity. Further, in its dispersion, awaiting the Messiah kept its national self-awareness alive. On the other hand, the anthropological foundation of their distant ethnic character was preserved by their religious commands and requirements. There was always hope present in their spiritual home. Amidst the dissolution and birth of peoples and religions, the Jews preserved the ancient form of monotheism. In order to defend themselves against pagan polytheism, they had established a number of rituals. The more the existence of a particular Jewish community was threatened, the more seriously the members observed these rituals. The act of following the word of the law defined the intellectual horizon of Jewish monotheism. As Erich Kahler stated, "The fact that the Jews survived dispersed all over the world has been explained by the unparalleled unity of their strict and universally religious idea and by their physical insistence on rituals."[10]

For the Jews, "Jewishness" was not a "question" since the intellectual content of the religion answered "the question" with the doctrine of the "chosen people" on the one hand and in a belief in redemption on the other. And so, in facing modernity, European Jews embarked on a dialogue with fate because the notion of a choice of being Jewish or not was excluded by the spirituality of their religion and by its rituals. Both the presence of and the emancipation of the Jews comprised primarily a problem of their environment—in particular, a problem for those who felt compelled to decide whether the Jews were a people or an unreformed religious community. More exactly, the problem emerged at that point when emancipation exceeded the stages of traditional tolerance and experimented with the idea of complete equality before the law.

Emancipation related not only to the Jews. Instead, it referred to the abolition of mutual religious intolerance. Jacob Katz[11] was justified to point out John Locke's passage in "Letter about Religious Tolerance" that if we consider a human being a human being, neither pagans, Muslims, nor Jews can be excluded from the republic of civil rights.[12] The word *emancipation* fitted everyday experience and the legal language when the English Parliament debated the issue of political representation of Catholics. It also fitted the situation of the Jews.[13]

The pure idea of "emancipation" was problematic for Dohm's opponents. Arguing with him, H. E. G. Paulus proved that the Jews had already been emancipated by their medieval privileges (Schutzbürger). It created access to offices, and expanded freedom would not be emancipation in the original sense of the word. The neo-Hegelian philosopher, Bruno Bauer, developed a definition of "Jewish question" in one pamphlet. Bauer resented the fact that the phrase was now shining in the company of such great phrases as "Liberty" and "Human Rights," basking, as it were, in borrowed light.[14]

An exemplary figure of the Enlightenment, Moses Mendelssohn, argued that while there was the eternal validity of a divine revelation in the Jewish religion, the rituals were short-lived and it was necessary to renew them. A unique form of philosophical dialectics prevailed in his work, "Jerusalem." The Jewish belief was just as much a natural religion as Christianity, he argued.

Therefore it too could be understood by reason. As far as the rituals were concerned, they required tolerance only since they did not partake of the characteristic of a missionary religion, and did not contradict social laws of coexistence. Mendelssohn formulated the message "be a Jew in your home and a human being outside it" which was accepted by such philosophers of the Enlightenment as Lessing and his pen-pal Immanuel Kant.[15]

Although various European emancipation struggles tried to accommodate an outcast community, they did so at the expense of getting rid of the Jews as a community. During the French Revolution Clermont-Tonnerre, who was the first to profess the equality of the Jews, declared that "...we do not give them anything as a nation but will give them everything as individuals who want to become bourgeois."[16]

Clermont-Tonnerre and Mirabeau, who participated in the same discussion, emphasized that the Jews wanted to become bourgeois, and the "bourgeois"—in the context of the Enlightenment—was an individual who decided his own fate. A bourgeois who responded to the universal command of morality could render homage to different gods or follow any kind of ritual, but was still equal before the law. Neither Mirabeau nor Clermont-Tonnerre professed anti-Judaism. All each wanted was to eradicate those Jewish rituals from public life which were sectarian in nature or contrary to reason.[17]

The Enlightenment clearly defined the dilemma of emancipation: as a community, the Enlightenment project considered the Jewry a medieval remnant. As a religion, it considered Judaism as a historical phase predating Christianity. Finally, in its customs, it considered the Jews as barbarians. However, the Enlightenment offered the chance to modernize religion or a denomination, and offered the protection of civil law and order for individuals. It did not denigrate the religious community. Instead, it created a new community of "citizens." Only an individual could grow to become a citizen.

The Bipolar Model of Emancipation

Numerical figures demonstrate the success of emancipation. At the end of the 18th century, demographic data recorded two and a half million Jews in Europe. This number increased to nineteen and a half million by the end of the 19th century—the largest minority increase within the European population. Although Jews lived disproportionately in the Ottoman Empire, Northern Africa, and Europe, the success of integration was marked by the fact that eighty percent of the Jewry settled in developed countries, and—as Jacob Katz said—different German, French, and English Jews made their appearance.[18] And later, since these perpetual wanderers always recognized new opportunities, migration spread to the East.

The Jews were not the only group that ought to belong to the state and the political nation. Bavarian minister von der Pfordten, reflecting on the "tribal nature" of the Jews and the phenomenon where the "national state" was the most important promoter of the political state, wrote the following: "Nowadays our runaway imagination makes us believe that a state and a nation living in that state ought to be fully identical. History, however, refutes this idea. There is not a single state in Europe which would be based on a single nation and we have to interpret this fact in the context of European cultural development. A complete isolation of nationalities belongs to the infancy of statehood." And from this respect, the Jews was not an exception. "I cannot accept that there is no difference between a German and a Polish or a Bavarian and a Prussian Jew." If these differences did not disappear, it was because emancipation had not advanced far enough and because civil society had not fully implemented state measures into practice.[19]

The almost century-long march of emancipation released peculiar energies in the European Jews who had been limited in their social relations and were discriminated against in their legal status.

Emancipation was the social measure of the irresistible breakthrough of modernity. Through emancipation the Jew finally was included in history from his pre-social and pre-historical state. Jewish groups, professional circles, and individuals became actors in their given societies. Their milieu wrestled with the issue whether in terms of group dynamics a civil society emulated the state that only controlled the legal framework of community coexistence.

Emancipation was part of the disintegration and transformation of feudal society at a time when new ties and connections were formed. Therefore, even if it is true that emancipation was the legal measure of development, the new legal framework did not reflect the status of social prejudices. In the most developed capitalist state, England, the processes of acculturation and assimilation preceded legislation.[20]

The prolonged process immediately incited resistance in those opposing the Enlightenment project. The birth of nation-states broke down old walls and ravaged community relations, violated pre-existing interests, and created new winners and losers. A German author wrote in 1833 that not even baptismal water could free them from the Jews. Another one elaborated that the Jews was a peculiar part of the population, not similar to any other race since his characteristics were unchangeable and eternal under any climate and in any century. The Jews' fertility and mortality rates were different, they suffered from different diseases, and their moral and intellectual behaviors were also different from those of other peoples.[21]

Although with a different force, the whirlwind of history had also affected European Jews by the middle of the 19th century. Jewish communities, in touch with one another but with only temporary permission to reside where they were, were gradually gaining the protection of their civil rights. A great historian of the Jews, Simon Dubnow discovered a prevailing centrifugal force in the process of the Jewish emancipation. Their internal relationships had become loose and their integrating forces had been torn away by secularization. By opening several venues to individual success, the emancipation "offer" had torn certain representatives of the Jewry away from their roots and customs. Emancipation had already been preceded by a certain assimilation while, ironically, the demand to assimilate became the condition of emancipation.[22] Dubnow complained that the "young Jewish generations' had begun to adapt to the new European culture and the life styles of those nations now reviving around them."[23] To a certain degree, this adaptation was a beneficial and necessary development because in this way the Jew was able to emerge from his isolation and approach the surrounding Christian environment. However, this rapprochement was often immoderate and followed extreme excesses.

The question is whether the emancipation process could have been implemented without "excesses." In certain countries, the granting of various rights occurred in the form of government dictates such as Joseph II's edict of tolerance which rendered compulsory the teaching of Jewish children in secular schools.[24] This "dictated enlightenment" increased the tension between progressive and orthodox Jews with, mostly, the Galician orthodox Jews devising several clever plans on how to evade government orders.[25]

Dubnow and, in his stead, Raphael Mahler and Shmuel Ettinger outlined the so-called bipolar model of emancipation. Many individuals and groups were cast out from traditional Jewish communities during the emancipation process. A new type of Jew—socially adapted and modernized—appeared and matured to become a burgher/bourgeois who remained a Jew only in his memories at most. The centrifugal force of emancipation had caused this new type to drift far from his original community. At the same time, affected by forces opposing emancipation, a new centripetal force emerged which sought to pull back into their original communities those who had left. They searched for consolation in memories and in solidarity with the Jewish past and with the whole Diaspora. And, due to the halting process of modernization, they also tried to re-establish their broken contacts with their primary communities.[26]

The bipolar model of assimilation began with the fact that the emancipation contract was really not completely executable. As Dubnow delicately claimed, it would only prevail through excesses and detours. Note, however, that the terms had been set by the rights grantors. While the Jews could not be moved collectively into the details of a constitution, emancipation still won legal reforms of the Jews' unique conditions by demanding of them religious reforms, more relaxed rituals, and adaptation to the national culture. In the age when the idea of national identity was being created, dual identity would have been a difficult notion to comprehend. The reorganization or even the creation of national states did not favor such ambivalence as the retaining of an earlier "Jewishness" or the creating of an unambiguous character of a new French, English, German, or Hungarian Jew.[27]

In the center of the bipolar model, at the meeting point of centrifugal and centripetal forces, the idea of a "Jew" obviously changed. The foreign tribe, the pariah people who rejected accepting the national religion, could gain a new identity only by connecting to the European intellectual Enlightenment—by shedding, often voluntarily, their old identity.[28]

The "Ahasuerus" Idea of "Jewishness"

Up to the Eighteenth century the population of Europe considered the Jews as an ethnic and religious minority. Semantically, the "Jew" implied certain occupations and behaviors. As a swear-word it meant a merchant, a banker—a usurper. Even in the 1960s Isaac Deutscher complained that the Oxford Dictionary listed a secondary meaning of the word "Jew" as a blackmailer and a tough businessman.[29]

In the Nineteenth century, a new meaning for the word "Jew"—indicating religion—was added with the ideas of *Jewishness* and *Jewish mentality*. "Judaism" appeared in the vocabulary of the renewed Protestant theology—partly as a response to Jewish emancipation. Individuals originating from Jewish communities gradually acquired legal protection and, at the same time, Jewish communities gradually became mere religious denominations. Independent "Judaism" and the "Jewish mentality" established a new horizon over the religious and civic lives of Jews. An assumed "Jewish mentality" restrained and obfuscated Jewish acculturation and assimilation. The German Constantin Frantz's pamphlet published in 1844 newly paraphrased the legend of Ahasuerus. Frantz portrays Ahasuerus urging Jesus to hurry up walking towards the Golgotha as applying to every Jew. "*The Jewish people is itself the eternal Jew.* It ousted the Redeemer and was therefore scattered around the earth and cannot find peace anywhere. It wants to merge with other nations in order to contaminate these peoples but eventually is unable to do it. …" In another place Frantz wrote that "The Jewish people is the embodiment of Ahasuerus who cannot have peace—not even that of the grave—as it is unable to die. Truly, the myth of Ahasuerus was founded in reality."[30]

Nineteenth century Germany resurrected the Ahasuerus symbol. The Jewish Ahasuerus appeared as a counterpart to the new image of the bourgeois Jew and as a "different" cursed immortality—the circular motion as opposed to the linear one. The 'eternal Jew' was the opposite of the Christian *anima mundi* (world spirit). As Hans Mayer stated, "der ewige Jude ist eine durchaus unjüdische Gestalt;" that is, "the eternal Jew is fundamentally a non-Jewish phenomenon."[31] This is ironic not only because the historical Ahasuerus (in the books of Ezra and Esther) was a Persian king and an enemy of the Jews, but also because the new legend has the condemned Ahasuerus as a symbol of eternal return. As Siegfried Kracauer explained in the essay "Ahasuerus or the Puzzle of Time," Ahasuerus would be the only person to witness both creation and mortality in world history.[32]

The Ahasuerus motif appears in the second act of "Parsifal." It is evident from Wagner's anti-Semitic lines that he saw Ahasuerus as the negation of the world spirit and a principle negating the Christian ethos. "Judaism is the bad conscience of our civilization," he wrote in reference to Heine and commented on the radical steps necessary for assimilation to succeed. "Remember, there is only one way to free yourself from the weight of their curse: the Ahasuerusian redemption—that is destruction."[33] In Wagner's terms this meant that Judaism could redeem itself by a complete repudiation of its Jewishness and by becoming part of the modern western civilization through this act. As Wagner declared, such a redemption was not easy because it entailed immense suffering. The worth and loyalty of the Jews to the receiving community had to be proved a thousand times.[34]

Verjudung, or the fear of encroaching Judaization, was a special neologism of the time and was a Wagnerian invention.[35] Part of it was the notion that Ahasuerus as the spirit of counter-history was so strong that its contagion would weaken newly forming national cultures. Jewish emancipation held a very thin line between complete isolation and total integration. An anti-modernization ideology developed which tried to block the road to economic headway by the Jews, their one area of success outside of politics.

The French Count Gobineau, father of modern racial theory, openly identified the Jews with profiteering. Gobineau wrote that "The unbearableness of total tolerance" characterized the France of the Louis Philippe period. Gobineau revealed his motivation by saying that "the Semitic peoples essentially created the consumer society."[36] Gobineau argued that the Semites were a race with historically cursed characteristics. As long as they created a closed ethnic-cultural unit, they did not endanger their surrounding environment. However, in the Diaspora they became a disintegrating force.[37]

The Place of the Jew in the Anthropology of Enlightenment

The German Enlightenment discovered the outsider, the unredeemed, and the one not to be redeemed in the spirit of Ahasuerus. Kant and Herder viewed the Jews as a people, a tribe, and a "foreign nation" and, although they did not protest emancipation, they did assume a certain separation between the enlightened German nation and a Jewish community that adhered to pre-enlightenment customs.[38]

Beyond religion, the Jewish "mentality" represented some kind of "essence" of the "chosen people" and critical philosophy considered this mentality in the Jewish question. Similar to criticism from other religions, the new-Hegelians' religious criticism investigated the idea of "substance," "essence," and *Wesen* primarily on the "testing ground" of emancipation in Germany. It was Ludwig Feuerbach's *On the Essence of Christianity* that began the chain reaction that led to the infamous Bruno Bauer-Karl Marx debate.[39]

Hegel and, similar to several of his students, Feuerbach also accomplished a remarkable conjuring trick by elaborating on the dialectics of appearance and reality. Feuerbach hypostasized a new God-image and pointed out that rational foundations of belief could be discovered: "The consciousness of the infinite being is nothing else but a human being's consciousness about his own infinity ..."

The critique of religion, a phenomenon accompanying the unique experience of secularization, fixed the undivided status of state and church in its musings. Bruno Bauer debated Jewish emancipation on this basis.[40] A Jew could be a citizen with equal rights if he could abandon his religion since the Christian state could not offer protection to believers of an antagonistic belief.[41] In their isolation, the Jews could not participate in making history and, therefore, they are not a historical (or, as Marx later said, history forming) people. They do not want progress; indeed, they want conservation.[42]

Bruno Bauer knew well his master Hegel's views on Jews as a "non-historical" people. Hegel subjected Jewish political emancipation to the condition that the Jews not declare themselves a people and a nation but instead only a religious denomination. "Formal law … was against the Jews at the time when they were not given even civic rights. The assumption was not only that they view themselves as a different religious denomination, but also that they not view themselves as a foreign people. Noise created by this and other viewpoints, however, did not consider that they are first of all *human beings,* which is not an abstract quality. Rather, it entails that self-esteem is created by granted civic rights. People with rights count in a civic society and the balance of ideas and emotions originates from this infinite root which is free from everything else."[43]

However, Hegel himself viewed Jewish religion and history in the mirror of his own evolutionary theory.[44] The Jews used to play a role in the realization and success of the world spirit. However, in modernity, theirs remained a "ghost religion" without any substance and essence but as a collection of rituals which are bound to disappear and burn to ashes in the fire of history. Ahasuerus' people could find peace only in dissolution and their earthly course could come to completion only through disappearance.[45]

In their national backwardness many Germans envisioned an utopia of an ideal state where virtue was mediated by that state, whose course would inevitably advance, and which retained only a rational seed of any religion adverse to reason.[46] Kant, Hegel, and Marx were advocates of emancipation while they also viewed real Jewish communities with the contempt and disdain of prophets.[47] The Jews' stubborn monotheism, bound by traditions, did not seem to be reconcilable with the Cult of Reason. The rational philosophers metaphysically rationalized the Jews' social situation by saying that it was a tribal union between the God of the Jews and His believers, containing obsolete and cold ceremonies.[48]

As Feuerbach demonstrated by elevating a new notion of the human being beyond any controversial definitions, the Enlightenment worked out a new category of the human in opposition to any form of religious constraints. This new category was the discipline of anthropology. Hegel's comments about Jewish emancipation allude to this discipline, as did Herder who made equally controversial statements about the Jews. Herder's marginal remarks, at different points in time, are connected by the fact that his views elevated the abstract concept of "human" to be the paramount *substantive* category beyond any other. As Herder wrote, "What a huge topic it is to demonstrate that a human being does not have to be a Jew, an Arab, a pagan, a savage, a martyr, or a pilgrim in order to become what he wants to become."[49]

In this concept-building process the *universal* conquered the *particular* while the individual, that most particular notion, was raised to become the universal. Law was rendered to individuals. Instead of communities, it protected individuals because an "individuum" meant both an individual and its universality at the same time. It is not by mere chance that freedom's theologians such as Hegel, Bauer, and Herder were also representatives of critical theology.[50] They could vindicate the universality of reason against the universality of religion only through this criticism.

The idea of a universal human being, however, removed bipolarity, ambivalence, and duality only in appearance. It tried to systematize such notional (and practical) counterparts as pagan/religious, believer/heretic, and Christian/Jew by destroying the old system and forming a new one. Within the ideal type of a bourgeois state, these contradictinctions belonged within the orbit of individual decisions while public life created that "neutral" or "semi-neutral" sphere which Jacob Katz had perceived as the social pre-condition for emancipation.

A semi-neutral society meant that the legal obstacle to assimilation was removed and that the public sphere could view with indifference any Jewish social roles. Thus several layers of the public could freely practice real discrimination against individuals assumed to be Jewish. At the same time, the assimilation contract also meant that the contracting parties mutually kept their eyes closed over the real situation concerning occasional examples of discrimination.[51]

The triumph of this concept of human being and the abstract generality of law in European society resulted in a "semi-neutral" society as a matter of course. Secularization became one of its fundamental trends including the formation of a private sphere and the delegation of religious questions to the civic sphere, something which proved to be a controversial process. In a legally neutral field, this offered a free choice of ideas but also left untouched the survival of prejudices and pre-existing conditions. The state allotted only negative obligations to its citizens. These were, as early advocates of natural rights professed, *obligationes imperfectae*—imperfect obligations. Namely, the state would hinder any group or individual from violating others' rights.

Therefore emancipation was a legal contract with assimilation and integration as issues only "on the side." From that respect, emancipation relied upon the language of the "Bildung," upon the cohesive force of the language, and upon public morality. However, the "pacta sunt servanda"—the validity of the contracts—does not apply to the civilian sphere but only to the modern state. Instead, public contexts and civilian ethics decide such things.[52]

In states where civil society was more backward and feudal and a dispersed administration apparatus prevented the bourgeois state from achieving its centralizing ambitions, popular revolts and pogroms challenged emancipation goals. In England, where legislation was slow to stabilize the real situation, Jewish acculturation and integration preceded legal measures.[18]

The bourgeois state is the guardian of human rights and of the citizen's rights: it provides supervision for the citizen while committing some human relations to the civilian sphere. However, the assumed civilian spheres—the spheres of freedom of conscience and religion—were violated right from the beginning of the emancipation struggles. Prussian theologian Friedrich Schleiermacher wanted to endow the state with moral power as a remedy for the loss of religious influence. Fichte, for his part, saw the state as the embodiment of positive right and moral and economic power.[53]

Obviously, theories opposing the idea of a neutral state targeted minorities such as the Jews who could not gain any office and who had no political representation. Moreover, if the state had not created a "semi-neutral" environment providing for equality before the law, the state as the highest moral authority would have been unable to grant this equality.[54] Interestingly, it was the young Marx's famous pamphlet "On the Jewish Question" which defended the bourgeois state from the attacks of religious pietism with the theory about the *citoyen*'s heavenly and the citizen's "earthly" face.

According to Marx, the neutrality of the state was only appearance. The state is not a neutral organization striving to balance different interests. It is the embodiment of interests which dissect society into its constituent atoms in order to turn its citizens into goods.[55] Its neutrality is not founded on any social contract. The reality underlying this false equality was manifested by the fact that the modern state had created the principles of tribal Jewish characteristics. That is, the modern state was itself "essentially" Jewish—it embodied the spirit of extortion and usury.[56] Applying Hegel's *Wesenlogik*—and his substantive dialectics—Marx declared: "Since the Jew's real substance is generally realized in bourgeois society, bourgeois society could not convince the Jew about the non-reality of his religious essence which is itself nothing else but an ideal view of a practical necessity. It is not only in the five books of Moses and the Talmud but also in today's society that we find the essence of the Jew—not in abstraction but rather in empirical essence, and not in the limitedness of the Jew but rather in the Jewish limitedness of society."

The modern bourgeois state, said Marx incarnated the Jewish mentality. Emancipation had taken place by emancipating the whole society to itself (under its terms) and by deciding its norms. Therefore according to the dialectic conclusion: "The social emancipation of the Jew is the emancipation of the society from the Jew."[57]

With youthful zeal Marx revealed the Judaization of the modern world and developed the argument that became a frequent weapon for both left and right wing anti-Semitism.[58] *Verjudung,* that is fear of Judaization, assumed two things: an empty religion (money is the God of the Jews) and the efficacy of international power.[59] Economics subjugated politics to become its serf, as Marx analyzed. Marx considered Christianity a direct continuation of the Jewry because the Jews' "world God" of today agreed with the reality of Christianity; indeed, it expressed its essence. "The Jews emancipated themselves by Christians becoming Jews"[60]

Another major argument concerned the Jews' indifference towards art, history, and human beings and how this indifference indicated the money makers' real consciousness. Marx identified the Jews with plutocracy, thus revealing the Jew's "real self." He created a history for the extra-historical Jew by indicating that, thus far, marginal activities had now become central in a society of commodity producers. Through plutocracy, the spirit of a traditional community of Jews spread all over the world.[61]

Marx's pamphlet illustrated a number of anti-emancipation views and it illustrates the fact that political equality produced its own poison which then spread into a stream of anti-Semitism. It was not really the contradictions of emancipation but rather the controversial issues of cultural adaptation that Marx's arguments revealed. He emphasized features of assimilation which must have existed in embryonic form but which seemed insignificant to observers during the emancipation struggles. A key component for Marx was the reaction of the surrounding society to the "Great Transformation"—the dissolution of corporations and orders and the appearance of the individual. As several of Marx's analysts have pointed out, Marx warned about the interaction among the different interest groups that were fighting for possession of the state. In the process of feudal disintegration, there was a chance for a "foreign" prototype, the Jew, to influence the public atmosphere.[62]

During the course of the debate over the "Jewish question," the notion of what constituted "Jewishness" received several new features. The secondary semantic circle which identified Jewish stereotypes (profiteers, usurers, etc.) was darkened by adding the shadowy idea of the "spirit" or "essence" of Judaism. The voice of Jewish representatives was suppressed by demagogy which, for the first time in European history, connected the "Jewish question" with the "social question." By the end of the 19th century, anti-Semite people's tribune Otto Glagau declared, as a slogan, that the Jewish question was identical with the social question.[63]

The *Bildung*—the Ennoblement of the Jews

During the emancipation struggles, the question of whether the Jews were a religion or a nation kept coming up. Was the Jewry Chimera, a ghostlike nation, as Bauer and Marx claimed or a religion whose commandments were to be forgotten or relaxed in order for isolated Jewish communities to be gradually integrated into the modern nation-state? This prompted a further question: would *Bildung*—the program of education embracing the whole nation—be able to transform the Jews? Applying *Bildung* caused the Jewish question part of the task of civil society to form the new citizen's personality and character. The result was a personalized moral code that, at the same time, postulated a communal ethos. From this viewpoint Herder professed that *Bildung* ended human inequality of opportunity since it stressed bourgeois virtues against aristocratic privileges.[64] *Sittlichkeit,* that is virtue, became associated with the concept of *Bildung* and became the watchword of German minorities. The virtuous or moral road held out the promise of integration into the wider society.

Acculturation was an interim step between emancipation and assimilation. Introducing new customs into the traditional Jewish communities would create the chance for a social dialogue even without the Jews abandoning their religion. This was the reason why a part of the German Jewish community flew the *Bildung* flag; it was a cultural tool used to become a citizen. Rabbis spoke about the *Veredelung der Israeliten,* the Jews' ennoblement, to indicate that they had joined the secular religion of reason. "What else would be the meaning of virtue than to conquer our passions by our minds?" professed the *Sulamith,* the Jews' newspaper in Germany.[65]

The program of "Bildung," however, was a double-edged sword in the citizens' hands. On the one hand it raised the idea of bourgeois civilization and, on the other hand, it offered tools that could be used to discriminate and brand outsiders. The concept of "Veredelung" as ennoblement originated from the fact that people currently "ignoble" but expecting to be "ennobled" would remain outside the norms of civilization until the time of their ennoblement. According to Koselleck, ennoblement typically ought to be interpreted as a set of "asymmetrical" counterparts which would lead into a system of conditions whose fulfillment the "educator" would verify. Historically, the "educator" was embodied by the majority consensus which could have changed the conditions of the unspoken contract at any time according to the nation's assumed needs.

The Enlightenment believed in the backwardness and decay of specific peoples and nations. Its program focused on progress and the acquisition of a culture which would serve as a general "language" for communication within a nation. For the Enlightenment, the most important historical example of decay was that of the barbaric Jews, the people who spoke a foreign language. Several anti-Semitic entries in Voltaire's *Lexicon of Philosophy* maligned the unenlightened ancient religion, monotheism, which had paved the way for Christianity. But it was precisely the Age of Enlightenment which considered education to be the best medicine for society. "Let us change the Jews' education in order to change their hearts. It has been a long time since we kept repeating that they too are human beings. They are first human beings and only then Jews. … Jews were born with the same abilities as were we."[66] was Abbot Grègoire's last argument for the emancipation of the Jews.

A moral rebirth was the general program pushed by the Enlightenment. In Germany, Wolf and Schleiermacher developed a reform program for religion including such slogans as that "moral and political" improvement is both the condition and consequence of emancipation. The legal and political considerations of emancipation were obscured by the fact that assimilation was to occur within the lines of a nation's culture. From a historical perspective, it entailed the impossibility of assimilation. During the Enlightenment, the major authoritarian European states, in a loose union, molded a special blend of elements into a new type of political and cultural nation. As Isaiah Berlin said, the way nationalism and etatism entwined together resulted in nationalism entering into alliance with its "former sworn enemy," the forces trying to advance industrialization and modernization.[67] The emancipation movement explored the internal debate within etatism at the time when representatives of the majority and minority cultures voted for legal or cultural equality.

From Germany to the Carpathians, assimilation became the basic condition of emancipation. At this point we cannot elaborate on its far-reaching consequences. However, an amalgamation of legal and cultural spheres played decisive roles in developing the conditions of the Modern Age. At the end of the Nineteenth century, the historical misinterpretation that assumed the blending together of languages and races and created the "enemy typology" of "Semite and Asian" peoples also contributed to the Modern Age.[68]

On the other hand, various opinions and theories to prove the unreformability of the Jews also appeared. Opponents of emancipation argued that a nation could not be a member of another nation.[69] Even Bruno Bauer argued that, in order for a Jew to be ennobled into a human being, he should give up his religion and—hence the Marxian expression, *chimera*—his evanescent nationality.[70]

The asymmetry of the agreement also included an underlying rejection of the original community. More exactly, the original community was forced to resign from certain legal spheres. Mendelssohn was justified when he remarked that one of the conditions of integration was for the Jewish community to renounce its right of "damning."[71] Therefore, the program of *Bildung* imposed the cost of stricture by Jews towards their own community as a set price for the success and integration of the individual, since *Bildung* placed the community beyond state and cultural norms.

What is more, *Bildung* could also be interpreted as a "heavenly mirror" of the Jews' economic success. While developing a bourgeois mentality, the Jews had looked up to aristocratic ideals, hence their gravitation towards classicism. Dizzied by the dynamics of rising on the social ladder, the Jew, longing for middle class status, looked up to the nobility and tried to imitate its culture. There was only a quick passage between pariah and parvenu. Based on the eagerness of those involved, it might have seemed that cultural emancipation was nothing more than an attempt to legitimize financial and social success.[72]

The *Bildung* was two-faced both in its content and historical evolution. During the first phases of the Enlightenment, the *Bildung* connected education and self-education to virtue since only by enhancing the ability to ennoble the self did the man of Enlightenment reach a higher level of virtue. The secularization of morals was aimed against dogmatic religion while external dogmas were regulated by the individual's internally controlled development of concealed or dormant abilities. Establishing the ideology of secularization and individualization was the historic mission of the *Bildung* program. David Sorkin described the concentric logic of secularization as "The unity of human existence and essence was to be achieved by a self-induced process where a human being could be his own model."[73]

In the second phase of the Enlightenment the program of individual self-education conquered the traditional religion-based "virtue-fantasy" and then allied itself with a newly-born *aesthetic feeling*. *Taste* took over from *virtue* and moral education was replaced by artistic education. In German language areas, all this took place with the encouragement and help of the state.[74]

It would lead us too far astray to analyze the social role played by the development of state mentorship since the social groups had sworn onto the *Bildung* and the state bureaucracy tried to enhance its own role at the expense of the aristocracy and landowners. The "Bildung's" tendency to focus on virtue and the improvement of one's aesthetic sensibility originally served to enhance social dialogue and social mobility while also developing the basis for a new type of separation. For example, it deepened and secularized the theological assumption that the Jewish religion was inferior to the Christian religion and converted it into the doctrine of the moral and artistic inferiority of Jews and other minorities.

Various models of Jewish emancipation and assimilation, all quite uniform although different in essential details, collided with the idea of "Bildung." Sorkin remarked that in England and France, theories of natural law defined individual freedom vis-à-vis the state. Followers of natural law in Germany came to a different conclusion: the security of freedom lay with the state.

Central and East European models gave a favored role to the state. Both Dohm, the first significant theoretician of emancipation, and Wilhelm von Humboldt were state officials. In the wake of the French Revolution, states struggling to develop either absolutist governments or forms of limited representative governments utilized the idea of equality so as to dismantle old privileges and barriers in order to allow new privileges and power allotting systems to develop. The privilege of enacting legislation significantly increased the powers of state bureaucracies and their systems of representation. The sometimes faceless representative of the "regime" ruled over Catholics in Protestant countries and over Protestants and Jews in Catholic countries.

The modern state that wished to abandon its feudal privileges and barriers was, unfortunately, founded on contradictory principles. On the one hand, it was built on the trans-national idea of equality. On the other hand, it was built on the idea of the bourgeois nation, a concept given an historical and mythical weight by homogeneity, common traditions or language, or possibly the same ethnicity. Therefore, emancipation was first referred to as *naturalization.*[75] Opponents of naturalization argued that since the Jews had no homeland and since their religious laws forbade mixed marriages, it would be easy for them to transfer themselves and their possessions to another country. Proponents of naturalization turned this argument around saying that since the Jews did not have a country, settling them where they were was the most appropriate approach.[76]

All the arguments for a "rational state" came out in the debate. England's program for settling the Jewish question was first drawn up in an invitation to all Protestants of the world. However, practical considerations defeated these ideological arguments for racial homogeneity—even in John Toland's writings. The issue at stake was the Jews' possessions at the time when the "state" still had to wrestle with the privileges of the aristocracy. The group which offered its loyalty with relatively few constraints could have adapted most easily. And this would be that group which had only an imaginary country for its homeland.

Naturalization, similar to the oath of allegiance, meant that the individual would be admitted into the state. Even the 1867 Hungarian Emancipation Law discussed naturalization along with settlement and offered equal rights in return for several years of residency. During the Reform Age in the first half of the nineteenth century, Enlightenment zealots interpreted the notion of belonging to a state on an even less practical ground, that is on the basis of natural law. In 1840 Péter Vajda wrote, "Birth gives the right to life indelibly. Consequently, one has the right to live on the land one was born in. And since every land belongs to a country, every newborn has a country."[77]

The process of extending rights always entailed the idea that the state was independent of social forces or at least kept social forces in balance. This idea is the basis of ambitions which were intended to invest the governing power with moral authority.

Jewish emancipation has become part and symbol of the Enlightenment process extending all over Europe. This symbolism became increasingly eerie with the intensification of conflicts kindled by the expansion of rights. As Hannah Arendt wrote: " Deeper, older, and more fateful contradictions are hidden behind the abstract and palpable inconsistency that Jews received their citizenship from governments which in the process of centuries had made nationality a prerequisite for citizenship and homogeneity of population the outstanding characteristic of the body politic."[78]

This contradiction settled down in a newly inspired anti-Semitism. Jacob Katz explained the difference between the traditional and the modern anti-Semitism by indicating that the latter aspired to a quasi-metaphysical dignity. The modern anti-Semite not only tried to protect the Christian religion from a group that rejected Redemption by Christ. He also attached a whole system of stereotypes and prejudices to the religious aversion which pursued the movement of emancipated Jews while still hiding all the antipathy of a still hostile environment. Both religious and anti-modernity tendencies became inseparably intertwined in order to oppose any role for the Jews in society. Their relative isolation as well as their integrating efforts could have become subjects of criticism.[79]

The breadth of anti-Judaism corresponded to the situation created by the nature of equal rights extended by nation-states. The Christian hope of the millennium—expecting a second coming of Jesus when the Jews converted—was incorporated in the modern principle about the expansion of human rights. Thus, the promise of assimilation would play the drama of redemption within the framework of a secular state. The grade, mode, and speed of integration was a continuous measure of a worldly catharsis. Most of the contradictions of the liberal dream could have been included in the "Jewish question" because it could have coded both success and failure in its premises. So every member of the Jewish community, although deemed unredeemable, would still manage to get through the "eye of a needle." Thus, it promised victory while an occasional revival of any of the stereotypes would verify the total failure of this process even though ingrained and fated from the very beginning.

Internal contradictions and the historical trap of emancipation prevailed in the peculiar double-faced appearance of political interests. The ambition of the French Revolution—that it would extend equal rights to Jewish individuals as well while not to the Jewish community as a whole—translated into practice with the state extending and depriving privileges as if it were a zero sum game. It offered settlement to certain Jewish groups and imposed taxes on others, extended the right of assembly, but did not permit the operation of the religious community. It destroyed the inner autonomy of Jewish communities but, as Hannah Arendt also verified, "it consciously kept the Jews as a separate group in society."[80] Bureaucratic autocracy could hide within the "bestowed" rights while the bureaucracy's short term interest might intersect the strategic goal of the unification of the nation-state.

Protestants and Catholics, both included in process of emancipation, lived in groups integrated in the society. Besides the Jews, there was no order or class in Europe which would have begun its acculturation and assimilation through emancipation. Consequently, their existence depended upon the grace and protection of the state in return for financial and other services, participation in international organizations, and the collection of taxes. Therefore, preserving both equal rights and social separation was in the interest of the state.

The new bureaucracy concealed this double-faced nature of the modern state, although it hardly changed its absolutist practices. Absolutist rulers like Leopold I and Maria Theresa hesitated between mercantile interests and religious pressures. These were rulers who had first driven out and later, after imposing suitable taxes and limitations, called the Jews back into their country. The expulsion ordered by Leopold I began by driving out non-taxpaying beggars and scientists from Vienna. Before another forced emigration and during a thirty-day moratorium, all the assets and liabilities of the Jews were recorded. When, however, the Turkish-Italian-Polish trade chain broke and the supply of Crown horses was interrupted, a few rich Jews (Oppenheimer and Wertheimer) were called back. Maria Theresa declared that "I do not know a more dangerous plague for the state than this nation" [that is, the Jews]. And yet, she relied on her court Jew whose advice she listened to from behind a folding-screen—so that her face would not be glanced at by a Jew.[81]

The difference between the German-Austrian and the English emancipation and assimilation models also points out that there was a complex and delayed interdependence between the political emancipation of the Jews and their integration. The German model hid the fear of assimilation behind emancipation struggles while in the English model the assimilation process preceded political emancipation.

It was characteristic of English liberal laws that English society did not experience any nullifyings even in times of political change while in German territories, the partial retraction of rights extended to Jews frequently occurred.[82]

In England the state religion of Puritanism was based on a comprehensive study of the Old Testament. Certain Protestant theologians professed that the advent of the millennium depended upon the conversion of the Jews. They saw neither the embodied Satan nor the "eternal Jew" that they saw in contemporary Jews. Rather, contemporary Jews were the stray sheep who must be lured back to the flock. There was a special connection between Protestant and Jewish Messianism which facilitated Jewish integration into English society.[83]

The history of the settlement in England is exemplary in several respects. The Jewish problem was a sub-chapter of the Catholic or "papist" issue. If we accept that the practice of tolerance began in the French Revolution with the extension of equal rights to the Protestants, then the legal expansion of the bourgeois transformation was finalized by the political acceptance of the Catholics and the Jews by the English. In England the role of the Jews as pariahs was transferred to the Catholics since they were disparaged by the same stereotypical accusations as the Jews were in Germany. As Coleridge wrote in 1825, "Emancipation of the Catholics would lead to the moral breakdown of the nation."[84]

In England the political equality of "foreigners" before the law was also hampered by the fact that the national state was joined to a national church. According to a noteworthy remark which a Member made in the English Parliament, one could not expect loyalty from the Jews because during the Egyptian campaign Napoleon promised Palestine to them. "A Jew can never be English even if he were born here a hundred times. He considers himself the subject of another empire and has more sympathy and solidarity towards a Paris or Warsaw Jew than towards Christians or citizens of his homeland living in the same town."[85]

Yet many views on the emancipation of the Jews put forward in the English debate resembled many German views. Shlomo Avineri's article about Marx also alludes to Thomas Babbington Macaulay's arguments which were published in the *Edinburgh Review* in the same year as the pamphlet "On the Jewish Question."[86] "The Jews were not ostracized by the political power. They possess power and as long as they are entitled to accumulate wealth they will have it. ... What is a bigger power in a civilized society than that of a creditor over taxes?"[87]

The agreement between Marx and Macaulay is just as puzzling as trying to interpret the Jews' own role in the various emancipation movements having, as they did, different methods but the same goal. Apart from the short episode of Protestant philo-Semitism in England, an almost identical stereotypical image of the Jew appeared across all national borders and political systems. While traditional Christianity had a typical Jewish image in Ahasuerus, modern anti-Semitism had its own image in Shylock. There are no other universal Jewish characters in European literary mythology than those of Ahasuerus and Shylock. Both of them were created from an old Judas image and split into two separate but cognate images. Shylock is really Ahasuerus' successor.[88]

The Unredeemable Jewry

The secularized public earnestly criticized the backwardness and isolation of Jewish communities in those states where the Enlightenment program was well established. For example, one could hear the voice of enlightened rabbis urging religious reforms. However, the content of this criticism can only be understood by taking its "asymmetric counterpart" into consideration. The denunciation of religious backwardness was often just a semantic code for targeting the Jews' corporate privileges and economic activities which invaded the pre-existing feudal and guild-based society from the "outside." The role of outsider or foreigner was fulfilled by the "usurer" and the "profiteer." And Jews played these roles since a Jew must be the foreign money lender in the rigid, limited feudal system where money was still unable to break away from the church. Stereotypes preserved the Jews' roles in connecting and serving as intermediaries between different social classes that had been frozen as still pictures, and were then passed over by the dynamics of development.

As Macaulay observed, economic power had some compensating political and social power for certain representatives of the Jews. Emancipation sought to complement this economic power with political rights in order to divert the process into its normal course and to draw together the interest groups under the control of the state. Jews had specific functions in the pre-capitalist society which was now being transformed and diversified during the Western European stage of capitalist development. Money management ceased to be an exclusive Jewish privilege. The new capitalist market surpassed the economic function of the Jewish agents. Jewish communities and "Jewish mentality" had lesser roles in this transformation than suggested by anti-emancipation advocates and later social analysts. The view that countries left by Jews therefore fell into economic decline, or countries settling them therefore began to thrive had no basis in reality.[89] Sombart argued that Israel flew over Europe like sunshine; its coming initiated prosperity and its departure started decay. In contrast with this assumption is the fact that Jews fleeing to Turkey in large numbers never launched any prosperity there while the presence of the Jews in Holland did not prevent its 18th century decline.

Sombart defined anybody with a Jewish ancestor as a Jew.[90] According to him modern civilization developed when this southern nomadic people, with its wandering and eternal Jewish instincts, encountered the northerners. The city became the new desert where Jewish instincts prevailed.[91]

The assumption of the existence of a Jewish "essence," "Wesen," and "mentality" supported those arguments which saw the resurrected eternal Ahasuerus in every Jew, but mostly in the form of Shylock.[92] Although Sombart rejected biological anti-Semitism, he replaced it with a kind of "spiritual anti-Judaism."[93] However, he did believe that the Jewish "unchangeable essence" had been dispersed among the host people and became manifested as a contagion. The "Jewish mentality has transformed all the exterior framework of our existence and is *present* even when Jews are not present. In other words, the Jewish mentality is inside us and becomes objective in thousands of measures and in practice: in our laws, constitution, our life-styles, and economy."[94] Sombart is not content with a simple fight against Judaism. Instead he envisaged a necessary spiritual "de-Judaization" of the German people.

Such an historical role for a minority as was played by the Jews was unparalleled in Europe. Sombart developed his effective formula about the economic role of Jewish influence as a parallel to Max Weber's classic theory about the spirit of Protestantism. Sombart explained the Jews' financial success from the force of their anti-stigmatization struggle and from the stimulation that the pain of discrimination caused.

In the history of European anti-Semitism, anti-Judaic views on assimilation often combined protests against the expansion of capitalism with the stigmatization of the Jews. Texts by the young Hegelians, from Fichte to Gutzkow to Marx, did not characterize the Jews as a sociologically demarcated group. Instead, the Jews were characterized as traders and profiteers, presaging Werner Sombart.[95] Therefore, we can raise the question whether anti-Semitism, which had begun with emancipation, was in reality also a generalized code for anti-capitalism and for protesting a global historical transformation by making stereotypes of the activities, life styles, and mentality of a traditionally stigmatized community.

This theory is reinforced by the fact that even those who honestly demanded political equality still used the language and thinking of stigmatization. The fact that several Jewish authors dramatically described the decay of the Jewish community in order to support the necessity of the Jewish community to renew itself and to break with dogmatic traditions supports the argument. In this way, a historically peculiar situation occurred when European Jewish communities were suddenly at the intersecting point of several diverse historical trends. The rising national bourgeoisie looked at the Jews as historically privileged forerunners of the money economy. Yet the feudal groups of national states played the Jews against the national bourgeoisie in order to preserve those privileges of the feudal classes that still retained some influence.

The ultimate paradox of emancipation was the fact that by the time political equality has been achieved, the Jews' special social role—as a group that played a well-defined role in the economy—ceased to exist. By the time numerous social interest groups had the chance to occupy and modernize many branches of the money economy in the developing capital and market economy, the Jews—alienated and with an imposed shameful memory of this activity—carried the stigma of these activities which, by then, everybody practiced without being stigmatized.

That is the reason why the foreign archetype—the "other" one who is a mirror image of every vice—was embodied in the Jew. Divine Grace allows the eternal Jew to live and die as the new

Ahasuerus—about whom an Eighteenth century German dramatist wrote the new story of redemption.[96]

Consequently, a Jew did not always mean a *Jew* in the age of emancipation. Following the French Revolution, in countries where attempts had been made to reinforce the national state, one could detect a *cognitive dissonance* stemming from the conflict between the idea of equality and an awakened national spirit. In the revolution, "Patrie" became identified with "Liberté." Europe experienced the Napoleonic wars as a period of self-determination, self-defense, and self-definition. Patriotism welded together commoners and nobility—fighting for their birth privileges—as fellows-in-arms. The stigmatizing discrimination against the *foreigner*—along the line of traditions proven useful in Christian communities for centuries—was the only available cognitive trick. The Jew, the displaced minority who had different cultural and ritual customs, offered an obvious target. "The Jew" was a historical enemy of redemption and, therefore, this figure could assume mythical dimensions. However, the reality was more threatening than the myth. It was an ousted and isolated community that both the Christian Goethe and the Jewish Heine described in horror following their visit to the Frankfurt ghetto. Anti-Judaism fitted both the conservatives' and the liberals' cognitive model since their starting point was the backwardness, depravity, and medieval appearance of the Jews.

Dohm's argument in his description of the emancipation contract that the "Jew was rather a human being than a Jew" also meant that "human" or "humane" were asymmetric counterparts of the Jew. Some researchers believe that this statement included both a wish for improvement and the continued presentation of the Jew as an antithesis to a human being.[97]

The cognitive model that permanently identified the Jews with everything that manifests as social "evil" was possible only if its generalizations referred to some specific things that could be identified. From this respect, as Max Weber's work on the history of religion showed, the European Jewry was a peculiar creation. It was a caste in a casteless society. The Jews were a nationless nation and an ethnic group defined by their religion. Yet their social functions also filled a social vacuum: they were usurers in places where capital movements were forbidden and were money lenders where—due to their "neutral" situation—material goods received from a Jew did not carry social obligations or stigma.[98]

The multiple and multi-faceted social roles of the Jews can be described by opposing pairs of ideas. The structure of feudalism conserved their economic power by allotting them certain social positions. As Henri Pirenne and later Jacob Talmon said, Jews who revolted against society were lawless and homeless.[99] However, two Jewish types, the pioneer and the usurer, originated from this circle. The two roles often intertwined. Polish kingdoms lacking large cities, the Ottoman Empire, and the Hungarian aristocracy all used the wandering Jews who were willing to settle in certain places and so help to revitalize population growth, craftsmanship, and trade.

Economic Rationality and Emancipation

Assimilation was not merely a "Jewish question" in Europe but was also a general problem of integrating non-conforming groups. Economic development imposed a forced standardization on the modern nation-state: the exchange of commodities and trade called for equal rights, contractual stability, and the assurance of social mobility.[100]

This economic pressure, however, should have been manifested most forcefully in countries with more developed industries. Whereas, the fact is that a demand for assimilation emerged with most urgency and full of conflicts in the less developed countries tilting towards state absolutism. It happened mostly in countries where the revolution did not take place on the barricades but in men's minds—with apologies to Marx—such as in the German principalities, in Austria-Hungary, and in Russia. There were several demographic and historical reasons for this development. Developing industrial and trade interests forced the Jews to the "East," an area of lower population density. Ninety percent of the Jews of the East originated from the Ashkenazi ethnic group of the German territories. The Ashkenazis had acquired two "foreign" cultures during their migration: biblical-Talmud traditions on the one hand, and the Yiddish language on the other.[101] Both of these were closed cultural heritages which helped retain the difference between the sacred and mundane everyday communication.

The European Jews did not have a unified history until the emancipation period. Statistically, their community might be measured by two indicators: absolute numbers of people and relative part of the total population. At the end of the 18th century, the Dutch Jewish population of 50,000 amounted to 2.5% of the total population. The second largest European Jewish community, that of Hungary, totaled one hundred thousand but was only 1.4% of the population.[102]

Jews were forced to migrate East by the general European situation. Where no central power existed, it was up to the decision of the person exercising local legal power to decide whether the Jews could settle or whether they would be driven out of the country. The Jews also were a point of contention in the debates among kings, principals, and municipalities. Maria Theresa had the Pozsony [present Bratislava, Slovakia] Jews driven out but in three years, she permitted their resettlement. Or again, a group of Jews might be allowed to settle in one town but not get permission in a neighboring municipality. Or the Jews might not be able to spend a night unpunished in Pest, while they might be able to do so in Buda.[103]

Consequently, it seemed that the Jews' status was solely decided by economic rationality. Where their money management and later tax collecting activities were needed, the Jews received privileges but no rights. The Jews were also an issue in the debate between the city bourgeoisie and royal authority. Lajos Venetiáner summarized the situation, "Cities were well aware that kings needed a city bourgeoisie against the landowners and with increasing royal needs to keep their independence, they needed the Jews. In this unfair battle only the Jews would fare badly."[104] However, lacking a "unified" history due to the division of Europe, ideological-religious considerations ruled over economic rationality. The Jews' existence in the punishment of dispersion proved Christian justice. At the same time, the promise of redemption was extended to every people of the earth—including the Jews.

The Jewish Diaspora symbolized the punishment meted out to God's killers. Underlying the decree which said that a Jew could not have a Christian servant was the understanding that the Jews were the Christians' eternal servants. Saint Augustine's theology demanded that the Jews be saved and spared while at the Resurrection they, as the devil's disciples, were allotted the role of witness.[105]

Emancipation as a potential right to be given to the Jews did not originate solely from the needs of economic rationality either. The money changing and custom collecting activities of Jewish communities had not contributed as profoundly to the development of a commodity producer society as fashionable turn of the century theories described. For instance, Werner Sombart attempted to discover the qualities that had allowed this community to deceive these "foreigners." He argued that Judaism permitted a different morality towards "foreigners" than towards its own fellow sufferers. In such a context, cheating or extortion might be considered as the fulfillment of religious duties.[106] Sombart argued that capitalism developed under the influence of the Jews as if that minority had been preparing to take over power. Although Sombart's ideas were vulgarized and thus taken further by other authors, the idea of capitalism as a "foreign" phenomenon was already haunting German romanticism.

Historical facts, however, prove that Jewish *commercium*—trading and money lending—was more connected to the ancient and medieval forms of money circulation than to modern finance capitalism. Max Weber also noticed that isolated Jewish communities feared industrialization and the exchange of goods, an attitude fostered by Jewish traditionalism. It was not only their circumstances that confined Jews to money changing—or usury—but the fact that this profession provided more free time for studying the sacred books. As for Sombart's theory about Jews being vanguard capitalists, Weber decisively criticized it and, indirectly, Marx as well. "What is characteristically new in either the modern economic *system* or in the modern economic *disposition* is not characteristically Jewish. Rather, the ultimate theoretical reasons are again connected to the Jews as a pariah people having a pariah religion."[107]

Similar dispositions and actions against the Jews revealed more critics' prejudices and the role of ideology than the role of economic rationality. Jewish economic and moral dispositions could not be characterized as a capitalist "focus rationalism." Instead, they revealed the behavior patterns associated with the "pariah religion" syndrome. As far as the Jews' economic activities were concerned, state protection of certain religious community privileges was motivated more by concerns for state financing than for rational risk-taking. That is why in other writings Weber examined the Jews' economically "irrational" businesses.[108]

Every form of emancipation was a political concomitant of the "focus rationality" of the modern commodity producing economy. The Jews' distinguished role in this process stemmed from the fact that through their religion, isolation, and economic activities, they were considered the most backward community. Their integration and assimilation were the touchstone of state and national integrating ambitions.

It is interesting to note that communities breaking away from feudalism and living under autocratic rule experienced assimilation as a form of acculturation. This probably took place in countries where bourgeois development and the issue of the nation were strongly entwined and where state independence had been achieved before the need for democratization emerged.

In contrast to Anglo-Saxon political nations, autocratic-feudal states and federations of states were organized on a more cultural basis. On the one hand, nurturing a national language might prove to be a force stronger than that in a loose economic union. While on the other hand, the equalizing and emancipating aspect of belonging to a nation might revive patriarchal subordination. In less developed countries, nationalism became the carrier of modernity.

Therefore, the emancipation of minorities fitted into a large equalization process with both legal and cultural content. As Ernest Gellner wrote, in the age of early nationalism "in order to become a full citizen, either one adjusted to the ruling higher culture or changed the political framework of one's life to assure that one's own culture became the decisive culture of the new entity."[109]

Religious Reform

The pre-emancipation Jew was a mythical foreigner who belonged to a separate sub-group identifiable even after his political emancipation. Yet, after he adjusted to modernity, only religious memories connected the Jew with his ethnic group. However, his religion preserved many of the traditions of his people, even though liturgical reform attempted to "de-nationalize" the Jews. German reform rabbis, like those in Hungary, disclaimed the Jews' transnational constraints and the differences between the people of Israel and those of other nations. As Abraham Geiger, from Breslau, said, "Jerusalem ... has dimmed in our memory."[110]

Jewish religious reform ambitions—and the Jewish Enlightenment itself—came not merely in reaction to the conditions of integration nor were they acts of compromise concluded within the religion by an ethnic-cultural group. Rather, the renewal of Jewish theology was tied to the deep stream of the Enlightenment and built a bridge to secularization by negotiating between the Words of Faith and of Reason. This period of time produced not only Jewish theological reform. Both Catholic and Protestant reform movements (by supplanting Jesuitism with sweeping Jansenism) also showed that every traditional religion struggled with the influence of the Enlightenment.[111]

Jewish philosophy gave diverse responses to the dilemmas forced upon the Jewish people and the Jewish religion. Spinoza considered Judaism a political religion, saying that the Mosaic faith was the political constitution of the ancient Jews. It was not their God that chose the Jews, but the Jews who chose a "political leader" for their state. Thus, state and religion coincided. This is what Spinoza called theocracy, where civic rights and religion unified in blind obedience to God. For him in such a situation, only a life lived in isolation was possible.[112]

In the Diaspora, the traditional religion preserved the ghost-country that, according to Heine, every Jew carried in his bag. Admission to the Jewish nation was through religion so that anyone who deviated from this religion fell out of that nation.[113]

Spinoza envisioned a new universal religion, with the state as its keeper, to replace the historical religions. As Jacob Katz has stated, Spinoza had anticipated the utopia of complete assimilation.[114]

The urge for universality strengthened in the age of Enlightenment. Just as Spinoza substituted a general morality of mercy and compassion for the traditional dogmatic religions, so other reforms also strove to apply the principle of universality.

During this period of tempestuous nation-state development, maintaining universality necessitated immense intellectual efforts. Battling religious universalities also consumed a lot of intellectual energy. The leaders of the Enlightenment, such as Voltaire, rejected the historical Jewish religion saying that it was tribal and particularized. Montesquieu claimed that Judaism had lost its territorial and political power and, being short of a nation, could only claim the status of an archaic religion.[17]

Jewish reform movements attempted to respond to these issues and to other accusations as well. Even in the mid-Nineteenth century Rabbi Abraham Geiger dismissed Christianity, arguing that its culture was too abstract and spiritual. He said that its words appeared in dead and rigid languages (Latin and Greek) in the period of decline of the great and noble Greek and Roman civilizations while Judaism became law in a living nation and by means of a living language. "Judaism was born as a closed and separate entity. Yet it successfully transmitted its basic ideas to humanity as universal heritage. And, when artificial dividing walls finally come down, it can retain its universality during its whole history. Therefore, let us cast a glance back at our former national existence with pleasure. It was an essential transitional period of our history when the life of the Jewish nation took root in fertile ideological soil."[115]

While such argument laid the foundation for "Jewish sciences," Geiger and his predecessors were also responding to century-long debates in their theological discussions.[116] As a follower of universalism Stanislas de Clermont-Tonnerre professed that the Jews could not be tolerated as an independent political (national) formation since a nation within the nation could not be allowed to exist in the French homeland.[117] Fichte, in the spirit of German criticism of the Enlightenment, made similar statements. He allotted new "ideological," intellectual, and spiritual ground as a new home for Judaism, tied to the Enlightenment through universality, and as a carrier of a universal cultural heritage to the wider society. Historically, Judaism took its place based on a universality that provided a home for a nationless and homeless cultural community within the family of peoples.[118]

Their customs and religion lent a core to the cohesion and, in modern terms, to the group dynamics of the Jews. In addition to the Diaspora experience, the Jews also had in common an unquestioned and established Messianism that, even if it made the pariah people passive and resigned, also "elevated" them above history and carried them over into a quasi-mythological timelessness. European Jews do not merely have a history. Instead, they have a redemption history, since rites had arrested time.

"Jewish Science"

In response to emancipation movements, a number of intellectuals established an intellectual enterprise called "Jewish science." It was a chronicle of the Jewish people and Jewish religion placed in their historical contexts. Intellectual "proofs" that the religion could be cleansed of sediments of customs and that the original religion could be discovered replaced Divine Revelations. The ultimate motive for this enterprise was to show that emancipation was not happening to a pariah-nation. The young Leopold Zunz, Heinrich Heine, and their friends founded the association *Verein für Kultur und Wissenschaft der Juden,* which became a cultural circle to study the religion, life, and customs of the Jews. *Wissenschaft,* that is "science," here clearly means "history."[119]

"Jewish science" was one of the responses Jewish intellectuals gave to the question of assimilation. In this way, one of the important Jewish groups adjusted to the long march of the Enlightenment. The process was necessarily controversial: the more urgent the task of catching up with secularization, the less likely that groups within the world of the pariah people would complete the task. Jewish culture (defined by modernity as a religion) had only the arena of reforming its own beliefs as an available playing field.

As has already been mentioned, there is a significant difference among the English, French, and German assimilation models. Yovel Yirmiahu defined the difference between the German *Aufklärung* and the French *Lumière* by saying that the former "did not defy the justice of religion, instead it tried to rationalize it as much as possible."[120] In Moses Mendelssohn's works elements of "historizing" the religion appeared. In his response to Spinoza, the German thinker claimed that after the destruction of the Temple in Jerusalem the identity of politics and religion ceased to exist. Therefore, nobody could be excluded from the community. Jewish religion was not the result of a proclaimed belief but that of the proclaimed law, and acceptance of the law was voluntary.[121]

Mendelssohn tried to dissolve an epistemological trap by dividing reason from will, the same way that he separated justice from belief. He argued that reason and revelation move along different paths and the historical demand to follow laws should not hinder the paths of reason and knowledge.[122]

In conclusion, emancipation cannot be characterized as a simple "settlement" because its process ought to be visualized as a bilateral movement. The *Zeitgeist* not only forced the "players" to rethink the context of social coexistence along the lines of self-interest. The intellectual and moral force of the Enlightenment as well as various interests in accelerating social mobility were also factors in reaching equilibrium.

Notes

1. See Alex Bein, *Die Judenfrage: Biogaphie eines Weltproblems,* vol. 2, (Stuttgart: Deutsche Verlags-Anstalt, 1980).
2. Jacob Toury, "The Jewish Question: A Semantic Approach," *Leo Baeck Institute Yearbook* XI (London, 1966): pp. 85-107.
3. A. M., *Beiträfe zur Lösung der jüdischen Frage* (Deutsche Viertelsjahr-Schrift, 1838, Heft 1), pp. 248-263.
4. Christian W. v. Dohm and Franz Reuss, *Über die bürgerliche Verbesserung der Juden: 2 Teile in 1 Bd* (Hildesheim, New York: Olms, 1973), pp. 200, 376, and 105; English version, *Concerning the Amelioration of the Civil Status of the Jews*, trans., Helen Lederer (Cincinnati, 1957).
5. Jacob Allerhand, *Das Judentum in der Aufklärung* (Problemata, 86, Stuttgart-Bad Cannstatt: Frommann-Holzboog).
6. Horst Möller, "Aufklärung, Judenemanzipation und Staat. Ursprung und Wirkung von Dohms Schrift 'Über die bürgerliche Verbesserung der Juden," in *Deutsche Aufklärung und Judenemanzipation,* ed., Walter Grab, (Tel Aviv, 1980), pp. 119-149; and Robert Liberles, "Dohm's Treatise on the Jews: A Defense of the Enlightenment," *Leo Baeck Institute Yearbook* XXXIII (London, 1988): pp. 29-41.
7. Robert Liberles, "From Toleration to *Verbesserung*: German and English Debates on the Jews in the Eighteenth Century," in *Central European History*, (1989), p.3.
8. H. D. Schmidt, "The Terms of Emancipation," *Leo Baeck Institute Yearbook* (London, 1956): pp. 28-33.
9. Paul P. Bernard, *The Limits of Enlightenment: Joseph II and the Law* (Urbana: University of Illinois Press, 1979).
10. Erich Kahler, "Forms and Features of Anti-Judaism," in *The Dynamics of Emancipation*, ed., N. L. Glatzer (Boston, 1965), p. 44.
11. Quoted by Jacob Katz, "The Term 'Jewish Emancipation': Its Origin and Historical Impact," in *Studies in Nineteenth-Century Jewish Intellectual History*, ed., Alexander Altmann, (Cambridge, Mass., 1964), p. 5.
12. John Locke, *A Letter Concerning Toleration.* Latin and English text. Ed. Montuori, Mario, (The Hague, M. Nijhoff, 1963)
13. See Todd M. Endelman, *Radical Assimilation in English Jewish*

History, 1656-1945: The Modern Jewish Experience (Bloomington: Indiana University Press, 1990).

14. Ernst Barnikol and Ralph Ott, *Das Entdeckte Christentum in Vormärz: Bruno Bauers Kampf gegen Religion und Christentum und Erstausgabe seiner Kampfschrift,* 2., wesentlich erw. Aufl., (Aalen: Scientia, 1989).
15. Jacob Katz, *Jewish Emancipation and Self-Emancipation,* 1st ed. (Philadelphia: Jewish Publication Society, 1986), p. 12.
16. Quoted by Arthur Hertzberg, *The French Enlightenment and the Jews: The Origins of Modern Anti-Semitism,* 1st Schocken paperback ed., (New York: Schocken Books, 1970), p. 360.
17. Paul A. Meyer, "The Attitude of the Enlightenment Towards the Jews," in *Studies on Voltaire and the Eighteenth Century* (1963), pp. 1161-1205.
18. Jacob Katz, *Zur Assimilation und Emanzipation der Juden: Ausgewählte Schriften* (Darmstadt: Wissenschaftliche Buchgesellschaft, *Jewish Emancipation*), p. 5.
19. Quoted by Reinhart Rürup, "The European Revolution of 1848 and Jewish Emancipation," in *Revolution and Evolution—1848 in German-Jewish History*, eds., G. E. Mosse et al., (Tübingen: J. Mohr, 1981), p. 44.
20. Todd M. Endelman, "The Englishness of Jewish Modernity in England," in *Toward Modernity: The European Jewish Model*, ed., Jacob Katz, (New Jersey, 1987), pp. 225-226.
21. Quoted by Rainer-Erb-Werner Bergman, *Die Nachseite der Judenemanzipation—der Widerstand gegen die Integration der Juden: Deutschland 1780-1860* (Berlin: Metropol), p. 51. The quoted writing from A. Escherich, *Die Judenemanzipationsfrage vom naturhistorischen Standpunkte* (Deutsche Vierteljahrschrift, Heft 4), pp. 97-118.
22. Simon Dubnow, *Die Grundlagen des Nationaljudentums* (Berlin: Jüdischer Verlag), n. d.
23. Simon Dubnow, *An Outline of Jewish History* (NewYork, N.Y.).
24. Joseph Karniel, "Die Toleranzpolitik Kaiser Joseph II," in *Deutsche Aufklärung und Judenemanzipation*, ed., Walter Grab, (Tel Aviv: Univ. of Tel Aviv, 1980), pp. 155-178.
25. Raphael Mahler, *A History of Modern Jewry 1780-1815* (New York: Schocken Books, 1971), p. 338.
26. Shmuel Ettinger, "The Modern Period," in *History of the Jewish*

People, ed., Ben Sasson, (Cambridge, Mass, 1986), pp. 730-733.

27. See also Todd M.Endelman, *Comparing Jewish Societies* (Ann Arbor: University of Michigan Press: The Comparative Studies in Society and History Book Series, 1997).
28. Michael A. Meyer, *The Origins of the Modern Jew: Jewish Identity and European Culture in Germany, 1749-1824* (Detroit: Wayne State University Press, Wayne Books; WB32, 1979).
29. Isaac Deutscher, *The Non-Jewish Jew* (Oxford, 1968), p. 38—"extortionate usurer, driver of hard bargains—to cheat, overreach."
30. Constantin Frantz, *Ahasverus oder die Judenfrage* (Berlin, 1844), p. 47 and quoted by Bein in Alex Bein, *The Jewish Question—Biography of a World Problem,* trans., Harry Zohn (Rutherford, Herzl Press, 1990), p. 479.
31. Hans Mayer, "Von Ahasver zu Shylock," in *Aussenseiter* (Frankfurt am Main: Suhrkamp, 1975), p. 312.
32. Siegfried Kracauer, "Ahasver oder das Rätsel der Zeit," in *Schriften (Aussenseiter)* (Frankfurt am Main: Suhrkamp, 1975), pp. 148-149.
33. Quoted by Jacob Katz, *The Darker Side of Genius: Richard Wagner's Antisemitism* (Hanover, NH: Tauber Institute for the Study of European Jewry, 5, 1986)
34. Jacob Katz, *ibid.*
35. Christoph Cobet, *Der Wortschatz des Antisemitismus in der Bismarckzeit* (München: W. Fink, Münchner Germanistische Beiträge, 11, 1973), p. 147.
36. Quoted by Mária Ludassy, "Fasizmus francia módra—Adalékok a jobboldali radikalizmus történetéből 1797-1937," [Fascism a la France—Additions to the History of Right-Wing Radicalism: France, 1797-1937], *Mozgó Világ* (Budapest, 1998,1): p. 102.
37. See also Leon Poliakov, *The Aryan Myth: A History of Racist and Nationalist Ideas in Europe,* ed., C. Columbus, *Columbus Centre Series: Studies in the Dynamics of Persecution and Extermination,* (New York: Basic Books 1974).
38. Thomas Nipperdey and Reinhart Rürup, "Semitismus und der sekuläre Begriff des Juden als Vorassetzungen," in *Geschichliche Grundbegriffen,* eds., Werner O. C. Brunner and Reinhart Koselleck (Stuttgart, 1972), p. 131.
39. Ludwig Feuerbach, *Das Wesen des Christentums*, ed., Werner Schuffenhauer (Berlin, 1956).
40. Bruno Bauer, *Die Judendfrage* (Braunschweig, 1843), pp. 224-245.

41. Ernst Barnikol – Peter Reimer et. al, *Bruno Bauer. Studien und Materialien: Aus dem Nachlass ausgewält und zusammengestellt von Peter Reimer und Hans-Martin Sass,* Hrsg. Vom Forschungsinstitut der Friedrich-Ebert-Stiftung, Bonn-Bad Godesberg und dem Internationaal Institut voor Sociale Geschiedenis (Amsterdam: Assen,1972).
42. Jacob Talmon, *The Unique and the Universal* (New York: G. Braziller, 1966), pp. 151-152.
43. Georg W. F. Hegel, *Rechtsphilosophie* (Stuttgart, 1952).§ 270.
44. See also Shlomo Avineri, *Hegel's View of Jewish Emancipation* (Jewish Social Studies, 1963, 25), pp. 145-151.
45. Georg W. F. Hegel, ed., H. Nohl, *Theologische Jugendschriften* (Tübingen, 1907) and in English, *Early Theological Writings,* trans., T. M. Knox (Chicago, 1948).
46. Emil E. Fackenheim, *Encounters Between Judaism and Modern Philosophy* (New York, 1980), pp. 89-90; Fackenheim, *To Mend the World-Foundations of Post-Holocaust Jewish Thought* (Bloomington, 1989), pp. 103-147; and Paul Lawrence Rose, *German Question/ Jewish Question—Revolutionary Antisemitism from Kant to Wagner* (Princeton, New Jersey, 1990), p. 109.
47. See also Jacques Derrida and Moshe Ron, "Interpretations at War: Kant, the Jew, the German," *New Literary History*, (1991), p. 39.
48. Albert S. Lindemann, "German Question/ Jewish Question: Revolutionary Antisemitism from Kant to Wagner," *Ethnic and Racial Studies*, (1994), p. 722.
49. Johann G. Herder, *Werke,* ed., Suphan, Vol. IV. (Stuttgart, 1962), p. 365.
50. Godwin Lämmermann, *Kritische Theologie und Theologiekritik: die Genese der Religions- und Selbstbewusstseinstheorie Bruno Bauers.* (München: Kaiser, Beiträge zur evangelischen Theologie, vol. 84, 1979).
51. Jacob Katz, *A Social Background of Jewish Emancipation, 1770-1870.* (Cambridge, Mass: Harvard University Press), Ch. XIII.
52. Amos Funkenstein, "The Political Theory of Jewish Emancipation," in *Deutsche Aufklärung und Judenemanzipation,* ed., Walter Grab (Tel Aviv, 1980), p. 17.
53. George L. Mosse, "German Jews beyond Judaism," in *The Modern Jewish Experience* (Bloomington-Cincinnati: Indiana University Press; Hebrew Union College Press), p. 13.

54. See Shulamit Volkov, "Juden und Judentum im Zeitalter der Emanzipation," in *Die Juden in der Europäische Geschichte,* ed. W. Beck (München: Beck, 1992), pp. 86-108.
55. See also Helen Fein, "Insiders, Outsiders, and Border-Crossers: Conceptions of Modern Jewry in Marx, Durkheim, Simmel and Weber," in *Antisemitismus und jüdische Geschichte: Studien zu Ehren von Herbert A. Strauss,* ed., Rainer Erb and Michael Schmidt, (Berlin: Wissentschaftlicher Autorenverlag,1987), pp. 479-494.
56. See Hollace Graff, "Political Discourse in Exile: Karl Marx and the Jewish Question," in *Ethics* (1993), p. 612.
57. Karl Marx, "Zur Judenfrage," in *Deutsch-Französische Jahrbücher* (1844). In English, Karl Marx, *Early Writings*, trans., and ed., Tom Bottomore (New York: McGraw Hill, 1964), p. 40.
58. Joseph Gabel, *Réflexions sur l'avenir des juifs—racism et aliénation* (Paris: Méridiens Klinksieck, 1987).
59. Steven E. Aschheim, "'The Jew Within': The Myth of 'Judaization' in Germany," in *Culture and Catastrophe* (New York: New York University Press, 1996), pp. 45-69.
60. *Ibid.*, p. 373.
61. See also Helmuth Hirsch, *Marx und Moses: Karl Marx zur "Judenfrage u. zu Juden* (Frankfurt am Main: Judentum und Umwelt—Bern—Cirencester, UK: Lang, vol. 2, 1980).
62. Robert Misrahi, *Marx et la question juive* (Paris: Gallimard, Collection Idées 259, 1972),..
63. Edmund Silberner, *Kommunisten zur Judenfrage: zur Geschichte von Theorie und Praxis des Kommunismus* (Opladen: Westdeutscher Verlag, 1983); Silberner, "Was Marx an Anti-Semite?" in *Essential Papers on Jews and the Left*, Ezra Mendelssohn, ed.,(New York: New York University Press, 1997), pp. 361-402.
64. David Sorkin, "Wilhelm von Humboldt: The Theory and Practice of Self-Formation (*Bildung*), 1791-1810," *Journal of the History of Ideas*, (1983, January), pp. 55-73.
65. Quoted by George L. Mosse, "Between Bildung and Respectability," in *The Jewish Responses to German Culture—From Enlightenment to The Second World War,* eds., Jehuda Reinharz-Walter Schatzberg (Hanover-London: Clark University, 1985), pp. 1-17.
66. Quoted by Leon Poliakov et al., *The History of Anti-Semitism* (New York: Vanguard Press, 1975), vol. 3. p. 155.
67. Isaiah Berlin, *Against the Current: Essays in the History of Ideas*,

Selected Writings, vol. 3, 1st ed., (Berlin-Oxford-New York: Clarendon Press, 1991), p. 345.

68. See Leon Poliakov, *The Aryan Myth: A History of Racist and Nationalist Ideas in Europe* (New York: New American Library, 1977).
69. Eleonora Silberner, *Er ist wie du. Aus der Frühgeschichte des Antisemitismus in Deutschland* (München, 1956).
70. Bruno Bauer, *Einundzwanzig Bogen aus der Schweiz,* vol, I, (Zürich, 1843), p. 71.
71. See also David J. Sorkin, *Moses Mendelssohn and the Religious Enlightenment* (Berkeley: University of California Press, 1996).
72. Leon Botstein, *Essays zur Rolle der Juden in der deutschen und österreichischen Kultur, 1848-1938* (Wien: Böhlau, 1991).
73. David J. Sorkin, *The Transformation of German Jewry, 1780-1840* (New York: Oxford University Press, Studies in Jewish History, 1987), p. 15.
74. Peter Pulzer, *Jews and the German State—The Political History of a Minority, 1848-1933,* ed., David Sorkin (Oxford: Blackwell, Jewish Society and Culture,1992).
75. Jacob Katz, "The Term 'Jewish Emancipation': Its Origin and Historical Impact," in *Studies in Nineteenth-Century Jewish Intellectual History,* ed., Alexander Altmann, (Cambridge, 1964), p. 5.
76. John Toland, *Reasons for Naturalizing the Jews in Great Britain and Ireland on the Same Foot with all Nations* (London, 1714) and the new edition, (London, 1914).
77. Quoted by Ernő Ballagi, "A magyar zsidóság harca az emancipációért" [The Hungarian Jewry's Struggle for Emancipation], *IMIT évkönyv*, (1940), p. 135-167.
78. Hannah Arendt, *Antisemitism—Part One of The Origins of Totalitarianism* (New York: Harcourt, Brace and World, 1966), p. 11.
79. Jacob Katz, "Anti-Semitism Through the Ages," in *The Persisting Question—Sociological and Social Contexts of Modern Antisemitism,* ed., Helen Fein (Berlin-New York: Walter de Gruyter, 1987), pp. 52-53.
80. Hannah Arendt, *ibid.* p. 12.
81. David Kaufmann, *A zsidók utolsó kiűzetése Bécsből* [The Jews' Last Ousting from Vienna] (Budapest, 1888).

82. Israel Finestein, "Jewish Emancipationists in Victorian England: Self-imposed Limits to Assimilation," in *Assimilation and Community—The Jews in Nineteenth-Century Europe,* eds., Jonathan Frankel and Steven J. Zipperstein (Cambridge: Cambridge University Press, 1992), p. 43.
83. Norma Perry, "Anglo-Jewry, the Law, Religious Conviction, and Self-Interest (1665-1753)," *Journal of European Studies*, (1984, XIV, 2).
84. Quoted by Mária Ludassy, "A római katolikusok és a zsidók emancipációja" [The Emancipation of the Roman Catholics and the Jews], in *A toleranciától a szabadságig* [From Tolerance to Liberty] (Budapest, 1992), p. 81.
85. Robert Inglis, Sir, *Parlamenti beszéd* [Parliamentary Address] (May 22, 1883), quoted by Ludassy, p. 90.
86. Thomas B. Macaulay, ed.; G. T. Bettany, *Essays Historical and Literary from the 'Edinburgh Review' by Lord Macaulay,* pp. 171-172.
87. Geoffrey Aldermann, "English Jews or Jews of the English Persuasion? Reflections on the Emancipation of Anglo-Jewry," in *Paths of Emancipation—Jews, States, and Citizenship,* eds., Pierre Birnbaum and Ira Katznelson (1995), pp. 138-139.
88. Hermann Sinsheimer, *Shylock—The History of a Character,* 2nd ed., (New York: Benjamin Blom, 1953), p. 117.
89. Léon Abram, *The Jewish Question: A Marxist Interpretation* (New York: Pathfinder Press, 1970), p. 177.
90. Werner Sombart and S. Z. Klausner, *The Jews and Modern Capitalism*, Social Science Classics Series (New Brusnwick: Transaction Books, 1982), p. 30.
91. T. Fritsch and Werner Sombart, *Die Juden im Handel und das Geheimnis ihres Erfolges: Ausgleich eine Antwort und Ergänzung zu Sombarts Buch 'Die Juden und das Wirtschaftsleben,* 2, durchgesehene Aufl. Ed., (Steglitz: P. Hobbing, 1913), p. 308.
92. Martin D. Yaffe, *Shylock and the Jewish Question*, Johns Hopkins Jewish Studies (Baltimore: Johns Hopkins University Press, 1997).
93. See also Werner Krause, *Werner Sombarts Weg vom Kathedrarsozialismus zum Faschismus,* 1. Aufl. Ed. (Berlin: Rütten & Loening, 1962).
94. Werner Sombart, *A New Social Philosophy* (New York, 1969), pp. 177-179 and in the original, *Deutscher Sozialismus* (1934).

95. Hal Draper, "Marx and the Economic Jew Stereotype," in *Karl Marx's Theory of Revolution, I: State and Bureaucracy* (New York: Monthly Review Press, 1977), pp. 591-608.
96. Christian F. D. Schubart, "Der Ewige Jude," in *Gesammelte Schriften und Schicksale* (Stuttgart, 1839), vol. 4.
97. Daniel J. Goldhagen, *Hitler's Willing Executioners: Ordinary Germans and the Holocaust,* 1st ed., (New York: Alfred A. Knopf, 1996), p. 57.
98. See also Arnaldo Momigliano, "Le judaisme comme 'religion-paria' chez Max Weber," in *Mélanges Léon Poliakov,* ed., M. Olender, (Brussels: Complexe, 1981), pp. 201-207.
99. Jacob L. Talmon, *The Myth of the Nation and the Vision of Revolution: The Origins of Ideological Polarisation in the Twentieth Century* (London: Secker & Warburg; Berkeley, CA: University of California Press, 1981), p. 180.
100. See also Eric J. Hobsbawm, *Nations and Nationalism since 1780: Program, Myth, Reality*, 2nd edition (Cambridge, England—New York: Cambridge University Press, 1992).
101. Jacob Lestschinsky, *Jewish Migration For the Past Hundred Years,* YIVO English translation series (New York, N.Y: Yiddish Scientific Institute, YIVO, 1944), vol. 2, p. 2.
102. See also Jacob Katz, *Exclusiveness and Tolerance: Studies in Jewish-Gentile Relations in Medieval and Modern Times* (Westport, Conn: Greenwood Press, 1980).
103. Sándor Büchler, *A zsidók története Budapesten a legrégibb időktől 1867-ig* [The History of the Jews in Budapest From Time Immemorial to 1867], az Izraelita Magyar Irodalmi Társulat kiadványai [Publications of the Hungarian Israelite Literary Society], vol. 14, (Budapest: Franklin Nyomda, 1901), pp. 332-335.
104. Lajos Venetiáner, *A magyar zsidóság története—különös tekintettel gazdasági és művelődési fejlődésére a XIX. században* [The History of the Hungarian Jewry: With Special Emphasis on Its Economic and Cultural Development in the 19th Century]—a modified edition of the 1922 publication. (Budapest: Könyvértékesítő Vállalat, 1986), p. 34.
105. Joel Carmichael, *The Satanizing of the Jews: Origin and Development of Mystical Anti-Semitism,* 1st U.S. ed, (New York: Fromm International Pub. Corp, 1992), pp. 52-53.
106. Werner Sombart and S. Z. Klausner, *The Jews and Modern*

Capitalism, Social Science Classics Series (New Brusnwick: Transaction Books, 1982), p. 230.

107. Max Weber, *Economy and Society: an outline of interpretive sociology,* (New York: Bechminster Press, 1968)
108. Max Weber, *Gesammelte Aufsätze zur Religionssoziologie* (Tübingen: J.C.B. Mohr, 1988)
109. Ernest Gellner, "Nationalism and Politics in Eastern Europe", *New Left Review*, (1991, 9/10)
110. Max Weiner, ed., *Abraham Geiger and Liberal Judaism: The Challenge of the Nineteenth Century* (Philadelphia, 1962), p. 74.
111. David Sorkin, "Enlightenment and Emancipation: German Jewry's Formative Age in Comparative Perspective," in *Comparing Jewish Societies,* ed., Todd. M. Endelman (Ann Arbor: University of Michigan Press, 1997), pp. 89-113.
112. Benedictus Spinoza, *Chief Works of Benedict de Spinoza; a theologico-political treatise.* (New York, Dover: 1955)
113. Steven B. Smith, *Spinoza, Liberalism, and the Question of Jewish Identity* (New Haven: Yale University Press, 1997), XVII, p. 270.
114. Quoted by Yovel Yirmiahu, *Dark Riddle: Hegel, Nietzsche, and the Jews* (Pennsylvania: Penn State University, 1998).
115. Abraham Geiger, "The Developing Idea of Judaism," in *Ideas of Jewish History,* ed., Michal A. Meyer (Wayne State University, 1987).
116. Julius Carlebach and Hochschule für Jüdische Studien Heidelberg, *Wissenschaft des Judentums =[*Hokhmat Yi*sra*el]: Anfänge der Judaistik in Europa* (Darmstadt: Wissenschaftliche Buchgesellschaft, 1992).
117. Patrick Girard, *Les Juifs de France de 1789-1860: de l'émancipation et l'égalité.* Diaspora (Paris: Calmann-Lévy, 1976), p. 139.
118. Max Weiner, *Abraham Geiger's Conception of the Science of Judaism* (YIVO Annual of Jewish Social Science, 1956/57), XI, pp. 142-162.
119. Yoseph H. Yerushalmi, *Zakhor—Jewish History and Jewish Memory* (Seattle and London: University of Washington Press, 1982), p. 84.
120. *Ibid.*, p.10.
121. See also Edward Breuer, "Politics, Tradition, History: Rabbinic Judaism and the Eighteenth-Century Struggle for Civil Equality," *Harvard Theological Review*, (1992).
122. David Sorkin, "The Case for Comparison—Mendelssohn Moses and

the Religious Enlightenment: A Contextual Integration of Jewish Societal and Cultural History into an Expanded Historical Discipline," *Modern Judaism*, (1994), 14(2), pp. 121-138.

The Liberal Pact of Assimilation

The precondition of the agreement on assimilation in the classical age of liberalism was that the minority should master the language of the recipient majority. The language as a criterion of admission commands two kinds of further criteria, a general and a specific one. What was specific in Hungary rested on the country's political and administrative relations with Austria. Those assimilating masses who spoke Hungarian and consequently declared themselves Hungarians contributed to the numerical increase of the Hungarian population and the feeling of superiority in the Hungarian minds. By the increase of the population the country rose higher in the cultural hierarchy of nations. Linguistic integration is the first condition of cultural assimilation. It is a gate which leads to the adoption of a new mother tongue. By submerging into the linguistic abyss, the individual will be fully exposed to the attractions and forces of the recipient culture.

The Hungarian movements of independence generally appeared in the form of a struggle for linguistic independence, since the interests of admission and independence coincided. National pride was fostered by the love of the mother tongue, this being in itself a pledge of independence.

Vernacular creates the range of communication indispensable for bourgeois development. The language of commerce is money, but language is, in practice, the currency of communication and the exchange of ideas, as Turgot, a pioneer of the Enlightenment explained.[1] The dialogue between individual ethnic groups of the population extends urbanization even to the villages and detached farms. Scholars rightly call, therefore, the learning of the common language "naturalization."[2]

The first Jewish association serving assimilation was founded by medical students in Pest in the summer of 1843. Its members urged the application of the "political numerical science," i.e., statistics to the demographic and occupational distribution of the Jewish population. By the time the first calendar of the association was published in 1848 by the printers of Landerer and Heckenast, it became obvious that "Magyarization" indicated that the former Jews of trading and commerce had turned toward the handicrafts as well, not only as itinerant vendors but as artisans, though they were not yet admitted into the guilds.

There were among them tanners, makers of frieze capes, makers of cordovan leather, oil-pressers, loop-makers, pipe-makers, croppers, copper-smiths, tinder and quilt-makers, and others. Although they were not allowed to work among the Christian population, their mastery of the language of the majority helped them to find their place in industry.[3]

Széchenyi and Linguistic Assimilation

The new generation of the Reform Period (The name given to the belated Hungarian Enlightenment) tried to create a national state or nation-state out of the political one by urging the use of Hungarian as the mother tongue of the nation. In feudal society identity was not defined by the language a person spoke, as Viktor Karády points out.[4] The common language of the nobility was the privileges they shared, and it was only the forced Germanization of the Josephinist era that made the ruling elite realize the collective force and the political advantages of a linguistic self-consciousness. The fact that all this served to create a nation within the political boundaries was proved by Count István Széchenyi's offer for assimilation.

Széchenyi, a nobleman of resources and anglo-phile reformer, believed that the Hungarian language embodied a political nation, and it was this fact that governed its attraction. "But if I speak to Slovaks, Germans, and other races of this country, I tell them the following: 'You have a fatherland of your own outside this country, but we have none. On the other hand, you have no constitution, which we do have, so let us come to an agreement whose main points of which could be the following: let everyone speak his own Slovak, German, Wallachian, Greek, Latin, French or Sanskrit mother tongue in the intimate circle of his friends and family.... In exchange for this wonderful concession, however, all that falls within the realm of public life should be discussed in Hungarian....'"[5]

In his work *Kelet népe* [The People of the East] Széchenyi repudiated assimilation by force and voted for an agreement with the minorities. His argument indicates that linguistic assimilation was both a political and a cultural necessity, and it also served to make the position of the minorities legitimate in society. In Saint Stephen's Hungary the Hungarian-speaking population constituted a minority, so the political elite of the multi-national state felt it absolutely necessary to follow the liberal model of assimilation as shown by the proposal of Széchenyi to distinguish between the private and the public spheres. The proposal was meant to ensure considerable advantages to those who undertook assimilation in this way, promising them upward social mobility.

The attractive invitation of the country's influential aristocrat Széchenyi was, however, declined by the minorities. The statistics based on the distribution of the population as regards the mother tongue prove that "the rate of those speaking Hungarian rose above half of the population only as late as 1900, and it did not reach fifty-five per cent even by 1910."[6] The assimilation of those to whom Széchenyi offered his hand contributed to the overall rise in the rate of assimilation only by ten per cent, while those whom he neglected or refused to take into consideration played a leading role in the process of Magyarization, ensuring them majority status in the Hungarian nation of the dualist monarchy.

It was not the native, though foreign-speaking minorities called *hungarus* that were assimilated rapidly but rather the newcomers. The number of Jews speaking Hungarian doubled between 1880 and 1910. Three quarters of the Jewish population constituting six per cent of the country's population in the beginning of the century, came to be Hungarians.[7] As Viktor Karády stated, "Taking only the naked facts of the population growth into consideration, the balance of linguistic assimilation is positive only as regards the Jews in Hungary."[8]

Széchenyi's idea of the nation was different from that of the romantic philosophers like Herder in that he did not think a person's belonging to a nation was a mythic or even a prehistoric bond. He advocated the building of nations, and defined the criteria for being Hungarians not merely by the exclusion of enemies; he believed that civic virtues and enlightened minds were the prerequisites of creating a nation.[9] Being an ardent follower of the Enlightenment, whenever he criticized the Jewish community, his aim was to criticize their religious orthodoxy.

Political Assimilation

Assimilation is a marriage of convenience between the established recipients and those accepted into a society. The nineteenth-century Hungarian poet Csokonai, an admirer of Rousseau once said the following in his rough and simple manner: "Do not dare to do any harm to the Jews in the future, for the landlords need them."[10] Beyond such interests, however, love can also grow in the hearts of the couple. The social motivation behind accommodation cannot be described only in terms of money. The process of bourgeois development is not only an attempt at modernization taking place in the economic sphere but a mode of communication, in which various patterns of behavior, beliefs, prejudices, and cultural preferences are involved.

The "parvenu factor" also played a part in social accommodation in the sense that belonging to the liberal nobility lent a peculiar gentlemanly tint to the upstart. The Jews had to conform not to the cits turned gentlemen but to the nobility who favored free enterprise or to the gentry in control of commerce through their administrative power in everyday life. In his novel *Kivilágos kivirradtig* [Until the Small Hours of Morning] Zsigmond Móricz, a major writer in twentieth-century Hungary offered a clinical picture of the rising Jewish landowner wishing to enter the world of the farm-bailiff, the district doctor, and the postmaster by acquiring a doctor's degree at times even when contrary to his own interests.

The noted historian of the dualist Monarchy Péter Hanák questions why it was not the majority of the German population of Hungary that assimilated to the Hungarian nation while ahead on the road to developing bourgeois values, but rather the Jews, who might have been more attracted by Vienna from both a linguistic and an economic point of view.[11] The question can naturally not be answered fully in the framework of the present chapter. It is, however, interesting to note that the relative backwardness of Hungary paradoxically contributed to the solidarity of the Jewish population of the country, for example, in the war for independence of 1848-49. The Jews hoped to be defended by the Hungarians against the anti-Semitism of the more "developed" Germans of the Hungarian cities, says William O. McCagg, Jr., a distinguished scholar of the Jewish-Hungarian symbiosis.[12]

The dualist era offered the possibility of linguistic as well as social assimilation for rising into the middle class. At the same time, it exercised a strong cultural attraction.

From the point of view of those wanting to assimilate, a further impetus was given to them by the crisis of their own cultural background. As Aladár Komlós pointed out, Jewish orthodoxy had created a cultural void by the nineteenth century and had become an enemy of modernization. "The self-imposed seclusion of

Rabbinism had by the early nineteenth century degenerated into nonproductivity, landing the Jews in a situation where the only thing they could do was to assimilate by force of the law of *horror vacui*."[13] Assimilation also meant breaking free of the ghetto, just as the modernizing or neological "revolution" in the field of religion turned the Jewish faith into a "Hungarian religion", and turned the members of this new "second community" into a group choosing linguistic and cultural assimilation.

So the majority of the assimilants accepted and even supported the new collective image of the nation. The leaders of the religious communities addressed their members in a circular prior to the Bill on Emancipation of 1867, inviting them to learn the Hungarian language, and they held a memorial service to commemorate the death of the aristocrat István Széchenyi, notorious for his anti-Semitic statements.[14] A truly ironic if useful gesture.

Some advocates of constitutional reform did not, or actually could not, integrate the political concept of the nation into their way of thinking in the period of Hungarian Enlightenment. The young Kossuth, later a leading liberal called the Jews a fungus that drew off the vital assets of its environment, and could not be patriotic, its religion being "theocracy" that "Would not be reconciled with the present order."[15] Even the later Kossuth maintained that emancipation was a reward for assimilation, and he did not reconsider his views, similarly burdened with prejudices as those of Széchenyi, until the Jews themselves began to show efforts to assimilate voluntarily.[16]

In the debate, lasting from the Reform Period to the Compromise of 1867, on whether it should be the recipients who offer emancipation or the assimilating party who should express its loyalty first, Baron József Eötvös expressed his unequivocal views as follows: "...Granting civil rights to the Jews is not rewarding them for their merits but putting an end to an outrageous injustice...." Eötvös did not deny that "... the Jews had not shown sympathy for our nation so far...," but wondered if they were to blame for that.

"Tolerated because of their money, hated by all in this country, excluded from all offices, expelled from certain towns and municipalities, ridiculed and despised wherever they go, why should they love this country at all?," asked József Eötvös.

Called a doctrinaire by some conservative politicians, Eötvös reached a liberal definition of patriotism just through his analysis of the conditions of the Jews: "Our fatherland is not just the piece of land where we were born, ... it is more than that. It is the place where we feel free ... , where we are not considered aliens."[17]

The national minorities of Hungary declined Széchenyi's offer to assimilate, but they accepted that of Eötvös, since it stressed the liberal idea of the equality of opportunity. When Eötvös introduced a bill in November, 1867 on the emancipation of the Jews, it was passed by both houses of the parliament and a new successful chapter of Jewish assimilation began.

Cultural assimilation

"Look up to the sky and then to the ground:
This is where the Promised Land is found."

These are the words of the first truly emancipated Jewish poet of Hungary, József Kiss.[18] In his poem *Az ár ellen* [Upstream] he sings a hymn to the sun so that "corn should be twice in the ear and wines should mellow twice a year."[19]

József Kiss was a poet of both Jewish songs and Hungarian ballads. He was an exceptional figure in that he managed to integrate into an alien society without giving up his identity. He did not seek to avoid the drama of assimilation, and his double allegiance was not the result of a mere compromise. In his novel in verse entitled *Jehova* the tension is between the father dedicated to the study of the Jewish Bible in a rural community and the son's enthusiasm about the new ideals of the cities. In the closing canto of his last verse novel called *Legendák nagyapámról* [Legends of My Grandfather] Reb Meyer talks with a Hungarian country bumpkin nicknamed Foolish Steve on their common fate. Foolish Steve was as emblematic figure of Hungarian misfortune as Reb Meyer of that of the Jews.[20]

Emancipation rarely brought about concrete results for those wishing to assimilate, so uncertainty necessarily led to excessive demonstrations of loyalty. A sketch of Kálmán Mikszáth, the nineteenth-century novelist, a Hungarian classic on the Jews in Szeged expressed his view that assimilation was a slow but certain way of losing one's identity, as experienced by the Jews some time back in the "golden age."

"There are no Jews in Szeged any more. There is only a separate traditional Hebrew religion and its followers. Jewish people speak and think of Jehovah's greatness in Hungarian... ... Rabbis preach in the synagogue in Hungarian and quote Vörösmarty to support their points. Girls in love express their sorrow in Hungarian popular songs, and the portrait of the late rabbi in Jewish homes is covered with a cloth in the red, white and green colors of the Hungarian flag. The younger generation in Szeged may even think of Jehovah as an old man wearing a Hungarian short coat with gold lace...."[21]

Mikszáth's sketch was written in 1879, one year before the Tiszaeszlár blood-libel trial. Although the sketch was but a short piece of prose and not a carefully elaborated, significant writing, its importance goes far beyond its size and genre, since it reveals an aspect of assimilation as seen through the eyes of the recipient majority and influencing its attitude. As Viktor Karády said, common education and the extension of human rights involved several socializing elements[22], including the ironic and forgiving gesture, with which Mikszáth accepted the newcomers.

In the 1880s clouds were gathering above the process of assimilation. The rise of anti-Semitic political parties and the charge of ritual murder were the response of Hungarian conservatism to the success of assimilation. József Kiss, waking up from the ecstasy of emancipation, wrote the following in a poem entitled *Új Ahasvér* [A New Ahasuerus] in 1875:

"You may build cottages,
You may accumulate wealth,
You will still not have a home in this country."

The cynical Mikszáth described the situation after the ritual murder-case Tiszaeszlár through his conversation with the defense attorney in the great trial, Károly Eötvös. "It is a pity you entered into this comedy," Mikszáth said, "Once the whole Hungarian nation is angry with the Jews, why should we not be angry as well, as it is proper?" "What nation? Let me see that nation!," said Eötvös bitterly, "It is but the proletarians who are irritated and the decaying gentry, that's all."[23]

Proletarian is here presumably the synonym for the parasite, just as in the famous play of Csiky or for the mob. The gentry hostile to modernization and the mob so easily misguided were, however, given political representation in the anti-Semitic party of Győző Istóczy. The full integration of the Jews thus came to a stop, and even the successes of the previous years seemed to be questioned, especially because the economic, legal, and social pact of assimilation came to be impugned by the religious and racial aspects of the charge. Integration came up against a special obstacle called by Viktor Karády a primordial, irrational system of stigmatization, causing the objectively assimilated Jews to play the role of the scapegoat at times of crisis in the future too, and, thus forcing them to overfulfil the obligations imposed on them by the "pact."[24]

The relative success of assimilation placed the Jews into a social void. Istóczy viewed even the division of the Jewish community along orthodox and modern lines as a plot and as part of the Jewish aspiration at world hegemony.[25] His naive and harmful theory is worth mentioning only because the first organized wave of anti-Semitism threatened the Jews with dissimilation, i.e., the reversal of the assimilation process.

But the Jewish masses could not go back. As Péter Hanák remarked, "Both in the Dual Monarchy and later in the successor states anti-Semitism prevented the Jews in the process of assimilation from reaching a high level of social and national integration, from becoming absorbed within the recipient nations. At the same time, their achievement of middle-class status prevented them from finding a way back to dissimilation and from becoming a distinct nation or a national minority."[26]

It was not by chance that the first and the second anti-Semitic "world congresses" at Dresden in 1882 and at Chemnitz in 1883, aimed at nothing less than the social and economic boycott of the Jews. The participants were invited not to read the Jewish-owned press and not to join associations with Jewish members.[27]

Anti-Semitism exercised social pressure for dissimilation on an integrating social group that had nowhere to dissimilate. In effect, both its religious and its ethnic identity was offered to it as an option for dissimilation. The resulting social trap necessarily produced various strategies of compensation on both sides, generating a false ideological force field between two extremes. One made the full assimilation of the Jews a precondition of the equality of rights and of social integration, while the other questioned even the possibility of assimilation, and demanded the abolition of the Jews' civil rights and their emigration, as long as their extermination was not possible.[28] Istóczy was seriously considering this option as well.

The pitfalls of the ambiguous assimilation process had become obvious by the turn of the century. Zionism was, after all, a movement resulting from the perceived impossibility of assimilation in the Diaspora. There is a ghastly consonance between the proposals of Győző Istóczy and Theodor Herzl with emigration as a solution for the problems of the Jews unable to integrate. The Zionist Herzl does not set out from the impossibility of assimilation but rather from his awareness of the fact that integration would mean the total loss of identity in a country where forced assimilation and pressure as well as distrust and the arbitrary modification of the preconditions of assimilation can equally occur. It was, therefore, not accidental that the young Herzl suggested first that the Jews should be converted *en masse* in order to make their full assimilation possible. Herzl wished to obtain the consent of the Pope to the mass conversion of the Jews of Vienna on the square before the Cathedral of St. Stephen.[29]

When Herzl finally found the solution for the ambiguity and the discontinuity of assimilation in an independent Jewish state, i.e., in exodus as the extreme form of dissimilation, he noticed also the overfulfilling aspect of Jewish assimilation in Hungary and the efforts of the Hungarian Jews to comply with all preconditions of assimilation. In 1903 he wrote to Ernő Mezei, a Hungarian MP as follows: "The hand of fate shall also seize Hungarian Jewry. And the later this occurs, and the stronger this Jewry becomes, the more cruel and hard shall be the blow, which shall be delivered with greater savagery. There is no escape."[30]

The western type of assimilation based on strictly liberal ideals, urging the majority to ensure an equality of rights and social integration for those wanting to assimilate and at the same time making it possible for them to preserve their identity, could not be realized in the Austro-Hungarian Monarchy. There was an urge for compensation from two sides in the ideological force field mentioned by András Gerő. On the one hand there was the jovial and condescending cynicism of Mikszáth who in his novel *Szent Péter esernyője* [St. Peter's Umbrella] ridiculed a small country town called Bábaszék saying that it tried to outrival the neighboring Pelsőc and improve the fame of the town by importing an old Jewish woman for want of someone better. They even assigned a plot for an Israelite cemetery and a synagogue to orient strangers by, although they had only that single “honorary Jew.”

On the other hand there was liberal joviality also showing signs of compensation and wishing to brush aside the anti-Semitic threat. The ballad *Salamon bácsi* [Uncle Salamon] by Andor Kozma in 1892 is an example of that.

“Uncle Salamon is a Hungarian except for his faith
He speaks no alien language even on weekdays.
His speech is clear and fully Hungarian,
His manners are like those of the Hungarians.”

Uncle Salamon has no trouble at all as long as the newspapers do not start the old animosity again, although he thought it had already died out completely. “The commonest of the common” start to scold the Jews anew, but the farmers place a sentinel in front of Uncle Salamon’s house. He has a conversation with the sentinel and the next morning he is greeted by all with the old cordiality again.

“Last night was but a dream, a bad dream and nothing else,” Uncle Salamon says with relief.

Emotional elements are also used as a strategy of compensation in the struggle against prejudices. The poem *Bosszúálló zsidó* [The Avenging Jew] by Antal Váradi in 1900 applies tragic irony to describe the fate of a Yitzhak whose house is set on fire and who, while running to save his own life, saves the son of the arsonist.

“‘Take the child, ... I’ve saved him...’
And the mob stands amazed...
While the burning cottage collapses in sparks,
The old beggar staggers away, leaving home.

The flame makes the sky bright,
And the exile slackens the pace of his walk.
He can hear the crowd shouting from afar:
‘Fraternity! Unity! Liberty vivat!’”

The Cultural Aspect of the Jewish Question

The more obstacles were removed from the way of the political and administrative assimilation and integration of the Jewish population, the higher the impalpable walls rose around it. Marcell Benedek admitted that he had written his contribution for the conference of the periodical *Huszadik Század* on the Jewish question on the very day when a Jew was offered a portfolio in the cabinet. "There still exists an unfathomable but significant emotional, psychological and cultural Jewish question," he said. There is racial pride in the Jews on the one hand, and there are prejudices in the Hungarian mind on the other.

Marcell Benedek did not realize how contradictory his words were. While speaking of a Jewish racial pride, he also states that "the emotional side of the Jewish question looks roughly like this: here is an ethnic group deprived of its self-respect as a race, dressed in the characteristics, prejudices and even in the national extravagance of another race at times, ridiculed by it for this grotesque robe and kept at a distance socially."[31]

The emotional obstacles of admission and integration could grow so high because the persisting preconditions of assimilation went much beyond the original pact. The requirements included not only linguistic assimilation and social integration but identification with the national traits and the fate of the nation. Marcell Benedek was mistaken in presuming that all the constitutional or legal and economic preconditions of assimilation were given. These preconditions could prevail only as long as they did not endanger the leading role in political life of the landowning nobility. And this role was guaranteed by what Marcell Benedek called an anti-Semitism "unter uns." The "secret clause" of emancipation, i.e., full admission was prevented by the prevailing ideology defining the Hungarian nation by its national characteristics and stressing the importance of pure blood rather than as a political nation. In András

Kovács's words, "in the age of nationalism only those who were considered legitimate representatives of the national interests had a chance for any kind of political leadership. The political hegemony of the landowning nobility could only be guaranteed if the bourgeois middle class of Jewish origin was not accepted as Hungarian despite all its efforts at assimilation. They were to remain Jews, that is, aliens. This was why the obviously exorbitant demand of acquiring Hungarian national traits and mentality came to be stressed again and again."[32]

There were still many ways of escaping the pitfall. The tainted social force field became polarized along conflicting political intentions, which offered strategies for modernization and reform. The requirements of pure blood and national character belonged so much to the conservative side that radicalism could offer a reasonable alternative: fight instead of resignation. "For the acceptance of the Jew was not a full acceptance, it existed only on its face but not in everyday social life. True integration can only be reached through love, and it was through the lack of love that the Jews were burdened by the prejudices of the society around them, saying that the Hungarian nation was the chosen people of God and not the Jews, the Jews were not people of full value, etc.," Aladár Komlós wrote.[33]

Assimilation Deferred

The birth of modernism in literature gave rise to a new pact of assimilation. When the periodicals *Hét* and *Nyugat* were founded, it became obvious that the Hungarian efforts to block assimilation were actually the rear-guard battles of the nobility and the gentry in the guise of patriotic slogans. The Jewish population found, beyond doubt, a new strategy of assimilation in this revolt against conservatism. Géza Szilágyi expressed the wish for full assimilation in his erotic poetry, Jenő Heltai did the same through his cynicism, and

Ignotus through his elegant prose and his struggle with the official aesthetics. When in a debate on Ady organized by the periodical *Toll* Lajos Zilahy ventured to say that Ady, as a characteristic representative of the upper classes between the Compromise and the revolution, had sold himself to the Jews, the reply of Lajos Hatvany revealed the essence of the earlier pact of assimilation: "In the heart of our late friend [the poet Ady] the grievances of a deposed gentleman turned into love toward all despised classes, races, and strata. There were Jews who returned this love, whose hearts were opened by their own grievances in the forefront of the 'despised classes,' and who realized the miracle of assimilating to the Hungarian people through this love of theirs."[34]

The social upheaval of modernization established a new bond between Ernő Osvát, Hatvany, Miksa Fenyő, and Ignotus on the one hand and Ady, Babits, and Móricz on the other, uniting the prewar *Nyugat* in a particularly strong way that predicted the birth of a new civil society. As citizens enchanted by art, they celebrated the miracle of union. Aladár Schöpflin wrote as late as 1937 that "Hungarian life has a peculiar assimilative force of its own that foreign observers also notice. ... Immigrants adopted the Hungarian language very soon, in one or two generations, and did their best to assimilate in other aspects as well."[35]

However, the lost war and the Trianon peace treaty transformed the "miracle of assimilation" into an age of dissimilation focusing on the conservative criticism of modernism. János Horváth, who attacked Dezső Szomory's un-Hungarian idiom as early as 1911, wrote in his essay *Aranytól Adyig* [From Arany to Ady] the following: "The *Nyugat* is a gathering of Jewish and definitely philo-Semitic writers, representing the Hungarian nation with its assimilated Jews. Assimilation completed."[36] Professor Gyula Farkas from Berlin, a former student of János Horváth charged Ignotus with "taking the formation of a Hungarian-Jewish society as an accomplished fact."[37]

The volume *Három nemzedék* [Three Generations] by Gyula Szekfű reviewed the problem of assimilation in 1920. Szekfű held large-scale immigration responsible for the decline of three generations. He thought that emancipation meant granting privileges to the Jews, and those who had come to this country earlier helped the newcomers arriving from Galicia out of love of their own race. The Jewish press had established its empire over their souls, he believed, and assimilation was a pact concluded with the declining Hungarian race.[38]

Szekfű was not the only one to draw up such new concepts. István Lendvai adopted the slogan of the "new conquest," a more refined formulation of the notion that the Hungarian was an endangered race in his own homeland.[39] Endre Zsilinszky spoke of a "national and racial renaissance" and of the necessity of uniting "northern morals and the Turanian forces of nature."[40] The recent past was equally criticized by the politicians and the press. In Szekfű's words, yesterday's political elite accepted only the liberals, while today liberalism is considered suspect and alien to the nation. The change in the political idiom was so fundamental, and its pressure on the language was so strong that even Babits allowed himself to say in 1919 that "the outcasts of the peoples appeared again, the *blasé* of cultural life, the enthusiastic and obstinate Jews wanting to make a clean sweep."[41]

The new concepts could naturally express only an ambiguous revision. The ethnic overtones of the new concept of nation expressed irredentism. Minister of Cult and Public Education Kunó Klebelsberg said of the trend called "protection of the race" that its followers wanted to save the Hungarian nation not from Petőfi or the German Munkácsy but from the Jews alone.[42]

Race and Nation

This indoctrination with the new concepts was so profound that it affected even those who had been immune to such a way of thinking before the First World War. The protection of the race sought scientific justification not only in the pseudo-biology of Professor Méhely but found its way into several systems of reasoning as their unquestionable precondition, irrespective of their definition of race.

Rather than ties of blood, the concept of race or species came to be determined by a common fate and history. It was thought to be a community, whose members should "cherish the historical traditions beneficial to the whole nation deep in their hearts... and irradiate the ancient Hungarian spirit..."[43]

The relationship of race and literature was widely discussed by Hungarian intellectuals from Dezső Szabó to the conservative academy. Even the *Nyugat* dealt with it more than once. In 1929 Ignotus replied to Klebelsberg's experiences in Berlin. Klebelsberg, Minister of Cult and Education insisted that art can only be "racial and national,"—a ghastly *déja vu,* since Ignotus had already fought this battle regarding the national character of literature against an authority like Kálmán Mikszáth.[44] Only the introduction of the concept of race would be a novelty for him. His argument was, however, not very successful, since race and nationality were the natural breeding-ground for literature in those days. "...It is natural and goes without saying that art must go back to and have its roots in blood, race, and nation, since it is individual in character, and the more individual it is, the more typically it represents the race the author belongs to. I still do not know what policy of art and literature I should derive from that. Shall artists be *ordered* to represent their inner self, i.e., their race?"[45]

Ignotus was among the first to become a typical outcast on whom the new principles of "race protection" were exercised. He is said to have been the original of the journalist in Mihály Babits's novel *Timár Virgil fia* [Virgil Timár's Son]. In any case, the figure of Vilmos Vitányi represents the new perception, of which Ignotus could only be a negative example. In the Cistercian grammar school, young Virgil Timár "had a new Hungarian book in his hand that created a sensation in those days. It was written by a Jewish writer and was full of witty articles and aphorisms expressed in a free and skeptic spirit. ... The Catholic literary periodicals criticized the book in lengthy and embittered articles, saying that it made fun of sacred things in a light-minded way, and gave a malignant interpretation of everything, relying on the superficial knowledge so typical of journalism. Furthermore, it flirted with Catholicism starting from idle Jewish aesthetic points of view and, in its sad lack of principles, it expressed dismal scepticism."[46]

It was naturally not Babits who spoke these words but a fictitious narrator who adopted the jargon of the day and expressed the opinions of the characters of the novel on journalism and aesthetics. Whatever his points of view were, they were not far from the spirit of the age. Vitányi "... thought of his bandy-legged small figure and oriental face ... In spite of all this, he was a man of the world, a master of life, a lady-killer, and an *arbiter elegantiarum*. He wished his poor grandfather, an old Jew in a caftan, could have seen this in the candle-light one Friday evening."

The chameleon character of Vitányi, his adaptability, and flirtation with Catholicism were almost a parody of an assimilated person. The strong disgust of *Timár Virgil fia* is worth mentioning, because it reveals the same strategy of compensation as that of Ignotus, though from quite another aspect. Ignotus ignored the actual pressure of the situation after Trianon beyond the frequent calls of "race" and "nation," while Babits tried to blame the "chameleons," the press, and the false assimilators for the liberal failure in the war. The hatred of the press was again a code for something else, and many could not avoid that pitfall. Where the decimation of the press was concerned, the lack of freedom meant compensation by squeamishness and self-justification.

When the first anti-Jewish Act was adopted, the Hungarian intellectual elite protested. Bartók, Géza Féja, Kodály, Móricz, Schöpflin, Tersánszky, and Zilahy were among the intellectuals who raised a protest, but Babits and Illyés were unfortunately missing. Illyés, a leading poet and noted populist writer gave a curious explanation for his absence: "The lackey-playwright, the author of slipslops, the gambler on the stock exchange, the newspaper hack living by economic blackmailing, the publisher of trash, the film producer, the film writer, the theatrical agent whom language fails us to describe, the manager of chorus-girls, and the white-slave trader all lament the Hungarian culture and urge us to die a hero's death for it, since we also have championed culture, democracy, the freedom of the press, and the free propagation of ideas. ... It may really happen that we will sacrifice ourselves, but the way we do it must be worthy of us and must serve our own good. When we have kept our palms clean of their handshakes, posterity should not find our bones in a common grave with such beasts."[47]

It goes without saying that in his otherwise brave cultural struggle Illyés took the wrong side this time. His remark deserves mention only because his peculiar indifference reflects the mentality of the age. In the atmosphere of a short circuit in communication the mentality of society was characterized by individual manias and unjust judgements made by special circumstances rather than by logical arguments.[48]

It is actually irrelevant after the event, if Illyés protested against the discriminative racial laws or not. The fact that his signature was missing or refused is only an episode in his life. It is much more important that as the editor of *Magyar Csillag* [Hungarian Star] he refused to enforce any restrictive measures. It is quite another matter that it was he who linked anxiety for his people with the withdrawal of the "pact of assimilation" when the populist movement was born, calling attention to the deterioration of the villages in Transdanubia and the practice of having only one child in the families of certain Transdanubian villages. Literary historians are not in agreement as to when the populist-urbanist controversy unfolded.

Aladár Komlós and Pál Ignotus reckoned it from the publication of Illyés's article *Pusztulás* [Doom], while Miklós Lackó puts it at the spring of 1934, and attributes it to the Jewish question.[49] No matter which standpoint one adopts, it is Illyés's opinion and attitude that matter. Beyond its actual subject matter, the article *Pusztulás*, touched two important problems, namely the situation of the German minority and the deterioration of the language.

Mentioning the German minority in the autumn of 1933 had no political implications, and the fact that half a million ethnic Germans gained ground in Hungary would most probably support the claim of decay. Also here is the opinion of the sociologist Róbert Braun, who argued in the debate over *Pusztulás* as follows: "I consider the article of Gyula Illyés especially harmful, because its moderate urbane tone and literary quality make it suitable for influencing public opinion against the rural German population, though they are sure to set an example to be followed by the Hungarian peasants for a long time to come, owing to their economic achievements."[50]

Róbert Braun was, however, not in a position to notice that the "expansion of the German population" and the confrontation of the "true-born Hungarians" with the assimilated but alien minority were codes which illustrated the shocking facts of the decay of the population. Aladár Schöpflin also hinted in the debate over *Pusztulás* that the system of having only one child in a family, i.e., deterioration, also affected the German population.

Aladár Schöpflin noticed another aspect of the article, namely its anti-Budapest and anti-city attitude, expounded by Illyés again and again at the time of the introduction of the anti-Jewish Act.

Illyés believed that deterioration in the countryside was born out of a pessimism causing the exodus of the rural population, while in the cities it manifested itself in the destruction of the language. "It is the destruction of the people from below, and the influence of Pest poisoning the Hungarian language from above... "[51]

The complaint about the deterioration of the language would not be so conspicuous, were it not for an article on assimilation where it is mentioned. The mastery of the language of the majority was, however, the primary political and cultural precondition of assimilation. Considering it a failure means that the whole process of assimilation is in question. Aladár Schöpflin's polemic essay is a proof of the contemporary awareness of this aspect of Illyés's writing: "I was astonished to see how the radically enlightened Illyés let his suppressed nationalist sentiments come to the surface in this article. It was not his discussion of the decay of the Hungarian people in Tolna and Baranya that made it obvious ... but what he wrote about Budapest and the language..."[52] "Some linguistic rules make us speak a foreign language right now," Illyés said. "A language is not made up of words only. It is the pattern organizing the words themselves that matters. ... A nation lives through its language... If it is really true, one can really be fearful for the future of this nation."[53]

Aladár Schöpflin was not deceived by the colorful metaphors. He asserted that Illyés's pessimism was exaggerated and "Budapest was just as Hungarian as the countryside, only the ways of thinking, the feelings, and their linguistic expression were different. Different but not inferior.... Budapest society was born as a conglomerate of Hungarians coming from the country, and of assimilated Germans, Slavs, and Jews in the last fifty or sixty years, and it has not melted into a unified whole since then. Such a process needs generations. In any events, it has taken the right course, and the Hungarian citizens of a future Budapest will be metropolitan but not less Hungarian for that. Unless history interferes in a tragic manner, they will be like any Hungarian citizen of Tolna or the Great Hungarian Plain."[54]

It was naturally not the language that was being talked about. Linguistic assimilation was considered to be only the first step toward the concept of the homogeneity of culture, while the representatives of Hungarian culture are now divided into "authentic" and "spurious" characters from the point of view of radical populism. In other words, into "newcomers" and "Hungarians to the bone."

Striving for homogeneity was a natural reaction to an actual threat. Being afraid of the decay of the Hungarian ethnic was part of the Trianon complex of the day concentrating on the linguistic isolation and defenselessness of the Hungarians. The withdrawal of the "assimilation pact" within the contemporary Hungarian borders was a response equivalent to the forced assimilation of the Hungarians outside the borders of Hungary.

However, when Schöpflin's objective mind noticed that in Illyés's thought radical enlightenment was united with clandestine nationalism, he understood the roots of the cultural pessimism and the efforts at homogeneity of the populist trend. He realized that the radical enlightenment of Illyés had been forced to incorporate the arguments of conservatism, keeping them alive in the eyes of the public.

A significant writing by Zsigmond Móricz proves that this is not an arbitrary interpretation. Móricz published his article *Az irodalom és a "faji jelleg"* [Literature and "Racial Characteristics"] in *Nyugat* in 1931. He argued with László Négyesi, who also demanded "racial character" from Hungarian literature. Had the conservative way of thinking not changed at all since Ady? Was it enough for Négyesi to draw upon the old weapons and phrases? "The world around us has, however, changed in the meantime," Móricz said. "First of all, because of Trianon." There is, for example another generation growing up in Slovakia. "Young people have grown up in foreign schools, studied in a language their parents do not understand, and so they have had to find new criteria for their Hungarian identity. They have to become more social-minded, more cultured, and closer to the European standards. They have never heard the slogan *extra Hungariam non est vita*."[55]

The idea of Móricz about the integration of the Hungarians living sporadically as a minority and their preserving identity at the same time was, of course, self-deception. His lines still reflected a new theory of assimilation called later by István Bibó "contractual" as opposed to the "organic" one. Knowledge gained in a foreign language on the one hand and preserved cultural identity on the other are the core concepts of a polyphonic culture. Again, it was not by chance that Zsigmond Móricz was one of those who protested against the first anti-Jewish Act.[56]

Concept of the Nation with Variations

As has been stated, the concepts of the nation divide roughly into two contrasting types, i.e., into contractual and organic concepts. "The first type," as Ferenc Fehér suggests, "is based, at least theoretically, on the actual or fictitious agreement of free individuals... With the other type, the concept of the fatherland is always strained emotionally, and demands that the subjects accept their assigned status as something 'deeper' than the one they have chosen for themselves. Those who are unable or unwilling to do that, will remain aliens forever..."[57]

It follows from this that the question of assimilation was never independent of the political image of the nation created by the recipient or majority entity. In the first phase of assimilation the idea was supported by the hope of increasing the numbers of those speaking Hungarian. However, in the period between the two world wars, when assimilation came to be suppressed, the prevailing ethnocentric ideologies emphasizing the dangers threatening the historical races pushed the already assimilated masses toward reassimilation or dissimilation. They reverted toward a previous condition.

Paradoxically, the ruling class of the Hungarian nation aiming at a homogeneous culture and cultural identity was unable to outline and put into practice those requirements of assimilation that would have offered to the various religious and national minorities the possibility of a successful integration on a contractual basis.

As Bibó once put it, a community becomes a real recipient one only if it turns into a defending community, and the preconditions of assimilation are clear, since the community has clear-cut social requirements and ethical norms. In many cases, however, those who wished to assimilate had nothing to assimilate to. In Gyula Gombos's words, assimilation in Hungary "differed from the usual one in that it was too fast and too large-scale, and the assimilants had hardly more to adopt than the language and the patriotic rhetoric of the day."[58]

The "context" of assimilation had, therefore, been false from the beginning, stated Bibó daringly.[59] "The Hungarian nation lived under such political and social circumstances, where a spade could not be called a spade; facts had to be interpreted not in terms of cause and effect but from the point of view of inappropriate presuppositions and political expectations; ... there were no objective standards to measure the correctness of actions, and the standards of moral values were built on ancient fears and grievances."[60]

Bibó presumes that this was why the dominant society of the dualist period could not give a clear-cut definition of its requirements concerning assimilation. Recent research has, however, pointed out that these requirements were not executable, anyway. András Kovács argues that from the 1880s on there was an ideological pressure to make the people reject modernization with all its cultural consequences, declaring those very spheres alien to the Hungarian nation in which the assimilants had been successful.[61]

As a consequence of the pressure against modernization, those cultural fears and grievances divided the intelligentsia and offered fixed points for self-identification that could be realized only to the detriment of their opponents. Let me mention here only the notorious conflict between populists and urbanists.

In spite of the unfavorable context, a new kind of culture evolved from the assimilated masses, namely, an "interactive" type of culture that can be observed in the works both of the assimilated intellectuals and in the recipients. The poems of Géza Szilágyi reverberated in those of Ady, Béla Balázs in Bartók, and the poems of Milán Füst in those of Illyés.

In the contradictory and paradoxical history of Hungarian liberalism even the partially successful assimilation of the day is an integral part of Hungarian cultural history.

Notes

1. A. R. J. Turgot, "Réflexions sur la formation et la distribution des richesses, [1766]," in *Oeuvres*, vol. 1, (1913), p.45.
2. Cf. Etienne Balibar, Immanuel Wallerstein et al., *Race, Nation, Classe. Les identités ambigues* (Paris, 1988); József Bayer, "Nacionalizmus egykor és most" [Nationalism Then and Now], *Kritika*, (May 1993) 12.
3. Lector Judaeus, "A magyar zsidóság száz év előtt—Statisztikai kistükör" [Hungarian Jewry One Hundred Years Ago—A Statistical Sketch], *Magyar Zsidók Könyve*, (1943): p.25.
4. Viktor Karády, "Egyenlőtlen elmagyarosodás, avagy hogyan vált Magyarország magyar nyelvű országgá" [Disproportionate Magyarization: How Hungary Became a Country Speaking Hungarian], *Századvég*, no. 2 (1990), p.6.
5. István Széchenyi, "A' Kelet népe" [The People of the East] (1841), in *A mai Széchenyi*, [Széchenyi of Today], selected by Gyula Szekfű, (Budapest, 1935), p.255.
6. See Viktor Karády, *op. cit.*, p.14.
7. Yehuda Don, Georg Magos, "A magyarországi zsidóság demográfiai fejlődése" [Demographic Development of the Hungarian Jews], *Történelmi Szemle*, no. 3 (1985): p.436-469.
8. Viktor Karády, *op. cit.*, p.15. Cf. also Ludwig Gogolák, *Zum Problem der Assimilation in Ungarn in der Zeit von 1790-1918*, (Südostdeutsches Archiv, 1966).
9. See Endre Kiss, "Széchenyi a modern nemzetté válásról" [Széchenyi on Becoming a Modern Nation], *Valóság*, no. 2 (1994): p.71-80.
10. *Csokonai Vitéz Mihály összes művei* [Collected Works of Mihály Csokonai Vitéz], (Budapest: Genius), vol. 3, 339; quoted in Jenő Zsoldos, "A romantikus zsidószemlélet irodalmunkban" [The Romantic Attitude toward the Jews in Our Literature], *IMIT évkönyv* (1935): p.268.
11. Péter Hanák, "Polgárosodás és asszimiláció Magyarországon a XIX. században" [Bourgeois Development and Assimilation in Hungary in the Nineteenth Century], *Történelmi Szemle*, no. 4 (1974): p.520.
12. William O. McCagg, Jr., "The Jewish Position in Interwar Central Europe: A Structural Study of Jewry at Vienna, Budapest, and

Prague," in *A Social and Economic History of Central European Jewry*, Yehoda Don, Victor Karady, eds., (New Brunswick, 1990), p. 64.

13. Aladár Komlós, "Zsidóság, magyarság, Európa" [Jews, Hungarians, and Europe], *Ararát évkönyv*, (1943): 24.
14. László Gonda, *A zsidóság Magyarországon, 1526-1945* [The Jews in Hungary 1526-1945], (Budapest, 1992), p.115-116.
15. Lajos Kossuth in *Pesti Hírlap*, 5 May 1884. See also István Barta, ed., *Kossuth Lajos ifjúkori iratai* [Papers of the Young Lajos Kossuth], (Budapest, 1966), p.179-180.
16. See Jacob Katz, *From Prejudice to Destruction. Anti-Semitism, 1700-1933* (Cambridge, Mass., 1980), p.236. For Kossuth's argument against the social emancipation of the Jews see László Bányai, Anikó Kis, "Történelmi bevezetés" [Historical Introduction], in *Hét évtized a hazai zsidóság életében* [Seven Decades in the Life of Hungarian Jews], Ferenc L. Lendvai, et al., (eds.), vol. l, (Budapest, 1990), p.104.
17. Baron József Eötvös, *Költemények—tanulmányok* [Poems and Essays], (Budapest, 1934), p.104.
18. József Kiss, "December huszadikán" [On the Twentieth of December]. First published in the volume *Zsidó dalok* [Jewish Songs] in early 1868, a few months after the Emancipation Act had been adopted.
19. Cf. Aladár Komlós, "Zsidó költők a magyar irodalomban" [Jewish Poets in Hungarian Literature], *Ararát évkönyv*, (1942): p.164.
20. Cf. Aladár Komlós, "A századvég költői" [Poets of the fin de siècle], in *Tegnap és ma* [Yesterday and Today], (Budapest, 1956), p.151 passim.
21. Cf. István Radó, "Zsidó vonatkozások Mikszáth műveiben" [References to Jews in Mikszáth's Writings], *IMIT évkönyv*, (1913). For the quotation see Jenő Zsoldos, (ed.), *Magyar irodalom és zsidóság. Költői és prózai szemelvények* [Hungarian Literature and the Jews. Selected Poetry and Prose], (Budapest, 1943), p. 84-85.
22. Viktor Karády, "Asszimiláció és társadalmi krízis" [Assimilation and Social Crisis], *Világosság*, no. 3 (1993): p. 37.
23. Kálmán Mikszáth, *Az apró füvek* [Short Grass], (1883). Cf. Mór Krausz, *A zsidó Mikszáth Kálmán munkáiban* [The Jews in Kálmán Mikszáth's Works], (Budapest, 1910).
24. Viktor Karády, "Asszimiláció és társadalmi krízis" [Assimilation and

Social Crisis], *Világosság*, no.3 (1993): p.38. Cf. also Béla Vágó, (ed.), *Jewish Assimilation in Modern Times*, (Boulder, Colorado, 1981).

25. Győző Istóczy, *Országgyűlési beszédei, indítványai és törvényjavaslatai* [Speeches in Parliament, Motions, and Bills], (Budapest, 1904), p.16-18.

26. Péter Hanák, "A lezáratlan per" [The Undetermined Trial], in *Zsidókérdés, asszimiláció, antiszemitizmus* [Jewish Question, Assimilation, and Anti-Semitism], Péter Hanák, (ed.), (Budapest, 1984), p.374.

27. Jacob Katz, *op. cit.*, 280. See also Judit Kubinszky, *Politikai antiszemitizmus Magyarországon* [Political Anti-Semitism in Hungary], (Budapest, 1976), and György Szabad, "A polgári jogegyenlőség elleni támadás és kudarca" [An Attack Against the Equality of Rights and Its Failure], *Társadalmi Szemle*, nos. 8-9 (1982).

28. See András Gerő, "Liberálisok, antiszemiták és zsidók a modern Magyarország megszületésekor" [Liberals, Anti-Semites, and Jews at the Birth of Modern Hungary], in Mária M. Kovács, Yitzhak M. Kashti, Ferenc Erős, *Zsidóság, identitás, történelem* [Jewry, Identity and History], (Budapest, 1992), p.19. Cf. also Viktor Karády, "A zsidóság polgárosodásának és modernizációjának főbb tényezői a magyar társadalomtörténetben" [Major Factors of the Embourgeoisement and Modernization of the Jewry in the Social History of Hungary], in *A zsidókérdésről* [On the Jewish Question], Balázs Fűzfa, Gábor Szabó, (eds.), (Szombathely, 1989), p.95-137.

29. Theodor Herzl, *Tagebücher*, vol. 1 (Berlin, 1922), 8. Quoted by Carl E. Schorske, *Fin du sičcle Vienna. Politics and Culture*, (New York, 1981), p.161.

30. Quoted by Randolph L. Braham, "The Uniqueness of the Holocaust in Hungary," in *The Holocaust in Hungary: Forty Years Later*, Randolph L. Braham, Bela Vago, (eds.), (New York, 1985), p.186.

31. Contribution of Marcell Benedek, in *A zsidókérdés Magyarországon. A Huszadik Század körkérdése* [The Jewish Question in Hungary. The All-Round Inquiry of the *Huszadik Század*], (Budapest, 1917), p.44-48.

32. András Kovács, "Az asszimilációs dilemma" [The Dilemma of Assimilation], *Világosság*, nos. 8-9 (1988): p.608.

33. Aladár Komlós, "A zsidó lélek" [The Jewish Soul],(1927), in *Írók és elvek. Irodalmi tanulmányok* [Writers and Principles. Literary Essays], (Budapest, 1937), p.171.

34. Lajos Hatvany, "Baloldali művészet—jobboldali politika" [Left-Wing Art, Right-Wing Politics], in *Emberek és könyvek* [People and Books], (Budapest, 1971), p.300.
35. Aladár Schöpflin, *A magyar irodalom története a XX. században* [History of Hungarian Literature in the Twentieth Century], (Budapest, 1937), p.35.
36. János Horváth, *Aranytól Adyig* [From Arany to Ady], (Budapest, 1921), p.45.
37. Gyula Farkas, *A magyar szellem felszabadulása* [The Liberation of the Hungarian Spirit], (Budapest, n.d.), p.333.
38. Gyula Szekfű, *Három nemzedék és ami utána következik* [Three Generations and After], (Budapest, 1935), pp. 335-336, 360. The first edition appeared in 1920.
39. István Lendvai, *A harmadik Magyarország* [The Third Hungary], (Budapest, 1921).
40. Endre Zsilinszky, *Nemzeti újjászületés és sajtó* [National Revival and the Press], (Budapest, 1920), pp. 93, 117.
41. Mihály Babits, "Magyar költő kilencszáztizenkilencben" [Hungarian Poet in 1919], *Nyugat*, (September 1919). Cf. Tamás Ungvári, "Babits 1919-ben" [Babits in 1919], in *Ikarusz fiai* [Sons of Ikaros], (Budapest, 1970), p. 247-282.
42. Kunó Klebelsberg, *Neonacionalizmus* [Neo-Nationalism], (Budapest, 1928), 129. Cf. Rolf Fischer, *Entwicklungsstufen des Antisemitismus in Ungarn 1867-1939. Die Zerstörung der magyarisch-jüdischen Symbiose*, (Munich, 1988), p. 144.
43. *A magyar parasztság levele a művelt fiatalsághoz. Röpirat* [A Letter From the Hungarian Peasantry to the Educated Youth. A Pamphlet], (Miskolc, 1938). Quoted by Gyula Juhász, "A magyar szellemi élet és a zsidókérdés a második világháború előtt és alatt (1938-1944)" [Intellectual Life in Hungary and the Jewish Question Before and During the Second World War, 1938-1944], in *A háború és Magyarország 1938-1945* [Hungary and the War, 1938-1945], (Budapest, 1986), p. 78-79.
44. Ignotus, "Hazafiság és irodalom—egy kis polémia.—Scarron (Mikszáth Kálmán)" [Patriotism and Literature. A Debate with Scarron (Kálmán Mikszáth)], *A Hét* (1904). Reprint in Anna Fábry, Ágota Steinert, *A Hét, 1900-1907*, (Budapest, 1978), p. 208-215.
45. Ignotus, "Faj és művészet" [Race and Art], *Nyugat*, vol. XXII, no. 11 (1 June 1929): p. 717.

46. Mihály Babits, *Összegyűjtött munkái* [Collected Works], vol. 6 (Budapest, n. d.), p. 46-47.
47. Gyula Illyés, *Magyarok. Naplójegyzetek* [Hungarians. Diary Notes], (Budapest, 1939), p.276-277. First published in *Nyugat* (May 1938).
48. Cf. Asher Cohen, "The Attitude of the Intelligentsia in Hungary toward Jewish Assimilation between the two World Wars," in *Jewish Assimilation in Modern Times*, Bela Vago, ed., (Boulder, Colorado, 1981), p.57-74.
49. For the differing viewpoints see Gyula Gombos, *A magyar népi mozgalom* [The Hungarian Populist Movement], (Budapest, 1989), p.191.
50. Róbert Braun, "A hivatalos statisztika" [The Official Statistics], *Nyugat*, no. 5, vol. 24 (1 March 1931): p.179-281.
51. Gyula Illyés, *Magyarok* [Hungarians], p.17.
52. Aladár Schöpflin, "A nép, a nyelv és a főváros" [The People, the Language, and the Capital], *Nyugat*, no. 19, vol. 26 (1 October, 1933): p.272-274.
53. Gyula Illyés, *op. cit.*, p.17-18.
54. Aladár Schöpflin, *op. cit.*, p.19.
55. Zsigmond Móricz, "Az irodalom és a 'faji jelleg'" [Literature and "Racial Characteristics"], *Nyugat*, no. 5, vol. 24 (1 March 1931): p.286.
56. Zsigmond Móricz, "Zsidótörvény" [Jewish Act], *Pesti Napló*, (8 May 1938)
57. Discussed in detail by Ferenc Fehér in his essay "Bibó István és a zsidókérdés Magyarországon" [István Bibó and the Jewish Question in Hungary], *Holmi*, no. 6, vol. 3 (June 1991): p.727, passim. – Cf. The English version in *New German Critique*, no.21 (Fall 1980) pp. 3-46.
58. Gyula Gombos, *A harmadik út* [The Third Road], (Budapest, 1990), p.68.
59. István Bibó, "Zsidókérdés Magyarországon 1944 után" [Jewish Question in Hungary after 1944], in *Válogatott tanulmányok* [Selected Essays], (Budapest, 1986), p.722-754.
60. István Bibó, *op. cit.*, vol. 2, p.603.
61. András Kovács, "A 'Zsidókérdés'," in *A hatalom humanizálása. Tanulmányok Bibó István életművéről* [Humanization of Power. Essays on the Oeuvre of István Bibó], Iván Zoltán Dénes, ed., (Pécs, 1993), p. 204.

The "Jewish Question" in the Shadow of the Trianon Treaty

Awakening Hungarians

The situation of the Hungarian Jews changed radically in the shadow of the Trianon Treaty. Towards the end of World War I anti-Semitism, with all the features of a witch-hunt, intensified. There was a famous discussion in the review *Huszadik Század* debating whether the Jewish question existed at all any more, concluding, however, in the affirmative.[1] Péter Ágoston's pamphlet *A zsidók útja* [The Road of the Jews] launched the debate. Originally it was prepared in defense of the Jews but later evolved into a bill of indictment under the "pressure of the times."[2]

After the lost war, anarchy in the country created favorable circumstances for anti-Semitism to grow, and people disappointed with revolutions blamed the Jews for their role in the Hungarian Soviet Republic of 1919.[3]

One of the secrets of the counter-revolution's success against the Soviet Republic was in conjoining the different streams of "popular" and political anti-Semitism. Official politics was both sanctimonious and hypocritical. During the Paris peace talks the nation was pro-Jewish to the "outside" world while supporting the "commandos" inside Hungary. According to historian Gusztáv Gratz, who was active in establishing the counter-revolutionary governments, "intensifying anti-Semitism posed quite a number of difficulties for the government."[4] Minister of Justice Lajos Pálmai of the first so-called Arad government of the counter-revolution was "of the Jewish religion." According to Gratz, intrigues against Pálmai led to the downfall of Gyula Károlyi's government as well.

Gratz said the following about Pálmai's resignation speech: "He was aware that the majority of them was patriotic and all of the Jews could not be blamed for the sins that some of the Jews committed against the country. However, one needs to understand that the ever-intensifying anti-Semitic atmosphere was in reaction to the destructive work of the National Council, the People's Republic, and the proletarian dictatorship whose devastating operations were mostly directed by Jews."

During the counter-revolution, government forces—described as moderate—stepped up activities to prevent atrocities and at the same time, moved by their own rhetoric, undertook the reprogramming of public speech and brought about the lowering of the public's threshold of sensitivity. Post-Trianon governments professed an ideology of being threatened by a "national menace." The feeling of deception and *ressentiment* offered the government absolution for the duality of its foreign political image and its rigid internal activities. Secret associations patterned on Free Masonry, such as the *Egyesült Keresztény Liga* [United Christian League] and the *Etelközi Szövetség* [Etelköz Alliance], organized by Károly Wolff, influenced domestic politics pushing it more and more to the right.

Many secret organizations showed open anti-Semitic programs. In the *Vigadó*, at the assembly meeting of the *Ébredő Magyarok Egyesülete* [Society of Awakening Hungarians], Catholic priest Gyula Zákány demanded that the Jews resettle in Palestine or be dispersed among the civilized nations by population ratio.[4]

Many secret societies drew a theoretical dividing line between groups representing Hungarian and those representing foreign interests. On the one hand they espoused the slogans of a defensive national unity. In the shadow of the humiliating Peace Treaty, a member of the negotiating delegation and later Prime Minister, Pál Teleki, called upon the people: "Let us not see parties, let us not see classes today, and let us not see differences between one Hungarian and another Hungarian."[5] However, belief in an internal and external enemy and the rupture between the ideology of patriotism and internationalism amplified all of these "differences." For example, although Teleki professed that the Hungarian working class was "blood of our blood," at the same time he declared that "everybody ought to understand that internationalism is a sin in Hungary and if somebody claims to be an internationalist in the present situation of the country, the country—for the sake of its own existence—has to take measures against him as if he was a criminal."[5]

On the other hand, the *Awakening Hungarians* supported the international organization of anti-Semites.[6] The *Society of Awakening Hungarians* and the *Keresztény Nemzeti Liga* [Christian National League] participated in the Vienna conference on the promotion of anti-Semitic and Christian "world solidarity."[7]

A wide spectrum of counter-revolutionary ideas developed. Forces advocating violent repression and those advocating political consolidation both insisted on placing the "Jewish question" and its solution at the center of political thinking. The extreme right launched a full frontal attack. István Milotay summarized their program: "We will reclaim the land, whether small, medium, or large holdings, from the Jews who had grabbed them from us during the past fifty years. We will also reclaim the threatening power, castles, and organization of Big Capital. We will wrench away the press from their hands, retake theaters and literature, and we will monopolize trade and big industry. We will close schools and universities to them and eliminate them from public offices …"[8]

The reason for all this was the failure of assimilation. The post-War revolutions proved that the liberal dream was a delusion. The more successful the Jews were, the less they felt the necessity of integration. Milotay wrote the following about the balking assimilation process: "…similar to the increasing rate and high measure of their economic, cultural and social expansion, the Jews gave up on assimilating as Hungarians and on their inclination to join the nation and the state… . The Jews, in the possession of this huge cultural and political power, abandoned the idea of assimilation and became a state within the state."[9]

István Milotay announced a program of renewal for the trueborn educated Hungarians and swore to fight for a Christian intellectual hegemony. He succinctly formulated the regime's ideas, but viewed them as a long-range program, not as a regime. Certain historians present Milotay as a reform conservative and a right-wing populist,[10] even though his "social sensitivity," acquired in the 1920s, was an attempt to create a mass base in the peasantry and rural professional classes for his proto-fascist radicalism. In response to the permanent revolution of the right-wing, Milotay attacked the ruling regime of Admiral Horthy, regent of Hungary from the extreme right, coming into conflict with prime-minister Bethlen who had fought for consolidation and who, in Milotay's view, had sold out the country to the Jews. Milotay would have continued with the post-war intransigence and racial politics and did demand an ultimate changing of the guard. He began with the view that the urban Christian intelligentsia and white-collar middle class had sunk to the level of an impoverished proletariat.[11] Consequently, it was of crucial importance to force the Jews to retreat in every field and, especially, in education.[12]

Milotay's fight to increase the political influence of the middle class was the so-called quest to define the role of the genteel middle class. The increase in the number of the educated work-force and their post-war unemployment crisis offered adequate reasons for an ethnic interpretation of social tensions.[13] It was Bethlen who incorporated the gentry, civil service, and military officers into his power base, but his regime regime was constantly besieged precisely by the army of malcontent professionals, clerks, teachers, administrators and officials of local administration. Anti-Semitism became a tool of their radicalization.[14]

The "Jewish question" was entwined in a general attack on liberalism. The slogan of "Christian Hungary" was connected with the idea of curbing vulture capital and with the utopia of social reform. As Béla Bangha said, "We have to reform our thinking and to eradicate the defilement that spokesmen of the past fifty-sixty years of journalism, national economic divergence, and organized anti-social mentality have implemented. We will literally have to burn the liberal idols that we have admired until now."[15]

According to Béla Bangha, a Jesuit priest and public writer, the October Revolution and communism "were no more than a conspiracy of destructive Jews planning to annihilate Christian and national Hungary." The Jews would have to be forced out of both economic and cultural life. "...If it is possible, the countryside should not see any Jews."[16]

Milotay's and Bangha's paths diverged after a momentary alliance but theoretically they were connected in criticizing the "regime" from the right. They were dissatisfied with the implementation of the Christian regime's program. Bangha argued that if the Christian national direction failed, all Hungarians would fail since the country's external and internal enemies would strangle its very existence. The external enemy was known but the internal one did not yet have a definite program. "We have worked with commandos in our social reorganization attempts and it resulted in separation and dissension."

The Jewish question was the first among the ambiguous issues. Would the Christian and national trends have institutional protection in the fields of public education, press, and literature? "The six or seven percent Jews in Hungary—down to the last shop-assistant—know what they want. We, the big majority, are helpless. We do not even know exactly what we want." And later, "... we do not dare to face the facts bravely and independently, and do not dare to name the child by its name. Even when we attack liberalism, we throw respectful curtsies toward liberal rhetorical idols and want to build up Christian Hungary under Jewish slogans."[17]

It seemed that a "third Hungary" was to be created by connecting the action against liberalism with the Jewish question. In the preface to his book, and under the same title, its prophet, István Lendvai, envisioned the agony of two "phony" Hungaries—one in war and one in revolution. There was a historical Hungary reborn in 1867 which, however, no longer ruled and there was another one, "the Hungary of foreigners," which raised its head from grubbing among the molehills only in 1918.[6] "I summarize the two countries in two names which represent them: Count István Tisza and Oszkár Jászi-Jakobovits." Lendvai saw the gentry Count Tisza as a father figure for the country but with the star of destruction planted on his forehead. The gentry have "grown too old for the Hungarian existence."

The Hungary after Trianon was the *tertium datur,* that is a third chance for an independent people's state. Hungarians strayed in two different directions but could only venture out on a new road if they broke free from the binding pincers. Otherwise, the union between the "Tarnopol" (Jewish) Hungary and the Vienna (Austrian) power had drifted the country into its fate and the blind "Tisza Hungarianness" was annihilated by the "Semite drift." This is why the two false Hungaries "had to burn" in the red death.

The Memory of Revolutions and the New Anti-Semitism

The post-war revolutions broke out as a result of the conspiracy of the international Jewish union. This statement was an unquestioned platitude of the rightwing press. Mihály Károlyi and Béla Kun, heads of two consecutive revolutions, were the governors of Jewish interests, so it was said. As it was reported by sources of the counter-revolution, eighteen of the twenty-six commissars were Jewish.

Here is how the Tharaud brothers, anti-Semites of international renown, described the revolution in the respectable *Revue des deux Mondes*: "Within two weeks a number of foreigners managed to turn everything upside down—at least in Budapest. A new

Jerusalem grew up on the banks of the Danube, devised by the Jewish mind of Karl Marx and built by Jewish hands. The notion of the ideal city—where there are neither rich nor poor and where perfect equality and justice rule—has been haunting the imagination of Israel's sons for centuries. Dreaming about the coming of the Messiah in the wild ghettoes of Galicia, they had nursed this thought for a long time before their descendant, Béla Kun, strove to establish it on the banks of the Danube."[18]

Writings accusing the Jews of having a revolutionary and Messianic spirit, in effect actually criticized the liberal agreement under the pretext of condemning those Jews who followed communism. Budapest, which was branded a revolutionary place, acquired Lueger's characterization of "Judapest."[19]

Voicing the fear of "jewification" was an idiopathic way of raising anew the old "Jewish question." The fear of "jewification" was fostered by the notion that Jewishness is a pestiferous mentality. It was claimed that its behavior patterns were so strong and its social influence so penetrating that it contaminated its entire social environment. Several sources claimed that even though the Jews had given up their national ambitions by accepting assimilation, immigration continuously replenished Jewish racial characteristics.

The anguish caused by the fear of "jewification" was difficult to support by arguments based on logic or experience. In the shadow of Trianon, theories of decadence mushroomed and the vision of a universal decay seemed to offer the appropriate corrective for the dismemberment of the country. Social Darwinism, the prevailing intellectual trend, created a nightmare image, yet one premised on a scientific concept. On the one hand, the notion that Hungarians were deteriorating had to be pointed out in order to speak about contamination. On the other hand, newer proofs were needed to explain the impossibility of Jewish assimilation.

As János Makkai, a sociologist of the period, said, "There is a larger or smaller, teeny-weeny Jew living in all of us. In order to get rid of him, it is not enough to be anti-Semites and it is not satisfactory to sever social contacts. Instead, we ought to recognize the Jewish influence and its major manifestations."[20]

Peace Talks

Hungary's international situation hindered a large-scale attempt at "dejewification." Albert Apponyi, leading delegate at the Paris peace talks, sent a message to the national assembly cautioning against extremism and calling for the curbing of atrocities.[21] "More and more frequently, news reaches us that in our country private militias set out, on a denominational basis, and violate the civil freedom that is assured by public law. By resorting to force, they endanger people's lives." And this is dangerous because they put at risk the main argument of the peace delegation that "through territorial reorganization, millions of people would be shifted from a community on a higher level of culture to a state at a more backward level."[22]

During the peace talks, Apponyi kept silent about the fact that atrocities were barely controlled in his country and that discrimination had been elevated to the level of state policy.[23]

Sándor Szimonyi-Szemadam read Apponyi's letter in the national assembly and added: "Believe me, hatred against and antipathy towards the Jews are not worth as much as the integrity of Hungary. Please, sacrifice all your moods and antipathy at this big moment … and believe me … that the national course is not negative and nor is it the base of hatred. A real Christian national regime cannot be a hated-based denominational regime."[24]

However, the sometimes careful voice of Parliament was suppressed by the commandos' noise. Rolf Fischer characterizes the double standard the following way: "During their conferences abroad and first of all at the peace conference where the detached territories and the ethnic composition of the population were the issues, Hungarian politicians applied the argument that the majority of the Jews had assimilated as Hungarians. However, the same politicians spoke about the assumed necessity of dissimilation when back in Hungary. Pragmatism was outdistanced by cynicism."[25]

The Jews' patriotic loyalty played a significant role at the peace talks. Pál Teleki participated in writing a memorandum which said: "They proudly mention that Turkish Khazars, many of whom took the Jewish faith, assimilated into the conquering Hungarians... Most of them completely assimilated as Hungarians ... They produced outstanding Hungarian writers, scientists, and artists. With regard to their assimilation to the Hungarian national spirit, we have to acknowledge that, from a racial point of view, Hungarian Jews are not Jews any more."[26]

Obviously, the Hungarian delegation attempted to argue for preserving the pre-war borders of Greater Hungary. However, in its backup strategy, it also considered allowing referenda to be held on the territories to be detached from Hungary. Apponyi indicated that their priority would be to vote for territorial integrity based on historical and natural law but, if needed, they would offer the option of a referendum "on Wilsonian principles."[27] Thus, it needed to be proved that the majority of the population in areas to be joined with other countries were Hungarians. The number of Jewish Hungarians on the already occupied territories was 460,000. Forty-five percent of the population of Munkács and 31 percent of Ungvár's population could have been considered both Hungarian and Jewish.[28]

There existed a real "Jewish question"—whether the Jews of the detached territories now part of Czechoslovakia or Romania would continue to declare themselves Hungarians and, furthermore, whether they would apply for minority rights as assured by the Peace Treaty or would instead adhere to the assimilation "contract." According to the latter option, Judaism was an equal denomination with other established religions. Therefore, the advocates of anti-Semitism played a dangerous game since alienating the Jewish community would have hindered the flow of foreign loans and enforcing restrictive minority laws would have threatened the international political status of the Hungarians.

The population of the detached territories lived under double pressure. People's identity underwent a special crisis as Aladár Komlós, under the pseudonym Álmos Korál, wrote from now Slovakian Eperjes: "And if you still doubt it, we can prove it to you experimentally: strike the Hungarians in front of us and we are in pain… . Strike the Jews and it is even more painful. We can doubly ache."[29]

The Jews of the detached territories were in a "double minority" status.[30] The newly-created states devised different strategies for changing the assimilation pressure on them according to their social standing and social opportunities.[31] Numerous approaches were tried, from claiming themselves to be Hungarian Jews to declaring an independent nationality.[32]

The Jews' political situation in the detached territories was also delicate. Professional studies warn us about the dubiousness of the census results of these areas. For example, declaration of nationality and mother tongue would have been threatening to the Slovak Jews since they possessed minority rights.[33] The political pressure also launched a "dissimilating" process which included a search for a new Jewish identity. Consequently, the Kassa Jewry, Hungarian at heart, did not declare solidarity with the mother-country. Instead, they declared solidarity with the Hungarians who were a minority in Slovakia.

In Slovakia as well as in Transylvania, Zionist movements gained ground and, the politicians of the Hungarian homeland especially blamed the Jews even though their taking on minority status in the detached territories could have hindered assimilation to another new culture. This explains the statement of József Fischer, president of the Transylvanian Jewish National Association, that "during the last five years, history has beaten down Jewish political thinking towards assimilation. The Jews living in Transylvania have irrefutably demonstrated that they have turned back to their own nationality. They do not declare themselves either Hungarian or Romanian but Jewish..."[34] However, arguments supporting this statement only explained the Jews' choice on the level of political reality. The fact is that Jewish nationality hampered the assimilation of the Transylvanian Jews in Romanian society at that specific time. The forces fighting for "Hungarianness" in the detached territories could hardly win considering the low number of Jews, although cooperation between the two nationalities would have produced a moral victory.[35]

The Transylvanian Jews, as well as the majority of the Jews in the homeland, declared themselves to be Hungarian. The scholarly rabbi of Nagyvárad, Lipót Kecskeméti, preached the Word of God on behalf of the detached territories: "Jewish religion is not a Jewish nation. Our national sentiments are with the Hungarians. We are Hungarian Jews even under the new rule and we persist with our Hungarian feeling eternally."[36]

In 1920 at the ratification of the Peace Treaty, József Schönfeld, editor of the *Zsidó Szemle,* mourned for the Jews of the detached territories: of Pozsony, Kassa, Nagyvárad, Munkács, Ungvár, and Temesvár. He found consolation by saying that "Even if the Jews of the occupied areas formally belong to other countries, culturally they will remain identified with the Jews of dismembered Hungary." The Zionist Schönfeld believed the Hungarian Jews had a special calling. "Jews, organized in the name of the Jewish national idea, will be an invisible force that will topple artificial borders while our cultural ties will establish economic connections among us." Then he added, "We will overlook accusations and harassment and, while suppressing our sorrows, fulfill our Jewish and Hungarian obligations."[37]

The Dilemma of the Jews

In the shadow of Trianon the Jews lived under the threat of pressure toward non-assimilation. If qualified as a nationality, they would have been a minority in Hungary that could hardly have counted on having any political influence. As a religious denomination, however, they could have expected a whole series of discriminating measures. The dilemma between nationality and religion was part of the threat anyway since it was the ruling elite who decided whether religion or nationality, as qualifications, would be to their own political advantage. In 1929 an essay summarized the dilemma: "The Jews are a separate nationality, if it entails the predominance of a minority. However, the Jews are part of the nation when so much intellectual and material capital would be missed or when Hungarians talk to the outside world. But they are second-class citizens when it comes to the question of rights and equality before the law. The Jews become a race when wide contradictions between worldviews are to be proven. Finally, Jewishness becomes a religion when the issue at stake is patriotic feelings and sacrifice."[38]

The vast majority of the Jews declared themselves Hungarian even during the post-war revolutions and when the alleged "internationalism" broke loose. Lajos Bíró, a well-known writer and later under-secretary of state during the 1918 revolution, expressed the view of the community: "In this critical moment we, Hungarian Jews, are obligated to make all the sacrifices, with unchanged warm love and multiplied unselfishness, that a homeland might demand from its loyal sons. Many of our brothers have connections with the leading minds and organs of European cultural life. These Jewish brothers of ours should immediately set out to do everything they can in order to warm up the icy climate towards our Hungarian nation during the period of the peace talks."[36]

On August 28, 1919, after the fall of the Hungarian Soviet Republic, the magistracy of the *Pest Israelite Community,* headed by Ferenc Székely, made a solemn declaration. "During good times and bad times, we firmly stand by our country and nation, ready to sacrifice all, confiding in the Hungarian laws that have made us equal citizens of this country." The statement of the Szeged Jewish community, publicized on June 26, 1919, said the following: "We do not tolerate and, wherever it comes from, we refuse any pretext that insinuates that we, the Jews—due to our denomination—are not loyal to our Hungarian homeland and the Hungarian nation. We served the idea of the Hungarian nation in the past and we are at its service today and any other day as well, with unwavering loyalty and dedication."[39]

The Jewish community realized that the counter-revolution could not have occurred without the help of the Jews also. Lajos Szabolcsi thought it was timely in 1940 to quote from the archives (attorney Ármin Balassa's collection) about the counter-revolutionary activities of the Szeged Jews. According to one document Gyula Gömbös, a politician known for his racism, proposed the admission of two Jews into the counter-revolutionary committee. On May 7, 1919, fifteen Jewish soldiers participated in the reoccupation of the Mars Square barracks.

Lajos Szabolcsi also mentioned that a local notary public, "our Jewish brother" Lajos Pálmai, assumed the Minister of Justice position in Count Gyula Károlyi's government which was organized by the Arad counter-revolution and established on May 5, 1919. Later Pálmai became the Minister of Food in Szeged and Chief Rabbi Immánuel Lőw greeted this event from the pulpit. Szabolcsi made the following statement on behalf of the Jews: "According to biased and one-sided presentations, we did not have anything to do with the 'Szeged idea.' Some want to argue away from us the fact that we are also part of the Szeged idea and that we were also present at its birth. There are some who think that the Szeged idea was a Hungarian program excluding us and, what is more, against us, although the Szeged idea evolved into a counter-revolution and we bravely participated in it."[40]

The support given to an anti-Semitic counter-revolution by the official Jewry was justified by both constitutional and experiential considerations. Jewish spokesmen refused to accept the one-sided termination of the results of assimilation policies since they had continuously proved their loyalty to the Hungarians and the nation. We cannot discuss here how much of this was due to illusion and how much of it was a belief in the law. However, the period of revolutions, later called the period of "Jewish rule," really threatened in the name of a fundamental atheism the religious life of Jews that had already been weakened by assimilation. The pressure towards proof distorts it since the anti-religiousness of the dictatorship served as a denial of the legend about Jewish racial solidarity. Religious community president Sándor Léderer remembered 1919 the following way: "The rule of the reds and the unrestrained behavior accompanying this disaster paralyzed every regular function. Even holding council meetings was forbidden. Some public buildings were reserved for commissarial offices. The Dohány Street synagogue was designated to become a concert hall. The pension fund was confiscated …"[41]

The Jewish denomination assumed a constitutional position from the beginning of the counter-revolution. Moderates on both sides applied standards of moral conviction and legitimacy to the Jewish issue, urged that the law should settle the Jewish question, channeled excesses into favorable directions, and "civilized" behavior. The *numerus clausus* was directed not only against the Jews, but was also a means to intellectually disarm the "commandos" that Gyula Andrássy's and Miksa Fenyő's debate had illuminated in the columns of the *Új Magyar Szemle* and the *Nyugat.*[42]

Swept up by the spirit of the times, Gyula Andrássy seemed to have found the roots of the "Jewish question" in pre-war liberal politics. It was the basic idea and hope of liberal politics that justice and equality would assimilate the Jews so that they would gradually integrate as Hungarians. However, this hope was never fulfilled and the Christian middle class was in a depressed condition while the Jews had been getting rich during the war. Consequently, the Jewish question had to be solved and Andrássy counted on the cooperation of the Jews.

Miksa Fenyő was "deeply saddened" by Andrássy's article. If the writer of the article was right, the "Jewish question" would be solved only by pogrom-like actions "because that is how one can break the habit of almost one million Jews who stubbornly declare themselves Hungarians in order to succeed in either economic or scientific fields." How could Andrássy wish that the Jews would pursue a Hungarian national policy when they are driven out of every career by the "policy of hatred?" Fenyő pointed out the traps in Andrássy's reasoning and predicted its consequences. "What do the people generally think and what kind of existential opportunities do they allot to the Jews when they say, 'We will drive you into the background economically, both institutionally and by force, and we will not allow you to become a civil servant, a teacher, a judge, a doctor, a lawyer, or an engineer. Only Herod could solve this problem."[43]

Andrássy, similar to Milotay's *Magyarság* which came into existence with his help, acted on behalf of the new middle class and the Christian intellectuals. This group was more moderate than Milotay or Bangha but acted in the same spirit as far as their goals were concerned. Andrássy wrote, "It is also the intelligentsia's task that propaganda against the Jews be kept within the boundaries of fairness and wise foresight and not let hatred, which has undoubtedly spread, become the chief motif." This propagation could not be confined to intellectual areas. Neither should the financial capital and financial management be in the hands of people who could easily succeed in other countries. Instead, "...the ones who are our flesh and blood ought to gain power in the financial world—those whose lives are inseparably connected to this country and can develop only here and nowhere else."[44]

The Jews defended themselves on three fronts. To prove loyalty to the state was the first issue, especially in the debate about the number of Hungarian Jews who died on the front, the proper number of Jewish soldiers, and their proportionate losses. Lajos Szabolcsi sued and, with the help of his attorney Ernő Ballagi, won the "war of numbers" debate with Representative Elek Avarffy who contested the number of Jewish soldiers who died in the trenches of World War I.[36]

The second debate front opened up on the question of religion and race. While the official Jewry, unequivocally and concordantly with their political position, declared themselves a religious denomination, there were those who tried to reconcile the trio of race, religion, and national loyalty. Tamás Kóbor, the famous novelist and publicist wrote: "As much as I fiercely contend the idea that the Jews are not Hungarians, I recognize their racial difference. It is impossible to deny and just as superfluous. During centuries, the Jewish community has maintained its racial characteristics in addition to its religion."[45]

The acceptance of the racial aspects of Jewishness was rare among applied Jewish defense strategies, especially from a community condemned to be driven out even though, by the end of the War, it had become clear that the dream of liberal assimilation was dead. The Jewish masses had not merged into the Hungarians without any trace, not even in cultural fields. Moreover, the illusion had caused the development of ambiguous psychological attitudes and peculiar social behavior patterns. Converts to Christianity were considered to be traitors by the official representatives of the Jewish community. This was logical if, as in their view, the Jews represented a denomination and nothing else. However, the characteristics of this conflict depended on the kind of model of assimilation used to inspire religious loyalty.

On the question of converts, the left-wing advocated the democratic principle of free choice. In the course of the debates, which had revived at the beginning of the 1930s, Rusztem Vámbéry effectively explained that religious loyalty by itself was not an answer to anything and nor did it offer any refuge to the "Hungarian" Jews. "...The debate whether the Jews who were baptized under Bolshevism or after Bolshevism were discreditable is futile because not only a motivated Jew's bravery and self-respect are concentrated in his spur but also his judgment. It is more important for him to be able to sew frogs and loops on his caftan and tulips on the wall of the ghetto than to remove the caftan and break down the walls of the ghetto."[46]

The contradiction in the Jewish existence multiplied after Trianon. The dilemma which Aladár Komlós, under the pseudonym Álmos Korál, discussed still remained: are we Jewish or Hungarian? Even if the generation that was raised in liberalism voted for Hungarian, it thus denied its dual bonds in a self-mutilating way. "...Time and again the Jewish blood sees through the Hungarian skin" of assimilated writers and poets. Aladár Komlós very openly stated it behind the pseudonym, "There is Jewish blood circulating behind Ferenc Molnár's heroes' skin. ...Ignotus stands on a Hungarian nationalist basis but in his extreme liberalism he involuntarily fights for Jewish interests. And the way he fights, his dialectics and rhythm of thoughts, are unparalleled Jewish. ... Ernő Szép always feels that he is from a different world and not from the Hungarian people's world. And as a Jew, he would consider it a little false if he dedicated himself to populism without restriction."[47]

A writer of the right-radical press, István Lendvai, accused Ernő Szép for the same thing he was praised by Komlós. In Ernő Szép "there is a complete and impenetrable, that is eternal, foreignness." When Jewish writers described Hungarian mansions and peasant houses, it was all counterfeit. They write "In the foreign light of Hanukkah candles which they probably cannot help and which is probably unconscious since it is stitched into their flesh and bones with the thread of millennia."[48]

However, the comparison of the similarity of Komlós' and Lendvai's opinions paradoxically emphasized their differences. What was a cultural community for Komlós was race for Lendvai. While Komlós considered the Jews capable of a new assimilation through self-criticism and cleansing, Lendvai believed that there was an unbridgeable difference between the Hungarians and the Jews.

Wherever the revision of the assimilation project began, it could not solve this issue of a dual trap—Hungarian and/or Jewish. Instead, it intensified it. Jewish self-reflection became the new program of the Jews—from Aladár Komlós to Károly Pap—against external criticism.

Aladár Komlós, a noted literary historian and critic, differentiated between two types of assimilating Jews. On the one hand, there were those who adopted Hungarian habits, wore Tyrolese hats, and became drunk time and again. "But these, superficially assimilated gentry Jews, are really the ugliest ghetto Jews" in whom there was a bad mixture of the ghetto Jew's amorality and gentry shallowness, as he saw them.

However, the ideal type of the assimilated Jew was foreshadowed in the post-Trianon catastrophe: "the Jew who has nurtured in himself the backbone and delicate sensitivity of the cream of Western Christianity and, therefore, does not lower himself by falsely imitating shallow superficiality, but quietly and bravely declares himself a Jew."[49]

Postulating the existence of two types of assimilated Jews was a desperate attempt to revive and maintain the process of an arrested integration and cultural symbiosis. The idea that there were "two types of Jews" also surfaced in a more moderate "ethnic" ideology. Publications and theoretical writings about the "Jewish question" between the two world wars, from the politician and journalist Bajcsy-Zsilinszky to the essayist and critic László Németh, portrayed the Komlós-Korál ideal type as a minority within Jewry. As

Endre Bajcsy-Zsilinszky wrote, "I know very well that there were and are great numbers of Jews who are not only exemplary patriots and valuable contributors to the Hungarian cause, but who also want to and are able to merge into the way of thinking of the Hungarian race. It is most unfortunate, however, that this cannot be stated about the masses of today's Jews."[50]

Miksa Falk, Mór Mezei, and Lipót Vadász, high officials in the "Golden Age of the Compromise" were classified as "good" Jews by Endre Bajcsy-Zsilinszky while Lajos Bíró, Pál Kéri, Zsigmond Kunfi, Oszkár Jászi, and Lajos Hatvany, free-floating intellectual, scholars and journalists in some cases turned politicians, were categorized as "bad" Jews who, after achieving power in 1918, fostered the Jews' distinct views, thinking, and goals in revolutionary times.

There was a threatening occasional concurrence between the critics who censured the roles of the Jews from the "inside" and those who denounced them from the "outside." While the official representatives of Jews shifted all the responsibility to the internationalist Jewish intellectuals who participated in revolutions, Jewish critics of past assimilation attempts worked on developing new conditions for a renewed assimilation endeavor by accepting the general Hungarian slogan for a national moral revival. Vis-à-vis assimilation, which was considered hypocritical in retrospect, they showed the possibility of a humanist Jewish consciousness which would open a new road towards Hungarians. Being Hungarian with a Jewish consciousness seemed to be the new assimilation contract proposed by the Jewish intellectuals. The starting point of this new assimilating contract, based on a hidden and unspoken agreement, was acceptance of the theory of the "two kinds" of assimilated Jews.

As Lajos Hatvany, the best example of a Jew disapproved by everyone during the inter-war period, said: "I am and remain—in my Jewish self—Hungarian." He was among the first to publicize abroad Hungary's plight and suffering under the shadow of Trianon in his book published in German with a telling title: "The Wounded Land."[51]

From his exile, he continuously sent professions of love to Hungarians, written in a defensive and hysterical tone. In one article he envied the rabid anti-Semite Dezső Szabó because Szabó was able to condemn the regime without the word "Jew" being thrown at him. And if Hatvany acknowledged Szabó, the Jews would laugh in his face for having offered himself to the racist. The world was open to him and to others, yet the novelist and playwright Sándor Bródy and Ignotus, emigrèes like him, kept sending their warm professions of love back to their homeland.[52]

The post-Trianon situation again raised the issue of the "parvenu" and the "pariah." During the pre-war period of the Hungarian-Jewish tension and during the time of an assumed successful assimilation, breaking away from the Jewish community was seen as the measure of adjustment to the Hungarians. Jewish awareness of identity had faded or was retained only in the collective unconscious.

From the hosts' perspective, social acceptance did not accompany assimilation. The pseudo-feudal social structure did not facilitate integration. The Hungarian-Jewish conflict often walked in disguise: when identified as a denominational difference, it allowed the cultural community to refuse to deal with it. In addition, the developing urban lifestyle brought about an antagonism between "foreign" Budapest and the "Hungarian" countryside. Further, literary modernity developed the stylized theme of a confrontation between a popular-national past and a decadent modernity. As Viktor Karády described it, the paradox of the first, pre-Trianon, phase of assimilation did not defeat the primordial stigmatization of Jews and, as a result, "every Jewish initiative towards fundamental group solidarity and cultural subsistence was followed by suspicion."[53]

The balance between integration and keeping traditions was tipped during the war and the post-Trianon period. The anti-assimilation group was strengthened while the war caused a social crisis, an ideal situation for scapegoating. The war made it difficult to achieve assimilation or status mobility especially because Hungarian liberalism was built on the 1867 Compromise and social compromises were undermined by recent events. The eminent historian Miklós Szabó considered "ressentiment" the strongest motivating force behind Hungarian anti-Semitism. "Ressentiment" conveyed the emotional reaction that the Jews had attracted against themselves more dynamically than any other social group.[54] Identifying capitalism with the Jews was a projection of insecurity about the social mobility issue. Finally, the representation of *ressentiment* was taken up by the advocates of political anti-Semitism.

Signs of crisis among the Jews and uncertainty about the sensibility and possibility of various goals multiplied in the atmosphere of *ressentiment.* The assimilation crisis manifested itself in the Jews experiencing a continuous irritation and a certain understandable over-sensitivity. The chronic identity-duality forced Jewish intellectuals into paradoxical situations. As Anna Lesznai characterized it in the debate of the *Huszadik Század,* this duality not only manifested itself in a Jew's social situation but also internally since "the Jew is a Jew for himself as well." Consequently, *"the Jewish psyche developed under contradictory influences as opposed to Christians living under normal circumstances.* The Jews' religiousness and ancient traditions became social handicaps. Plus they hold their nationalist affiliation (their Hungarian, French, or German pride) as well." A Jew has to be ashamed of his wealth and his brains in order not to evoke any antipathy. His latent ghetto-fear shifts into shame. *"He is unable to coexist with a Christian social group at his cultural level without denying himself to a certain degree."*

Fathers and Sons

The two types of Jews originated in this situation, "the two extreme attitudes of an excluded man who does not belong anywhere and the man who is humiliated in his self-esteem"—the snobs, gentry imitators, and adjusters on the one hand and the iconoclasts on the other.[55]

It is worth examining the two types in a specific historical context. The Jewish generation that was successful in its economic mobility could certainly be classified as the "fathers" who had integrated into society even at the expense of hypocrisy while the war and post-Trianon generations experienced their dual bind as an identity crisis. The latter also considered a new alternative, universal internationalism, hoping it would solve social injustices and the "Jewish question," which had been driven into the background but which many still experienced. In his above quoted article, McCagg considered the radical universalistic experiment a possible solution to the dilemma between integration and loyalty to tradition, a revolt against the fathers' first assimilation attempt.[3] More exactly, those "sons" who suffered in the war rejected the assimilation strategies of earlier generations. The secularization that had accompanied the fathers' status mobility created a proper foundation for a different bond with the radicalized Christian intellectuals.

It is appropriate here to introduce the principal actors in the unfolding drama of Hungarian modernity. The advocates of renewal grouped themselves round a literary review poitedly named "Nyugat," "The West," thus disclosing their political and intellectual orientation. To follow the example of the West, of the more advanced countries in Europe was the professed goal of the review. The editor-in-chief of the periodical, however, entitled his introductory article in 1908 "Kelet népe" [People of the East] referring to Hungarians as of oriental origins linguistically related to the Finns. The occidental orientation of "oriental" people was the program of the witty journalist, poet, raconteur and organizer who had hidden himself behind the pen-name Ignotus. Born as Hugo Veigelsberg he was the epitome of the assimilated Jew.

Ignotus reached out to the new talents growing up in the provinces and adapting to the buzzing life in Budapest, the capital. The names he protected, discovered adn interpreted are legion, the foremost among them Endre Ady (1877-1919), the emblematic figure of turn-of-the century modernity. a descendant of lesser nobility Ady became a symbol of radical thinking. Decadent and revolutionary, a true-born Hungarian and philo-Semite—the relationship to Ady was the scale on which political opinion was scaled. Even after his early death the relationship to his legacy located literati in the sometimes parochial battles on either side of the fence.

Nyugat the periodical was breeding all the new talents—now classics—of Hungarian literature. One of its financial backers adn authors was baron Lajos Hatvany. Trained as a classicist, publishing his scholarly works in German and Hungarian, Hatvany was a combatant critic of conservatism and the financial source of the bohemian escapades of Endre Ady.

Both Ignotus and Hatvany became emigrants after the First World War and the revolutions. *Nyugat* was taken over by a triumvirate of editors. One of them, the exquisite poet and essayist, Mihály Babits was a devout Catholic, and, as we will see, was tainted by some side-remarks about "Hungarian-Jewish symbiosis." The *Nyugat* achieved success first by fraternity and aestheticism, or more plainly said, by brushing the "question" under the carpet. Behind the cavalier attitude (or neglect) there was an undercurrent of "knowing," a secret "who's who" by descent or affiliation. Suppressed and erupting after Trianon, palpable discrimination shadowed public discourse due to the influence of the prophet of anti-Semitism Dezső Szabó.

A trained linguist of Finno-Ugrian languages Dezső Szabó was the trensetter in blaming the alliance of liberalism and the Jews for the decay of Hungary. A sharp and witty a pamphleteer and orator he spread hate among his youthful followers. It must be mentioned here that he started his writing career in the review *Nyugat*.

In the aftermath of the war and the revolutions the achievement of the *Nyugat* was drastically re-evaluated. In the eyes of conservatives or representatives of the vision of cultural decay *Nyugat* embodied the symbiosis of "foreigners and true-born Hungarians."

It was not by chance that the Ady-Ignotus and the Ady-Hatvany unions around the review *Nyugat* were criticized by the new conservatives. They embodied the cooperation between "foreigners and the pure-bloods" which was recognized and attacked in post-Trianon Hungary. The union was not a simple affair and did not lack for obstacles in the first decade of the century. Aladár Komlós warned that the "Jew-like" term describing the attitude of Ady appeared in Babits' and Kosztolányi's early correspondence around the turn of the century.[56] Differences stemming from origin, taste, and possible prejudices were settled by the idea of an alliance to promote modern Hungarian literature. As the conservative literary historian Gyula Farkas wrote, "Writing for and even reading the *Nyugat* counts as a political confession and excludes 'the offender' from the 'patriotic' nation. The poet-contributors of the review bear its odium because it is not politics which is important to them but literature as such. In this way, however, rapprochement is difficult for those who cannot or do not want to separate the two: literature and politics. They become more and more isolated and become independent of the support group of radicals, the Jewish intellectuals."[57]

Such a historical separation of the "national" and the "artistic" was the vice of the conservatives, something also acknowledged by Gyula Farkas. After the war, however, the role of the accuser and the victim were reversed and then the radical intellectuals were charged of expropriating artistic innovations. Ignotus, forced into exile, was blamed that he had not really understood Ady while Hatvany was accused of financially corrupting Ady. Farkas also discovered that beneath the harmony of an undisturbed "Jewish-Hungarian" symbiosis, differences erupted time and again, even if they did not mature into full-fledged conflicts. Still, in 1914 Zsigmond Móricz underestimated the role Ignotus played around Ady: "Whoever wants to understand this poet, not only does he have to live in this man's 'Life-grove' *but must also live in the millennial jungle of the Hungarian race....*" It must have been evident to the perceptive reader that the above did not apply to Ignotus.[57]

"Ady-expropriation" was one of the most significant ambitions between the two world wars since it hid one of the justifications for the racial theory. Ady's masterpieces, however, were really not up for bargaining. When János Makkai wrote in the publication, *Ifjú szívekben élek* [I Live On in Young Hearts], "We have learned [from Ady] that Hungary belongs to the Hungarians and it is the Hungarian race's hegemony that should lead to victory," Komlós, staunch defender of liberal values responded in the columns of the *Századunk.*[58]

The Ady Expropriation

According to Komlós, Dezső Szabó initiated the counter-revolutionary Ady-expropriation. Komlós must have known that the Ady image had changed a lot in Dezső Szabó's work: during the revolutions he still celebrated the universal Ady,[59] while later on he hailed in Ady the true-born Hungarian genius.

Komlós might as well have added that it was Szabó who had warmed up the "racial issue." In the 1910s, dormant since the turn of the century, the chief motive of his articles, written under a pseudonym, was to scourge those Jews believed to be settling on the national body. The Jews' goal "is to chew up the roots of the Christian and national culture, to cut the past from under Hungarian feet, and to establish the rule of the Jewish race on the carcass of a religiously, morally, and financially destroyed nation." His pamphlets teemed with such expressions as "the Semite race that grew extremely bold."[60] The "racial" question became inflamed just at the end of the War. After Ady's death, in the memorial volume of the *Nyugat*, Tibor Déry still held it against Ady that he was the last one to speak about the "national idea," since "primary human characteristics are universal."[61]

As if to respond to that, in 1920 Mihály Babits, one of the most respected poet of his generation, co-editor of *Nyugat*, wrote that, "Through his deepest roots, Ady was the poet of a nation's self-esteem and its race..."[62] Then Babits proceeded to explain the essence of this "racial issue" which was far removed from any exclusionary policy and which would only be distorted by "teasing Hungarians."

Dezső Szabó reevaluated the achievements of the *Nyugat* from the perspective of the racial issue. In the revolution of the best among the contributors to the *Nyugat,* he celebrated the rise of the true Hungarians. "All the important talents of this literature, except for the one Southern Slav Babics (*sic.*), were flesh and blood Hungarians." He was as naturally Hungarian as nobody else was before him. If they were attacked in their Hungarianness, it was because the "Jewish nationality writers" joined them. The Jewish writers, as opposed to their Hungarian brethren "clowned away the Hungarian language with grimaces and tasteless gambols ..."[63]

The *Nyugat*'s separation of writers into true Hungarians and Jews was Dezső Szabó's own invention. However, in order to rewrite literary history he had to cope with Ady's giant shadow. It was a difficult task to squeeze out any verification of racism in Ady, the prophet of assimilation. As his surviving brother stated about Ady, "It was his conviction until his death that the integration of a few hundreds of thousands lively, agile, and teachable Jews among the talented but sluggish and slower blooded Turanian millions would result in a mixture of races, beneficial not only to the Hungarians but to all mankind."[64]

Obviously, Endre Ady was also a son of his time. When he became irritated in company, similar to the Hungarian gentry, he let his tongue loose and made remarks which would qualify as racist. On the occasion of a visit to his wealthy editor's mansion, which Ady mightily envied, he wrote the poem called *Zikcene, Zakcene, satöbbi* [Zikcene, Zakcene, et cetera] mocking Yiddish counting.

"Beauty and dream,
In their possession,
Zikcene, Zakcene, I am scared,
Future, women, and life are all theirs."[65]

On this, Aladár Komlós reflected that "Irritations, sometimes awakened towards each other by sons of alien races, might have inflamed Ady's nerves and there might have been some anti-Semitism within his heart of hearts. But let us not worry about the word 'race.' It all depends on what you do with your theory of racism. …Yes, it could easily happen that the yellow flame of racism (hatred of Swabians, Jews, Galicians, etc.) flared up in Ady. …However, Ady rejected, despised, and fought against any sign of racism. ... However, what the racist placed on an altar—his inferior sentiment—the poet rejected with disgust."[58]

Even there, Ady's example was undeniable. He also expressed his faith in assimilation by identifying with the persecuted as his poem *Bélyeges sereg* [Army of the Yellow Star] so well exemplified. In the Hungary between the two world wars, this kind of identification was more and more difficult and any solidarity with minorities faced several obstacles. For example, Babits' poem from the beginning of the 1920s identified anyone persecuted with the Jews:

"Ouch, I have been smeared with mud,
My kind watches me in disgust,
And I wear what Jews used to:
The ugly rags with a yellow patch."[66]

The *Nyugat* and the Race Issue

Although the post-Ady *Nyugat* of the 1920s moved away from its apolitical liberalism, it never gave way to counter-revolutionary ideas. Even in the question of "race," it withstood the trend of the times, although it had to be aware of the "semantic field" that the post-Trianon slogans had contaminated.

Ignotus could not help responding to Kunó Klebersberg who had given an account of his experiences in Germany where the importance of national and racial characteristics of poetry had dawned on him. Ignotus' article well exemplified how disturbing for the thinking of the time the issue of "race" had become. Ignotus hurled around dozens of names to demonstrate how difficult it was to separate national from racial qualities, while he himself mixed up the ideas. He acknowledged that "art starts where it is rooted in blood, race, and nation, and cannot be different by the nature of the uniqueness of art itself because the more unique one is, the more a typical embodiment of his kind."

From there, Ignotus concluded that racial and national characteristics were primordial and could neither be stimulated nor tricked into being. "Shall I order the artist to make his art originate from him, that is from his own kind? It is futile. Art stems from there anyway… . Art, racial art, and national art exist, but dictated art has never been art."[67]

An obstinate defense of literary freedom and autonomy made Ignotus word his thoughts loosely. A co-worker of the *Nyugat*, Zoltán Szász, ventured to realign them. He stated that under "race and kind," Ignotus mostly meant nation and people. "Ignotus speaks about French, German, and English races and 'raciality' and, in the same breath, about belonging to the French, German, and Hungarian nations." This false identification might lead to disturbing consequences. "The fact that somebody is a Jew is not simple enough of a matter to say 'a Jewish kind' … because in my view, kind and race are worlds apart from nation and people."[68]

The occasional debates in the *Nyugat* on race and racial characteristics always focused on separating the question from actual politics. With its apolitical nature, its concentration on art, and its literary ambitions towards modernity, the *Nyugat* offered a historical brake on the debate about "national" and "cosmopolitan" and, leaving that vicious circle, declared it null and void. The liberalism of the Compromise limited the question to intellectual issues and hardly allowed one of its hidden aspects—assimilation—to be revealed. While assimilation was considered to be a necessary consequence of liberalism in the world of the Nineteenth century, influential ideologues of the post-Trianon historical situation, from Gyula Szekfű to László Németh, viewed liberalism as a consequence and distortion of assimilation.

A Stroke of Lightning

Political radicalism was one of the ways out from under a faltering and dismantled assimilation project. At the same time, the liberalism created by the Compromise of 1867 was a balanced model for assimilation. But it was a fragile equilibrium, one toppled by the War. The war experience induced several generations to reconsider the whole political system and the role of the severely disappointed Jewish intellectuals. In the light of a worldwide catastrophe, they had a glimpse of the failure of assimilation. Their revolt was against the Hungarian-Jewish symbiosis, whose hypocrisy and aimlessness they experienced in the duality of resignation and appeal. Looking back from the post-Trianon period, the fates of the integrating parvenu and the revolting pariah seemed equally hopeless.

The Jewish pariah and parvenu conflict was the dominant theme of a novelist of post-Trianon liberalism, Béla Zsolt. Journalist, playwright, pamphleteer Zsolt was an emblematic figure of Hungarian literature between the two World Wars. Maligned for identifying himself with the Jewish cause he was, in the meantime, a resolute critic of the assimilation process. He chastized Jews for conformism and false acculturation to the worst features of Hungarian society, and the Hungarian middle-class for being insensitive hosts to those who ascertain their identity as Hungarians.

One of Béla Zsolt's autobiographical novels, *Villámcsapás* [Stroke of Lightning], was an authentic mirror of this dual disappointment. As Zsolt explained, in post-Compromise Hungary, most of the Jews dressed up as Hungarians. "It was certainly in the interest of the plutocrats, Jewish university professors, and lawyers engaged in politics that Jewish assimilation would seem to be genuine and convincing because in their business connections with the ruling classes and in their professional careers, they needed the support of the fiction about a 'Hungarianized' patriotic Jewry. Probably, that is why the newly created Jewish press fell into the trap of chauvinistic exaggerations of Hungarianness… . The Jew of the third segment of the century became the domestic political Jew of historical Hungary. Therefore, the Jews of the previous generation had become conservatives—in compliance with the spirit of historical Hungary—before they became Hungarians."

The post World War I generation became Hungarian in a different way. "We felt that our fathers were not honest Hungarians. Instead, they were accomplices of the ruling classes, representing Hungary's authority, and we wanted to make good this Jewish sin. That is the reason why we became radicals and socialists. We became Hungarians and is it possible to love a nation more honestly than through its people? Our generation did not have any specific Jewish goal… The October Revolution was not only aimed at historical Hungarians. It was also the young Jewish intelligentsia's own fight against their fathers…"[69]

This retrospective explanation of radicalization pinpointed its foundation at Trianon. In the light of its failure, it exaggerated the first generation's sins and justified its participation in the revolutions by appealing to an abstract love of the people. The loss of the dual illusions certainly supports the self-flagellation that arose from this bitterness. Béla Zsolt, a child of the post-Trianon era, internalized the acceptance of the "Jewish question" and the fact that it was the task of the Hungarian public life to find a remedy for this centuries-long problem.

Jewish Self-Hatred

The revolutionary inclination of the Jews, so sensitive to moral absolutes, has been analyzed by numerous historical essays. At the beginning of the 1930s Theodor Lessing's book, *Jüdischer Selbtshass,* was also discussed in Hungary. Through six Jewish life-stories including Maximilian Harden and Otto Weininger, it discusses the internal discord of six outstanding representatives of the Jews.

As Theodor Lessing argued, modern Jewry was an "at risk" group whose energies were wasted in a fight for survival. This community had always been forced to believe in a higher idea, to fix their eyes on a utopia, and to define themselves as pure ethic will instead of simply enjoying the immediacy of life. "The turbulent malcontent, the tyrant of justice, and the angry fanatics arrived instead of the favored of life."[70]

The rebellious Jew was a type who came from the community in crisis. The second type of Jew denied himself and found every mistake *in himself.* Therefore, he annihilated himself. The third type of Jew was the one who completely cast himself aside and identified with others. However, as György Kecskeméti, commenting on Lessing stated, this type of assimilation remained completely external. "The fugitive did not become what he would have liked to be. He did not find a new life but simply lost the old one."[71]

Kecskeméti continued with the argument that the Hungarian Jews did not need an excessive assimilation. This was different from the German assimilation where the emancipated Jewry adjusted to a high culture because, in Hungary, the Jews were the creators of genuine culture. Thus, they could not feel like a foreign body since they had played a lion's share in the Hungarianization of the cities and in the process of the Hungarian language becoming dominant. "Here anti-Semitism has been, and is being, energized by what is so exceptional in the historical role of the Jews—the Jews' comfortable settlement within the Hungarian middle-class."[72] As opposed to other European assimilation processes, "when the Hungarian Jews became members of the Hungarian bourgeois civilized society, they did not sit down to eat at a foreign table. Instead, they began to appreciate the fruit of work they had actively participated in."

Kecskeméti's arguments not only delicately reveal the self-identity crisis of Hungarian Jews, but they also pointed out the essential characteristic of the post-Trianon anti-Semitism whose focus included not only the Jews but the developing Hungarian bourgeoisie. The disowning of the Jews showed that post-Trianon Hungarian politics—an ethnocentric, interventionary, feudal, and free-market limiting system—also wanted to break with liberalism.

Anti-Semitism—Anti-Capitalism

The Jewish question and the attack on "capitalism" were closely inter-linked in the parliamentary debates of the early 1920s. As opposition representative Rezső Rupert said in parliament, "the anti-Bolshevik fight spread over to the field of the anti-bourgeois fight."[73]

In the 1920s the number of parliamentary bills urging limits on property and curbing free-market capitalism increased. Representative Béla Fangler proposed a "national Jewish survey" which would have divided religious denominations into "guilty" and "not guilty" categories. The property of the guilty would be confiscated and the living quarters of the suspected would be limited to one room. If a Christian wanted to open a shop, he could legitimately point out a Jewish shop to be confiscated.

Thus Hungarian legislation looked for an ethnocentric solution to the overproduction of the educated professionals and the problems faced by the middle-class which had fled from the detached territories. As statistician Alajos Kovács stated[74] there was a 50% increase in the number of civil servants teachers and clerks in dismembered Hungary. This fact elicited a sort of "blood of my own blood and flesh of my own flesh" reaction in many Hungarians. There could not be any constructive work with such rootless clerisy. "After all, it is not immaterial from what layer of society come intellectuals, the leading elements of a nation. Nor is it immaterial whether they are identical with the national body in origin and blood or whether they are driven by the same feelings and desires as the universal nation. In other words, do the intellectuals have roots in the nation and are they a perfect spiritual essence of it or, rather, do they originate from alien and non-assimilated blood, permeated by a foreign spirit, and are a distant part of the nation body far removed from national ideals?"

A statistician counts ethnicity based on "racial criteria." A statistician would ask whether it is justified that a country, 94% Christian, should allot one quarter of its leading positions to elements of "foreign origin" "whose special racial characteristics, traditions, and ways of thinking are at complete variance with (or at cross-purposes with) what we call the Christian spirit and morality."[75]

It is surprising that certain leaders of the 1918 Revolution (called bourgeois or democratic in various interpretations or Octobrists), such as Oszkár Jászi or Pál Szende, surrendered to the pressure to raise the "Jewish question." As a prominent figure in the October revolution, Jászi wrote the following in his first book in exile in 1920: "The Jewish question does exist in Hungary and it has to be healed." The Jewish question was created by the peculiarity of Hungary's historical development. And Jászi continued, using the vocabulary of the regime that he had vehemently criticized, "Somehow the blood contact between the highest intellectual values and the deepest human terrain ceased to exist. ... The Hungarian spirit had proved to be more and more barren and the sparse ranks of culture's army became filled by aliens, primarily Jews. And these were Jews with the highest level of skills of adapting to the system of exploitation popularly called the Hungarian state. Therefore, the noisiest, most disrespectful, and least scrupulous representatives of *Junkerdom* succeeded and the most disgusting spiritual synthesis in the world came into existence as the cross-section of Budapest's leading intellectuals. It was a mixture of the arrogant, show-off, superficial, and idleness of gentry mentality mixed with the amorality, cynicism, and lecherous nihilism of *Lipótváros* [Leopoldtown, a Jewish district of Budapest]."

Jászi's unusual remark can only be explained by his acceptance of the "lingua" and semantics of the period. The above lines, written in Vienna, harmonize with the anti-feudal and anti-Semitic "Jew-criticism" of the Austrian Left and Marxism[76] which sought to use elements of the social aspects of anti-Semitism in order to expand its mass base.

The anathematized Jakobovits of the regime, Oszkár Jászi, announced the failure and derailment of assimilation without realizing that with the October Revolution he had already experienced the failure of the revolt against assimilation. Therefore, by the 1920s the assimilation contract had been terminated by several sides. By being in alliance with district administrators and with capitalists, assimilation had become "a very enraging mixture of Turanian indolence and yeshiva-boys' relativism."[77] A part of the Jewish community that stayed in Hungary withdrew into a religious identity while the regime reacted by developing several explanations for the fact that the main reason why the country had disintegrated was due to the assimilation attempt and the Jews' role in the revolutions.

The community in exile wanted to expose the regime by pointing to its alliance with Jewish banking capital. As Pál Szende, another emigrant wrote, the victims of the white terror were always poor little men and never rich capitalists. "The more autocratic a regime is, the higher the level of corruption is, and smart Jewish merchants reap the huge crop." He mentioned a case when the brigantines shot a Jewish-looking banker. In this case, the assailants were brought to justice while, in cases involving poorer Jews, they went on acting unpunished. The situation had turned upside down, characterized by the following: "It may sound unbelievable, but the most ferocious anti-Semites are really philo-Semites, friends of the rich Jews," while "in the Hungary of today, there is no place for a Jew with a moral foundation." The Jews were nostalgic for the golden days of István Tisza "when Jewish capitalists not only become rich but were able to stay patriotic."

In the spirit of Austro-Marxism the exiled liberal, Pál Szende, analyzed the situation of the Jews in counter-revolutionary Hungary and concluded that the regime absolved the rich and struck the poor. Arguments referring to the economic situation hardly considered the impact of having no rights and the humiliation and social consequences of being outcasts. Szende did not recognize the end of assimilation and envisioned that rubbing shoulders with the gentry world could continue, albeit perhaps in different forms. "Does anti-Semitism exist in Hungary? The answer is 'yes' and 'no.' With regard to the rich Jews it is 'no;' with regard to poor Jews or Jews who possess moral and intellectual values, it is 'yes.' ...Hungarian communists were mostly Jewish and yet they wanted to wage a lethal fight against Jewish capitalism. Leaders of the new Hungary were Christian and anti-Semitic, yet, they acted according to the interests of Jewish bankers."[78]

Szende, just like Rudolf Diner-Dénes in Paris, tried to explain to the outside world Hungary's mysterious contradictions, the role of the Jews in the revolution, and why the regime, which wanted to reclaim Greater Hungary, found its leading ideology in anti-Semitism. The French socialist Leon Blum admitted honestly that for him the new Hungary was a mystery and an anachronism in the modern world.[79] According to Rudolf Diner-Dénes the leftists in exile hoped that a Western orientation would gain the upper hand, in the spirit of a new compromise between the Hungarians and the Slavs.

The ambitions of the exiles were in sharp contrast with works created during the "Trianon shock" of the 1920s. The most influential, Gyula Szekfű, promulgated a Hungarian orientation towards the "German spirit" while conservative historiographers such as Dávid Angyal and Henrik Marczali, scholars of Jewish extraction argued for the Hungarians' historical rights to the Carpathian Basin. Kuno Klebelsberg even raised "Hungarian cultural superiority" to a political level.[80]

Numerus Clausus

The "Trianon experience" entailed a radical revision in Hungary's minority policy and in the assimilating practices of the Monarchy and Hungarian liberalism.[81] The 1920 introduction of the *numerus clausus* became the revision's symbolic and concrete promulgation.

The ratification of the *numerus clausus* had been preceded by the anti-Jewish demands of right-wing radical student movements "to clean up" the universities.[82] This movement was stimulated by difficulties young people had in adjusting to their arrival home from the front. The drafting of the bill was the result of the central government's taking an exemplary series of measures, under pressure of the students and with the submission of the universities to the curtailment of their autonomy, that compromised with extreme right radicalism.[83]

The Bill was prepared in two stages. Several parliamentary committees first discussed the criteria by which students should have the appropriate "moral and patriotic reliability." Then, a motion on "the proportionate number of races and nationalities" was introduced. Finally, multiple hearings were held connecting patriotism and the racial question in a syntactically innocent and disguised way, although its anti-Jewish edge remained obvious. The enacting clause of the Act listed the rates of the nationalities allowed in, including the rate of the Jews, based on statistical calculations. Therefore, the Jewish community was re-classified by law from a religious denomination to a nationality.

The *numerus clausus* Act was attacked equally from the Right and the Left. The radical extreme right demanded that Jewish instructors not teach subjects dealing with national history and culture. In Gömbös' 1923 proposal Christianized Jewish students would be declared Jewish.[84] From the liberal and social-democratic sides, several proposals were offered to modify the Act. Their partial success became the milestone of prime-minister Bethlen's endeavor introducing a moderate course, the so-called consolidation.

The introduction of the *numerus clausus* had a symbolic significance. It introduced the ethnic and cultural affiliation of an individual as a distinctive social and political principle. Viktor Karády was justified to say that the *numerus clausus* arrested the emancipation process developed by Hungarian national liberalism, by the restoration of certain feudal collective rights and the charging of the Jews with a collective absence of rights.[85]

The law of discrimination and exclusion was eventually damaging to the privileged groups in Hungarian society by arresting the liberal version of the ubiquitous rule of law. As Karády observed, it deepened the non-Jewish intellectuals' crisis.[86] Ending professional rivalry with the Jewish intelligentsia by such political intervention led "to the moral corruption of certain layers of the

Christian middle class." Restraining the educated Jews opened up the way for the privileged groups in society to drift towards fascism.

While the privileged were damaged, the *numerus clausus* reinforced the motives among Jewish intellectuals to un-assimilate and to emigrate. Karády viewed this emigration as a forced flight and a positive experience because, paradoxically, by curbing their social mobility, the Jews were forced to accumulate a knowledge-capital useful anywhere in international markets.[87]

Minority Rights

Discussions about the *numerus clausus* issue raise the question of why opponents of the law did not appeal to the League of Nations. There were two ways to oppose the law: on one hand to try to enforce stipulations of the Trianon Treaties with regard to minorities and, on the other hand, there was the constitutional position keeping the pact of emancipation: equality and religious tolerance.

This question was not merely theoretical. The Council of the League of Nations had a significant influence in awarding foreign loans to respective countries. If it could be proved that Hungary had not complied with the terms of the Trianon Treaty, it would have adversely effected the extension of stabilization loans.

Mária M. Kovács raises the question of what could have encouraged the Entente Powers to secure minority laws in a separate treaty.[88] The answer is probably the recognition that new nation-state borders redrew the "minority map" of the area. Compared with 1914, the percentage of nationalities condemned to minority status decreased from two thirds to one third of the total population of the area. A certain historical change-over took place and, in the course of the process, large minority groups found themselves in states with newly acquired sovereignty.

The victorious powers extended collective rights for these minorities while the Hungarian *numerus clausus* was an example of collective disfranchisement in a situation where Hungary, itself a defeated nation, suffered under the limiting measures of the Peace Treaties. While in other successor states international guarantees of minority rights were combined with the declaration of a new sovereignty, in Hungary assuring the same rights violated the state's sovereignty, even if the latter was never declared.

Therefore, external intervention in the Jews' interest would have involved great risk. The discriminated-against Jews also had to face a decision of whether to fight internally against the violation of their civil rights or to turn to international forums. Jewish leaders finally decided on the former course and abandoned the idea of foreign intervention. Their decision was based on the expectation that the government would take a definite position against the extreme right and that the center of politics would remain moderate. It also was based on the expectation that the *numerus clausus* was an open violation of civil rights, a retraction of the policy of liberalism. During the discussion of the Bill in the national assembly Gyula Zákány admitted that withdrawing community rights was unusual in modern jurisprudence. However, he added that a state's interest might overrule certain civil rights. The Jewry had contributed to Hungary's culture so extensively that it had become a catastrophe for Christians.[89]

Such public talk narrowed the scope of activity both for the government and for the leading opposition parties. In addition to that, curbing atrocities and discrimination was especially difficult because moderates like István Bethlen, who had been forced into giving concessions to the extreme right wing, and the scientific anti-Semite Pál Teleki considered it the task of consolidation to solve the "Jewish question." "I recognize that presently there exists a Jewish question in this country, but its solution is in the economic sphere. We should be the same without them as we are with them.

It is also in their interest because the moment they become dispensable, harmony will have been restored."[90]

The "we" and "they," "others" and "the ones who belong to us," belong to the "natural" tone of Bethlen's text. However, it ought to be kept in mind that Bethlen as prime minister of "consolidation" after the counter-revolutionary period was experimenting with a rational explanation in a sober voice. He spoke about an "economic" and not about a "racial" basis for solving the issue. Therefore it had a calming effect on the aroused anti-Semitism.

Consolidation after the counter-revolution began when representatives like László Budaváry and Béla Dánér, too eager to implement the *numerus clausus* and having released an anti-Semite pamphlet, were voted out of parliament after the 1922 elections. Sober politics got fed up with the bombing attempt against the Jewish members of the *Erzsébetváros Circle* and, at least verbally, stood up for the victims although without mitigating or revoking the discriminating law of the *numerus clausus.* The restoration of law and order was on prime-minister Teleki's agenda and, later, on Bethlen's agenda too, although his government tolerated legally controlled anti-Semitism. Protesters against the law were justified in pointing out the obscure wording and euphemisms of the Act of *Numerus Clausus* (Act XXV of 1920). The first paragraph discussed university admission of students who were reliable with regard to patriotism and morality while the third paragraph discussed the ratio of "youth belonging to certain ethnic groups and nationalities in the territory of Hungary." Religious community leader Gyula Gábor proved the contradictions of the Act with legal arguments. His pamphlet recommended the establishment of a Jewish university. Consequently, a Bill for doing this was brought before parliament by a Jewish deputy Pál Sándor.[91] Yet, the idea died away because, in effect, it was only supposed to prove the absurdity of the current law. However, Gábor revealed the secret motivation behind the legislation. "The true goal was to lay the foundation-stone for a Jew-free Hungary and to establish a Jew-free university since the Jew is not capable of living where learning opportunities are closed to him."[92]

The League of Nations and the Jewish Question

International organizations placed the case of the *numerus clausus* issue on their agenda. The League of Nations asked Hungary to report on the application of the law. On behalf of the London-based "Joint Foreign Committee," journalist and diplomat Lucien Wolf, League of Nations deputy of the English and French Jews, several times attempted to take the question of the limiting law, which contradicted several items in the peace treaty, to an international court.[93] Bethlen and the Hungarian government suspected treason by those who sent documents to the League of Nations claiming that Hungarian Jews were hostages in that the improvement or deterioration of their lives was dependent on how their brethren abroad fought for a favorable image for Hungary and for territorial revision of the country. Bethlen complained that "the Jews abroad think it fit to push this unfortunate country even deeper with their propaganda—just because there is anti-Semitism here."[36]

In 1925 chief delegate Lucien Wolf wanted to take the issue of the *numerus clausus* to a qualified court of the League of Nations. The Hungarian government issued a "theoretical" response as clarification of the question, arguing that race, religion, and nationality were mixed in the Jews with a different dominant characteristic in each country. Therefore, the argument went on, in the Act being contested, religious references were deliberately omitted because one could consciously decide about and change his religion. Therefore, religion cannot determine the character of a national minority.[94] Klebelsberg, an aristocrat holding different cabinet-posts voiced similar arguments claiming that the law was temporary, a consequence of Trianon, and that as soon as Hungary gained back its economic stability, the Act could be cancelled.[95]

Klebelsberg reached an agreement with the delegates of the League of Nations stressing anew that the measure was temporary justified by the extraordinary social situation, and made a promise to modify the Act.

Eventually the League of Nations referred minority regulations to the Hungarian government's own jurisdiction, supposedly because the Act was not literally executed in terms of statistical rates and exceptions.[96] Lucien Wolf could not fulfill his mission to enforce minority rights according to the text of the peace treaty. The League of Nations, as it so frequently did in its history, backed off in this suit.

Bethlen himself prepared the official position of the Hungarian Jews in the "Geneva suit" and then transferred it to deputy Pál Sándor. "The Hungarian Jewry declares that it has not and does not turn to the League of Nations in the issue of the *numerus clausus.* The Hungarian Jewry considers it its own internal issue and refuses any foreign intervention. The Hungarian Jewry declares that it has not authorized anybody to represent its issue in Geneva and abjures the lawfulness of the submitted petition. The Hungarian Jewry hopes that the Hungarian government will shortly modify the Act of the *numerus clausus*."[36]

The official representatives of the Jews accepted the spirit of the text inspired by Bethlen, even if they did not interpret it literally. Learning from the Geneva suit, Klebelsberg must have realized that the *numerus clausus* Act was indefensible in international forums. As Klebelsberg wrote to Bethlen, "Therefore we have to revise the Act not by pouring thousands of Jewish university students onto the nation but by saving the essence of the Establishment with a certain rational appeasement."[97]

Jewish official circles had little chance to influence events, and foreign countries were skeptical about the Jews' "proofs of

Hungarianness" and their protest against the Geneva suit since the essence of the report was that they suffered under special pressure and discrimination.

Between the two world wars, the *numerus clausus* debate molded the official position of the Hungarian Jewry. On the 30th anniversary of the recognition of the Jewish religion, the official position was expounded by a former advocate of that legal recognition, former minister of justice, and staunch defender of Jewish interests, Vilmos Vázsonyi. He declared that the Jews had never had and presently did not have to represent their own religious concerns separately since these were combined with general human and national issues. If democracy and equal rights prevailed, there was no separate agenda of justice. "Here at home those whose vision and thinking have been obscured by the greatest curse, which the Old Testament also mentions, the Egyptian darkness, do not understand us. Often, neither do our brethren abroad because, first and foremost, we declare ourselves Hungarian. We are not Hungarian Jews but Jewish Hungarians."[98]

In connection with the Geneva suit, Vázsonyi also spoke in the National Assembly and summarized his position about the Trianon Treaty. "The universal meeting ... of Hungarian citizens of Jewish faith has brought the resolution that they have not and will not consent to any foreign intervention in order to seek the retraction of the *numerus clausus* no matter how antagonistic it is with the official recognition of that faith. The meeting has brought the resolution and declared that, even if the known item on the Trianon Treaty demands that there will not be any national or religious discrimination among citizens, they will not refer to this item because the Treaty has dismembered Hungary. That which is the sorrow of the nation cannot be the source of rights for Hungarians of Jewish faith."[98]

Although full of pathos, Vázsonyi's words hid disappointment. It was as if Klebelsberg, after arriving home, had forgotten about his promise to the League of Nations and continued to speak about maintaining the *numerus clausus.* In the National Assembly Tibor Eckhardt provoked Vázsonyi by saying that if Jews entered universities, "we" would be there—probably armed, as Vázsonyi perceived.

Bethlen could have counted on a similar protest had he tried to mitigate the Act under foreign pressure. Both university students and the *Awakening Hungarians* announced that they would, by all means, enforce the original law.

The *numerus clausus* issue also contributed to the deterioration of the international connections which a lonely Hungary needed. The League of Nations feared that Austro-Hungary's successor states would follow suit. As if to prove this point, the first 1927 post-Trianon Treaty alliance—with fascist Italy—determined the foreign policy orientation of Hungary and paved the way to the catastrophe of World War II.[99]

During all his regime's tenure, István Bethlen was compelled to balance between the demands of the extreme right-wing and the interests of banking and big capital, which were perceived as Jewish, who in times of economic pressure were called an ally. As Lajos Szabolcsi summarized, "Jewish industrial capital stands by its oath to Bethlen."[36] Other than that, Bethlen was the embodiment of gentry anti-Semitism. In his memoir, Bethlen admitted to his own prejudices when analyzing Gömbös, "[Gömbös] was an anti-Semite deep in his soul, but not more so than any other good Hungarian in response to the Mihály Károlyi and Béla Kun periods when everybody was disgusted by the behavior that the majority of the Jews demonstrated."[100]

Bethlen tried to activate Hungary's recovery with the help of foreign aid. In 1923 and 1924, the followers of pro-racist and pro-economic radicalism supported the new financial policy. The President of the Hungarian Telegraphic Agency Miklós Kozma wrote in his diary in 1924, "Restlessness began in the right-wing which resented the idea of a loan and heavily criticized the government's financial and economic policy. Not quite unreasonably, they blamed this policy for the fact that during the so-called "Christian course" the Jews had gained economic territory in an unparalleled measure."[101]

President of the National Union of Industrialists Baron Ferenc Chorin, Director of the Hungarian Iron Works Baron Mór Kornfeld, Directors of the Hungarian Coal-Mining Joint Stock Company Barons Adolf Kohner and Jenő Vida, Executive Director of the United *Izzó* Lipót Aschner, and textile factory owner Arnold Goldberger were all to be found in Bethlen's court.

After the parliamentary elections of December 1926, seven Jewish representatives entered parliament. Immánuel Lőw and Koppel Reich, representatives of the reform and orthodox Jewry, became members of the Upper House. Consolidation had truly created a delicate situation, one of *realpolitik* that had persevered under the constant threat of its own ideology.[102]

However, the prevailing winds had changed by the 1930s. The solution to the "social question" could not be postponed any longer since many intellectuals had seen several ominous signs about the extent of the problem. The debate, at the incentive of Lajos Fülep and Gyula Illyés, about the "only child syndrome" of a few Trans-Danubian villages ignited the new village exploration literature. Official politicians spoke about reform in a way that joined land reform with the Jewish question. Social demagoguery and anti-capitalist rhetoric were amplified following the earlier "anti-Bolshevik" anti-Semitism. As Béla Zsolt characterized the situation, "National socialism conquered in Germany and there came to us the Gömbös regime, the reform generation, and popular and racial myths which overnight shifted the center of gravity of Jewish sins from responsibility for the anti-capitalist revolution to responsibility for the abuses of capitalism."[103]

The election of Gyula Gömbös as Prime Minister was the moment when this "shift" from anti-Bolshevism to anti-capitalism occurred.[104] Gömbös, who had the reputation of being an inexorable racist, promulgated reforms and reconciliation with the Jews.[105] "And I will honestly tell the Jews that I have revised my position. I want to consider the Jews who avow a common fate with the nation and the Hungarians as my brethren."[106]

Obviously, the speech had been devised with the intention of "pacifying" many people. Gömbös had not changed and, at best, he made concessions to certain groups for which Bethlen systematically attacked him from his right wing racist position. Gömbös could not help mentioning the Jewish question at an informal meeting with certain writers, organized by Lajos Zilahy, which acquired a dubious repute later on. When the idea of organizing a scientific society came up, Gömbös interrupted the review of names saying, "No Jew, please, because then I will not discuss the matter any more. I have my reasons. I think now the way I used to."

The religious peace promulgated by the government was not to last long. Gömbös' successor, Kálmán Darányi, submitted the Bill for the first Jewish law.

Notes

1. "A zsidókérdés Magyarországon" [The Jewish Question in Hungary] (Budapest: Huszadik Század, 1917), in *Zsidókérdés, asszimiláció, antiszemitizmus* [Jewish Question, Assimilation, and Anti-Semitism] Péter Hanák, ed., (Budapest, 1984).
2. Péter Ágoston, "A zsidók útja" [The Road of the Jews], in *A Jövő kérdései, II.* [The Questions of the Future] (Nagyvárad: Nagyváradi Társadalomtudományi Társaság, 1917).
3. William O. McCagg, "Jews in Revolutions: The Hungarian Experience," *Journal of Social History*, vol. 6, no. 1, Fall (New Brunswick, 1972): pp. 78-85.
4. Gusztáv Gratz, *A forradalmak kora—Magyarország története, 1918-1920* [The Age of Revolutions—The History of Hungary, 1918-1920] (Budapest: Magyar Szemle Társaság, 1935; Reprint ed., 1992), pp. 210 and 254.
5. Quoted in Lóránt Tilkovszky, *Teleki Pál—legenda és valóság* [Pál Teleki—Legend and Reality] (Budapest: Magvető, 1969), p. 62.
6. Zoltán Csellényi, *Az Ébredő Magyarok Egyesülete (ÉME) működése, 1918-1920* [The Operation of the Society of Awakening Hungarians, 1918-1920] (The Scientific Publications of the Károly Eszterházy Teacher Training College, 1991:20), pp. 51-67.
7. Tibor Zinner, *Az ébredők fénykora 1919-1923* [The Golden Age of the Awakening Hungarians, 1919-1923] (Budapest: Akadémiai Kiadó, 1989), p. 114.
8. István Milotay, "Remények és csalódások" [Hopes and Disappointments], *Új Nemzedék* (April 11, 1920).
9. István Milotay, *Nemzetgyűlési beszéd* [Speech in the National Assembly] (September 18, 1920).
10. Tibor Löffler, "A jobboldali modernizációs ideológia a huszas évek végén" [The Right-Wing Ideology of Modernization at the End of the 1920s], *Valóság*, vol. XXXVII, no. 8 (Budapest, 1995,): pp. 50-65.
11. István Milotay, *Tíz esztendő: Cikkek, kortörténeti jegyzetek 1914-1924* [Ten Years: Articles and Historical Notes, 1914-1924] (Budapest: Pallas, 1924), p. 354.
12. See also Péter Sipos, *Milotay István pályaképéhez* [To István Milotay's Career] (Budapest: Századok, 1971, 3-4).

13. See also Tibor Hajdu, "Az értelmiségi számszerű gyarapodásának következményei az első világháború előtt és után" [The Consequences of the Numeric Growth of the Intellectuals Before and After World War I] *Valóság*, XXII, 7 (Budapest, 1980): pp. 21-34.
14. See also Miklós Sticr, *Uralkodó elit: Kormányzati hatalom—kormányzó réteg a Horthy korszakban* [Ruling Elite: Governing Power and the Governing Class of the Horthy Regime] (Budapest: Századok, 1983), pp. 434-443.
15. Béla Bangha, *Magyarország újjáépítése és a kereszténység* [Reconstruction of Hungary and Christianity] (Budapest: Szent István Társulat, 1920). It is to be newly published in 2000/8, p. 50.
16. See Péter Sipos, "A 'kirekesztés' Magyarországon: Zsidókérdés a két világháború között" ["Exclusion" in Hungary: Jewish Question between the Two World Wars] *História* (Budapest, 1998/1): pp. 20-22.
17. Béla Bangha, *A kurzus bajai* [The Problems of the Regime] (Budapest: Magyar Kultúra, 1921), pp. 14-27.
18. J. e. J. Tharaud, "Bolchévistes de Hongrie. II. Michel Károlyi et Béla Kun," *Revue des deux Mondes* (April 15, 1921).
19. István Deák, "Budapest and the Revolutions of 1918-19," *Slavic and East European Review* (January 1968, 46, 106): pp. 129-140).
20. János Makkai, "A bennünk lakó zsidó" [The Jew Within Us], in *Az úri Magyarország* [Gentry Hungary] ed. Pál Léderer, (Budapest: T-Twins, 1993).
21. The *Nemzetgyűlési Napló* [Journal of the National Assembly] (Budapest, 1920/21), p. 123.
22. "Az Apponyi-levélhez" [To the Apponyi Letter] *Múlt és Jövő* (March 26, 1920): pp. 9-10.
23. József Galántai, "Az Apponyi-szózat hamis hangjai. 'Szomorú ceremónia' (Trianon 1920-1990)" [The False Sounds of the Apponyi Manifesto (Trianon 1920-1990)] *Magyar Nemzet* (Budapest, 1990, 53, 129): p. 8.
24. Quoted by Walter Pietsch, "Trianon és a magyar zsidók" [Trianon and the Hungarian Jews] *Múlt és Jövő* (1990, 4, 4): pp. 40-53.
25. Rolf Fischer, *Entwicklungsstufen des Antisemitismus in Ungarn 1867-1939: die Zerstörung der magyarisch-jüdischen Symbiose* (München: Südosteuropäische Arbeiten, 85, R. Oldenbourg), p. 169.
26. Márton Vida, ed., *Ítéljetek!—Néhány kiragadott lap a magyar-zsidó életközösség...* [Judge!—A Few Selections from the Hungarian-Jewish Community ...] (Budapest, 1939).

27. Ignác Romsics, *Gróf Bethlen István politikai pályája 1901-1921* [Count István Bethlen's Political Career, 1901-1921] (Budapest: Magvető, 1987), p. 218.
28. Alajos Kovács, *A zsidóság térfoglalása Magyarországon* [The Jews' Expansion in Hungary] (Budapest, 1922), pp. 14 and 60.
29. Álmos Korál (Aladár Komlós), *Zsidók válaszúton* [Jews at the Crossroads] (Eperjes, 1921), p. 17.
30. Ernő Gáll, "Kettős kisebbségben" [In a Dual Minority] *Korunk* (Budapest, 1991,8): pp. 957-969.
31. Viktor Karády, *Csoportközi távolság, réteghelyzet, a zsidó-keresztény házasságok dinamikája Erdélyben a világháborúk között* [Cross-Group Distances, Classes, and Marriage Dynamics in Transylvania Between World Wars] *Korunk* (Budapest, 1991,8): pp. 941-954.
32. Moshe Carmilly-Weinberger, *A zsidóság története Erdélyben (1623-1944)* [The Jews' History in Transylvania, 1623-1944], ed. Géza Komoróczy, (Budapest: Hungaria Judaica, Judaic Research Group of the Hungarian Academy of Sciences, 1995), p. 278.
33. Éva Kovács, "Zsidók válaszúton" [Jews at the Crossroads], in *Varietas Historiae—Tanulmányok Juhász Gyula 60. születésnapjára* [Varietas Historiae: Essays on Gyula Juhász' 60th Birthday] (Budapest, 1990).
34. Quoted by István Haller, *Faj-e a zsidóság, vagy felekezet?* [Is the Jewry a Race or a Denomination?] (Budapest: Apostol nyomda), p. 26.
35. Gábor Gaál, "Az erdélyi zsidóság az első világháborút követő időszakban" [Transylvanian Jewry in the Post-World War Period] *Korunk* (Budapest, 1991, 8), pp. 1029-1034.
36. Quoted by Lajos Szabolcsi, *Két emberöltő: az Egyenlőség évtizedei, 1881-1931: emlékezések, dokumentumok* [Two Generations: Decades of Equality, 1881-1931—Memories and Documents] (Budapest: Hungaria Judaica, 5, Judaic Research Group of the Hungarian Academy of Sciences, 1993), pp. 306, 316, 353, and 374; Originally an article by Lajos Bíró, "Egyenlőség" (November 21, 1918).
37. József Schönfeld, "A béke ratifikálása és a zsidóság" [Peace Ratification and the Jewry], in *Harcban a zsidóságért* [At War for the Jewry] (Budapest, 1920), pp. 53-54.
38. Béla Edelstein, "A külföldi zsidóság története a háború utáni években" [The History of the Foreign Jewry during the Post-War Years],

in *Évkönyv* [Almanac] Samu Szemere, ed., (Budapest: IMIT, 1929), pp. 295-337.
39. Quoted in Péter Ujvári, ed., *Magyar Zsidó Lexikon* [Hungarian Jewish Lexicon] (Budapest, 1929), p. 200.
40. Lajos Szabolcsi, "'A szegedi gondolat' és a zsidók" [The "Szeged Idea" and the Jews] *A Magyar Zsidók Lapja* (Budapest, March 7, 1940): p. 5.
41. Sándor Léderer, "A Pesti Izr. Hitközség tíz éve" [Ten Years of the Pest Israelite Religious Community], in *Zsidó Évkönyv* [Jewish Almanac] (Budapest: Pesti Izraelita Hitközség, 1927), p. 74.
42. Count Gyula Andrássy, "A zsidókérdésről" [On the Jewish Question] *Új Magyar Szemle* (Budapest, July 1920).
43. Miksa Fenyő, "Elmúlt hetekből" [From the Past Weeks] *Nyugat* (Budapest, January 1, 1921).
44. Count Gyula Andrássy, *A magyar értelmiség feladatairól* [On the Hungarian Intellectuals' Tasks] (Budapest: Magyar Kultúra, 1921), pp. 3-13.
45. Tamás Kóbor, "A zsidó kérdésről" [On the Jewish Question] *Múlt és Jövő* (Budapest, April 23, 1920): pp. 7-8.
46. Rusztem Vámbéry, "A becstelenség apológiája" [An Apologia for Ignominy] *Századunk*, vol. VI, no.1 (Budapest, 1931).
47. Korál, *op. cit.*, pp. 12-13.
48. István Lendvai, *A harmadik Magyarország—Jóslatok és tanulságok* [The Third Hungary—Predictions and Morals] (Budapest: Pallas, 1921), p. 151.
49. *Ibid.*, p. 23.
50. Endre Zsilinszky, *Nemzeti újjászületés és sajtó* [National Revival and the Press] (Budapest: Táltos, 1920), pp. 28-30.
51. Lajos Hatvany, *Das verwundete Land* (Leipzig-Wien: E.P. Tal and Co, 1921).
52. Lajos Hatvany, "Egy magyar zsidó monológja" [The Monologue of a Hungarian Jew] *Korunk* (Budapest, 1927): pp. 327-334.
53. Viktor Karády, "Asszimiláció és társadalmi krízis—A magyar-zsidó társadalomtörténet konjunkturális vizsgálatához" [Assimilation and Social Crisis—To the Business Connections of the Hungarian-Jewish Social History] *Világosság*, vol. XXXIV, no. 3 (Budapest, 1993): pp. 33-60.
54. Miklós Szabó, *Nemzetkarakter és ressentiment: Gondolatok a politikai antiszemitizmus funkcióiról* [National Character and

Ressentiment: Thoughts about the Functions of Political Anti-Semitism] *Világosság* (Budapest, 1981, 6): pp. 358-362.

55. Anna Lesznai, "Hozzászólás a Huszadik Század körkérdéséhez" [Remarks on the Public Opinion Poll of the *Huszadik Század*], in *A zsidókérdés Magyarországon, 1917* [The Jewish Question in Hungary, 1917], pp. 104-109.
56. Aladár Komlós, *Problémák a Nyugat körül* [Problems around the *Nyugat*] (Budapest: Magvető, Gyorsuló Idő, 1978), p. 32.
57. Gyula Farkas, *Az asszimiláció kora a magyar irodalomban, 1867-1914* [The Age of Assimilation in the Hungarian Literature, 1867-1914] (Budapest: Magyar Történelmi Társulat, Magyar Történelmi Társulat Kiadványai, Vol. III, 1937), pp. 246, 252.
58. Aladár Komlós, *Fajvédő volt-e Ady Endre?* [Was Endre Ady a Racist?] (Budapest: Századunk, 1929), pp. 308-312.
59. Dezső Szabó, *A forradalmas Ady* [The Revolutionary Ady] (Budapest: Táltos, 1919).
60. Gyula Gombos, *Szabó Dezső* (München: Auróra, 1969), p. 91.
61. Tibor Déry, "Az utolsó nemzeti költő" [The Last National Poet] *Nyugat* (Budapest, 1919): p. 344.
62. Mihály Babits, "Tanulmány Adyról" [An Essay on Ady] *Nyugat* (Budapest, 1920): p. 128.
63. Dezső Szabó, *Panasz—Újabb tanulmányok* [A Complaint: More Recent Essays] (Budapest: Ferrum, 1923), pp. 19-20.
64. Lajos Ady, *Ady Endre* [Endre Ady], pp. 232-234
65. Endre Ady, "Zikcene, Zakcene, Satöbbi" [Zikcene, Zakcene, et cetera], in *Összes Versei*, [Complete Poems] György Belia, ed., (Budapest: Szépirodalmi, 1972). p. 505. There are only a few translations of Endre Ady into English. See Endre Ady - G. F. Cushing, *The Explosive Country: a selection of articles and studies 1898-1916,* (Budapest: Corvina Press, 1977).
66. István Gál, "Babits-dokumentumok" [Babits Documents] *Tiszatáj* (1973, 11): p. 69.
67. Ignotus, "Faj és művészet" [Race and Art] *Nyugat* (Budapest, June 1, 1929, 22, 11): pp. 715-718.
68. Zoltán Szász, "'Faj és művészet'" ["Race and Art"] *Nyugat*, vol. II (Budapest, 1929): pp. 72-74.
69. Béla Zsolt, *Villámcsapás (Schwartz András önéletrajza)* [A Stroke of Lightning: András Schwartz's Autobiography] (Budapest: Pantheon), pp. 146-147.

70. Quoted by György Kecskeméti, "Ankét az önantiszemitizmusról" [Conference on Jewish Self-hatred], in *Ankétsorozat a zsidóság mai problémáiról* [Conference Series on Today's Problems of the Jewry] Simon Hevesi, ed., (Budapest: OMIKE, 1931), p. 9.
71. *Ibid.*, p. 10.
72. *Ibid.*, p. 14.
73. Quoted by Zsuzsa L. Nagy, *Bethlen liberális ellenzéke (A liberális polgári pártok, 1919-1931)* [Bethlen's Liberal Opposition: The Liberal Bourgeois Parties, 1919-1931] (Budapest: Akadémiai, 1980), pp. 31 and 33.
74. *Ibid.*, p. 10.
75. Alajos Kovács, *Értelmiségünk nemzeti jellegének biztosítása* [Securing the National Character of Our Intellectuals] (Budapest: Stephaneum).
76. See also Robert S. Wistrich, *Socialism and the Jews: The Dilemmas of Assimilation in Germany and Austria-Hungary* (Rutherford, NJ, London, East Brunswick, NJ: Fairleigh Dickinson University Press, Associated University Presses: The Littman Library of Jewish Civilization, 1982), p. 435.
77. Oszkár Jászi, *Magyar Kálvária—magyar föltámadás* [Hungarian Calvary—Hungarian Resurrection] (Vienna: Reprint Magyar Hírlap Books, 1920, and its 1989 edition), pp. 160-161.
78. Pál Szende, "Keresztény Magyarország és zsidó kapitalizmus" [Christian Hungary and Jewish Capitalism], in *Zsidókérdés Kelet és Közép-Európában* [Jewish Question in Eastern and Central Europe] Ferenc Miszlivetz and Róbert Simon, eds., (Budapest: ELTE, 1920), pp. 367-373.
79. Lee Congdon, "Trianon and the Emigré Intellectuals," in *Essays on World War I: Total War and Peacemaking, a Case Study on Trianon*, Béla K. Király, Peter Pastor, and Ivan Sanders, eds., (New York: Columbia University Press, 1982), p. 396. A selected bibliography of the Trianon literature in Béla K. Király - László Veszprémy, eds., *Trianon and East Central Europe: Antecedents and Repercussions*, War and Society in East Central Europe, vol. 32. (Boulder, Colorado: Atlantic Research and Publications, 1995), pp. 297-301.
80. See also Steven B. Vardy, *The Impact of Trianon: Hungary and the Hungarian Mind: The Nature of Interwar Irredentism* (Hungarian Studies Review, 1983, 10, 1-2), pp. 21-42.

81. Péter Hanák, "Trianon szubjektív tényezői" [The Subjective Factors of Trianon] *Világosság*, vol. XXXI, nos. 8-9, (Budapest, 1990): pp. 691-94.
82. Andor Ladányi, *Egyetemi hallgatók az ellenforradalmi rendszer első éveiben* [University Students in the First Years of the Counter-Revolutionary Regime] (Budapest: Akadémiai, 1981).
83. L. Nagy, *op. cit.*, p. 77.
84. Péter Tibor Nagy, "A numerus clausus—hetvenöt év után" [The Numerus Clausus—After Seventy-five Years] *Világosság*, vol. XXXVI, no. 2, (1995): pp. 72-80.
85. Viktor Karády, "A numerus clausus és a zsidó értelmiség" [The Numerus Clausus and the Jewish Intellectuals], in *Iskolarendszer és felekezeti egyenlőtlenségek Magyarországon (1867-1945)* [School System and Denominational Inequalities in Hungary (1867-1945)] (Budapest: Replika kör, 1997), pp. 235-266.
86. Viktor Karády and István Kemény, *Antisémitisme universitaire et concurrence de classe. La loi numerus clausus en Hongrie entre les deux guerre* (Actes de la Recherche en Sciences Sociales, 1980, 34), pp. 67-96.
87. Mária M. Kovács, "A kisebbségek nemzetközi jogvédelmének politikai csapdája. Vázsonyi Vilmos és a numerus clausus." [The Political Pitfall of the Legal Defense of Minorities. Vilmos Vázsonyi and the numerus clausus.], *Beszélő*, Apr. 7. pp. 28-30. See also József Galántai, *Trianon and the Protection of Minorities*, Atlantic Studies on Society in Change, no. 70. (Boulder, Colorado: Atlantic Research and Publications, 1992).
88. Gyula Zákány, "Nemzetgyűlési felszólalás" [Remarks at the National Assembly], in *Nemzetgyűlés Nyomtatványai, Nemzetgyűlés Naplója* [Papers of the National Assembly, Journal of the National Assembly] (Budapest, 1920), pp. 166-168.
89. Quoted in Róbert Barta, *A numerus clausus és a baloldali magyar zsidó politikai közvélemény* [The Numerus Clausus and the Left-Wing Hungarian Jewish Political Public Opinion] (Budapest: ELTE Btk, Sic itur ad astra, 1990), pp. 8-32.
90. Gyula Gábor, *A numerus clausus és a zsidó egyetem* [The Numerus Clausus and the Jewish University] (Budapest: Fráter Press, 1924).
91. *Ibid.*, p. 13
92. See T. J. F. Committee, *The Jewish Minority in Hungary* (London, 1926).

93. Nathaniel Katzburg, *Hungary and the Jews: Policy and Legislation, 1920-1943* (Ramat-Gan: Bar-Ilan University Press, 1981), p. 68.
94. Kuno Klebersberg, "Beszéd" [Speech] *Official Journal*, ed. L.o. Nations, vol. 7, (Geneva, 1926): pp. 148-153.
95. Thomas Spira, "Hungary's Numerus Clausus, the Jewish Minority, and the League of Nations," *Ungarn-Jahrbuch*, vol. 4, (1972), pp. 115-128.
96. Miklós Szinai-László Sándor, eds., "Klebelsberg Kuno gróf levele Bethlen István grófhoz 1926. nov. 3." [Count Kuno Klebelsberg's Letter to Count István Bethlen on November 3, 1926], in *Bethlen István titkos iratai* [Secret Documents of István Bethlen] (Budapest: Kossuth, 1972), pp. 256-257.
97. Vilmos Vázsonyi, *Beszédei és írásai* [His Speeches and Writings], H.-B. József Hugó Csergő, ed., vol. II. (Budapest: Vázsonyi Memorial Committee), pp. 441 and 445.
98. C. A. Macartney, "Hungarian Foreign Policy during the Inter-War Period, with Special Reference to the Jewish Question," in *Jews and non-Jews in Eastern Europe, 1918-1945,* eds., Bela Vago and George Mosse (Jerusalem: Keter Publishing House, 1974), pp. 125-137. See also Ezra Mendelsohn, *Trianon Hungary, Jews and Politics*, in H. A. Strauss, ed., (De Gruyter: Berlin - New York, 1993), pp. 893-916.
99. István Bethlen, *Emlékirata* [His Memoir], Ignác Romsics, ed., (Budapest: Zrínyi, 1988).
100. Miklós Kozma, "Belpolitikai helyzetkép, 1924 május (közli Romsics Ignác)" [Internal Political Situation: May 1924—published by Ignác Romsics] *Kritika*, (Budapest, 1924, 1986, 6), pp. 23-24.
101. See also Tibor Erényi, "Zsidók és a magyar politikai élet" [Jews and the Hungarian Political Life] Múltunk, vol. XXXIX, no. 4, (Budapest, 1994): pp. 3-31.
102. Béla Zsolt, "Zsidó nagytőke" [Jewish Plutocracy], in *Kőért kenyér—Vezércikkek 1921-1939 (1939)* [Bread for Stone—Editorials, 1921-1939 (1939)] (Budapest, 1937), p. 111.
103. Sándor Kónya, *Gömbös kísérlete totális fasiszta diktatúra megteremtésére* [Gömbös' Attempt to Establish a Total Fascist Dictatorship] (Budapest: Akadémiai, 1968).
104. Jenő Lévai, *Gömbös Gyula és a magyar fajvédők a hitlerizmus bölcsőjénél* [Gyula Gömbös and the Hungarian Racists at the Cradle of Hitlerism] (Budapest: Globus, 1938).

105. Gyula Gömbös, *A nemzeti öncélúságért* [For a National Self-Centeredness] (Budapest, Stádium, 1932), p. 41.
106. Gyula Illyés, *Naplójegyzetek 1919-1945* [Diary Notes, 1919-1945] (Budapest: Szépirodalmi, 1986), p. 83.

The Tragedy of the Pariah-Parvenu:
The Case of Szomory

There is no doubt that one of the main issues of Hungarian intellectual and cultural life between the two world wars was the "Jewish question." This issue, elevated to the level of state policy by the *numerus clausus* laws, did not leave the general Hungarian society unaffected. In fact, irrespective of origin, religion, attitude towards the Jews, or political ideology, a certain slant on viewing the events in this period became a permanent part of society's interpretation of the "Jewish question." Social and/or political players could either ignore the facts or look them straight in the face; these two attitudes forced different intellectual strategies on the Hungarian elite. Even the strategy of negation—denying the existence of the "Jewish question"—can be interpreted, ironically, as the acknowledgment of its existence.

The ones most affected were the ones with the least chance to have an impact. After Hungary became independent, although mutilated, and had shed her Habsburg chains, it became inconceivable for even completely assimilated Jews to accept formerly irrevocable premises. The responsibility of certain numbers of the Jews who had been involved in the tragedy of the dismemberment of the country was apparent to everyone. Their actions were seen as the collaboration of anti-national forces with agents of foreign powers.

The ruling ideology of the twenties in Hungary was based on territorial revisionism in order to reclaim the lost territories. Greater Hungary remained the dream in post-Wilsonian Eastern Europe. Those who renounced "international revisionism," the rearrangement of borders between Hungary and Romania, urged "internal revisionism"—a Hungarian awakening and the establishment of a new identity. Yet both standpoints were related. The "internal revisionism" camp held out the uniqueness of Hungarian culture and included a dose of anti-Semitism almost as an integral ingredient. *Új Élet*, the student newspaper of the Association of the *Székely* University and College Students, described the situation as: "Nowadays the Hungarians fight on two fronts. One front is against the Jews and the other one is against the irredentist. The first one is mostly economic and moral. The economic superiority of the Jews, which decides the fate of our country and rules us, can be conquered only by means of competition and rivalry. Our negligence, our past, and our tendency to rule distorted the work done in trade and 'business'—at which the Jews excelled—and we have not had or developed skills for these professions. Simply, we have not. What is to be done? We have to create these skills by influence and through education."

The rhetoric of this article both advocates cultural advance and also specifies its content. The ruling race ought to assume the role of the Jews by influence and education.[1]

Right-wing movements cannot be measured simply by their politically effective impact. Their intellectual influence expressed through journalism or academic authority was more important than their direct political influence. The Hungarian extreme right suffered numerous political defeats between the two world wars. The victory of the small-holders at the elections of 1920, the breakthrough of the liberals in 1922, and the Budapest advantage enjoyed by the social democrats all testify to the fact that the extreme right did not advance without meeting resistance. Gömbös and the "Race Protector" party were pushed into the background in 1927, while a more tolerant social atmosphere prevailed until 1932.[2]

The liberals and the social democrats, however, remained continuously defensive and kept a low profile on the so-called "Jewish question." As Zoltán Szász argued at the end of the 1920s, anti-Semitism was not the determining principle of Hungary's state ideology. The old state ideology was replaced by a unique *etatism* in which bourgeois radicals were content with the representation of only certain layers of the Jewish community.[3] During the debate to modify the strict orders of the *numerus clausus,* social or political moderates had little chance in the twenties. The "center" was attacked from both sides: the liberals attacked it because of concessions to the "race protectors," while the extreme right charged them with giving away concessions to the Jews. Gyula Gömbös once again announced his "race protector" program in Parliament. "I want—and it is a legitimate demand—that in Hungary every leading position of economic or political influence belong primarily to the sphere of influence of the Hungarian race." He also declared that "the only rational function" of the Jews of the country was to awaken and to keep awake Hungarian racial self-esteem.[4]

Expulsion from the Stage

During the parliamentary debate in 1927, the radical right demonstrated against the revival of Dezső Szomory's play, *A nagyasszony* [The Grand Dame]. The theater performance was disrupted by stink-bombs with the police trying to control the rushing and swaying crowd. The demonstration was aimed both at the director, Sándor Hevesi, and at the author, and the attitude of the mob was indisputably anti-Semitic.[5]

Many have described the demonstration and its political connotations. Aladár Schöpflin, writing in *Nyugat,* ventured the following criticism: "Barbarism incited immaturity and made the revival of *The Grand Dame* an unprecedented scandal in the history of the Hungarian theater." It was unparalleled because it was an insult to the writer and made the actors pay the price. Here "insane and blind hatred" defiled a writer and an institution.[6]

However, the hatred was not senseless. In fact, the "immature" crowds were mobilized by a conscious will. This was revealed in István Milotay's article. Milotay joined the debate concerning the cancellation of the *numerus clausus*, commenting on the liberal argument that the mitigation of the *numerus clausus* could sway the western countries towards considering a revision of the peace treaty. In Milotay's view, this was hopeless. Although Lord Rothermere in England sought out Hungarian allies, France had changed its 1920 policy and had now placed Hungary under a "moral" quarantine after the revelation of Hungary's forgery of the franc. (In the early twenties some high officials were caught red-handed in dispersing counterfeit French francs.) This did not allieve Hungary's post-war isolation. International public opinion was influenced more by its own interests and less by the decisions of the Hungarian government. "And now they come up with the *numerus clausus*, believing that it would attract the support of international public opinion and that of the world powers for us. Why don't they say that performing the Szomory play is also demanded by world public opinion which will not trust us until Szomory and company have marched into the National Theater to establish the *numerus clausus* for their own benefit and at the expense of Hungarian play-wrights and the Christian public.... This is how we arrived at a point that, in the name of reversing the *numerus clausus,* a Jewish director and a Jewish playwright carried the last bastion of the Hungarian theater by assault and staged a private national holiday within themselves and with their own audience. And, for whose protection, half of the police force was mobilized while, outside, a pale and ragged-clothed Christianity looks on and screams during the October night under the strokes and cuts of police swords and mounted attacks. Inside, however, similar to banks, factories, other theaters—and tomorrow or the day after tomorrow to the universi-ties as well—the same conquering crowd, in the name of integrity and peace revision, fills in the spaces and drives us out of the remaining positions of mutilated Hungary into the October night of destitution and hopelessness…"[7]

Right-wing radicalism felt threatened by the reversing of the *numerus clausus*, by the "Jews' conquering the world," and by Jewish "expropriation" of Hungarian intellectual life. And so it denied Szomory the registered noble suffix of his name (the *y* at the end) and used his play as a pretext in big politics. It is also typical of an artist to whom this world was alien and who was elevated to a romantic distance from reality that he thought the demonstrating crowd had arrived to celebrate him. Dezső Szomory had irritated conservative critics for a long time. His vocabulary and his unique language were stumbling-blocks for them and stood as symbols against nationalism. "The linguistic vagrancy that settles into others' property with the unabashed cold blood of a usurper, the insolent consistency in the way this strange element goes from nest to nest to drop its cuckoo-eggs, and the meek tolerance with which the Hungarian audience watches its language being defiled day by day—what is more, they even applaud it—all the above boils your blood and calls for a whip!"[8] The respected János Horváth characterized this period of right-wing radicalism as follows: "…Our writers of Jewish ancestry cannot complain. Their situation is so favorable and the road to their prosperity and success is so unobstructed; something that has never occurred for a Hungarian writer. They have the audience and from their point of view that is what counts."[9]

Szomory certainly had his audience, but he also had his own share of discrimination and suspicion as well. Whenever he was criticized for the peculiarity of his art, he was attacked for his Jewishness. At the publication of *Levelek egy barátnőmhöz* [Letters to a Girlfriend of Mine] in the same year that the *The Grand Dame* scandal took place, István Milotay mocked Szomory's description of a spiritual Judaic-image. "Who was the man that was my father? What pasts and yesteryears of my heritage, what inevitable echoes of Jehovah's worship and, later, that of the Greek breezes flowing from the direction of Epyrus via Phrygia and Hellespontus over to the plain lands of Media over grim exoduses towards the banks of the Euxius!..."

Szomory evoked the image of several thousand years of wandering. Mockery was the response. Greeks? Distant past? Milotay ridiculed these dreams. "One would think that in the past if somebody wanted to come from Galicia to Mátészalka, he would either come from the direction of Tarnopol or via the Lemberg-Sianki line via Ungvár and Beregszász, or the last station could have been Kisvárda as well."[10]

The inspiration of five thousand years of wandering was turned into Tarnopol, Galicia, in the eyes of this hostile world.

"Who is an Antisemite?"

Szomory received most of his insults in the year of *The Grand Dame*. Contemporary criticism rarely judged his origin or his Jewishness. It was actually one of Szomory's ambitions to distance himself from his ancestors. Still, they kept accusing him that his baroque exaggerations were examples of penetrating Jewish racial characteristics. The young Gábor Halász (who later perished in a forced labor camp) also accused him of ignorance when Szomory missed a Latin suffix in a poem and introduced somebody as Cicero's lover instead of his son-in-law. Halász also elaborated on Szomory's Jewishness and generally on Jewish literature.[11]

Antal Szerb (who was killed in the same labor camp as Halász) also went to extremes in his criticism of the *Letters to a Girlfriend of Mine* when in 1927 he wrote the following in the *Pandora* edited by Lőrinc Szabó: "The literary scholar of the future, who certainly will not question Szomory's value and uniqueness, will be embarrassed to try to find Szomory's niche—will it be within Hungarian literature or within that of the national minorities."

Szerb further asserted that Szomory had elevated the Pest language just like the classic János Arany had elevated the vernacular a century earlier. Nevertheless, even a witty explanation could not dispel the special underlying meaning of "national minorities."[12]

Young Hungarians on the left seemed to have agreed with the conservatives only in the case of Szomory. Even though János Kodolányi generally stood at the extreme left (and later on the extreme right), he agreed with the right wing on certain issues when they said "…that Dezső Szomory ought to be wiped out from Hungarian literature and if they hear only a few shreds of his melody, polyphony, and gradation, nervous restlessness, anger, and rigid resistance overwhelm them. We have to understand them… Never has a style signified the human being himself so well and never has a human being so utterly signified the class and race of his origin."[13]

Szomory rarely took issue with his opponents arguing that "only a Jew can feel anti-Semitism." However, whenever his childhood or family came up, his wounds burst open. "Who are anti-Semites? Directors, bankers, soldiers, painters and conductors, jockeys and popes, everybody from cardinals to prebendaries and vestrymen, to parish clerks, coroners, and the church mouse—whoever has a little good sentiment. Józsi Hódl is anti-Semitic and so am I, as is every artist for whom it is very useful since it fills up and enriches the content of the soul and covers the emptiness…"[14]

Szomory's outburst is a unique posture—that of exaggeration and extravagance. He chose the role in society of loneliness and isolation. Now this is not unknown in a given resisting medium. In the days of old, the one who stood out from his community, the *Schutzjude* (the protected, head-money Jew, the Imre Fortunatus) was the one who—in the possession of feudal privileges—acted as a middleman between his kind and the aristocrats. Szomory was just such a *Schutzjude*, but born after the demise of feudalism, a Hungarian dandy fashioned after Oscar Wilde. In Paris he dressed as an abbot and in his home he had to be addressed as "Your Lordship." It seems he attempted to avoid social constraints by role-playing.[15] He invented newer and newer poetic identities for himself: a stylized childhood and unusual trips. He responded with the attitude of a "stranger," a grain of artificial mystery, and disguises to counter the suspicion of strangeness. He used the recurring image of running and escaping. "I just walked and walked with the same momentum I started out with but in the opposite direction, just as you run down from a mountain on the other side of happiness … and I accompanied my shadow under the bushy-topped acacias, on the wooden floor, along the ditches, walking by a perfume shop where loitering Israelites did not watch my Christian rambling."[16]

On other occasions the "loitering Israelites" are the bearers of grim and tragic grandeur. Szomory wrote that little Margit loves András Nagy-Barnabás. "'It is a shame,' he said very simply, 'it is a great shame that you are of another nationality, my sweetheart. That is, that you are Jewish.'" The atmosphere of the long day spent in the synagogue completely moved Margit's whole self. "The great breeze charmed her and she absorbed the lurking rapture with quivering nostrils. The noise also stupefied and tortured her and swept her away towards old moods and familiar melodies where an unforgettable ring or an eternal word separated her soul from the immediate vicinity. I am at home, she thought. I am in the depth of my existence and András is a completely different person."[17]

Margit meets András one more time, which turns out to be the last time. The love which had not been realized connected two different worlds. There is only a slight hint as to why it did not. The difference is insurmountable.

Reward of Assimilation: Loneliness

Szomory rarely confessed directly about the obstacles to and difficulties of assimilation. Yet the disappointment of one who wants to be integrated sizzles in his feverish lyric, in his celebration of solitude, and in the painful revival of bygone times. The bygone yesteryear is evoked by the flickering light of a candle. "On such occasions our poor heart understands that our life—under the disguise of eternal remembrance—was not different from eternal oblivion and our fondest and dearest memory is not different from the burial of our dearest possession."[18]

The present which absorbs the past and the buried yesterday were the inspirations for Szomory's painfully secessionist and symbolist lyricism. We are not mistaken to say that the lost childhood and ecstatic solitude are roles that a Jewish author may experience. "The free actually escape from themselves" he wrote in one of his short stories.[19] Imagination and its roles parted with the everyday.

In Szomory's writing, emotional insecurity and the avoidance of self-definition sometimes overflow into irony. The narrator of *Lőrinc Monakóban* [Lőrinc in Monaco] is a former journalist and a recent silk merchant with the firm "Lévy et Afganisztán." "...and besides selling Lyon silk and wool, the firm was a zealous backer of the anti-Semitic league since both Mr. Calman Lévy and Moise Afganisztán were Israelites. Due to this mere pleasant chance, every Sunday afternoon I had to drink coffee and lash out at the Jews with my bosses at the Café Mazarin thus fortifying me in my position."[20] The merchant's friend, Lőrinc, rushes directly to the Grimaldi Palace and tells us that he has informed the Prince of Monaco that there was another Grimaldi "who was a grocery shop owner in Laudon Street under the name of Izidor Grün."[21]

For Szomory, travesty and grotesque are the styles of disappointment and the very opposite of prayers. Szomory despised the everyday parvenu and dreamed himself into the role of a transfigured pariah.

At the end of his career this ironic tone replaces the lyric one and is the underlying tone of his romantic short story series *Horeb tanár úr* [Professor Horeb]. Homér Horeb, a teacher steadfastly faithful to his religion, and Kálmán Varjassy, a careerist who has exchanged his ancient religion for a new one, fight over a woman, Dóra Zuckermandl and, in the process, explicate their philosophies. Horeb who was forced out of the scientific world, and the go-getter Varjassy play the comedic roles of assimilated pariah and parvenu for the forty year old charms of Dóra. Horeb's unceasing hunger for speaking and Varjassy's inferiority reveal a certain interdependence: the parvenu and the pariah represent the same fate. It was not by accident that in his criticism Lajos Hatvany felt this story was about him as well.[22]

Andor Kellér's essay described another Lajos Hatvany story of Szomory. Walking along *Margitsziget* (Margaret Island), Szomory exclaims while pointing at barren trees, "You see, that is how I live in my numb loneliness among barren trees, fallen dry leaves, and branches in the forest litter. I am alone in the world with my pain." Then theatrically raising his hand towards the sky, he exclaims: "*So ein grosser Dichter*—that is who I am!"[23]

In desperation the pariah transforms himself into a parvenu and plays both the dignified gentleman and the rebel. Szomory dressed in a cowl played the organ in his tower room, extended appointments to himself, haughtily refused any presents although he lived in wretched poverty, and played the role of a prince while being a beggar: *so ein grosser Dichter.*

A more recent anecdote by Kellér illuminates Szomory's peculiar "sin." Kellér argued that Szomory's Habsburg dramas and provocative behavior violated certain rules that his fellow human beings tacitly observed. Ferenc Molnár, who mockingly called Szomory a "frenetic junkman," told Lipót Hermann that "We Jewish artists—Adolf Fényes, Béla Iványi-Grünwald, Szomory, and I started out with a relatively similar suitcase of gifts. Although we made great efforts to reach the fullest of our abilities, all of us, hundreds of us in the world, reach only the fence and never get *inside*! Inside, to where we cast longing glances and where only a few walk, the Dantes, the Goethes, the Balzacs, and—well, I do not mind—Ady as well. The geniuses! And then comes Szomory, walking on top of the fence, ready to jump; he does his utmost, and wants us to believe that he belongs inside."[24]

Let us accept the anecdote as authentic since it originates from literary folklore—even if from a dubious source—and might become true by constant repetition. Molnár accepted Richard Wagner's theory which, in turn, was accepted by contemporary public opinion: that Jews lack artistic abilities and demonstrate the difference between a hack or a genius serving the audience and the nation. However, the image of "outside" and "inside" draws even more boundaries very similar to the invisible wall of assimilation. Sometimes Szomory climbed up the wall and sometimes he fell off it. It was only his fluctuating moods which revealed the invincible resistance he had to overcome. Time and again in his loneliness he came to realize that he was not needed or heeded by anybody. Therefore he played the role of a literary marquis. Szomory and others believed in his role. For instance, Kellér quotes the director Árpád Horváth as saying that "They believed him because he himself believed and still believes it. His country did not claim him and neither did his race. He fled from his benumbing loneliness to an even thicker solitude—the posture of refinement."[25]

The Birth-defect

The marquis, the dignified gentleman, and the imagined ability to rise in society are distinctive assimilating behaviors. Dezső Szomory dreamed of an ideal world where the obstacles of origin could be overcome. He radically adopted the *Nyugat*'s identity gospel and engaged himself as its voluntary prophet. Another Kellér anecdote has Szomory saying that "if I had been born Christian, I could have become the king's Master of the Horse." The fantasy of this author of royal dramas was set in motion by ranks, titles, and possibilities mainly because he was excluded from that very world.

In Szomory's writings, stylization and poetry were elevated beyond reality, accompanied by a certain inspiration towards the royal dynasty. He celebrated the tragic majesty in the Habsburgs. He hoped to reach Franz Joseph in his drama where the deserter beseeched the king for a pardon reaching out from his seventeen-year long Paris exile. There are several possible explanations for the biographical details of this time in Szomory's life. For instance, a gossip biography, which can hardly be taken seriously, declared his love for Mari Jászai, two decades his senior, as the reason for his escape to Paris.[26]

But the emperor had mercy on him. Pál Réz's biography published one of Szomory's letters written to Mór Jókai[27] in which the deserter—a dandy in civilian life—regales the reader with his homesickness. The playwright of Habsburg dramas seeks to become a *Schutzjude*: the emperor has read the play. In 1910 (and not in 1914 as Pál Réz mistakenly notes on p.87) Szomory wrote to Miksa Fenyő, an editor of the *Nyugat,* "Dear Mr. Editor, the King was most kind. He promised to subscribe to the *Nyugat.* Warmest regards to you and Mr. Osváth (!)—Dezső Szomory."[28]

Obviously, he had never spoken with the king. And it seems most improbable that Franz Liszt leaned over Szomory's cradle in Király Street just as another suggestion that he was thought to be Liszt's child in Paris—is quite improbable. Szomory quotes one of Liszt's books in the *Letters to a Girlfriend of Mine*. If Szomory had read Liszt's book, he would have known that Liszt—like Wagner—was a dedicated anti-Semite.[29] It is most remarkable to see Szomory wrestling with his Jewish origin among his revised and rewritten biographical details. The anti-Semitic attacks he received did not let him deny his origin but, as has been noted, he stylized this fact into a legend of origin. He did not claim to be born in Király Street but somewhere near the Euphrates. And he mentioned the cantor among his ancestors whose dearest wish was to sing to the king.

One of his first plays, the *Péntek este* [Friday Evening], was first performed in the Nineteenth century. The young wife of an old rabbi falls in love with the mysterious "black hunter" who knocks on their door. "The story of this little play goes like this: Darvay, a Christian landowner, elopes with the Jewish rabbi's wife on Friday evening" wrote the critic Sándor Hoffmann in the *Magyar Szemle*. Hoffmann later directed *The Grand Dame* in the *Nemzeti Színház* [National Theater] under the name Sándor Hevesi.[30]

All during the play the wind blows from the mountains creating moods in the manner of Ibsen and Maeterlink. However, Eszter's irrepressible admiration and attraction towards the representatives of the historical classes was the same as Szomory's. The *pariah* wrote the play while still in Paris and the *parvenu* reminisces: "At that time in my sorrowful absence, some of my small pieces were already being played at the Nemzeti Theater and, first of all, one called *Friday Evening* which, mostly because of its topic, held the Israelites' approval. I thought I would be clever this time and look for a topic that pleases the highest circles, and even the king himself, not these obvious outlaws."[31]

Szomory's commentary on *Friday Evening* could be considered ironic. However, his Israelites fare badly in the entire epistolary novel: either the five-thousand year old pain of the Israelites is given poetic exaggeration or else the Israelites are empty representatives of dark rigidity. "They do not seem to have come to the world in order to form a great state and a glorious nation. Oh, my God, no! According to the will of God their life is to fulfill their religious destination irrevocably. Like certain butterflies who are born to live for an hour [and then] to die. That was Jehovah's poetic idea for us."[32]

In Szomory's world, his father originates from a religious people incapable of forming a state while Ferenc Liszt claims the child as if an anti-Semite's touch could cleanse a chosen Jew. Szomory well exemplifies Hannah Arendt's statement that the Jew who wants to be fully integrated into his environment, and is consistent about it, has to adopt its anti-Semitism.[33] However, the writer of the *Letters* ... is not consistent. He would like to abandon the mark of his birth, would like to live on the aristocrats' level, and longs for Christian humility—just as the rabbi's beautiful wife of his first play yearns for the landowner. "But the people of Israel's tragedy is that their God survived them and they were left in the lurch. There still remain Israelites, yes indeed. They still pray and weep while their God became the God of the whole world in Christ. That is why I worship Christ humbly under the cross. Because we have the religion but we have lost the God. And human beings cannot be without God."[34]

As he spins on, "his perfect birth" deprived him of the Church's catechism but he compensated for this void with his feelings. Suffering is his Christian path. After all, Christian martyrs were also born pagan and birth is only important from a "feudal perspective." Emotional absorption, devotion, and suffering all offer redemption. "The ethics of the Christian religion is the gradation of pleasure, and pain is the greatest pleasure."[35]

The young Mór Weisz, (Szomory's original name), who went to a monastic school, was expelled and the famous Professor Maywald, who taught Greek, humiliated him. Individuals' histories and peoples' histories are all fortuitous and even mistaken. "In polite terms, it is only the Israelites' point of view that has no delusions if I look across History. ... Since they were equally persecuted and slaughtered in all periods of time, there had to be something intolerable about them."[36]

"A desperate longing for the eternally closed heaven" was the summary of Szomory's life while his hope was that devotion, solitude, and pain would save him from his imperfect birth. He chose the Deity without a religion, instead of choosing the religion which he declared had been abandoned by God.

His several postures saved Szomory from realizing the futility of his dreams. He noted about the yellow star that it did not suit a gray outfit. There came a point when he did not have anything to eat and he haughtily refused community aid. He respected the Jewish past and history and described it with poetic inspiration. But he did not like the Jew—even the Jew in him.

Szomory was not the only one to proclaim the role of the lonely prophet during the time of the *Letters* and *The Paris Novel.* The tone of contemporary pamphlets demanding the purification of the Jews, at this time, was at a high level of ecstasy. Ferenc Hevesi (the son of Simon Hevesi, the chief rabbi of Székesfehérvár) published a book entitled *Szenvedés, igazság* [Suffering and Justice] in which he said that everyone lived in a cold and dead world, "deprived of poetry." Poetry is kept at bay by business and there is no place for compassion, mercy, or pity or for the solemn harmony of sorrows and joys. God's name does not shine upon the forehead of today's man. The chosen people deserved the death of the sanctuary, an empty space devoid of faith. The role of faith is that of a musician and the Jewry is supposed to be the Deity's instrument. This image parallels that of a deified Szomory at the organ in his room in the tower.[37]

The concurrence of the styles, emotional intensity, and prophetic speech of the rabbi and the poet is startling.

There was also contemporary encouragement for Jews to accept the Christian "love" religion. The Újvidék doctor, poet, and playwright Árpád Fischer's pamphlet *Kiáltvány a zsidósághoz* [A Manifesto to the Jews] was published in the year of the revival of the *Grand Dame* and the publication of the *Letters*... . Inspired by

Buber's mysticism, the book analyzed Jewish sins and the connection between the Jewish and Jesus faiths. Similar to Buber, his student appearing from a successor state reclaims Jesus, the prophet to the Jews: Let us claim ownership of the gospels which were created among the Jews and which speak to the whole mankind. We have to realize Him in ourselves by abandoning our old lives and by realizing the Word of the Sermon on the Mount.[38]

Szomory's theory about the abandoned faith and religion and about the Christian purification of exaltation and morale was not stated in a lonely voice. The identity crises spared few.

In view of his desires, Szomory's fate is especially tragic. His old writer sibling was persecuted and he himself was branded a Jew by the yellow star he had to wear. He was moved to a so-called Swedish protected house where he presumably died of starvation in 1944.

Notes

1. István B. Bernát, "Adalékok a népi ideológia előtörténetéhez—a Barta Miklós Társaság előzményei" [Additions to the History of Popular Ideology—Antecedents to the Miklós Barta Society], in *A két világháború közötti Magyarországról* [From Hungary between the Two World Wars] , Miklós Lackó, ed. (Budapest: Kossuth, 1984), pp.403-404.
2. Miklós Szinai, "A magyar szélsőjobboldal történelmi helyéhez" [To the Historical Place of the Hungarian Extreme Right], in *Jobboldali radikalizmusok tegnap és ma* [Right Wing Radicalism Yesterday and Today], István Feitl, ed., (Budapest: Napvilág, 1998), pp. 114-122.
3. Zoltán Szász, "A demokrata párt és a zsidó hagyományhűség" [The Democratic Party and the Jewish Traditionalism], *Századunk*, vol. 9, (Budapest, 1928, 9): p. 557.
4. Quoted by Zsuzsa L. Nagy, *Bethlen liberális ellenzéke (A liberális polgári pártok 1919-1931)* [Bethlen's Liberal Opposition (The Liberal Bourgeois Parties in 1919-1931)] (Budapest: Akadémiai, 1980), p. 192.
5. Jenő Gáspár (J.G.), *A "Nagyasszony" botránya* ["The Grand Dame" Scandal] (Budapest: Magyar Kultúra, 1927), pp. 956-958.
6. Aladár Schöpflin, "Szomory Dezső a Nemzeti Színházban" [Dezső Szomory in the National Theater], *Nyugat*, vol. II, (Budapest, 1927): pp. 642-643, in *Válogatott* [Selected] (Budapest: Szépirodalmi, 1967), pp. 569-572.
7. István Milotay, "Békerevízió, numerus clausus és a Szomory-ügy (1927. október 23.)" [Peace Revision, *Numerus Clausus* and the Szomory Case (October 23, 1927)] in *A függetlenség árnyékában* [In the Shadow of Independence] (Budapest: Stádium, 1930), pp. 136-140.
8. János Horváth, "Szomoryzmusok a Nemzeti színpadján" [Szomorysms on the Stage of the National Theater], *Magyar Nyelv*, vol. 2, (Budapest, 1914): pp. 88-89.
9. János Horváth, "Kiadatlan írások a Két korszak határán című kötetből" [Unpublished Writings from the Volume Titled On the Boundaries of Two Periods], *Literatura*, vol. 1, (Budapest, 1993): p. 18.

10. For the debate see Ernő Ballagi, "Dezső Szomory's ötezeréves utazása Mátészalkáig" [Dezső Szomory's Five Thousand Year Journey to Mátészalka], *Egyenlőség*, (Budapest, July 30, 1927): p. 4.
11. Gábor Halász, *Szomory* (Budapest: Napkelet, 1927), pp. 786-794.
12. Antal Szerb, "Szomory Dezső: Levelek egy barátnőmhöz (Pandora, 1927)" [Dezső Szomory: Letters to a Girlfriend of Mine (Pandora, 1927)], in *A trubadúr szerelme—Könyvekről, írókról 1922-1944* [A Trubadour's Love—On Books and Writers, 1922-1944], Tibor Wagner, ed., (Budapest: Holnap, 1997), pp. 35-37.
13. János Kodolányi, "Szomory Dezső, avagy: pusztulunk, veszünk" [Dezső Szomory: We Are Destroyed and Ruined], *Élőszó*, vol. 2-3, (Budapest, 1927): pp. 106-110.
14. Dezső Szomory, "Egy levél alkalmából" [On the Occasion of a Letter], *Nyugat*, vol. II, (Budapest, 1917): pp. 257-268.
15. Endre Illés, "A mennyei küldönc—Szomory Dezső" [The Heavenly Messanger: Dezső Szomory] in *Krétarajzok* [Drawings in Chalk] (Budapest: Magvető, 1970), pp. 22-36.
16. Dezső Szomory, *Az irgalom hegyén* [On the Mountain of Mercy] (Budapest: Magvető, 1964), p. 355.
17. *Ibid.*, p.170.
18. *Ibid.*, p. 276.
19. *Ibid.*, p. 250.
20. *Ibid.*, p. 253.
21. *Ibid.*, p. 261.
22. Lajos Hatvany, "Szomory Dezső új könyve" [Dezső Szomory's New Book] (Budapest: Újság, January 16, 1935, 3-4) in *Emberek és könyvek* [People and Books], György Belia, ed., (Budapest: Szépirodalmi, 1971), pp. 158-164.
23. Andor Kellér, *Író a toronyban* [A Writer in the Tower], in *Író a toronyban* [A Writer in the Tower] (Budapest: Szépirodalmi, 1958), p. 40.
24. *Ibid.*, p. 90.
25. *Ibid.*, p. 138.
26. Imre Roboz, "Szomory Dezsőről" [On Dezső Szomory] in *Az irodalom budoirjában* [Within the Budoir of Literature] (Budapest: Rózsavölgyi and Co., 1916), pp. 195-208.
27. Pál Réz, *Szomory Dezső. Arcok és vallomások* [Dezső Szomory. Faces and Testimonies] (Budapest: Szépirodalmi, 1971), pp. 61-62.
28. "Szomory Dezső: Levelei Fenyő Miksának" [Dezső Szomory: His

Letters to Miksa Fenyő], in *Feljegyzések és levelek a Nyugatról* [Notes and Letters about the *Nyugat*] Erzsébet Vezér, ed., (Budapest: Akadémiai, 1975), p.439.

29. See Ferenc Liszt, "Liszt Ferenc a zsidóságról" [Franz Liszt on the Jews] *Magyar Fórum*, vol. II, no. 11, (Budapest, 1994): pp. 40-43. Also see *Letters,* 139; and see chapter XII, *Des Bohemiens et de leur Musique en Hongrie. Les Israelites.*
30. Sándor Hoffmann, "Nemzeti Színház: Egyfelvonásos színművek: Péntek este, Szomory Dezsőtől, Jefte lánya, Cavalotti Félixről" [National Theater: One Act Plays: Friday Evening, From Dezső Szomory, Jefte's Daughter, About Félix Cavalotti], *Magyar Szemle*, vol. 10, (Budapest, March 8, 1896): pp. 118-119.
31. Dezső Szomory, *Levelek egy barátnőmhöz* [Letters to a Girlfriend of Mine] (Budapest: Athenaeum, 1927), p. 103.
32. *Ibid.*, p. 77.
33. *Ibid.*, p.113.
34. *Ibid.*, p. 174.
35. *Ibid.*, p. 219.
36. Hannah Arendt, *Rabel Varnhagen: the Life of a Jewish Woman* (New York: Harcourt, Brace, Jovanovich, 1974), p. 224.
37. Ferenc Hevesi, *Szenvedés, igazság* [Suffering and Justice] (Székesfehérvár: Jenő G. Csitáry's Press, 1928).
38. Árpád Fischer, *Kiáltvány a zsidósághoz* [Manifesto to the Jewry] (Budapest: Ábrahám and Sugár, 1927).

The Lost Childhood:
The Hungarian-Jewish Symbiosis

The conservative literary historian, János Horváth viewed the *Nyugat,* a leading literary journal and a literary circle, as an example for Hungarian-Jewish cultural coexistence and as a type of assimilation for which the broader society was not prepared. Founded in 1908 *Nyugat* aimed at artistic excellence. Its politics was quality. There was truly no division between writer who came from provincial town or, for that matter, they were second or third generation from the ghetto. The conservative literary historian sensed the danger in such grouping. "The *Nyugat* is a gathering of Jewish and markedly philo-Semite writers; a Hungarian group saturated with Jewish assimilation; a completed Jewish assimilation."[1] Horváth explained that more indolent Hungarians had not noticed the rise of this new way of thinking among Hungarian Jews. A Jewish reading public had rallied to the symbolist poet Ady and his fellow writers while a now drained patriotic-Hungarian conservatism had not recognized its own interests.

Acculturation

The reader should note that a deeper hidden meaning of Hungarian and Jewish cultural coexistence and symbiosis might have unfolded. After all, assimilation is a complex historical process which might have included the "Hungarianization" of minorities and religious communities and the integration of isolated small settlements, market towns, and larger country centers into trade and industrial development. The process of assimilation could have entailed the "mutual discovery" of different social classes, the borderland and the city, Catholics and Lutherans, Christians and Jews, Hungarians and Slovaks and Serbs. The "Hungarian-Jewish coexistence" that was realized in the *Nyugat* was not an experiment in assimilation that took place as a result of the quick intellects of a cosmopolitan and politically emancipated Jewry pushing ahead using pure blooded Hungarians as a shield, as it had been claimed between the two world wars by Gyula Szekfű, János Horváth, László Németh, and Géza Féja. Rather, it was a part of a universal process that included the revival of liberalism in Hungary and marked a new period in the development of bourgeois thinking. At the turn of the century and through the 1910s, a defensive conservatism infected society with the virus of the "Jewish question" because this seemed to be the only ideology that could compromise the move towards modernity.

The assimilation of different groups and nationalities into Hungarian society was not complete by the turn of the century. "...And if there are some who wish that Hungarian poetry is national in the sense that French poetry is national, and if what they want is possible and beneficial, then it is not the poets who should be harassed by these political wishes but it is the politicians who should be so harassed. Politics should create—if it is capable, has the strength, ideas, courage, honor, generosity, and impartiality—a homogeneous national society that can create a homogenous national literature." Ignotus wrote this in *Kísérletek* (Experiments)[2] as the program of the *Nyugat.*

A national literature rises from assimilation itself and from the discovery of a common but unique voice. "Is today's Hungarian literature national?" Ignotus kept investigating the question. His response was ambiguous. "It is and it is not. It is a national literature in the sense that there is uniformity between even remote phenomena concerning social classes, races, and individuals who have become Hungarian in their language. These are similarities that we ourselves hardly see but which a foreigner would notice just as he would also consider Hungarian people of diverse ranks and origin mostly identical as well."

It is not difficult to decipher whom Ignotus writes about in connection with the classes and races who have become Hungarian in their language. There was a non-discussed and hardly ever surfacing problem hidden behind the battle fought using "persecution esthetics" over the question of "who is national and who is not." The future coexistence of Hungarians and Jews was to be realized through politics and the *Nyugat* had taken a chance by advocating this process according to Horváth's observation. Ever since the 1880s the "Jewish question" had lurked in the background of Hungarian public life. The *Nyugat* had stepped across the boundaries not by silencing the question but by "formulating" it.

An experienced drama, the advance that they had suffered for, and a cathartic cleansing experience helped them to go beyond the "question."

The Melting Pot

The innovation of the *Nyugat* writers was not only to develop a stylistic modernity but also to map up a new reality. They discovered unknown Hungarian scenery and elevated new objects to a literary level. The newly born Hungarian social novel described different forms of "socialization" and illuminated the behavior patterns of uniquely stratified groups in transition. These were responses to the challenges of the time.

"Hungarian-Jewish" coexistence was certainly realized on the everyday level as well. "My Ernő Szép is overtly ambitious, honest, Hungarian, and is a refined poet at the same time ..." Ady wrote in the first decade of the twentieth century and "Hungarian" is a loaded word within this utterance.[3] Endre Ady's dearest poet was Ernő Szép,[4] the son of a country teacher who sold his violin to be able to educate his son. Several times Szép invoked his dressmaker mother and compared her needle-pricked fingers to his own pen-imprinted "tool." As World War II approached he recalled the memory of the Friday evening candle-lighting with great poetic force in one of the *Ararát* almanacs.[5]

However, Ernő Szép's Jewishness did not only appear as a "theme" in his oeuvre. It was also present in his apologetic irony, in his lack of self-confidence, and in his withdrawal into childish naivete. Aladár Komlós hears the tune of self-defense in Ernő Szép's lyrics as if he had no right to a serious tune. Komlós also adds, "Ernő Szép is the child of a people lacking self-confidence, a people that created the self-mockery of Heine."[6] In a later essay Aladár Komlós characterizes Ernő Szép with "The Jewish shyness appears in his self-deprecating grimace. His eyes are full of the colors of the Hungarian landscapes and his ears are full of the voices of the Hungarian language and folk poetry."[7]

In a different vein, Sándor Scheiber seems to have discovered one of the motives of Jeremiah's laments. He was summoned as a child to be the prophet of destruction and tragedy of his people.[8] Both comparisons are true for Ernő Szép. He was Hungarian as Endre Ady declared and yet Jeremiah's pain and the uncertainty of assimilation lived on as Jewish motives within his art. Ernő Szép looked at life with a naive amazement and bombarded his social experience with questions of childish simplicity. "What I do not understand is why I have to be poor and Jewish when I have never asked for either. All I wanted to do is to sing as long as I live…" he wrote in one of his letters to Gyula Krúdy.[9]

Jewishness was a fate not chosen by the poet himself and that he occasionally experienced as a stroke of fate. "Look into a Jew's black eyes. No matter how shiny they are, pain remains in those eyes." To dream was to be released from the Jewish fate. The hero of the *Lila ákác* (Purple Acacias) fantasizes about a crazy beautiful world where the sweet music of a Venice night is heard but from which he is driven out of everywhere and in which he ultimately drowns in the Grand Canal. There was a barrier for Szép in "real life" as well. Hard as he tried to embrace the world, he seemed to hit his head against a ceiling. "I do not breathe the full air in Paris. Neither do I in London where all the good fortune I have are bargain and misery at the same time. In vain do I go to America or the Canary Islands. There will be a hotel where the chef might secretly despise me because I am a Jew! ..."[10]

In the play version of the *Purple Acacias,* Szép created a peculiar scene which takes place in the private box of the Casino. High spirited Master Lali enters Pali Csacsinszky's box where the thought rushes into his mind that he wants "to slap a Jew in the face." He demands from the waiter, "Get me a Jewish boy, I want to smack somebody's face today! I will give him such a sweet-smelling slap in the face ..." As it turns out there is no slappable Jew in the vicinity. Lali leaves the box and Józsi the waiter reports that "Mister Lali and a Jewish boy are outside in the corridor ... Are they boxing one another on the ears? No, sir. They are kissing."[11]

If there is a symbolic picture for the Hungarian-Jewish relationship, this seemingly unexplainable scene is it. Gentlemanly bravado calls for slapping a Jew in the face but the urge dissolves in a suddenly submissive kiss and a friendly embrace. The dynamics of assimilation is friction between social classes whose social experience with one another creates tension. It depends on circumstances and the sway of public atmosphere whether this friction concludes in melting into one another or in segregation. The former is demonstrated by the rapprochement and new solidarity of the *Nyugat*'s writers. When Ignotus announced the individual right of self-expression, he offered a particular absolution for the ones gathering in the *Nyugat* camp: both the release from—and a roundabout way back into—the community, the new republic of art.

In the parlance of the period around the turn of the century an individual and his individuality were the opposites of race and type.

Jenő Rákosi and the persecution-aesthetics movement demanded a national Hungarian representation in literature and then defined those capable of representing Hungarian intellectual life as residing within a narrow popular-national circle. Anti-Semitism was a natural part of their expressed chauvinism.

Frictions in 'Symbiosis'

It was not by mere chance that the authors of the *Holnap* (Tomorrow) anthology led by Ady originally chose *Hétmagyarok* (Seven Hungarians) as the title of their publication of new songs for new times. It was quite obvious that the *Holnap* would be radical and Hungarian.

One of Mihály Babits's notes about the Jewish question also reflects the contradictory interpretation of individuality and race. "Life is not a struggle of races; it is a struggle of individuals. And if the racial question is raised in life, its cause can be found in individual relationships. It is not the race that is resentful towards the Jews; it is the individual. And everybody is a little resentful towards the one he has to depend on."

Babits's handwritten notes—originally prepared for the *Zsidó Szemle* (Jewish Review) and which remained a manuscript—are radically honest and probably that is the reason why they have never been printed. The general Darwinian tone of the notes—the struggle of races and individuals—is misleading, speaking in the clichés of the time. This is because it originates in the social experience that reflects the bilateral grievances of assimilation.

In the eighteenth century, before the era of big money and the market economy, the assimilation experience was marked by unexpected integration and by the collision of isolated communities. These were not indifferent but so called allogeneous—ready to mix—groups. As István Bibó's classic essay informs us, the assimilation of the Jews occurred as a real social earthquake. Jews suddenly occupied important positions—thus far closed to them—and sometimes even positions of real power. At other times the closed nature of the conservative Hungarian society prevented them from many social and professional advances and accompanying integration. Legal equality did not eliminate social discrimination. The result was that mutual resentment and grievances required a new interpretation of social experiences, something hard to find. Bibó writes that the peculiarity of the phenomenon was such that "if certain insults, which the traditional hierarchy had sustained and endured from its usual potentates without much ado, came from the newly rising Jews or from any other emancipated people of "inferior" rank, these insults solidified as unforgivable offences and unparalleled humiliation for people who continued to live in a world of graded human qualities."[12]

The mobility of the Jews and other minorities threatened "Hungarian indolence" and that gentry comfort which loathed any kind of mercantile activity. In the Babits-Kosztolányi correspondence, Kosztolányi—already settled in the capital—celebrated the countrified Babits for his "virginity," for his abstinence from participating in the tumult of the capital. Isolation was a virtue. "Today, my dear, the times are different. I am living in a period of consciousness. They have purchased my body and soul..."[13] Glorifying activity and becoming drunk by his new found community, Kosztolányi flew on the wings of his new success. "They pay for every line I write," he wrote while celebrating his acceptance into a more dynamic community. Journalism signified social integration for Babits and Kosztolányi both of whom had arrived from the country and had come from a career in the bureaucracy.

"Country" and "city" lives ran according to different rhythms to the tune played by "foreigners" occupying independent positions. Suddenly upwardly mobile Jewish intellectuals and their audience were society's "bubbles" of effervescence. In 1920 Cholnoky wrote about this change in a pamphlet entitled

"Hungarian Literature and the Jewry." "Then the Jews started appearing. Life and a ceaseless come and go moved into editorial offices. While we Christians used to trick one another into reports and politics and all of us aspired to write comfortable literature or elegant theater criticism and would not leave our customary circles, young Jewish boys feverishly ran around in the city. They were everywhere. They knew about everything. And the editor of the political column spent almost all his life in the Parliament and in party circles..."

Assimilation pact revoked

László Cholnoky announced that the Hungarian press had become Jewish. The Jews' fault was a certain "loyalty to their ancestry;" they had not given up their emotional ties to their "own kind." The cause of the Hungarian press becoming Jewish was also to be found in Christian indolence: "the ratio between the Christians and the Jews should not have allowed for such an isolation ... Why is not there a special Jewish press in England or in the United States?"[14]

Social isolation despite assimilation, a restless haughtiness toward "mixing," and new groupings formed in the debate between "indolence" and "activity" all helped to create a social arena full of tensions. As Cholnoky stated, the Jews held a "loyalty to their ancestry."

In 1906 Babits was leafing through Ignotus' book *Olvasás közben* (While Reading It) and wrote the following: "Scratch the Hungarian and the 'melancholic Hungarian' (*búsmagyar*) appears." "A Hungarian starts by turning gray and ends up growing silent."[15]

It was troubling to the young Babits how he, a representative of "indolent Hungary," succeeded in an activity that social experience identified as a Jewish breakthrough. Babits, who agreed with Ignotus' statements, considered Ady's Hungarian-bashing farfetched and he unexpectedly declared his "loyalty to his ancestry." "I am Hungarian and come from a Hungarian noble family (and I am mighty proud of it) on both the paternal and maternal sides. From time immemorial my grandfathers used to be county officials (is there a more Hungarian occupation?) and my father was the first one who entered into state service. But officialdom notwithstanding, my father was an archetype of the Hungarian gentleman and lawyer. And I, who throughout my career and also through my learning, broke so far away from the family tradition and centuries old mentality, am every day more and more aware of how natural and of how close a continuation of my honest Hungarian ancestors I am…"[16]

Modernization offered to different intellectual groups the experience of struggle and appeasement, crisis and schizophrenia. Confronting the mutual grievances of Hungarians and Jews bred new personality traits in these intellectuals. For Babits it started with understanding Ady's role. Babits and Kosztolányi used to consider Ady an "empty poseur." Now Babits believed that Ady had welded modernity and "Hungarianness" into a unique unity.[17]

Endre Nagy, one of the teeming numbers of writer-journalists surrounding Ady, perpetuated the idea of the coexistence of communities and groups released from their former bondage. In the city of Nagyvárad, the Bihar county gentry, the spick and span soldier, the bishop, and the Jew lived together—"indeed, as if this city were a laboratory of the ideas of the world," Nagy wrote in his memoir, *A peceparti Páris 1900-ban* (Paris of the Pece River in 1900). Because of this, nowhere in the world did they utter the word *progress* so frequently as they did here.

According to census statistics, 35% of Várad's population was Jewish. But remove the center of the widespread market-town and it could reach to 80%. "Endre Ady used to say that it was similar to baking bread from eighty percent leaven and twenty percent flour."—as Endre Nagy stated.[18]

Nagy well illustrated the difference between statistics and social experience. It appeared to the gentry from Bihar county and the officer from Várad that the Jews had usurped certain occupations. Their presence was enlarged by the effect quoted by Bibó, that people who had been left outside of power now had managed to enter social circles formerly closed to them. That is why the "optics" of the situation became distorted and the so called "characteristics" of the newcomers became exaggerated.

"Every race has its good and bad traits," Babits wrote in his previously quoted manuscript. "But the Jew has strikingly good and strikingly bad qualities. I think anti-Semitism is rather caused by the good and not by the bad qualities. ...Obviously these qualities complemented the qualities of the Hungarian intelligentsia horrified by responsibilities and by free trade. They were needed and are still needed today."[19]

An irresistible socialization process had begun between the turn of the century and the 1910s: intellectuals from the outlying areas migrated to the city and met groups of people of different origins, cultures, and roots. Abandoning their distrust, changing the nature of "Hungarian consciousness," and struggling with the "Jewish experience" were all part of the transformation they experienced.

Similar to Babits, Dezső Kosztolányi, the son of a Szabadka high-school principal, proudly acknowledged his roots stemming from traditional historical Hungarians. However, one of the first signs of his new socialization is the fact that he immediately set out to protect young Jewish talents. When the *Budapesti Szemle* (Budapest Review) criticized Emil Makai, Kosztolányi—in a dignified way—disapproved, saying that the conservatives had "curtly rejected this rebellious Jewish boy who brought a new voice into Hungarian literature..." Makai's rebellion was that he had not worn a hat with feather-grass and had not written patriotic poems.[20] In the same year at the news of Sándor Bródy's suicide, Kosztolányi supported him "as a Hungarian" against his critics saying, "[Bródy] will always remain a Hungarian writer."

After the war and revolutions "the coexistence," János Horváth blamed on the *Nyugat,* disintegrated. The *Új Nemzedék* characterized the revolutions as "literary rat rebellions." This was penned by István Lendvai who also attacked Babits for his pacifism and Ernő Szép for his Jewishness, both in the same year.

According to István Lendvai, Ernő Szép and his influence was one of the most telling cases of the "intellectual megalomania of the Jews." In what manner did Szép dare to write about the Hungarian countryside in the *Patika* (Drug Store)?" Lendvai's answer was, "The complete, impenetrable, and instinctive—that is eternal—foreignness." Angels from paradise prohibited them from becoming Hungarians. What would they know about this people? "Even if they do, they slander them and incite against them with rage and impotence. They incite me, the stupid Hungarian." Lendvai also suggested a solution: "The Caesarian madness of the intellectual ghetto, which entertains that he is the only *civis europaeus* and everybody else is a stupid barbarian, wants to influence us all with this belief. This is something that should be terminated and its bones ought to be cracked."[21]

Babits was also vilified at the beginning of the counter-revolution.[22] There was a fragment of a poem among his first notes Lőrinc Szabó's estate kept hidden for a long time. Here Babits recognizes the parallels between his life and that of the persecuted Jew: "Oh, I have also been smeared with mud / my kind loathes to see me / and I wear as Jews used to / the yellow patched ugly suit."[23]

His "resentment" evoked a feeling of common experience with Jews. As if Babits had felt that the former Hungarian-Jewish "symbiosis" was to blame for the failure. He spun his novel, *Timár Virgil fia* (Virgil Timár's Son), from the wreath of these disintegrating flowers. Contemporaries recognized Ignotus—who had emigrated by then—in the character of one of his heroes, the cynical Jewish journalist who flirts even with Catholicism.

After the revolutions and the exile, Lajos Hatvany asks how it was possible that Babits was "a good Bolshevik" in April 1919 and "a counter-revolutionary chauvinist and a good anti-Semite in August 1919?" The cynic journalist Vitányi, the villain of the novel was a concocted paper figure. "Babits embraced the 'cliches' which emulated from the anti-Semitic slogans of the system or from the honest Hungarian racial attitude, also developed in the system. The Vitányi kind—Jewish monsters—are the creations of a counter-revolutionary atmosphere."[24]

During the counter-revolution of the early nineteen-twenties Kosztolányi edited the infamous "Pardon" column of the *Új nemzedék* (New Generation) and wrote some of the column's anonymous articles as if he were offering his *Zsidók kivonulása* (The Exodus of the Jews) as reparation for the Jewish review—*Múlt és Jövő* (Past and Future). The baby cried standing next to his mother / The full jug toppled on the table / The cattle mooed and backed on the hay / And the gate of the house was dark with blood."

For young Babits and Kosztolányi the "Jewish question" was part of the general issue of modernizing the Hungarians. They accepted the significance of the "Jewish leaven" for these Hungarians buried in "apathy" after the Compromise while both were aware of the deformities and outgrowths of the relationship.

Similar to Ernő Szép's literary hero, Babits' autobiographical novel *Halálfiai* (Sons of Death) held up a mirror to the other major type of Hungarian socialization of the period. As opposed to the Jewish boy, the country official's boy actively stares the Jews, who are foreigners to him, in the eye. He describes how the gentry became anti-Semitic after selling their estates to Jews. At Sót, where little Imruska Sátordy is raised, there used to be two Jews. By now there are several hanging around Schapringer, the town's capitalist. He has purchased the flooded fallow acres and hectares and brought in engineers to control the river.

In connection with the Dreyfus case Imruska is taught by his father that there is only one form of justice, and impartial justice at that. The young man "who felt a peculiar aversion when he had to shake hands with his grandmother's vine-dresser, indulged himself in imagining that the son of a grubby Jew (Dreyfus) could be a great and saintly man, holier than the Pope in Rome. What is more, Christ himself was a Jew …"

In the novel the story of socialization spins from Dreyfus and Zola to the recognition of the necessity of a Hungarian-Jewish alliance. At the university the Messiah-awaiting Rosenberg, full of optimism, steps to Imruska. "He is saturated with the restless idealism of his class, with a strong instinct towards culture, and with a freedom of thinking that a Christian would rarely achieve. Imrus—endowed by the exaggeration of youth—almost loathed the Christians in those days since he only had to compare Schapringer's erudition with that of one of his acquaintances. No wonder that he found friends among the Jews."

Until the end of his life Babits was tormented by the question why the number of his Jewish followers was so high. "Tell me Gyuszi."—by then mute Babits asked Illyés on a small checkered piece of paper, "why are all my followers and friends Jews? The Christians, apart from you, do not care about me and obviously do not like me while the Jews remain faithful."[25]

In Szép's play the character Lali was getting ready to slap a Jew in the face while Józsi, the waiter, who is himself Jewish, informs us about a secret kiss. Babits makes the following comment about the meeting of the two fellow-students: "And the descendants of the two ancient, eastern types—the Jew and the Hungarian—shook hands enthusiastically and with shining eyes in the name of the future and culture."[26]

After the *Anschluss* and in the shadow of World War II, Babits, on his deathbed made the following comment in one of the entries into his "talking" notebooks: "What is the news? Is it true that

Freud was arrested? Don't you think that something like that is possible here as well? We disappear and perish in the large German shadow. But what happens to Budapest without the Jews?"[27]

Ernő Szép wrote about his persecution in the Arrow-Cross hell in *Emberszag* (The Smell of Humans). It is as if history had refuted the shiny-eyed handshake that *The Sons of Death* eternalized. The poets of the *Nyugat* created the mythology of an innocent childhood. "I am playing with my two colorful eyes, / with my two dear, tiny hands, / I am playing with my playful self / a small child is a toy as well," Kosztolányi wrote in *Szegény kisgyermek panaszai* (The Complaints of a Poor Small Child). An antiquated world opens up here for us—the period of innocence in the countryside: that of Kosztolányi's in Szabadka, that of Babits' in Szekszárd, that of Gyula Juhász' in Szeged, that of Árpád Tóth's in Debrecen, and that of Ernő Szép's in Hajdúszoboszló. Rural Hungary becomes a symbol of pre-capitalist innocence, a world without frictions. As Ernő Szép wrote nostalgically: "Szoboszló is shrinking dressed in a veil, / we turn around a bend ... and see again / our tower like the upheld finger of a child." Rural Hungary had "to assimilate" into the town and modernity just like the outlawed Jewry had to do one day. The poets of the *Nyugat* headed by Ady were the "Jews" of a conservative Hungary, the outcasts and the ones washed ashore. The pain of the "dead-end history" of that Hungary appears by recalling one's childhood. The elimination of "country living" occurred before the liberty embodied in the "city" could be completely born. As Ernő Szép said: "I would like to run after my father, / who led me to the city, / and while I was gazing among the shops, / once he let my hand go."[28]

Just like the little Jewish teacher did with Ernő Szép, the country official father also let Babits-Imruska leave for the big melting pot that prewar Hungary represented. The symbol of childhood evoked the solitude of Hungarian progress to modernity and its lost chances, the still baffling nervous fever of the slap and the kiss.

We compared originally converging attitudes of two major Hungarian writers of the twentieth century. Their connection illuminates the dynamics of assimilation at the turn of the century and also the rupture of the twenties when influential writers dissociated themselves from the Jewish-Hungarian "symbiosis."

Mihály Babits died during the Second World War from cancer of the larynx. Ernő Szép miraculously survived the Holocaust. Much neglected by the new communist establishment and died in extreme poverty.

Notes

1. János Horváth, *Aranytól Adyig* [From Arany to Ady] (Budapest, 1919), p. 45.
2. Ignotus, *Kísérletek* [Experiments] (Budapest, 1910), pp. 82-83.
3. Endre Ady, "Könyvek és jóslások" [Books and Prophecies] (Budapest: Nyugat, 1914), pp. 71-72, in Gyula Földessy, ed., *Vallomások és tanulmányok. Ady Endre Összes Művei* [Confessions and Essays. Endre Ady's Complete Works], vol. III. (Budapest: Athenaeum, 1944), pp. 208-209.
4. Sándor Scheiber, "Ady Endre és Szép Ernő" [Endre Ady and Ernő Szép], in *Petőfi Irodalmi Múzeum Évkönyve* [Petőfi Literary Museum's Yearbook] (Budapest, 1961), pp. 119-121.
5. Ernő Szép, "Vidd el, hajó, levelemet" [Boat, Take My Letter With You], in Aladár Komlós, ed., *Ararát Évkönyv* [Ararát Yearbook] (Budapest: Országos Izraelita Leányárvaház [National Jewish Girl Orphanage], 1941), pp. 29-35.
6. Aladár Komlós, "A szépség költői" [The Poets of the Beauty], in *Az új magyar líra* [The New Hungarian Lyrics] (Budapest: Pantheon, 1928), p. 94.
7. Aladár Komlós, "Zsidó költők a magyar irodalomban" [Jewish Poets in Hungarian Literature], in János Kőbányai, ed., *Magyar-zsidó szellemtörténet a reformkortól a holocaustig. Bevezetés a magyar-zsidó irodalomba* [Hungarian-Jewish History of Ideas from the Reform Age to the Holocaust. Introduction to the Hungarian-Jewish Literature] (Budapest: Múlt és Jövő, 1997), p. 159.
8. Sándor Scheiber, "Emlékbeszéd Szép Ernő sírkőavatásán" [Memorial Speech at Ernő Szép's Tombstone Dedication], in János Kőbányai, *Scheiber Sándor könyve: Válogatott beszédek* [Sándor Scheiber's Book: Selected Speeches] (Budapest: Múlt és Jövő, 1994), pp. 307-309.
9. Pál Réz, "Szép Ernő", in *Úriemberek vagyunk* [We Are Gentlemen] (Budapest: Szépirodalmi, 1957), p. 11.
10. Ernő Szép, *Lila ákác* [Purple Acacias] (Budapest, 1919), pp. 60-61.
11. Ibid., in *Színház* [Theater], Pál Réz, ed., (Budapest: Szépirodalmi, 1975), p. 342.
12. István Bibó, "Zsidókérdés Magyarországon 1944 után" [The Jewish

Question in Hungary after 1944], in *Válogatott tanulmányok* [Selected Essays], Tibor Huszár, ed., (Budapest: Magvető, 1986), p. 701.

13. "Kosztolányi Dezső levele Babitshoz, 1906. jún. 24. után" [Dezső Kosztolányi's Letter to Babits after June 24, 1906], in *Babits-Juhász-Kosztolányi levelezése* [Correspondence of Babits-Juhász-Kosztolányi], György Belia, ed., (Budapest: Akadémiai, 1959), p. 131.
14. László Cholnoky, *A magyar irodalom és a zsidóság. Mi az igazság?* [Hungarian Literature and the Jewry: What is the Truth?] (Budapest: Garai Press, 1920).
15. *Babits-Juhász-Kosztolányi levelezése* [Correspondence of Babits-Juhász-Kosztolányi], *op. cit.*, Dezső Tóth-Kálmán Vargha, ed., *Új magyar múzeum* [New Hungarian Museum], (Budapest: The Institute of the Science of Literature of the Hungarian Academy of Sciences, 1959), p. 113.
16. *Ibid.*, p. 114.
17. István Gál, ed., *Babits Adyról* [Babits about Ady] (Budapest: Szépirodalmi, 1975).
18. Endre Nagy, "A peceparti Páris 1900-ban" [Paris of the Pece River in 1900], in *Ady-Múzeum* [Ady Museum] Gyula Földessy-Jenő Dóczy, ed., (Budapest: Athanaeum, 1925), pp. 76-78.
19. Quoted by István Gál, "Babits zsidószemlélete," [Babits' Attitude to the Jews](hereafter cited as *Babits' Attitude*), *The Annual Almanac of MIOK*, (Budapest, 1973/74): pp. 110-129.
20. Dezső Kosztolányi, "Makai Emil" (Bácskai Hírlap, April 9, 1905), in *Írók, festők, tudósok* [Writers, Painters, and Scientists], Pál Réz, ed., (Budapest: Szépirodalmi, 1958), p. 5-9.
21. István Lendvai, "Szép Ernő, Patika és egyebek" [Ernő Szép, Pharmacy, and Others] *Új nemzedék* (March 21, 1920) and, in *A harmadik Magyarország* [The Third Hungary] (Budapest: Pallas, 1921), pp. 145-153.
22. See Tamás Ungvári, "A szökevény próféta. Babits 1919-ben" [The Fugitive Prophet. Babits in 1919], in *Ikarusz fiai* [Ikarus' Sons] (Budapest: Szépirodalmi, 1970), pp. 247-282.
23. *Babits' Attitude.* Op.cit.
24. Lajos Hatvany, "A magyar értelmiség katasztrófája. Magyar író, magyar zsidó. I." [The Catastrophe of the Hungarian Intellectuals: Hungarian Writers and Hungarian Jews, I] *Jövő* (Vienna, December 3, 8, 13, 1922.)

25. György Belia, ed., *Babits Mihály beszélgetőfüzetei, II.* [Mihály Babits' Talking Notebooks, II] (Budapest: Szépirodalmi, 1980), p. 195.
26. Tamás Ungvári, "A regényíró Babits," in op.cit., *Ikarus,* pp. 282-301
27. *Babits' Attitude. Op.cit.*
28. Quotes from poems were collected by Gábor Devecseri, "'Tegezni az egész világot'—Szép Ernőről" [To Be on Familiar Terms with the Whole World—About Ernő Szép] in *Lágymányosi istenek—Összegyűjtött esszék és tanulmányok* [Gods of *Lágymányos*—Collected Essays and Papers] (Budapest: Magvető, 1979), pp. 470-476.

The Martyr and the Wandering Jew

Compensating Mechanisms, Taboos, and Amnesia

In the following chapter major figures of Hungarian literati of the thirties come on stage. For initiated readers to Hungarian letters the name of actors invoke an aura of familiarity. Baron Lajos Hatvany or László Németh were emblematic figures. The former represented liberal politics and a quest for modernity. The latter emerged as the conscience of the post-World War I generation. Their tormented relationship throws some light on the special undertone of their fights. The "Jewish Question" loomed behind their arguments, sometimes openly revealed, at others wrapped in allusions their readers understood too well. Their unfolding drama stretched over decades and helps to illuminate their ongoing debate over sensitive issues.

To László Németh, the leading mind behind the Hungarian populist movement of the nineteen-thirties, Lajos Hatvany embodied the wicked and bad Jew: a baron, a patron of art, an active supporter of the revolution of 1918, who intruded himself upon the national poet Ady. Baron Hatvany was seen in the new era after the First World War as an over-assimilated Jew who initiated a campaign against Németh, and who branded Németh a "briganti leader." Németh's pamphlet *Kisebbségben* (In Minority) alluded to Hatvany as the *bel esprit* "who has such high principles that he cannot differentiate a Jew from a Hungarian."

László Németh and Hatvany were relentless enemies at the end of the 1920s. However, by the time they reached an advanced age, they had reconciled. In the 1930s, it was Hatvany who reached out his faltering hand, through intermediaries, to Németh.

Visiting his exiled German friends in London in 1934, Hatvany wrote to the noted literary historian, authority on Ady, Gyula Földessy: "Tell László Németh once again that I will not respond to him publicly any more. Although I have a question for him and for his contemporaries: what separates them from the *Octobrists* (e.g from the revolutionaries of 1918—T.U.)? What is more, from the Galileans? Why don't they recognize the circle of the Social Science Society outside of the *Nyugat* as their true ancestors? … Why don't they mention Jászi and Kunfi with obligatory love? … Ignotus and Hatvany … and even Jászi, who disappeared from Hungarian life, would be finer and more becoming allies for their reform movement than the editors of the *Budapesti Hírlap* and *Magyar Figyelő,* who play around with reform slogans."[1]

The letter invokes names that were meaningful in themselves. These were the so-called bourgeois revolutionaries, who, after the collapse of the Austro-Hungarian monarchy, formed a government under Count Mihály Károlyi. The majority of these leaders were in exile by the time the letter was written to admit that any reform idea proposed during the interwar period owed a debt to the initiators of modern thought. This may have been the case, except that all these were *personae non grata* in interwar Hungary. Some of them were desperate to reach their former audience in Hungary, as Oscar Jászi was from his exile first in Vienna, then in Oberlin, Ohio, U.S.A., but his efforts failed. No intellectual status was allotted to failed revolutionaries.

The type of liberalism that Jászi, Kunfi, or Hatvany represented was outside of the reform movement's horizon as envisioned by László Németh. This assessment is reinforced by Ferenc Fejtő's analysis—written after World War II and which remained in manuscript form—that while the "urbanists" had aimed for general freedom rights, the popular camp had organized its progressiveness around the issue of land reform and had rejected the liberal tradition and the ideology of the European left.[2]

In László Németh's view, liberalism was the final stage of that aberration which had finalized the so-called "*Ausgleich*" the historical Compromise between Austria and Hungary establishing the dualist monarchy. László Németh was unwavering in support of his position, while Jászi and Hatvany offered to conclude an ideological alliance with even the populists. The latter would have been the correct political path to take: an alliance against the extreme right of the Horthy regime. As far as Hatvany was concerned, the offer was part of his conciliatory behavior which, quite a few times, revealed to his opponents his generosity and his intention to assimilate into the wider society. He opened his home to people he might have suspected of some anti-Semitism; both Dezső Szabó and Kálmán Sértő, rabid anti-Semitic writers were his lodgers.

Hatvany's attitude was not unique among the liberals who took the offer of Jewish assimilation seriously. In his autobiographical work, *Fegyvertelen* (Unarmed), József Erdélyi resolutely stated that when his racist poem about the alleged ritual murder of Tiszaeszlár, *Solymosi Eszter vére* (Eszter Solymosi's Blood), was published in a fascist Party journal *Virradat*, Miksa Fenyő, financier and writer, also one of the editors of the most prestigious review *Nyugat,* sent him one hundred *pengő*. "I told him that I could only accept it as a loan. Miksa Fenyő responded with a laugh: 'You will return it when you are a fascist king.'"

Erdélyi repeated this anecdote in his testimony to the People's Tribunal.[3] Fenyő considered it undignified to contest the statement and indicated that he did not want to increase Erdélyi's sentence. Why would he want to do that? With no evidence to the contrary and without trying to determine whose memory was stronger, we can infer that Fenyő also possessed a certain compensating mechanism.

How the compensating mechanism related to the "Jewish question" was revealed by a paragraph of the already quoted letter by Hatvany written to Gyula Földessy. "And he [Németh] ought to read my novel before he says that a Jew cannot exercise serious self-criticism. Babits may be a finer novelist than I am, but I do not think that he would have had a graver confrontation with his kind than the author of *Zsiga,*" (meaning Hatvany himself) and the assimilated Jews.

It was a vicious circle: why should Hatvany have had a "confrontation" with his kind and why does he call the novel that criticized Jewish assimilation a "confrontation"—even if only in a letter to Földessy asking him to show it to László Németh?

Imre Csécsy and the liberals who assumed responsibility for the *Octobrists*' heritage often complained that Hatvany did not support them but instead that he flirted from a distance with the popular reform movement just as did Oszkár Jászi.

One can list many examples to prove what must have been known by a few. The "Jewish question" was the Achilles heel of the Hungarian liberal ideology and of the "reform" represented by László Németh. Hatvany's or the exiled Jászi's tolerant, forgiving, and generous gestures stepped over the line of flexible political "*raison.*" A peculiar inferiority complex, a strange sense of self-sacrifice, and—possibly—hidden and unconscious Jewish self-hatred motivated them to unilateral assimilation.

During the thirties Hatvany became aware of the approaching world war and stated that "Simoom winds are blowing; one has to hide under camels' bellies." In another place he wrote, "One has to assume a ladybird's behavior when it pretends to be dead. I do not feel at all like emigrating once again … The gentlemen put a slur on me in my three capacities: that of an Israelite, a socialist, and a capitalist."[4]

It was difficult for Hatvany himself to harmonize the three roles. People compensated when visiting him in his Úri Street mansion in the Castle District of Buda as well. Gyula Illyés described in an obituary written on Kálmán Sértő's death how that peasant-poet boasted of his friendship with Hatvany and the fact that

Hatvany lived in a mansion: "'He is a true Hungarian' Sértő said about Hatvany. A smile hovered about his lips. I asked him why. 'At home he walks around in Hungarian costumes all day. His gown is all braids and frogs and loops.' I did not understand it. 'Even his shirt is like that.' Sértő wanted to convey to me that Hatvany considered his long night gown and his pajamas Hungarian gala costumes."[5]

The above anecdote was enhanced by Sértő's own essay *Vacsora Hatvany Lajosnál* (Dinner with Lajos Hatvany)[6]—revealing his hostile disposition towards Hatvany and his company. In the essay, the anecdote is preceded by another that happened at another social visit. An allusion was made to the poet's fine fingers which, according to Sértő, prompted a lady to ask him: "Aren't you Jewish?" In response the poet told her that his grandmother always shopped without money at the village shop ran by Uncle Ármin. In other words, it was possible that his father was half Jewish, "and then I am one quarter Jewish by all means ... And thanks be to God that there is Jewish blood in me ..."

Sértő, who died very young, was buried by the fascist Arrow-Cross Party. He might not have remembered the above remark in the last years of his life. However, what is interesting in what he wrote is his association of fineness and sensitivity with the Jews. He conveys the idea that "those" Jews are different and that the society is not able to recognize that a peasant could be refined as well. The text resounded as a *Korrobori,* the entwining dance of two peoples as exemplified by the way the Hungarians and the Jews are condemned to one another, just as Endre Ady had diagnosed.[7]

Discriminations

The peculiar tension and glitter of images and the continuous readiness to react to each other, enhanced by the differentiation between the Jew and the non-Jew, was a staple of popular talk between the two world wars. It eventually became ingrained in people's instinctive responses, and then into the deep currents of communicative interaction. The "Jewish question" became the secret code of many messages to be deciphered.

When his novel was published at the end of the 1920s, due to his feisty assimilated behavior Lajos Hatvany had to cope with the accusation of anti-Semitism leveled by the official Jewish press,[8] even from the assimilated Béla Zsolt.[9] Only Ignotus' words, who by then lived in Vienna, offered some consolation.[10] Hatvany responded to the accusation of anti-Semitism haughtily and bitterly.[11]

The complaining, hot-tempered, and easily forgiving Hatvany ("the depth of human sensitivity and irascibility" as László Németh characterized him in his obituary[12]) complained to his friends about the reception of his novel.

Imre Békessy, journalist and entrepreneur, who lived in Vienna by then, hastened to console him in a letter. They are typical lines. Békessy compares the breakthrough of the Jews with Árpád's conquest of Hungary. "The title of the book might as well be 'The Jews' Conquest of Hungary.' It is not only trickling from the village to Pest and the occupation of Pest which is shown with such plasticity in your book but the hard *necessity* also reveals that anything other than surrender to the Christians was not possible during the development."[13]

Comparing Árpád (the Chief leading his tribes to the place where Hungary was built) to the Jews and describing the process that defined assimilation as surrender were mirror images of the final reckoning, aimed at the Hungarian Jews only after the Trianon peace treaty when they had to prove their national status and legitimacy.

What made Hatvany's behavior problematic was precisely the fact that his earlier partner in debate, László Németh, was the one who had demanded the Jews' "adjustment." For László Németh, the new era of assimilation started with Trianon. In general, revolutions revealed that the Jews retained their internal smoldering. Therefore, a fresh oath of allegiance by them to the homeland was continually necessary. The Jews ought to be separated from their "guides"—that is, from the Ignotus and Hatvany type of leaders—because "if we [Hungarians] become more determined, they will adjust to us." Németh reiterated this idea in another article when he reproached the Jews that "from a Hungarian point of view, it is unnecessary and unreasonable for you to infringe upon the laws of adjustment."[14]

At the time few contested the necessity of adjustment since a new, limited assimilation arrangement was invaluable for a community on the defensive. Both anti- and philo-Semitism met on this narrow margin. Pál Teleki, Klebelsberg, and even Jewish official circles expressed sentiments along the same lines. The *Zeitgeist* called for Jewish understanding, reserve, and rationality. As László Németh professed, "a Jewry put in its place" is really a blessing. This was the statement that enraged Hatvany and branded László Németh a "briganti leader."[15]

Hatvany uttered taboo words in the debate by saying, "... as it is proper for a person like myself, I need to use a simile from the Old Testament to illuminate the modern mixture of vulgar anti-Semitism and subtle humanism existing in many types of people such as László Németh. It was Isaac who said, 'It is Jacob's voice and the hairy arm of Esau.' I am saying, it is the face of Plato and the arm of a thug leader."[16]

Let us ignore the details of this "commando" debate.[17] It might be enough to say that it inflicted wounds on both sides. László Németh viewed the debate as an outburst of Jewish racial solidarity. On the other hand, it dawned on Hatvany and friends, characterized as Shylocks, that the new arrangement of assimilation could easily be revoked.

This personalized debate precipitously deepened the gap between Christian reform intellectuals and defensive Jewish intellectuals. There was no more opportunity for an open airing of views. That was why the participants used a mesh of codes, taboos, and euphemisms, scattering around a series of allusions, the majority of them pointing to the "Jewish Question." From then on, every notion within the orbit of ideas about nation, religion, race, and calling became loaded with secondary meanings, and "forbidden" concepts.

It was in the shadow of these taboos that psychological compensating mechanisms sprang up alongside the more familiar phenomena of suppression, sublimation, concealment, and evasion which cast shadows on people's life-work and questioned their behavior and ideals.

The "briganti" debate was not only an episode in Németh's career. Exacerbated by his moral injuries, paralleled only by those of Hatvany's, the debate became one of the chief motives of his further works. Németh's anti-liberalism led him to the "Jewish question." Along with Szekfű, he also considered it a sin of Hungarian liberalism that, beginning with the "*Ausgleich*" (historic compromise between the Austrian and Hungarian governments), Jews gained excessive ground in the press and in literary organs. Németh attacked Ignotus because he was not the ideal spiritual leader to head a Hungarian burst of enthusiasm. He tore the Ady-Hatvany correspondence to pieces because he viewed the "baron" as a magnate and an evil enticer of Hungarian talent. In summary, Németh considered that, in their own country, liberalism's compromise had buried the Hungarians' own indigenous culture and had sacrificed a deeper "Hungarianness" for a more superficial one that would adjust to the different cadence of the "Ignotuses and Hatvanys."

At the end of the 1930s Németh did not believe even in limited assimilation any more. In his view, nothing but a total melting, that is a Jewish cultural amnesia, would offer redemption. The wandering Ahasuerus had to disappear in order to gain the chance for redemption.

Shylock in Hungary

There were several, sometimes contradictory, László Németh statements about the "Jewish question," alternating between the outstretched hand to giving fist-blows to the Jews.[18] In one of his letters, Hatvany called Németh a "scatter-brain." If it only meant that he was not a methodical thinker, his bilious injustice would be diminished. In reality, Németh was consequential only in his manias and idiosyncrasies such as in the martyr's role he assumed at the beginning of his career and in his self-tormenting passion which did not abate until the end of his life. A major issue that obsessed him was the "Jewish question," starting with the "briganti" debate and peaking in the "Szárszó speech."[19]

In these debates László Németh mockingly criticized the national Jewish laws just because they shifted the "Hungarianized" one-half Jews and one-quarter Jews towards full Jewishness. Therefore, these laws did not allow "the Jews to be Jews," that is to remain an unassimilated community. Because of the Jewish laws, however, "it is quite obvious that the vengeful Jews—lacking self-criticism—will have to fortify themselves during these four or five years against the strait-laced culture devotees. He who does not hear that Shylock wants the heart is very hard of hearing."[20]

This statement was never revoked. It remained a secret text, although its author purged it himself. It was kept in memory, however, even though it was never mentioned, much like a skeleton in the closet.[21]

The rest is dumb silence. In Németh's fiction shop, he created grand novels such as *Iszony* (Repulsion) and *Égető Eszter* (Eszter Égető). In them there is no hint of the "question" that so much concerned him in his youth and earlier adulthood, not even "retrospectively." Now and then he did mention that by swaying the youth away from the fascist Arrow-Cross with his ideas, he helped stem the destruction Hungary faced. But he did not even raise "the question" by mentioning the decimation that Hungarian literature experienced when Miklós Radnóti, Andor Endre Gelléri, Károly Pap, and Antal Szerb became victims, killed by fascists.

In *Égető Eszter,* the family's Jewish doctor and good friend walks towards the heroine during the period of persecution. "Eszter assumes that in his state of humiliation it would embarrass him—and would increase his humiliation—if she expressed her sympathy in any way. Therefore, she pretends that she does not notice him. Her sensitivity and female intuition conquered the temptation to recognize what was hidden in the depth of their doctor friend's "awkward" situation, let alone the perspective behind his individual fate."

The above was quoted by Vilmos Juhász in a passionate pamphlet published in an émigré periodical in the mid-1960s.[22] The pamphlet reveals that, from abroad, writers of significant influence between the two world wars adapted to the new regime. The compromises of the Kádár-regime induce one to raise the question: where were they in that earlier dictatorship when their Jewish fellow-writers were decimated?

"Although rooted in reality, there are questions which have by now become mythological. Their justice is mythological, similar to the truth of a fairy-tale, and that is why they are just as dangerous as demons. The Jewish question was alike in Hungary and generally in Central- and Eastern-Europe. To a certain degree, why the questions were mythologized rested with the intellectuals. The writers of the "half-Nazi" and "Nazi" periods did not do very much as *writers* to deplore this mythology. Writers *as writers* were generally silent," wrote Vilmos Juhász.

"I have long tried to find the reason for the absence of resistance by Hungarian writers and find only questions. Could one of the reasons be the fact that a part of the Jewish community financially supported the Horthy regime and, as such, in return received temporary protection from a regime that a major segment of writers considered an impediment to social development? Or is it due to the fact that some populist writers considered Jews active and foreign exploiters of the peasantry?," concludes Juhász

There is no obvious answer to these questions. After the war the left-wing branded the silence or the kind of anti-Semitism marked by Féja, Sinka, and Erdélyi as a betrayal of the profession of letters.[23] Social-democratic and liberal pamphlets did not spare Gyula Illyés or László Németh either.[24]

On the other hand, the leading writer between the two wars, Gyula Illyés, declared the following in 1945: "Our problem is not the past—which we did not choose of our own volition—but the future which we have to form on our own." Illyés advocated that writers funnel intense emotions towards this task, utilizing all the humane values available but avoiding confrontation or, perchance, a showdown.[25]

This cliché-sounding series of ideas was truly an offer of compromise. In the barrage of current attacks and because of the injuries of the attacked the past seemed to remain opaque. On the other hand, the offer of compromise complied with the goals of the communists who strove to monopolize power. The response of communist culture-czar, József Révai, parallels Illyés': "László Németh's primary responsibility is not for what he promulgated before 1944 but for the fact that he did not say a word after the liberation."[26]

World-famous philosopher, György Lukács, then a powerful party commissar, also offered to forgive the past for the promise of the future. "What does this world to be born want from the writers? It does not wish for the denial of their past or of their independence as human beings and writers. Neither does it want unproductive *mea culpa.* All the world wants is that they say a whole-hearted and genuinely felt *yes* to whatever is being formed today."[27]

The problem of the past was not only raised by Béla Zsolt and the social democrats. In a passionate article the chief secretary of the Peasants' Party, the rural sociologist Imre Kovács, also condemned—without any names—the right-wing peasant writers.[28]

Later József Révai's and György Lukács's meeting with Gyula Illyés and László Németh ended the attacks.[29] The communist party offered an alliance with the leaders of populist writers. Although these promises, like others, were eventually never kept, the gesture assured that any open probing of the past was terminated by the center. Béla Zsolt's rear action against the past remained an isolated attack, although the title of György Faludy's article did indicate what the literary turmoil was all about, *Az elsikkasztott történelem* (Embezzled History).[30]

"The past is another country," as Tony Judt said about people failing to confront the pre-war times. The social democratic left and the *Haladás* (Advance) circle around Béla Zsolt wanted to explore, with a certain taste for revenge, various intellectual mistakes made between the two wars. They never succeeded because, in the eyes of the communists, they represented the "rootless bourgeois culture." György Lukács and Márton Horváth and other communist officials branded them with the mark of *Lipótváros* (the upper class Jewish district of Budapest.)[31] Those affected did not have the chance to confront the past, while confrontation was not in the interest of the regime either.

Thus both the urbane Lajos Hatvany, who came back from external exile and was forced into internal exile, and the populist László Németh, as a country teacher, ended up in the infernal pockets of the Rákosi regime.[32] Since it is the right of the exiled not to absolve his martyrdom with confession, László Németh wrote that "For two years I have been asked for a statement that would underline my past. An honest writer—whether enticed or threatened—cannot make such a statement. But if they could see my inner self, just like you, they would see that I have shed those few thoughts and the whole life to which I had been enslaved for twenty years. And then they would rather bargain on my future instead of my past."[33]

This response was in keeping with our expectations—say yes to the future and shed the past. The past, his own past, had become a foreign land from which László Németh had become estranged but from which he would never distance himself. He avoided explaining his memories of the 1930s and 1940s as much as Eszter Égető avoided meeting the old friend of the family, the old Jewish doctor.

However, the barely coded message can still be deciphered from some of his autobiographical statements. At the end of his life he assumed responsibility for his *Szárszó Speeches* including the Shylock prediction. "I accept it ...what is more—defiance answers accusation—I consider it the greatest heroic deed of my life."[34] At other times he declared that he was more proud of his Szárszó declaration than of his greatest novel.[35] The source of that pride resided in the "predictive force of warning" He wrote that "Within 30 years, there will be no Jewish question in Hungary. The Jews will melt into thin air along with the responses of a childless well-being." This must have had a hollow effect, even after decades. It dissolved in the smoke of destruction. The interference of history with prediction cast a fatal shadow on such words.

The Rest is Silence

After the Second World War power interests removed the "Jewish question" from the public agenda. With unparalleled clairvoyance István Bibó pointed out that "Scarcely ever was the case of the Jews mentioned separately. Instead, it melted into the universal actions to eliminate fascism as if their suffering had been just one instance among several other sufferings of equal value. That is how the whole official public life wanted it ... the left and right wings of the coalition.[36]

Posterity reacted to the quoted passages of the *Szárszó Speech* as if they were taboos. Németh left out this response and the

Shylock comment from later editions of the text. Therefore, due to the taboo, how long it was between the time of the Jewish laws and the time of the vengeful "knife sharpening!"

Nor do we know whether it dawned on Németh that forgetting his past was a condition for continuing his work. In return for the future the intellectuals signed a pact of mutual amnesia. László Németh was no longer the writer of *Kisebbségben* (In Minority) or the prophet of the *Szárszó Speech.* Instead, to the public he became the author of *Repulsion* and *Eszter Égető* while a hibernating collective memory looked at the Shylock image with condemnation or respect—according to one's ideology.

The taboo, like a secret file, could be used for blackmail by the regime—whether by Lukács, Révai, Márton Horváth, or the culture czar of the post-1956 era, György Aczél. As Sándor Révész said, "Shylock became Németh's inner taboo. A duality formed that was not to be dissolved either in his soul or in his writing. It could only be hidden with compensating reflexes and with the consciousness of being persecuted."[37]

Compensation began with experiencing the past as a martyr. In addition to his "persecuted mindset," "an enormous self-deceit" was needed, as György Csepeli said, "especially after the Holocaust for somebody to continue to believe that anti-Semitism has a both sane and a mad version and, what is more, to believe that the former would control the latter from breaking out."[38]

In his rare statements about anti-Semitism, Németh writes, "I quite distinctly separated myself from the mad anti-Semitism of the Hitler era not only by being silent when it raged, but by fighting against its representatives. The reason why the young intellectuals, dissatisfied with the situation, did not change sides is due to four or five people: primarily to Dezső Szabó, then to Kodolányi, Sándor Karácsony, Péter Veres, and not the least to me. If they had changed sides, Szálasi or another perhaps less insane might have started their slaughter three or four years earlier. From this aspect, the

Arrow-Cross journalist who condemned my behavior was right: what I have been doing since 1934 was to protect the Jews…"[39]

The list of names is the most baffling part of the quote. Németh lists people who all unfurled the flag of racial theory, although it is true that none of them can be reduced to a common denominator with the Arrow-Cross, most of them were accused of a certain collaboration.

This may have been a defensive reflex while some notion of martyrdom may have instigated Németh's re-creation of memory. To this must be added the idiosyncratic public atmosphere of post-war Hungary which differentiated a "sane" anti-Semitism from mad racism, tolerating the former at least.

Most of the anti-Semites of the time took a strong line "in the interest of the Jews" against certain groups of the Jews. For example, ideas about "anti-Germanness" went well with certain suggestions for the solution of the "Jewish question." Gyula Gömbös, leader of a right-radical movement after the First World War, placed the "issue of the Jews" on the public agenda in the light of the German threat. "A drastic, perfect, and immediate solution to this question is not pressed by the hatred of the Jews but by the love of our kind" he stated. Gömbös, later prime-minister in the early thirties demanded a serious settlement so that Hungarian soldiers would not be sent to the front again in paper boots and that economic and moral sabotage would not dampen the strength of the people.[40]

The logic of "with anti-Semitism *for* the Jews" and "*against* nobody but *for* our kind" disclosed a complete paradox of the assimilation issue. Hidden in this logic was the idea that a rampant Jewry was a disaster and a controlled Jewry was a blessing. A crystal clear example of this lame reasoning was visible in one of Ferenc Erdei's letters written in 1938 to György Sárközi, who later perished. "I am not willing to become a crusader in defense of the Jews. However, I am ready to do anything for the Jews who are not

Jews any more but are otherwise Hungarians—not the ones who now pose as true Hungarians."[41]

Erdei, a noted sociologist was considered before the Second World War as a committed advocate of human rights issues. Sárközi , poet and translator, edited the review of the populist writers and was held in esteem by the predominant gentile circle of the populist thinkers and literati.

Erdei's argument: to do anything for the "Jews who were not Jews any more" indicated that even in left-wing circles only a full and complete assimilation was acceptable. Sárközi's martyrdom could have forced the slaves of this paradoxical logic to re-evaluate their ideas. However, neither their personal inclination nor their historic situation allowed them to do so.

This is how a process of successive compensations and a system of silencing, sublimation, and redrawn objectives began. History offered a very brief loop-hole for the survivors to escape. Ferenc Erdei, with a remarkable consistency, entered into alliance with a communist dictatorship that had sworn to eradicate the past for good. Anti-liberalism was another way out. The idea of a 'truer socialism,' instead of universal human rights, held the potential to marginalize that historical world event known as the Holocaust.

The awareness of martyrdom offered to some a self-torturing strategy incorporating others' martyrdom into one's self-relegation into the background and one's own sacrifice. Compensating mechanisms launched a series of timid bargains with the regime and the acceptance of a historical avoidance from hands which could reach out with a universal suppression of the "question."

It is not worth remembering László Németh's 1959 trip to the Soviet Union nor is there dignity in quoting his enthusiastic words in describing "really existing socialism" as the realization of "the revolution of quality." It was not the compromise—survival coupled with an awareness of martyrdom—that damaged Németh's reputation. Nor was it his occasional involuntary negotiations with the regime—in the person of the culture-czar György Aczél. After all, many shared this "vice." Rather, what damaged his reputation was his belief that such agreement would truly bring about "the revolution of quality" and that the regime could be influenced by those who declared themselves as dedicated representatives of the people.

Illyés, prominent during the years of dictatorship, was also convinced of this. Being in a privileged situation as a leading writer—with the illusion of equality—he was entitled to bargain with the regime. And Aczél proved to be an ideal partner in the roles of the beloved and the hated Other. Even during the war Illyés proclaimed that he would enter into an alliance with the devil himself for the sake of the people. Csaba Könczöl's fine analysis of Illyés' *Napló* (Diary) found that György Aczél was the poet's "secret hero" during his advanced years. Aczél's spirit hovered over the last decade of Illyés' oeuvre. It was the communist leader Aczél whom Illyés tried to get to intervene for the sake of minority Hungarians. It was also because of Aczél that Illyés never joined the dissident signature collections. In Illyés' work Aczél is "the unfilled space between words and lines, even if his name is not actually mentioned..."[42]

The bargain was realized in the complicated network of compensating mechanisms. Significant artists who started or matured between the two world wars came to terms with the consolidated Kádár regime—on a theoretical basis and not because of personal motivations. Since taboos were mutually observed, Tibor Déry was absolved of his former "leftism."[43] Illyés received the illusion that he had the capability to intervene in public affairs while László Németh was given guarantees against a Jewish revenge, and so the ideas in his work were rescued from condemnation.

Sándor Révész strongly criticized Németh's compromise. "László Németh was not looking for a compromise with existing socialism. Indeed, he tried to find a way to believe in existing socialism. He was not one of the compromise seekers; he was one of the protagonists..."[44]

Speaking about the post-revolutionary situation, Éva Standeisky was less critical, "The two most prominent populist writers, Gyula Illyés and László Németh, concluded an agreement with the Kádár regime after lengthy agony and due to tactical considerations. The platform of their rapprochement was the wish to realize socialism. This old wish made their agreement opportunistic. The populists were very much aware that their idea of socialism was not the same as that of the Hungarian Socialist Workers' Party. ...What was more, they took the oath of allegiance to the regime while their political comrades (first of all István Bibó) and fellow writers (first of all Tibor Déry and Gyula Háy) languished in prison."[45]

Németh and Illyés repeatedly tried to make the regime show mercy to the writers. The quality of their works also withstood attacks from the dogmatic left which "deactivated" numerous groups, attacking under the "communist" flag while also forcing them to the periphery of the regime.

However, their influence created the illusion of a false continuity which made it possible to ignore important issues, problems, and debates arising between the two world wars. Not a single one of Lajos Hatvany's writings which criticized László Németh was included in the growing number of his volumes.[46] Further, Németh's rivals, Pál Ignotus and Imre Kovács, were in exile while it was as taboo to say Jászi's and the *Octobrists*' names as to mention the "Shylock case."

Old and ill, Hatvany repeatedly visited Németh. Later, Németh wrote a moving eulogy about Hatvany—with more sympathy than mercy.

Their reconciliation occurred in the name of a catharsis that did not happen. Everything had been arranged, but nothing had been clarified. According to their interpretation of things, they played the respective roles of a Christ carrying his cross and of an Ahasuerus, the wandering Jew humiliating him on the way to Golgotha. They believed this drama could have evolved if Németh, the redeemer, and Hatvany, the wandering Jew, had shared the Passion-play rather than a conspiracy of silence.

Notes

1. Lajos Hatvany, "Földessy Gyulának" [To Gyula Földessy] (1934) in *Hatvany Lajos levelei* [Lajos Hatvany's Correspondence], (hereafter cited as *Hatvany's Correspondence*), Lajosné Hatvany and István Rozsics, eds., (Budapest: Szépirodalmi, 1985), pp. 172-73.
2. Ferenc Fejtő, "Pont egy viszály után, avagy: új fejezet a magyar szellem történetében" [Full Stop after a Conflict or a New Chapter in the History of the Hungarian Intellect] (1947), *Élet és Irodalom*, (Budapest, April 21, 1989).
3. "Fenyő Miksa nyilatkozata Erdélyi József vallomásáról" [Miksa Fenyő's Pronouncement about József Erdélyi's Confession], *Haladás*, (Budapest, May 1, 1947): p. 9.
4. Quoted by Endre Illés, "Hatvany Lajos portréja leveleiben" [Lajos Hatvany's Portrait in His Letters] in *Hatvany's Correspondence, op.cit.*p. 32.
5. Gyula Illyés, "Sértő Kálmán" (1941) in *Hírért megszenvedtem—Versek, napló, elbeszélések* [I've Suffered for Fame—Poems, Diaries, and Stories], Endre Medvigy and Tibor Tüskés, eds., (Budapest: Püski, 1996).
6. Kálmán Sértő, "Vacsora Hatvany Lajosnál" [Dinner at Lajos Hatvany], in *Hatvany's Correspondence, op.cit.*p. 261-262.
7. Endre Ady, "Korrobori" (1917), in *Jóslások Magyarországról* [Predictions about Hungary], Géza Féja, ed.,(Budapest: Atheneum), pp. 272-275.
8. Ernő Ballagi, "Hatvanyról" [On Hatvany], *Egyenlőség*, vol. 6, (Budapest, February 5, 1927): p. 4.
9. Béla Zsolt, "Zsiga a családban" [Zsiga in the Family], *Magyar Hírlap*, no. 6, (Budapest, January 9, 1927): p. 17.
10. "Ignotus Hatvanyról" [Ignotus on Hatvany], *Nyugat*, (Budapest, 1927): pp. 303-307.
11. "Hatvany Lajos levele" [Lajos Hatvany's Letter], *Egyenlőség*, no. 12, (Budapest, March 19, 1927): p. 3.
12. "Németh László Hatvany Lajosról" [László Németh on Lajos Hatvany], in *Sajkódi esték* [Evenings at Sajkód] (Budapest, 1961), pp. 336-341.
13. Imre Békessy, "Levél Hatvany Lajoshoz" [A Letter to Lajos

Hatvany], in *Levelek Hatvany Lajoshoz* [Letters to Lajos Hatvany], *op.cit.* p. 369.

14. Quoted in Gyula Juhász, *A háború és Magyarország* [War and Hungary], in the series, Kérdőjel, ed., Tamás Ungvári, (Budapest: Akadémiai, 1986).
15. László Németh, "Ember és szerep" [A Man and His Role], in *Kalangya* (Budapest, 1934), pp. 45-46.
16. Lajos Hatvany, "A szellem különítményesei" [Commandos of the Intellect], *Újság*, (Budapest, May 27, 1934).
17. László Németh, "Egy különítményes vallomása" [A Commando Member's Confession], *Tanú,* no. 9, (Budapest, 1934): pp. 277-284.
18. See a collection of László Németh's statements about the Jewish question, in Imre Monostori, "Újabb jelenségek Németh László körül" [New Phenomena around László Németh], *Kortárs*, no. 7, (Budapest,1991): pp. 62-66.
19. See also Ferenc Grezsa, "A *Kisebbségben*-metafora jelentésváltozásai" [Changes in the Metaphors of *In Minority*], *Kortárs*, no. 11, (Budapest, 1990): pp. 141-151.
20. László Németh, "Szárszói beszéd" [The Szárszó Speech] (1943), in *Az 1943. évi balatonszárszói Magyar Élet-tábor előadás- és megbeszélés-sorozata* [The 1943 Balatonszárszó *Magyar Élet* Camp Lecture and Discussion Series] (Budapest: Magyar Élet, 1943).
21. See also András Lengyel, "Németh László Shylock-metaforája. (Egy metafora értelme és eszmetörténeti szerepe)" [László Németh's Shylock Metaphor: The Rational and Ideological Role of the Methaphor], *Valóság*, no. 8, (Budapest, 1991): pp. 56-74.
22. Vilmos Juhász, "Az apák helyett—A mai magyar irodalom egy aspektusáról" [Instead of Fathers—On One Aspect of Contemporary Hungarian Literature], *Új Látóhatár*, no. 2, (1965), pp. 164-175.
23. Zoltán Horváth, *Hogy vizsgázott a magyarság?* [How Did the Hungarians Pass?] (Budapest, 1945).
24. László Faragó, *Írástudók árulása—írástudók helytállása* [The Betrayal of the Intellectuals] (Budapest, 1946).
25. Illyés Gyula, "Újabb szellemi frontot!" (1945) ["Let Us Have a Newer Intellectual Front!"], in *Ingyen lakoma* [A Free Feast] (Budapest, 1964), pp. 419-427.
26. József Révai, "Az összeesküvés tanulságai" [The Teaching of a Conspiracy], *Társadalmi Szemle*, (Budapest, March 1947): pp. 161-168.

27. György Lukács, "A magyar irodalom egysége" [The Unity of the Hungarian Literature], in *Irodalom és demokrácia* [Literature and Democracy] (Budapest, 1948), p. 188.
28. Imre Kovács, "Ellenforradalom az irodalomban" [A Counter-Revolution in Literature], *Szabad Szó*, (Budapest, December 12, 1945).
29. See Gyula Borbándi, *A magyar népi mozgalom—A harmadik reformnemzedék* [The Hungarian Populist Movement—The Third Reform Generation] (Budapest: Püski, 1989, 2nd ed.), p. 429.
30. György Faludy, "Az elsikkasztott történelem" [Embezzled History], *Népszava*, (Budapest, October 26, 1947).
31. Márton Horváth, "Illyés és Zsolt" [Illyés and Zsolt], *Szabad Nép*, (Budapest, April 13, 1947).
32. See Ferenc Grezsa, *Németh László vásárhelyi korszaka* [László Németh's Vásárhely Period] (Budapest: Szépirodalmi, 1979).
33. László Németh, "Irodalom 45 után" [Literature after 1945], *Tiszatáj*, (November 1976): pp. 5-6.
34. László Németh, *Homályból homályba* [From Twilight to Dusk] (hereafter cited as *Twilight*) (Budapest: Magvető and Szépirodalmi), p. 619.
35. László Németh, *Megmentett gondolatok* [Saved Thoughts] (Budapest: Magvető and Szépirodalmi), p. 640.
36. István Bibó, "Zsidókérdés Magyarországon 1944 után" [The Jewish Question in Hungary after 1944], *Válasz*, nos. 10/11, (1948): p. 263.
37. Sándor Révész, "A hit üzemanyaga" [The Fuel of Faith], *Mozgó Világ*, no. 9, (Budapest, 1994): pp. 110-115.
38. György Csepeli, "A népi gondolkodás paradox antiszemitizmusa" [The Paradox Anti-Semitism of Populist Thinking], in *A népi mozgalom és a magyar társadalom* [The Populist Movement and the Hungarian Society], Levente Sipos and Pál Péter Tóth, eds., (Budapest: Napvilág, 1997), pp. 180-186.
39. László Németh, "Kisebbségben" [In Minority], in *Twilight,* (Budapest: Magvető and Szépirodalmi, 1977), p. 628.
40. Gyula Gombos, "Egy református pap részére" [For a Protestant Minister], *Magyar Élet*, no. 6, (1939): p. 26.
41. "Erdei Ferenc levele Sárközi Györgyhöz," (1938), [Ferenc Erdei's Letter to György Sárközi], in Konrád Salamon, *A harmadik út kísérlete* [The Experiment of the Third Road] (Budapest: Eötvös, 1989), p. 34.

42. Csaba Könczöl, "A titkos főhős—Aczél György Illyés Gyula naplójában" [The Secret Hero: György Aczél in Gyula Illyés' Diary], *Népszabadság*, (Budapest, October 19, 1994): p. 23.
43. See also Tamás Ungvári, "Déry, Aczél és a börtön" [Déry, Aczél, and the Prison], in Ferenc Botka, ed., *D. T. úr X.-ben* [Mr. T. D. in X] (Budapest: Petőfi Irodalmi Múzeum, 1995), pp. 143-149.
44. Sándor Révész, "Illyés és Aczél, I, II" [Illyés and Aczél, I, II], *Mozgó Világ*, nos. 3, 4, (Budapest, 1996).
45. Éva Stadeisky, *Az írók és a hatalom* [Writers and the Regime] (Budapest: 1956-os Intézet, 1996), p. 460.
46. See also Péter Sz. Nagy, *Hatvany Lajos 1993,* (Budapest: Balassi), p. 104. See also István Cs. Varga, "Hatvany Lajos és Németh László—Egy kapcsolat útja a haragtól a megértésig" [Lajos Hatvany and László Németh: The Evolution of a Relationship from Anger to Understanding], *Napjaink*, (1981): pp. 20, 23, and József Tasi, "Hatvany Lajos és Németh László—Hatvany Lajos levele margójára" [Lajos Hatvany and László Németh: On the Margins of Lajos Hatvany's Letter], *Új Forrás*, no. 19, (1987): pp. 41-50.

Strategies of Assimilation

Literature dealing with assimilation, especially with the assimilation of the Jews, likes to use the concepts "success" and "failure" as measures, though they seem to be quite unsuitable for judging assimilation. Experts have considered the assimilation, for example, of the Jews in one-time Germany and Hungary the most successful, since there was a cultural assimilation in these countries even with such paradoxical situations as the rapid transformation of a former Jew into a Prussian *Junker* or the rise of itinerant Jewish vendors to barony in three generations.[1] In this context "success" means the total surrender of one's original identity and the identification of assimilation with a complete merger.

"Failure" is equally unsuitable as a measure. The persecution of the Jews in the middle of the twentieth century and the Holocaust itself seemed to have turned success into failure all at once, even more so since discrimination was retroactive. The Nuremberg laws went back to the grandfathers and questioned even their assimilation. So the historical concept of assimilation cannot be interpreted in terms of success or its opposite, since the historical process described in this way seems successful and victorious while in progress but unsuccessful in retrospect. If we want to avoid applying hair-splitting dialectics by calling the same thing once this, once that, we have to find other means of reconstruction and interpretation.

However, let us first examine the causes leading to the above approach of success and non-success. This dichotomy goes back to historical reasons and a double source. One of its roots goes back to the contract of emancipation. The struggle for emancipation starting with the French Revolution, as Jacob Katz proves it, went on under roughly similar circumstances all over Europe, both in the developed and in the less developed regions.[2] More precisely, the legal principles of emancipation were approximately the same everywhere. In Max Nordau's words, the Jews galloped into the realm of equal civil rights on horses bred in 1789.[3] Their acceptance was urged by political considerations, by beliefs regarding human rights, and by a zeal for enlightenment known already from the famous pamphlet of Dohm, namely the urge for the moral growth of the Jews, their rejection as a community, and the need for their rise as individuals.

So emancipation contained elements of a dictate everywhere, stipulations based on the power of the majority. The drawbacks of such a dictate were obvious but its advantages definitely meant a step forward. Emancipation is merely a part of the separation of state and church for a long period, part of the historical process of secularization, and the unifying tendencies of creating a bourgeois nation.[4]

It was not only the Jewish communities that were hurt during this transformation; not only was their identity offended, but so was that of all other ethnic groups or communities participating in the process. The whole process was still more a gain than a loss, since the Jews came to be qualified as a religious community during the great transformation in Europe called modernization. Thus it fulfilled its original aim of preserving for posterity the legalistic ideals of the revolution of a legal order in the world of nation states separating themselves from one another to an ever-growing extent, even at the expense of offering shelter for people persecuted both for their religion and their being a community separated only by religion from state affairs.

When in the middle of the twentieth century certain states in Europe started to disregard the contract of assimilation, they violated all other contracts leading to bourgeois growth and a common road to modernization, from parliamentary democracy to the civil rights of the individual. So if we consider assimilation unsuccessful from the point of view of the Nuremberg laws, we cannot think otherwise of the entire European development since the French Revolution, either.

This approach still offers a loop-hole of escape for the dichotomy of success and non-success. It allows us to believe that the most savage criticism of developments in Europe called, for brevity's sake, by the collective term "fascism," was born in countries where modernization was either belated or too quick, or had not been finished by the time of its appearance. Consequently, it seems logical that the faster a country caught up with the other constitutional states of Europe and the faster it managed to become one of them, the more spectacular it was in turning success into failure.

This kind of argument is, however, disproved by historical and theoretical counter-arguments. It is not true that the contracts of assimilation and the ideas of a constitutional state were violated only where the sphere of legislation was accommodated to the new, dictatorial order either openly or secretly. Let us only refer to the latest research results concerning the behavior of the Vichy government.[5]

The one-sided approach of success or failure will hardly explain the process of assimilation followed by the gravest form of dissimilation and fateful exclusion from society. Our new approach should, however, supersede assimilation and dissimilation as antagonistic concepts, transplant them onto another level, not explaining one with the other but taking them for two elements of the same process, and offering a complex view of this tragic story.

Instead of attempting to examine the process throughout Europe, so I shall concentrate on events in Hungary. However, it does not seem to be a great limitation, since the "Hungarian road" can be considered typical in many respects, as well as exemplary. The Hungarian Jews were among the first to establish liturgy in Hungarian and to found a society for the promotion of the

"Magyar" vernacular that could boast of the contribution of Jewish individuals to the national culture, while either losing contact with their original community or still maintaining its customs and faith.

Several authors have already called attention to the particularity of Hungarian development.[6] A recent Canadian dissertation has asserted the uniqueness of Hungarian Jewish assimilation.[7] The doyen of Hungarian essayists called the Hungarian-Jewish symbiosis a *histoire millénaire d'un couple singulier*, a unique bond of a thousand years.[8] A more guarded approach in numerous scholarly articles is that of Victor Karady who perceives the paradoxical nature of assimilation. The assimilation of the Jews in Hungary was much faster than that of the other ethnic groups considered alien there, but social discrimination remained. So it was only mutual hypocrisy that could deny tensions in social accommodation. In the atmosphere of non-success (after Trianon, for example), spasmodic, compensational forms of behavior prevailed.[9]

My starting point for examining the process of assimilation is cultural interaction. Several authors have already called attention to the reciprocity of the process but none of them has focused his attention exclusively upon this aspect. I call it inter-action, i.e., mutual acceptance and integration, because it is not only the culture, behavioral patterns and views of the majority that influence the adjusting minority but the customs and attitudes of the latter which also spread and influence the nation without identifying the donor.

The Jews and Modernity

Here I am sailing in troubled waters, and not without any fear and reservation, since the main charge of all racist theories was that Hungarian culture was assuming a Jewish character. A long list of false identifications followed, and not only in Hungary but in other European countries. Werner Sombart, an influential sociologist of the early twentieth century identified the Jews with greed and money-making in the wake of Max Weber's theory of Protestantism, and his ideas reverberated in the so-called Jewish debate of the periodical *Huszadik Század* (Twentieth Century), in the writings of Péter Ágoston.[10] The threat of a Judaized press in control of Hungarian public opinion was attacked by many in the mid-nineteenth century to László Németh and Gyula Illyés in our times. The truth behind these false accusations was the spirit of modernization that had also been promoted by the assimilating Jews, even if they, or at least many individuals of Jewish origin, did not wish to identify or name it.

However, the conservatives openly spoke of a "foreign heartbeat" behind modernity, namely that of the Jews. This is what literary historian János Horváth wrote about it prior to the First World War: "First of all one must accept as a fact ... that in the last few decades the Jews actually stormed our literary life. Is there anybody who would dare say that they did not bring new elements, valuable or harmful, into Hungarian literature that are definitely alien by blood? ...Is it not natural for conservative Hungarians to show reluctance in accepting this new element and in calling it Hungarian? Is it not natural that the Hungarians whose racial character could be fully expressed in literature and gain power only after so many hard struggles are now shocked, and they fight against the possibility of being driven out by a totally alien race and of either being deprived of full control over their own literature or of being forced to merge with it and tolerate the changes it may make?"[11] The author analyzes the besieging racial pressure exercised by the Jews wanting to dominate even while merging with the Hungarian race. In principle, however, Horváth did not preclude the possibility of assimilation, but with Taine's racial theory in view, an optimistic outcome is doubtful at best.

At the same time, the strategies of assimilation in the twentieth century did not reckon with the growing numbers of those wanting to break the contract, so it would be unjust to blame them in retrospect. "There is no Jewish question whatever," declared Lajos Blau, the learned rabbi in the famous debate in *Huszadik Század*, and from his point of view he was right.[12] If we take seriously the so-called reception law recognizing the Jews as a denomination, there is really nothing like a Jewish question, since the Jews as a reclusive religious community were recognized also by all contemporary anti-Semites. A Jewish question exists only if the Jews come forward as a spiritual factor as they actually did at that time. Their manifestations commonly called superfluous, cosmopolitan, or incapable of independent creation were described as "Jewish traits" by frail minds, and as "temperament" or "excessive agility" by the more intelligent. Ady had already written his famous article entitled "Korrobori" on the dance macabre of two interdependent peoples, when for Lajos Blau there was no Jewish question.

One of the strategies of assimilation was, therefore, the insistence on being a denomination. This attitude was justified historically and supported legally, and its followers mainly came from Jewish religious circles. These people were giddy with the success of the convert Baron Samu Hazai as Minister of Defense, of Vilmos Vázsonyi as Minister of Justice, and of the positions of the hatvani Deutsch, the Chorin, and the Weiss families in economic life. The official representatives of the Jews believed that the one-sided and stubborn clinging to the tacit contract of assimilation would reinforce it or at least ensure them the advantages of the innocent party.

The representatives of another strategy of assimilation forged a shield of modernity. Jenő Heltai, Géza Szilágyi, and later very emphatically also Ignotus, were rarely heard when they were attacked as Jews, assimilants, or advocates of modernity or decadence. Such attacks were quite common. Some of their opponents considered modernity rootless, and rootlessness is automatically a Jewish trait. Cultural anti-Semitism is actually a half-conscious or reflex-like mixing of the above elements and their conscious and deliberate re-coding. The essence of this strategy is coding itself. Can Ignotus, founding father of modern Hungarian literature be blamed for not wanting to concede this fact?

Young and ambitious assimilating Jews, finding their way into Hungarian literature through the periodical *Hét* (Week) edited by József Kiss also broke the contract with the Hungarian conservative gentry and resealed their contract of assimilation declaring their rights as fully qualified citizens and Hungarians, whatever their origin may be. The dual nature of their position was the subject of a significant debate on the pages of a Jewish monthly *Múlt és Jövő* (Past and Future) in 1929. Speaking of the Jewish poets of the 1890s, a leading literary critic of the interwar period, Aladár Komlós found the following differences from the earlier generations: "Full civil and human rights, that József Kiss felt to be a gift, were self-evident for them. The loud expressions of gratitude toward the Hungarian nation were just as alien to them, as their sense of dissimilarity was eclipsed by their coexistence with non-Jews. The Jewish poet of the nineties did not write patriotic or Jewish poems. He was both a Hungarian and a Jew at the same time, or neither of them."

These writers did not care for duality or ambivalence, so they chose to give up the attempts at breaking the contract of assimilation out of their interest in preserving their identity. Sándor Bródy, whose expulsion from literary life was the subject of a famous debate in the thirties, managed to become a Hungarian writer without being forced to deny his Jewish roots right up to the First World War. After the war, he could not recover from the shock of being an outcast, as his bitter letter to his fellow-countryman Géza Gárdonyi shows.[13] The shock nearly paralyzed the generation after the First World War. The official strategy of the Jews did not change a bit; they stood firmly by the contract of assimilation and rejected all interventions from abroad by various Jewish communities in foreign countries even in the case of *numerus clausus.*[14]

The writers, poets, and thinkers identified as Jews by the counter-revolutionary regime were, however, forced to find new strategies in the unexpected new situation. Although they could not realize that the newly independent Hungary, carved up in the peace treaty of Trianon, had now a single distinct minority, namely the Jews dissimilated by the new Hungarian attitude, they were sensitive enough to define their new orientation.[15]

Jewish Wounds – Jewish Vices

The concept of a Jewish-Hungarian symbiosis was enriched by two new elements in those years. One of them was the cautious expression of dual identity in the pseudonymous writing of Aladár Komlós,[16] and the other was self-reproach and a desire for reforms expressed in *Zsidó sebek és bűnök* (Jewish Wounds—Jewish Vices) by Károly Pap and in various writings of Béla Tábor.

If cultural anti-Semitism manifests itself really in the form of implicit codes, one has to take also the pieces written during the assimilation crisis not literally but decoded. Waking up from the dreams of assimilation was painful, and it is hard to retrace the confusion and uncertainty of thinkers reacting to the crisis. This is the cause of the strange contradiction that while Aladár Komlós struggled to reduce Bródy to his Jewish roots and to prove his own impartiality by it on the one hand, on the other he did his best to rally around the *Ararát* yearbooks all those whose brotherhood had been created by their being downgraded Jews.

We must not leave unmentioned those strategies of assimilation that can euphemistically be called Jewish self-criticism represented by the novelists Béla Zsolt and András Komor among others. Both criticized the assimilated Jews, and it was one of András Komor's writings that gave rise to the debate *Zsidó lélek az irodalomban* (Jewish Spirit in Literature) with the participation of Móricz, Schöpflin and Aladár Komlós. Móricz realized that a new wave was rising. Schöpflin remarked that “Hungarian writers of Jewish origin formerly refrained from touching this subject [e.g. Jewish life] and tried to prove their assimilation by pretending to belong exclusively to the Hungarian race and to have no links whatever with the Jews. There was obviously a certain amount of insincerity in this....”[17]

The discovery of the “Jewish motif” was welcomed by many and few of them could be said not to be sincere in retrospect. For Zsigmond Móricz’s naturalist and realist approach it is self-evident that only those experiences that come from within should find their way onto paper. But even he was embarrassed when he had to explain the message of his novel *Kivilágos kivirradtig* (Until the Small Hours of Morning), namely the impossibility of assimilation.

Gyula Illyés wrote positively about András Komor prior to the debate, but his realist experience is tinged by his belief that a community can be understood only by one who has been brought up in it. The praises are thus given a twist. “The mirror he[18] is carrying about is his small town shining bright and reflecting a sharp image as long as... how shall I put it ... Semitic profiles are seen standing in front of it. ... But as soon as hats with curled-up brims or Tyrolese ones with a tuft of chamois-hair on them or the traditional knickerbockers of the gentry appear, the outlines are blurred at once and none of the profiles is discernable any more.”[19]

Let us leave behind the above conviction of the day about the relationship of experience and literature, since it is not so much aesthetic as sociological and political problems that it concerns. The debate “Jewish spirit in literature” opened up a narrow path both for dissimilation and the belief that assimilation is impossible and can never be achieved; the instincts and cultural reflexes of the individual will inevitably revive. You can change religions but you can never change experiences and patterns that have been conditioned in you. While praising András Komor for his faultless reproduction of Jewish profiles, Illyés implicitly speaks of their inability to assimilate.

In his article written on the pamphlet of Károly Pap Illyés confirms our suspicion. He speaks of the Jews as a numerous race a "detachment" of which has settled in Hungary and adjusted itself to a feeble and mutilated nation. (If he had started from the great number of the Jews all over the world and their solidarity, he may even have been right.) Therefore Illyés rephrased the conditions of assimilation which were implied in the original version but which remained unsaid owing to liberal caution and a legalistic approach. So the Jews are "a huge and rich people with no illiterate persons among them. Half a million of this great nation can be accepted by a small and enfeebled one like Hungary only if this huge crowd fully denies all ties with its old community and is ready to share the fate of the new."[20]

One must not forget that the new debate over assimilation was started by the fact that the generation of the twenties and thirties witnessed the attempts at dissimilation and stopped to abstain from the criticism of the assimilating Jews as a response. This was a long historical process, stretching over the first half of the twentieth century. As George Schöpflin explains: "The falsity of the premise on which this assimilation was based—the façade augmentation of Magyardom began to emerge around the turn of the century with the growing recognition of the failure of the *Ausgleich* system. As Hungarian society increasingly feared the disintegration of historic Hungary, the Jewish attitude of combining democratic and assimilationist ideals grew more and more isolated from the rest of population. The collapse of historic Hungary in 1918-1919 resulted in the disruption of the entire tacit compact between the neo-feudal gentry and the assimilating Jews. The Horthyist restoration overtly professed nationalist, antidemocratic, and anti-Semitic views as a single, cohesive doctrine and argued that democracy, antinationalism, and Jews were interdependent."[21]

This was the specificity of eastern-European anti-Semitism between the two world wars. While in France anti-Semitism was a fringe political movement against a Republican State that had safeguarded the civil rights of Jews up to the German occupation of the country, in Hungary or in Poland the state injected ideology into its affairs and curtailed the civic rights of Jews and other minorities. Jews were never really allowed—with the exception of certain cases—to participate in political power or governance in Hungary thus their disenfranchisement by the state was eased by a century-long filter on acceptance. The more the official representatives of Hungarian Jews hailed their privileged status of equal rights, the less were they admitted to higher administrative circles. They could be agents of commerce and banking and exert a certain influence on economic matters, but they were in the meantime at the mercy of a state that found its strength through "ideological" legislation like barring Jewish students from entering the university.

After the first world war the pitfalls of assimilation became palpably visible. The Horthy-era established an etatism, a fresh political alliance of the nobility, the lesser gentry, and the so-called Christian middle-classes, establishing a coalition of interest-groups joining forces to reclaim the seceded territories mandated by the peace treaties, and finding their mutual enemy in the Jews. The liberal tradition was not strong enough to isolate groups otherwise critical of the ruling regime from the dominant politics of language. "The Jewish Question" was debated by leading intellectuals of the period. In different terms, granted, from the official and crude anti-Semitism. There was, however, an almost universal acceptance of a state of affairs in which the social role of the Jews and their responsibility for the distortion of the national spirit became an uncontested concept in arguments.

The common denominator among various groups—conservatives and populist alike—was the rejection of assimilation as a fait accompli, argued Asher Cohen. He claimed that anti-assimilationism did not necessarily lead to anti-Semitism. This must be true depending upon how one defines anti-Semitism. The crux of the matter, however, is the fact, that the Jews of Hungary were gradually discriminated against between the two world wars and the political atmosphere was poisoned by the "Jewish Question." Anti-assimilationism thus should be regarded as the first step toward discrimination.[22]

The Jewish response was scared, pathetic, and contradictory. The leaders of the community reiterated the legalistic argument. Jews are members of an accepted religion and they were constitutionally emancipated after a long process in both Houses of representation. Their unflinching loyalty to the Hungarian State was proven by numerous contributions of individual Jews to the cause of the counter-revolution of 1919 and 1920. To demonstrate that Jews are exemplary citizens a whole historiography of cultural heroes of Jewish extraction were written up in Jewish publications. A history of Hungarian Jews catalogued the achievement of the assimilated.[23]

A bitter irony has discredited this strategy. The true targets of the ideological witch-hunt were the assimilated Jews, or rather the crooked ways of assimilation. Any demonstration that Jews fared well in the past century in Hungary fueled the animosity of their detractors. It was, as they argued, a disproportionate expansion to the detriment of the "native" or "true" Hungarians.[24]

The situation was made worse by the appearance of racism in the writings even of those who were otherwise definitely against it. Even these writers accepted the commonplace idiom of the day as their second mother tongue.

The leading ideologist of the post 1920 period, Gyula Szekfű published a famous article entitled *A faji kérdés és a magyarság* (The Racial Question and the Hungarians) on the pages of *Napkelet* at the dawn of the consolidation following the First World War.[25] The above mentioned article by Illyés and several remarks of László Németh about Hungarian Jewish writers echoed its ideological approach. This was one of Szekfű's weakest articles, summarizing all that contemporary pseudo-scholarship advocated about a Dinaric and Turanian race, the Turkish origin of King Stephen the Saint, etc. It was in this article that Szekfű wrote the famous sentence repeated by Sándor Pethő and so many others: "Each assimilated person carries into his new community his own mental disposition that may come to the surface even in later generations and even after a most successful assimilation."

The race carries not only cultural but genetic codes as curses down to the seventh generation, which is the basic idea behind dissimilation. There is another question, not to be discussed in this context, namely, what concept of a nation arises from this supposition and from the one that says that belonging to a nation means fate and personal choice at the same time? The two concepts are fairly contradictory as illustrated also in the work of Tibor Joó, a follower of Szekfű, who dedicated volumes to reconciling them only to establish that those whose ancestors had come to this land with Prince Árpád were entitled to enjoy privileges because of that experience.

The mixture of fate and personal choice was, however, put into words not by Illyés or László Németh but by Count István Bethlen, the statesman of compromise, as Szekfű quotes it in his above mentioned article. This is why it is surprising to find the joined requirements of fate and personal choice in writings of Illyés, and definitely not in a conciliatory manner: "You may live outside a community if you are spiritually independent enough, but you can never belong to two communities at the same time, so how could a whole people do so? The echoes of the Hungarian countryside have already given the answer to the Jewish question. A pledge is taken seriously not when it is said but when a sacrifice is made for it."

The price of assimilation is total disengagement from one's original community. The Jews are more than a religious community. Illyés declares that nobody expects the Messiah to come any longer. All this is faultless logic, only the premises are unfounded.

Not much is needed to confuse community with race and nation with fate to reach the desired order of things. What is more, the national element was overshadowed by a certain class-consciousness both with Illyés and Németh, and also with Géza Féja naturally based on "scientific principles." Géza Féja refers to ethnographer Lajos Bartucz who "had proved" that alien ethnic elements are unable to assimilate; they preserve their racial characteristics and may, therefore, upset the harmonic life of a community. In his article *A "beolvadás"* (Assimilation) he speaks of dissimilation as early as the years of the Second World War. He says that the assimilation of the Jews took place from above and they did not adjust themselves to the majority people, so their adaptation was only exterior, consequently false.

"'Dissimilation' today is the result of this outward and seeming 'adaptation.' However, our Jews should not use this occasional 'dissimilation' to prove their having been 'assimilated.' The overwhelming majority of the Jews assimilated only superficially, used their pseudo-assimilation as a trump-card, and tried to leave their distinctive racial mark on our economic and intellectual life."[26]

The necessity of proof, mentioned by Géza Féja was practically useless in the midwar period. It was not by chance that Sándor Bródy's case preceded the debate "Jewish spirit in literature." His figure gained a symbolic meaning after his death, as if his fame was more than he actually deserved. At the same time, he was a symbol also for his supporters, that of a genius hindered in his development. In his funeral speech Ignotus said, "Your being a might-have-been can be explained by an unanswered love as is the case with so many men.... by the lack of requited love on the part of the public."

Bródy was born a "secondary citizen," Ignotus said. "He was on the wrong side of extreme emancipation through which the generous Hungarians ennobled all moneyed Jews. The Jewish writers, on the other hand, spent all the creative power they should have devoted to writing to apologize for their audacity in becoming

Hungarians. Their spirit of revolt that should have moved mountains was spent on forced smiles to avoid being taken for intruders."[27]

This kind of insistence proved, however, useless: László Németh speaks already of "two different peoples" when mentioning the Hungarians and the Jews.[28] Like Illyés, he too sees the true nature of Jewish literature as intrusion not wanting to retreat to its place determined perhaps by the numerical proportion of the Jews as in the case of *numerus clausus.* "Everyone has the right to live in his or her motherland, and a strong community cannot disown people once admitted. Disown they cannot, but they can force them back to their original place.... We have to do our duty, and the Jews will have no choice but to adjust to this great national duty... Hungarian Jewish literature, once assigned to its proper place and developing in the direction where its talents and problems lie, is felicitous, but a Jewish literature spreading above our heads and making us false-hearted is a disaster."

Such assertion laid a trap for the new identity of Jewish literature. It was not by chance that László Németh found his opponents among fiery assimilants like Hatvany and Ignotus, while his ideal Jewish writer was Károly Pap. Writers like him "developed in the direction where their problems lay" and they did not bother about the problems of the majority nation. As Aladár Komlós admits in an article, they were forbidden to do otherwise: "Since the war, Jewish writers are more and more paralyzed by a new obstacle, namely that they are forbidden to express their opinions concerning problems that the Hungarian public is most interested in. If they did so, they would not be given an ear. What is still more likely, their skulls would be cracked and their activity would only be detrimental to the cause they wish to serve."[29]

Repeated excommunication arriving from an unexpected corner was a surprise for Hungarian writers identified already as Jews. It was not the National Socialists but the populist trend of racism that started to advocate a strange mixture of nationalism and left-wing thoughts, threatening serious consequences if denied. Their racial theory was not expressed unambiguously, so it manifested itself in terms of origin and national characteristics. Ferenc Fejtő, a contemporary, characterized the turn of the late thirties as follows: "... the populists aimed at an exclusive, ethnic or true-to-race culture. It was perhaps Péter Veres who expressed this aim the most clearly saying that all cultures have to be primarily cultures of a given race. This was the reason why the Jews as persons having no purely Hungarian roots and not belonging to the Hungarians ethnically, and although assimilating but still alien, were to be eliminated from Hungarian literature, however touchy it is to draw this conclusion."[30]

The desperate attempt of Aladár Komlós to unite the writers identified as Jews in Hungary was a response to this trend toward elimination. It was the last of the strategies of assimilation before the Holocaust: pressure from outside forced the outcasts to express a solidarity they would probably never have done by themselves. The new Ignotus of the day, Aladár Komlós summed up the situation with exceptional common sense in an article entitled *Zsidó írók—zsidó közösség* (Jewish Writers - Jewish Community) in the 1941 volume of *Múlt és Jövő*. This article precedes his famous correspondence with Radnóti published as a *samizdat* in *Beszélő* later, where it was just Radnóti who refused to be considered as part of "Jewish literature." And he was not the only one, as Komlós writes in his article about writers who "declare themselves not to be Jews but merely writers, so to speak, writers by nationality..." On the other hand Komlós argued that when a tree that produces flowers is in danger, the tree is to be cared for first and not the flowers. So not the individuals but the Jews as such. "Since we had been taught over the past one hundred or one hundred and fifty years that there is no such thing as a Jewish people, we finally believed that there is nothing more urgent than to cut the strings uniting us to this allegedly non-existing community."

While in his earlier articles Aladár Komlós criticized the so-called overassimilation, here he discovers another original error: "The greatest sin of assimilation is that it robbed us of our faith that to be a Jew is beautiful, a splendid vocation. We have been proud and happy to belong to Jewry before, as if it were the most splendid place to be in the world. Assimilation taught us to be ashamed of it. In times past, the Jewish people was the first to believe it was the chosen people of God. Now it is the only one that lacks the sense of selectedness."[31]

This is already the sardonic tone of a man taking notice of discrimination fulfilled and fully aware of being threatened both as member of a community and as an individual.

So all strategies of assimilation seem to have failed, beginning with the assertion of loyalty to the Hungarian nation and the discovery of the independent character of the Jews. Even the "writers by nationality" suffered a defeat with Radnóti among them. Dissimilation actually built up the walls of an invisible ghetto to be followed by the building of the real walls with the help of the gendarmerie. One must not forget, however, that the death of such a great proportion of the Jews pulled down these walls. The perilous situation that called the attention of the assimilating Jews to their old links and the possibility of a double linkage earlier, has become now, after the Holocaust, and through the necessity of remembrance, an international standard among democratic nations. Paradoxically, it was advocated in Hungary uniquely just by Jewish writers and thinkers.

It was Imre Keszi who raised the question of the possibility of a double linkage in his article *Németh László és a zsidóság* (László Németh and the Jews): "You cannot be member of two football teams at a match at the same time, but you can absorb the values of two cultures."[32]

Even wider implications were raised by Aladár Komlós in his reply to Zsigmond Móricz in the course of the debate "Jewish spirit in literature," clashing with the spirit of the age and naturally creating a stir in a world of ethnocentric thinking. Komlós was aware that the ideal of the nineteenth century concerning the nation was extreme nationalism "not wanting to tolerate any racial, denominational or regional differences." This artificial unification was overthrown by riots, but "we still stick to national unity today, at the time of malignant particularism, even more than we did before the war..."[33]

At that point Aladár Komlós brought up a point that bore witness to exceptional foresight on the pages of *Nyugat* where his article was published. He argued that pluralism is possible only in the case of a different concept of the nation: the setting of the process of assimilation-dissimilation is the national state striving toward homogeneity, in the framework of which the problem can never be solved. As László Németh once remarked, it is not the Hungarian—Jewish antagonism that comes to the surface here, but the "Hungarian—Hungarian problem," i.e., the different interpretation of the concept of the nation and its theoretical and moral foundations. In his article Imre Keszi interprets László Németh's words so that belonging to a nation is a matter of both fate and active participation, and the fate of the Jews can indeed be harmonized with that of the nation accepting them. Komlós, however, realized that fate and personal choice are inadequate concepts in this context and that it would be imperative to formulate a new idea of the nation.

"The new concept will be more flexible than the old one. It will be formulated so as to keep in view the various communities within the nation. If these communities will unite to form a new and bigger one, the nation will not object to their preserving their distinct identities. It will not object to the Jews remaining Jews *too*, provided they are Hungarians at the same time."

If these are the words of a prophet or if they will remain a utopia forever, will be determined in our days and by the society we are living in.

Notes

1. Ludwig Gogolák, *Zum Problem der Assimilation in Ungarn in der Zeit von 1790-1918.* (Südostdeutsches Archiv, 1986).
2. Jacob Katz, "The Identity of Post Emancipatory Jewry," in *A Social and Economic History of Central European Jewry*, Jehuda Don-Victor Karady, eds., (New Brunswick :1990.), p. 13-33.
3. Max Nordau, *Bericht über den Zustand der Juden auf der ganzen Erde* (London: Gedruckt bei Wertheimer Lea & Co., 1900).
4. Arthur Hertzberg, *The French Enlightenment and the Jews; the Origins of Modern anti-Semitism.* 1st Schocken paperback ed. Schocken paperbacks, (New York: Schocken Books, 1970).
5. Eric Conan and Henry Rousso, *Vichy : un passé qui ne passe pas.* Nouv. éd. ed. Collection Folio/histoire ; 71., (Paris: Gallimard, 1996).
6. Jacob Katz, "The Uniqeness of Hungarian Jewry," *Forum*, vol. 27, no. 2, (Jerusalem, 1977): p. 45-53.
7. Vera Ranki, *The Politics of Inclusion and Exclusion. Jews and Nationalism in Hungary*, (Sydney: Allen and Unwin, 1999).
8. François Fejtő, *Hongrois et Juifs—histoire millénaire d'un couple singulier*, (Paris: Balland, 1997).
9. Viktor Karády, "Zsidó identitás és asszimiláció Magyarországon" [Jewish Identity and Assimilation in Hungary], *Mozgó Világ*, vol. 9, (1989): p. 47.
10. Péter Ágoston, "A zsidók útja" [The Path of Jews], *A Jövő kérdései*, vol. II, (Nagyvárad: A Nagyváradi Társadalomtudományi Társaság, 1917).
11. János Horváth, "Kiadatlan írások a Két korszak határán című kötetből" [Unpublished Writings from the Work On the Frontier of Two Eras], *Literatura*, vol. 1, (1993): p. 3-24.
12. "A zsidókérdés Magyarországon" [The Jewish Question in Hungary], *Huszadik Század* [The Twentieth Century], ed. In: *Zsidókérdés asszimiláció antiszemitizmus*, Péter Hanák, ed., (Budapest: 1984). Originally: (Budapest, 1917).
13. Sándor Bródy, "Levél Gárdonyi Gézához" [Letter to Géza Gárdonyi], in *A sas Pesten—Válogatott Írások*, (Budapest: 1954), p. 488.

14. Ezra Mendelsohn, "Trianon Hungary, Jews and Politics," in *Hostages of Modernization*, H.A. Strauss, ed., (Berlin-New York: de Gruyter, 1993), p. 893-916.
15. Ezra Mendelsohn, "Jewish Reactions to Antisemitism in Interwar East Central Europe," in *Living with Antisemitism, Jewish Responses*, Jehuda Reinharz, ed., (London, 1987), p. 269-313.
16. Álmos Korál, *Zsidók válaszúton.* (Jews at the Crossroads), 1921, Eperjes.
17. Zsigmond Móricz, "A zsidó lélek az irodalomban" [The Jewish Spirit in Literature], *Nyugat*, vol. II, (1930): p. 421-422. Schöpflin, (1930), #9626.
18. András Komor, *Zsidó problémák a modern magyar irodalomban* [Jewish Problems in Modern Hungarian Literature], OSZK kézirattár Komor András hagyatéka Fond 29, (1935).
19. Gyula Illyés, G., "Komor András: Fischmann S. utódai" [On the Novel Fischmann S. and his Heirs], *Nyugat*, vol. I, (1929): p. 831-833.
20. Gyula Illyés, "Zsidó sebek és bűnök. Pap Károly könyve" [Jewish Wounds—Jewish Vices. On Pap Károly's Book], *Nyugat*, vol. II, (1935): p. 37-41.
21. George Schöpflin, "Jewish Assimilation in Hungary: A Moot Point," in *Jewish Assimilation in Modern Times*, B. Vago, ed., (Boulder, Colorado: Vestwiew Press, 1981), p. 75-89.
22. Asher Cohen, "The Attitude of the Intelligentsia in Hungary toward Jewish Assimilation between the Two World Wars," in *Jewish Assimilation in Modern Times*, Béla Vago, ed., (Boulder (Co.), 1981), p. 57-74.
23. Lajos Venetianer, *A magyar zsidóság története: különös tekintettel gazdasági és művelődési fejlődésére a XIX. században* [The History of Hungarian Jews: a Special Focus on their Economic and Cultural Development in the Nineteenth Century], Reprint of the 1922 ed. *Tudománytár*, (Budapest: Könyvértekesítő Vállalat, 1986).
24. Viktor Karády, - István Kemény, *Les juifs dans la structure des classes en Hongrie. Essai sur les antécédents historique des crises d'antisémitisme au XX. siècle.* Actes de la Recherche Sociale, (1978. 21), p. 25-59.
25. Gyula Szekfű, "A faji kérdés és a magyarság" [The Racial Question and the Hungarians], *Napkelet*, (June-December, 1923): p. 801-820.
26. Géza Féja, "A beolvadás" [On Assimilation], *Magyarország*, (May,

11, 1942): p. 3.

27. Ignotus, "Bródy Sándor" [Sándor Bródy], *Nyugat*, vol. II, (1924): p. 180.
28. László Németh, "Két nép (Hozzászólás Papp Károly Zsidó sebek és bűnök című könyvéhez)" [Two People (Remarks on Károly Pap's Jewish Wounds—Jewish Vices)], in *Életmű szilánkokban I.* (1989), p. 418-429.
29. Aladár Komlós, "A magyar zsidó író útjai" [The Paths of the Hungarian Jewish Writer], *Ararát évkönyv*, (1939), p. 127-133.
30. Ferenc Fejtő, "Kérdések a Válaszról" [Questions about Válasz], in *Szép szóval*, Széchenyi Ágnes, ed., (1992), p. 104.
31. Aladár Komlós, "Zsidó írók—zsidó közösség" [Jewish Writers—Jewish Community], *Múlt és Jövő*, vol. XXXI, (July, 1941): p. 97-98.
32. Imre Keszi, *Németh László és a zsidóság* [László Németh and the Jews], (Libanon, 1937), p. 41-48.
33. Aladár Komlós, "A zsidó lélek az irodalomban. Válasz Móricz Zsigmond cikkére" [Jewish Spirit in Literature. Reply to the Article of Zsigmond Móricz], *Nyugat*, vol. II, (1930): p. 499-501.

The Assimilated Jew and his Talent

A Second Class Citizen

"There comes a painful moment in the 'early years' of every German Jew's life that he remembers as long as he lives, when it dawns upon him that he was born to be a second class citizen and neither diligence nor service will redeem him from this condition."[1]

This statement was made by Walther Rathenau, one of the most successful German industrialists. Later he became an Imperial State Secretary but was murdered only a few months after his appointment. The importance of the quote is underlined by the fact that it came from an assimilated Jew, one who had tried to overcome his "birth defect" by diligence and service. Marcel Reich-Ranicki collected such statements along with other ones including those by Arthur Schnitzler who made a similar claim in his book *The Vienna Youth.* Jewish representatives of European literature from Maximilian Harden to Hermann Broch held similar views. The frightening part of these statements is that the authors' life experiences did not belie these claims. Most of them came to a tragic end because their Jewishness—despite their intentions—predetermined their place and fate in society. During his wanderings in exile which came to an end only with his death, Kurt Tucholsky wrote to Arnold Zweig: "In the year 1911, I left Judaism. But today I know that this step is impossible."

Several of the European Jewish writers between the two world wars came to realize that it was impossible for them to be released from their Jewish existence. After the heat of the initial phases of the assimilation process had cooled down, certain European countries tried to revoke even their successful political emancipation acts. They then questioned those aspects of assimilation that were completed by offering new, but limited and essentially unfeasible goals.

Many Jews were forced to face this issue years and even decades after World War I and the Enlightenment programs had implemented emancipation and assimilation during the early phases of national development. It must have dawned on those involved that in nation-states, within the intellectual horizon of the Enlightenment, the situation and role of foreigners were not legally settled and that French universalist philosophers had claimed that if the viewpoints of a narrower community (homeland) and those of a wider community (mankind) clashed, it would lead to a moral crisis. To solve this dilemma, Rousseau voted for the approach of a larger human consciousness. On the other hand romantic critics such as Herder who appeared with a later wave of the Enlightenment, assumed the existence of a "*volkgeist*" and argued that the national ethos was paramount over all else.

Critics of the Enlightenment—like Hannah Arendt—repeatedly asked why an indigenous citizen of a state would have more rights than a foreigner and concluded that the Enlightenment inherently contained this conflict by separating the legal human being from the citizen.[2]

The Foreigner and the Indigenous

It is not only the wanderer knocking on an ethnic group's nation-state door who is a foreigner. An observer's approach to "foreignness" and "otherness" inherently contains his response to the theoretical question of whether ethnic heterogeneity or homogeneity leads to the improvement of a state-forming nation. The observer must consider whether the conflict between a foreigner and the indigenous and (whether the solution to this conflict) is part of the dynamics of the national spirit, as suggested by Freud's psychoanalytical explanations. Freud's antinomy indicates that the "*heimlich*," that is comfortable and intimate in society as well as internally in a human being, struggles with "*unheimlich*," everything that is homeless, foreign, threatening, and neurotic.

Historical investigation reveals that the conflict between a foreigner and a native is an expression of a larger, almost inherent, contradiction and conflict feeding on the differences between the idea of a human being and a citizen. This conflict spreads itself over the entire program of the Enlightenment. It was alternatively evoked or suppressed by real and concrete historical events and trends.

The permanence of anti-Semitism—its continuity, its alternately fading away, and strengthening—is a symptom of this same process, not its cause. It is of utmost importance to emphasize this idea because anti-Semitism does not have a long history. Instead, the European Enlightenment developed anti-Semitism as a special concomitant phenomenon which, by the power of its permanence and continuity, refers back to this basic contradiction within the Enlightenment.

In this context, the issue of the nature of the Jewishness of the Israelite Diaspora was raised because the answer dtermined whether Jews living in the territory of different nation-states counted as immigrants and foreigners or as a religious denomination connected to their ethnic or national origin through sublime memories and even rituals. Only anti-Semites mention race when speaking about the Jews, and if Jews do it, then they mean an ethno-cultural and religious community bound together by tradition and in loose relationships. During its history this community seems to have lost many people from its ranks. In fact, it has lost everybody who successfully left Judaism through mixed marriages and at the expense of raising future generations in a different tradition—something which would have been impossible, as Kurt Tucholsky testified, under the terrible circumstances prevailing during Europe's numerous shady decades.

Jean Paul Sartre, who began to fight against anti-Semitism after the War, came to the conclusion from his historical experiences that the Jews were defined, not from the inside but the outside, by the eyes of those who looked at them. Consequently, a Jew is anybody who is considered a Jew when a "look" defines him as a "foreigner" or "immigrant."[3]

The advantage of this definition of Jewishness is that it calls attention to the possibility of individuals or groups of people being defined externally, by social dynamics. Its drawback, however, is that it does not embark on a positive identification of the "issue" or even of the specific case. The self-definition of the Jew is completely missing also from the definition. In any case, would it have been possible during the bloody years of the war? Nonetheless, this definition carries the universal European experience of the Holocaust where many people were involuntarily identified as Jews even if they did not have anything to do with that religion, ethnic group, or tradition. Consequently, they carried their Jewishness hidden even from themselves until the "Law" branded them as such.

Thus a special aspect of the Freudian "*unheimlichkeit*" concept is when somebody involuntarily becomes part of a proscribed community. A peculiar state of existence evolves: a mixture of a person being thrown back to the world and being thrown out of this world at the same time when the chance to create one's own self-identity is denied.

The group downgraded to become Jewish and involuntarily identified with the Jews thus regenerates the category of the "non-Jewish Jew" which European history had recognized as the revolting pariah and the universalist revolutionary. This image has also been created "externally," via the looks of glaring eyes, as the modern version of Jewish Messianism.

The Negative Definition of the Jew

Between the two world wars European dictatorships within the orbit of fascism simply revoked the results of emancipation and assimilation and made preparations for a new version of the Egyptian and Babylonian captivities. The preparations began with the estrangement of the larger society from the Jews and with the forcing of the Jews back to the ghetto, first intellectually and later legally and physically. Finally, by utilizing several modern propaganda techniques, the dictatorships recreated the Ahasuerus symbol, the eternally homeless Jew.

A Holocaust survivor, the Austrian philosopher and writer Jean Améry, warned about the improbability of the Jews being allowed to create their own identity, saying that "If I say that I am Jewish, I mean the realities and possibilities embodied in the number tattooed on me in Auschwitz." Améry argued that the world was able to extend to him only a negative definition of identity because, when it imposed on him a Jewish identity from the outside, it never extended to him the possibility of rejecting the imposition and of being a non-Jew.

The new Diaspora Jew who lacks any kind of self-definition is Ahasuerus again, without the ability to die or to be newly born. According to Améry's suggestion, Ahasuerus is a being without positive definition, a catastrophe Jew who understandably has lost confidence in the world. "Without any confidence in the world I can only glance at my environment as a Jew who is a foreigner and lonely and who is unable to do more than to accept his foreignness as the decisive element of his personality and, then, who adheres to it as if it were his inalienable possession."[4]

Survival as a new identity is not new. The new Jew is really a radically peculiar character in the history of assimilation—that of the unfinished and unsuccessfully integrated person. The Jewish survivor's peculiarity, on the other hand, stems from the fact that he is the victim of world history's unique genocide without being able to explain his survival. Further, his current persona has already incorporated the anguish and neurosis of the Freudian "*unheimlichkeit*"—either in the form of guilt or oblivion.

The new Ahasuerus could cope with oblivion, if only he could forget what happened and if his environment would remember—if memory were the diploma for a new integration and a new opportunity. Whether it has or has not taken place depends on the individual history of each country. It would be irresponsible to conclude that the ratio of Jewish survivors conforms directly to the generosity of remembrance since it is precisely Germany that leads in legally outlawing Nazi remembrance and the so-called "Auschwitz-lie" and by integrating its remaining few thousand Jews while France truly tried to face its history only in the 1980s. Explosions and criminal attempts like the one in Paris' Rue Copernic are reminders of the existing Jewish community's past which is still unaccounted for by the liberated nation.

As long as it was squeezed by hostile pressures, the Jewish community could not fully cope with the issue of Jewish self-identity. Therefore, external definition became an inevitable historical event and does not allude only to the lack of Jewish self-consciousness. The so-called allogenic groups—who desire and expect assimilation but reach only a limited stage of integration—can achieve a decisive self-consciousness and sense of vocation only within the dynamics of their society and only in relationship with other social groups, since any kind of group consciousness-raising can not take place in a vacuum.

One can only guess—short of receiving complete reports—whether the post-war years made self-recognition and consciousness easier or more difficult. The most we can do is to judge by those symbolic gestures which evoke ghostly shadows. Among these are Kurt Thucholsky's suicide—between the two world wars and in exile—and the suicides of the great German poet Paul Celan, the Italian novelist Primo Levi, and Jean Améry. They were all concentration camp survivors.

Within the scope of Jewish self-definition even survival was considered to be a dubious triumph or moral certificate by those who were branded by it. As Primo Levi wrote, the real witnesses of the Holocaust were the perished victims and not the survivors. If Theodore Adorno's frequently quoted and frequently misinterpreted statement—"after Auschwitz there is no poetry"—is still discussed, it ought to be done within the context of Levi's suggestion. Victims do not speak and those who speak for the victims are the "catastrophe Jews," those who are not yet capable of self-definition, or those who are obligated to handle foreignness as the innermost determination of their characters until death or, more exactly, until voluntary death.

An appropriate representation of the Holocaust is difficult for several reasons. One of the reasons is the "fully negative" definition of the victims since they were punished for crimes they had not committed and became victims for something that their consciousness could only partially acknowledge. Beyond the difficulty of defining the characters of these victim-heroes, it is further aggravated by the metaphysical impossibility that, according to tradition, a holocaust was predicted to strike God's chosen people. Consequently, as Amos Funkenstein has asserted, the Jews experienced a godless world—unless we want to elevate their murderers to be servants of God's will.[5]

Although the walls of the Jewish ghetto had been re-built by national entities, they did not restore the *teodiceia,* the theology which connected the Jewish faith to its own polity and kept the Jewish people moving by the will of Providence. Coercion does not sustain religion. Another tentative reason for the post-Auschwitz muteness of poetry and, what is identical to it, for the difficulty in representing the Holocaust is the fact that reality has negated the events or preceded imagination. There was no mythical tale or barbarian saga which could have anticipated what actually happened. Therefore, descriptions of the events could only lamely follow the patterns of what happened in reality. The hesitation of observers about whether the Holocaust, by the power of its uniqueness, could fit into any historical process or whether it opens up metaphysical dimensions which arrest historiography also makes representation difficult.[6]

These questions are only tangentially raised here. But while elaborating on the problem, this analysis has aimed to discuss the nature of Jewish self-recognition, self-knowledge, and positive self-definition during the period of European assimilation while noting that survivors of the Holocaust—Jean Améry, Primo Levi, and Paul Celan—tell us with self-indicting and self-tormenting words of their lack of a positive self-definition.

Why the Jewish identity was mostly externally defined can be understood by noting the history of oppression that weighed heavily on the Jewish communities. The assimilation offer inherently included the intent to deliver the Jews from the Jew "within" and "living in his community." According to the Enlightenment program, moving over from the particularity of Jewish existence into human universality brings with it social acceptance, social rank, and also various chances—for those who look for new allies against old ties—and it also brings acceptance by a worldly society as opposed to the closed Jewish society. However even with this, a real transition appeared only in the imagination even during the period of "tolerance." In an 18th century German-Jewish novel, *Anton Reiser, A Psychological Novel,* Karl Philip Moritz described the life of a poor Jewish boy of the period. In this autobiographical work the boy becomes a compulsive reader and gains distinction for copying his enlightened pastor's sermon—but all in vain. He is redeemed by the theatrical world and roams the German principalities with strolling players. The theater group, however, goes bankrupt and our hero, once again, is forced to face reality.

The novel is quoted by Sander L. Gilman[7] who indicates that integration into society belongs to a fantasy world because foreignness accompanies the young man during his wanderings, even while he experiences an awakening of identity and a character ready to integrate into the society.

If Karl Philip Moritz's work is compared with Goethe's *Wilhelm Meister*, the fantasy world of theater during Wilhelm Meister's years of learning and wanderings represents the possibility of transformation from the everyday world to an ideal world. Wilhelm Meister is similar to the biblical Saul who went to look for his stray donkey and discovered a kingdom. Finding the kingdom is the detour back to the everyday world after gaining substantial experience. After Moritz' novel, there were very few 19th century literary works which equally described the Jews' possible wanderings into bourgeois society. Literary criticism has pointed out that literary description of the Jewish minority—from Dickens to modern short stories—usually amounted to caricatures even in the case of realistic figures like Fagin in *Oliver Twist*.[8] Evidently, a caricature addresses the issue of foreignness and the unknown and is the phenomenon that Fagin represents by breaking into the bourgeois world and acquiring the kind of power which his origin usually would preclude.

Michael Ragussis' book subtitled "The 'Jewish Question' and English National Identity" follows the esthetic, ethical, and social dimensions of Jewish representation from the "Maltese Jew" to modern times. He gives an account of various stereotypes tempting excellent authors from the utopian Harrington, who laid down the foundation of modern democratic thinking, through the converts' literature to the Disraeli phenomenon—the Jew who became British prime minister and who professed Jewish superiority and proto-racist theories, thus inducing a special anti-Semitic legend.[9]

Characterizing the nature of Jewish talent usually accompanied stereotypical Jewish figures. Several thousand years of the

Jewish spirit was considered to be unchanged and, as Werner Sombart said, the Jewish mind had been unaltered for thousands of years and as such was negative and destructive.[10]

By the turn of the 20th century it had become commonly accepted that the Jews did not have any imagination because a lack of imagination was one of the Semites' basic characteristics. Raphael Patai—who dedicated a whole book to the examination of Jewish thinking—testified to how widespread was the lack of Jewish imagination (according to Chamberlain),[11] so much so that even Hitler's positions were derived from them.[12] This view held that, in spite of all their apparent talents, the Jews do not have a real culture because they have absorbed everything they know from other cultures. This lack of creativity was given as a major example of the Jews' frequently mentioned negative characteristics. For example, according to the popular turn of the century theorist Lombroso, the number of degenerates was six-fold among people of Jewish origin.[13]

The widespread idea about the "degeneration" of the Jews, connected to the idea of a lack of creativity, described a new picture of "foreignness." The discrediting of Jewish talent was part of a theoretical task of differentiating cultures between "original" and "intellectual" ones or rather between "natural geniuses" and their "managers."

The Jew in Disguise

In Hungarian literature—following the Hungarian-Jewish symbiosis of the *Nyugat*—the historical debate about Jewish talent, skill, and genius acquired a special form during the years after the Trianon treaty.

There were two central arguments taking the forms of both compliments and accusations. The first one—formulated by László Németh in his remarks to Károly Pap's *Zsidó sebek és bűnök*

(Jewish Wounds and Vices)—claimed that, in the area of culture, Jews acted in disguise and were forced to engage in hypocrisy.[14] In the after-Trianon years, Németh said, "That the Jews were silent and that they lied shocked me. After all, it is his own greatness which is the most important thing for every writer. Once he has sacrificed all his life to writing, he owes his own sacrifice to the great word as well. This great word is the word of the great directing emotion in a perceived decisive moment. However, the Jewish writer covered his eyes in the most varied ways and it was precisely this decisive moment, which his greatness could have fed on, that he did not want to see. Moreover, he begged the non-Jew to imagine a silk scarf on the Jew's eyes. Many have wondered why there was not a real great Jewish writer with so many people, money, and opportunities around. Therefore the Jewish writer stands on impure ground for his fate." The idea of impure ground meant that the Jewish writer had not accepted his own origin and environment. Internal identification is certainly the thesis stated by the title, that there are two peoples living next to one another—the Hungarian and the Jewish—and it is merely the failure of assimilating "outreach" and integration that deprives the Jewish writer's work of its sincerity and, consequently, of its natural connections.

Obviously, there is an underlying value judgment in this remark. The uncertainty of that value judgment is testified to by the fact that, from among the Jewish writers, László Németh seemed to accept the mediocre Oszkár Gellért while leaving out Ernő Szép from his wide pallet, along with leaving out the heroes of the *Nyugat.* Ferenc Molnár, Menyhért Lengyel, and Dezső Szomory were just as conspicuously absent from the panorama of Hungarian literature as earlier ones like József Kiss and Sándor Bródy.

Németh sensed that there was a common sin which burdened the Christians and the Jews equally. "Nothing reveals to me more clearly the deep dishonesty of Hungarian intellectual life than the hypocrisy around the Jewish question." Here Németh is determined to criticize those individuals who brandish shameful truncheons at post-war universities and he even makes the allusion that their fate has several similarities with his own. “And then I was acquainted with the *Nyugat* where the Jew was the fellow-man of the best. Among so many great people I have not found the slightest evidence to indicate that there would be a different Jewish fate—different from ours.”

However, when László Németh drafts his own autobiography in concise shorthand, he indicates that these two fates do differ since Jewish talents fare worse in an atmosphere of bilateral dishonesty and among shameful lies. The Jew’s dishonesty obviously seemed more condemnable than the other’s dishonesty because “the Jewish is the strongest possible community of fate and there is no other human being on earth who can have more of a past than a Jew… We human beings not only serve our own needs but we also serve our own fate. And the Jewish fate is stronger than the needs connecting the average Jew to his receiving nation. The Jewish question has survived emancipation and is now more embarrassing than ever.”

Critics from Lajos Hatvany to Ignotus who clashed with Németh on the Jewish question argued that, his good faith notwithstanding, Németh would drive the Jewish intellectual into a new ghetto. Their common lot and fate would not allow them—even the ones who wish to break away from the Jews—to reach beyond their limits. Their fate and cultural ties would pull them back to national solidarity and to ethnic affinity. It is curious how many concordant responses came to the same idea from different directions. In his own benevolent way Zsigmond Móricz struck the right chord when he visualized an inevitable mask on Jewish writers: “At the end of the last century when talented Jewish writers began to occupy first class roles in literature, they felt obligated to adorn their characters with Christian color and glaze. There were only a few gaps that revealed their Jewishness. They used all sorts of typical

Christian names and tried to present life with an external glitter as if the secret—the spirituality that Jewish writers conveyed had been absorbed from their Jewish existence—did not carry any weight."[15]

It is quite obvious that Móricz did not wish to build a Jewish ghetto, nor did he want to suppress the Jewish intellect. Yet he reached the same position as Németh although from a different direction, that is, from his naturalist approach to the literary role of adventures and experiences. In a later found article Móricz argued against the disfranchisement of the Jews (in the *Pesti Napló* May 8, 1938) and tried to find common ground between the Hungarian and the Jewish fates while still protesting the first anti-Jewish law. Móricz claimed that he had learned his crystal clear writing style among Jewish journalists. The Jewish intellectual "was humane, had high cultural standards, and empathized with the masses suffering in the pits. … It was among these Jewish fellow-journalists that my eyes opened up to the thousand-year long misery and pain of the Hungarian masses. …Jewish editors were always at my assistance to help me discuss the most painful problems of Hungarian life with the clearest conscience."

While protesting the Jewish law, Móricz described the whole history of assimilation. Nineteenth century journalism carried the social spirit of the good old County Court judges. Democracy existed only for the gentry. Jewish journalism—whose style entailed logic and argumentation—struck a chord in Europeans since it did not differentiate among readers and spoke the same language to the peasant as to the university professor.

Therefore the Jews played a role in modernization after the abolition of serfdom when the peasants had to withdraw into their subdivided lots and the Hungarians were supposed to be transformed into skilled tradesmen and merchants at the same time.

> The Jews were very convenient in this transitional age because, during the previous two thousand years, Europe's every authority had trained them to appear

> whenever people were needed to do additions and subtractions. Armed with this exact skill the Jews set out to make up for what our Hungarians had not been trained to do and truly created both industry and exports which prospered and appeared on the world market. Mikszáth was right when he did not allow "Our Jew" to be harmed. The Jews brought in foreign capital and created a domestic industry. The Jews secured work and bread for the people who had fled from the countryside and who could not make ends meet in this land flowing with milk and honey. It was the historical role of the Jews to bridge a period which could have led to the annihilation of the Hungarians. From 1867 to 1914 the Jews' refined intelligence and organizing skills—developed during thousands of years of suffering—created the new foundation for a new life.[16]

The historical panorama and historical justice of their people touched upon the Jews' intelligence and organizational skills. However, both authors kept silent about the issue—which was raised a few years earlier of what role the Jews had in Hungarian arts and culture. This silence was due to the fact that cultural self-identity had been withdrawn from among the general rules of life since they were considered to be the source of an ultimate national identity. And on this issue, Móricz resembled Németh in his suppositions about the cultural role the Jews had played in the dismemberment of the country.

Various arguments and opinions coming from several places and for several different reasons converged on the common thesis that different sensitivities prevailed in literature than in ordinary life. Especially interesting was the fact that cultural anti-Semitism harmonized with philo-Semitism, the latter having been accepted on a legal basis. Further, the contemporary discussion of the Jewish question became the unexpected meeting point for divergent opinions. Among the first to applaud Móricz's opinion about the dishonesty of Jewish writers was the Zionist author József Patai. In his remarks at the evening discussion organized by the *Nyugat,* Patai mentioned Móricz by name when he declared that "The Jewish decline spreads from the West to the East. The Jews have been uprooted and became rootless. *Co-religionists have cropped up who do not profess their religion and do not face their fate.* Besides, they must have soon come to relize that they could not be fully transplanted into a different soil. And this caused restlessness, nervousness, and unconnectedness in them. Even the *chosen* strayed and staggered. As Zsigmond Móricz said, *Jewish writers avoided the Jewish soul* and Jewish psychoanalysis. It was not because they did not know them; it was because *they wanted to deny that they knew them.* A valuable human group, a race, and a people which had been able to reform the world from their own ancient land with their justice-seeking Words had started out on the road of decay."[17]

Zsigmond Móricz, László Németh, and József Patai especially agreed to reproach writers of Jewish or Hungarian-Jewish origin or those who had abandoned their Jewish heritage. These three critics admitted that the "Jewish question" had once again come into focus, especially because the independent, territorially dismembered, and now almost homogenous, Hungary demanded a new oath of allegiance from those people it did not consider to belong to the innermost identity of the new nation-state. The country lost 71% of its territory while 64% of its population was detached from the home-country.

This demographic tilt came along with the political restructuring and obviously it entailed a new "compact sealed with blood." The disintegration of historical Hungary was based first on ethnolinguistic identities because the new nation-state was 90-94% Hungarian. The Germans of Hungary decreased in size to half a million—5.1% of the whole population. Consequently and paradoxically, Hungary's modern national identity is the product of Trianon.[18]

The population ratio of the Jews changed according to changing classification requirements. When they were considered a denominational ethnic cluster, they numbered 473,000 in 1920 but only 401,000 in 1941. These numbers obviously do not include the converts, while the third Jewish Law, which cancelled the Act of 1894 permitting mixed marriages, raised the number much higher. Also, there seem to be discrepancies between the census returns of religious communities and the numbers in the state registries. Further, census returns did not reveal that the second largest ethnic group posed a special problem for the new state and did not show that several different solutions were proposed for the Jewish question. In László Németh's view, there were three options to solve the problem: assimilation, communism, or Zionism.

Assimilation—especially in post-Trianon Hungary—confronted special difficulties which were similar to those issues reflected by the census data. In the period when the census was being taken, it was incidental who was considered to be Jewish and what characteristics determined a Jew. As László Németh wrote,

> Even if Jews were more foreign to European peoples than they were among themselves, the common mother tongue could lure them deeper into the receiving culture. Thus, thrown between their past and current ideals, it is not surprising that their motivations drive them towards the latter. While a Hungarian *enters* the Romanian people and the German *enters* the Hungarian people, a Jew has to *change sides* no matter which European people is concerned. But is changing sides immoral if we want to dissolve an unclear situation in that way? I believe that it is not the conscious change which is immoral, but rather that opportunistic silence which enjoys the advantages of two common lots and does not really accept responsibility for either.[19]

Changing sides was a new offer of assimilation, one that truly wanted the abandonment of one common lot. Or—discounting the extremes of communism and Zionism—it was choosing one common lot by leaving behind the Hungarian-Jewish symbiotic identity and adopting one fate, either the Hungarian or the Jewish.

As with every offer of assimilation, this one also showed two organic faults. One was the inherent force and exclusiveness of an offer whose acceptance is tied by conditions. The second fault was the impossibility of executing it since changing sides involved assuming an "identity" that was not devised by the person who changed sides. Thus, he would have to remain a foreigner.

The Hungarian-Jewish short history that László Németh—based on Károly Pap's pamphlet—described about post-Compromise Hungary verifies the above. It is a laconic verdict: "We have built the post-Compromise Hungarian state with Jewish help and, when it collapsed, we made the Jews scapegoats for the collapse."

However for historical reasons, the Jews were allowed hardly any space in the newly constructed country. "Hungarians truly performed the reform of the nineteenth century with the help of those being integrated and mostly also for their benefit. The melancholic Vörösmarty and the brisk Schedel remained together during the whole century, and it was only by the end of the century that the ratio reversed between them. Hungary became the stock company of its immigrants and in this company, built on the exploitation of our people, the gentry became a well paid director figure."[20]

This was how the idea of "in the minority" was first formulated by László Németh to indicate that the Hungarians had become exploited natives in their own country.

The Hungarian Jewish community—ready for integration but found not to be mature enough for it—took on several forms. However, the dual bind, dishonesty, the ability for a diverse range of solidarity, and the profit from multiple binds—the constants of assimilation offers—were still inherently hidden in them and so were the continuous devaluation and ulterior retouching affecting the assimilating Hungarian-Jewish mentality. That was how in the Hungarian literary consciousness Ignotus became merely the crisis manager of the literary transition to modernity—the busy-body and brisk Jewish journalist who was the only one who was measured to Ady.

"The unsettled nature of the Hungarian-Jewish coexistence has been the most serious illness of our country since the War. But how could it have been settled, when the Jewish thinker refused to think about his own fate. The Hungarian Jews have superseded us in many ways. It is curious that they would lag far behind us in "envisioning their fate"—an inherently Jewish gift. Just compare Ady and Ignotus."[21]

Oh, but had it been only "envisioning the fate!" Surely, as if Ignotus had been Németh's *bęte noir,* Németh wrote an essay about Ignotus in 1927 where he stated his views on Jewish and non-Jewish talent for the first time. These views originated from a special attitude to race-consciousness. Thus they have to be presented extensively:

> Race characteristics are not like a constant profit with a fixed interest rate on the human being. There are human beings who, by their character, do not belong to any definite race because fate and mixed blood wiped out every trace of a single race in them. A person like that could integrate into any kind of people and if he is a genius, he could blend completely, and become that people's great creative force. Therefore I am not saying that lacking a definite racial identity would be such a great loss so that the human involved could not become a poet. If somebody does not have any love, she can still fall in love with her own husband. But if she wildly and desperately loves somebody else, how can she be expected to be a good wife to somebody she does

> not understand and even despises? The fact that Ignotus does not have a Hungarian character is not a tragedy. But he is driven by a fast-flowing different racial quality which would have bred at least nine Ignotuses out of ten children of a mixed marriage. Thus, how could he be a voice of Hungarian literature? It is the voice of an Ignotus who thinks so differently about homeland, family, and art that the host race would never be able to understand him. And yet, it is a clever voice because, if he were not clever, he would be cursed and ostracized.[22]

Therefore, according to László Németh's essay, talent, racial solidarity, racial characteristics, and personal character all played roles in his lagging behind Ady's vision of fate. But although it may be unjust to compare the two different talents, such evaluation is not necessarily unjust. Thus it seems that under a different constellation of circumstances, Ignotus could have thrived on his undeniable talent. But it was his tragedy that walking around in disguise in a host country, he almost contaminated the one he joined. "Strong individuals like Móricz and Ady became adorned with Ignotus' frills. After all, he was so inferior to the greater Hungarian writers of the *Nyugat* that even if it slightly overdecorated and distorted the deep will that time had ingrained in this generation, we ought to accept it as the shout and hope of pre-war Hungarians on the long run."

Skepticism about his talent was accompanied for Ignotus by the contemplation that he might cause intellectual contamination. The fact that the *Nyugat* did not become the organ of unequivocal development of Hungarian literary talents seems to be Ignotus' responsibility since he was a foreign graft on the Hungarian tree of life. This view is also revealed in an 1927 László Németh article about the Hatvany-Ady correspondence. And here again the Jewish question is in the forefront:

> This past month the whimsical profession of criticism threw two Jewish writers, Ignotus and Hatvany, my way. And it is as if I had found two types of the modern cultured Jew in these two writers. Ignotus is a more ancient and withdrawn soul who adapts to his environment only in expressions, keeping centuries of "ghetto-centrism" behind his modern mask. Hatvany, however, is more refined and well-intentioned. He honestly wants to integrate into the life of the host people. ...He wants to be useful but cannot break free from the role life has placed on him. Whatever he does, he remains a rich Jew. Others view him like that and again he hits his head against the bars raised by others' emotions. Ignotus is the disciplined and clever Jew who finally conquers. Hatvany is well-meaning, confused, and tragic.[23]

Life and fate become carved into the creative soul. Németh caught sight of the strange and entwining fate of two peoples in the Hatvany-Ady correspondence. And whatever was converted into an approach to literature and literary sensitivity in later decades, it carried forth these crystallized verdicts. Ignotus, Hatvany, and the others—talents who were sometimes pushed back into the Jewry—still do not occupy their worthy and definite place within the configuration of Hungarian literature because whatever was distilled into esthetics from contemporary views is still in effect today.

De-Judaization in Hungarian Literature

It was surprising how the different views intersected on the occasion of the first debate of the article *Zsidó lélek a magyar irodalomban* (The Jewish Soul in Hungarian Literature). And it is equally strange that in her essay *Zsidótlanítás a magyar irodalomban* (De-Judaization in Hungarian Literature), the post-Marxist and postmodern Ágnes Heller revives the literary topic of a "Jewish talent in disguise" and proposes a startling supposition: "In Jewish-Hungarian literature we encounter a peculiar case that needs our special attention. I am speaking about Hungarian-Jewish writers writing about Jewish life experiences and describing the ones they know internally and have known and have been able to interpret in their gestures, behavior patterns, psychology, and mannerisms since their early childhood." These writers, however, re-orchestrated their experiences and essentially falsified their own literary works. "They deny the Jewish identity of their figures and these Hungarian-Jewish writers describe Jewish figures as if they were not Jewish. They distribute ancient Christian documents among them—starting with the naming convention. In other words, they de-Judaize the Jewish characters in their novels."[24]

Heller takes three novels as examples: Ferenc Molnár's *Pál utcai fiúk* (The Boys of *Pál* Street), Tibor Déry's *A befejezetlen mondat* (The Unfinished Sentence), and Péter Lengyel's *Cseréptörés* (Peeking). In Heller's view "the 'Putty Club' is a kind of Jewish thing anyway. But the empty lot and its defense is a national affair." Accordingly, János Boka would represent the Hungarian nation and the relationship with the lot really represents the relationship with the homeland.

This is a most unusual thesis since Ferenc Molnár would have denied that the "empty lot" and the "putty club" had entered into his artistic system through Jewish socialization experiences and denied that he had really rewritten the story of the lot and the putty club from behind the mask of an assimilated Jew. The absurdity of the thesis might be revealed by other evidence. The first one has already been mentioned. Heller's observation—although very original in reference to the given piece of work—is not very original at paraphrasing the idea. The Jew behind a mask had become a commonplace literary topic, reinforced from several different sources, since the mid-1930s.(For that see Zsigmond Móricz's and László

Németh's statement analyzed above.) This, however, by itself did not contradict the thesis. However, Ferenc Molnár wrote one of the best novels of "Jewish Budapest"—entitled *Az éhes város* (The Hungry City)—published in 1900, five years before the *Boys of Pál Street*. In *The Hungry City* Molnár honestly and emphatically represents precisely the same pariah-parvenu contradiction that, according to Heller, the traitor Geréb as parvenu and Nemecsek as pariah represent in disguise in the *Boys of Pál Street.* A rich man Pál Orsovai, the converted protagonist of *The Hungry City,* goes to a painter to have his portrait painted. "Suddenly it dawned on the painter that he is dealing with a converted Jew and since one never knows whether they are anti-Semitic, he nonchalantly turned a painting of a Jewish woman—which had just been carried in—towards the wall." Then, in order to inform Orsovai about his religion, the painter called after his servant, "If His Excellency the Cardinal arrives, let me know immediately." It seems that Molnár very rarely denied his Jewish assimilation experiences. Otherwise, why would he have dressed the boys of *Pál* Street in disguise?

Jewish and non-Jewish architects are among those rubbing elbows with the converted Pál Orsovai. The first one whom Molnár characterizes as a notorious anti-Semite says the following: "I hope you will not have a Jew do this beautiful piece of work …" The other architect was a Jew and said: "I hope that you, as a good Jew, will have a Jew build the institute." In the end Orsovai declares that he is not Jewish.

The parvenu Orsovai is admitted to the Kisfaludy Society, whereas an old poet is not. "He is Hungary's greatest living poet. He was a poor Jew and the Kisfaludy Society did not want to acknowledge that it was not shameful to belong to Jesus Christ's kind. All of them felt that this old man was one of the purest poetic minds and, since the closure of literary histories, he was the only true poet of the Hungarian soil. But they did not need him—never, ever, ever. Yet the old man had applied for membership because it felt good to fail. After each such failure, he rose with glory ..."[25]

There are several of Molnár's remarks regarding Jewish assimilation that can be quoted. For example, there is the description of the occasion when the Minister of Commerce is not accompanied by his wife to partially Jewish parties.[26] And there is Molnár's very definite statement about the turn-of-the-century society such as the Prime Minister who is about to fail and who makes a final attempt to stay in power. "He had plenty of money. Rich Jews and aristocrats, irrespective of denominational differences, brought him gold to help."[27] It is difficult to fathom that Ferenc Molnár, who had made such honest statements about the Jewish question, would have suddenly de-Judaized his Jewish characters. Finally, Heller admits that Molnár is right and that this time "de-Judaization" has been transformed into an artistic virtue. As Heller says, through de-Judaization, the sociological dimension of the novel becomes insignificant and the writer elevates the story of young school-boys to a universal-existential level where every conflict is mythical. This time, de-Judaization raised the artistic value of the book—contrary to Tibor Déry's *Unfinished Sentence.*

The literary thesis of de-Judaization is a questionable thesis because at times de-Judaization can be viewed as an artistic virtue and other times as an artistic vice. As an esthetic value-judgment, this holds when social gestures, expressions, and characteristics that usually qualified as "Jewish"—are not considered to be factual. This means that the process of assimilation, even if it is incomplete, exerts a certain reciprocity. The sociological fact which has been mythologized as the "contamination" of the Jewish intellect paradoxically means that Ignotus, Hatvany, and Oszkár Jászi have exerted a real intellectual influence which did no harm to their "original talents." However, it is obvious that the Hungarian-Jewish symbiosis and the homeland the two groups built together have created certain standard ideas of everyday reality. What Ágnes Heller notices in Tibor Déry's book—the relationships within the Parcen-Nagy family—are really about the Leopold Town bourgeoisie, without "identifying" them as such. We are not about to follow Heller's complicated explanations here, but the accusation of de-Judaization in Hungarian literature is unfounded.

And it is unfounded in spite of the fact that its source is not only the right-wing. For example, András Komor, on the left, internalized the "disguise" accusation against the Jews. His lecture on Hungarian-Jewish literature described the symptoms of de-Judaization before World War II. His discussion of the pre-World War I literature of "assimilation" established that the Jew as a topic hardly ever occurred. "Hungarian literature certainly lost some colors from its palette when a veil was thrown over this topic area. Further, a problem—which probably was the problem of many—was completely lost. The same phenomenon appears on the other side of the coin as well. Thus, many writers present a rewritten version of their own Jewish experience and show their heroes from only one side and even then it is distorted."[28]

Many stories taking place in middle class environments leave behind a feeling of need. "The writer withholds something because, if he did not, the whole mechanical lifelessness would turn alive. The hero behaves in an especially perplexing way although it would be so easy to understand his behavior. Only a word need be uttered in order to explain so much. But literature exiled that word—'Jew.'"[29]

The assimilation program of the Jewish writer remained unsuccessful. András Komor was amazed that French-Jewish writers did not give away their origins while every line of Hungarian-Jewish writers reveals theirs. All the pain of unfulfilled assimilation can be found in his words; "...return to Judaism is not possible." Then he continues with a hand-written note:

> Time has torn us out of our Jewish environment where we do not fit any more. We cannot adapt to it, and we cannot identify with this Jewishness. Even if we wanted to, we could not be a Jew of ancient traditions any

> more. If we want to put forth roots, they do not reach ground anywhere. This is the gravest tragedy of our Hungarian Jewish self-identity. Involuntarily, we have dropped out of our Hungarianness, although spiritually and culturally we have much more in common with it than with the Jewish culture. János Arany is certainly nearer to us than Móses Maimonídes. We are not to blame for that. We used to be raised with the notion that we can be a Jew and a Hungarian at the same time, honestly at the same time and truly. Pre-War times educated us to be primarily Hungarians. The gap between the Jews and the Hungarians was not created by us. However, we might be predestined to eliminate it.

András Komor, whom Zsigmond Móricz and Gyula Illyés greet as a new discoverer of Jewish issues, demands an honest and critical consciousness, and first of all from himself. The accusation of "de-Judaization" voiced by Komor originated in the special experience of the "assimilation trap." Komor projected the "assimilation crisis" back into the past arguing that it was mostly due to the fact that Jewish writers of the past were not ready to face themselves. The experience of non-assimilation had hidden the key to the problem. The key was that they, as free individuals, had left the Jewish half of their past Hungarian-Jewish identity—a unique self-sacrifice—by accepting the promise of a complete integration. And these people, he argued, cannot be retrospectively reprimanded for the crisis of the 1930s.

Notes

1. Marcel Reich-Ranicki, *Über Ruhestörer. Juden in der deutschen Literatur* (München, 1993), p. 21, 23.
2. Mihály Vajda, *Hannah Arendt és a zsidó identitás* [Hannah Arendt and the Jewish Identity] (Szombat, 1996, par.2.), pp. 12-13.
3. Jonathan Judaken, *Jean-Paul Sartre and "the Jewish Question": the Politics of Engagement and the Image of "the Jew" in Sartre's thought, 1930-1980* (1997).
4. Jean Améry, *At the Mind's Limits: Contemplations by a Survivor on Auschwitz and Its Realities* (Bloomington: Indianan University Press, 1980), p. 95.
5. See also Amos Funkenstein, "Collective Memory and Historical Consciousness," *History and Memory*, vol. 1, no. 1, (1989): pp. 5-26.
6. See also Saul Friedländer, *Probing the Limits of Representation: Nazism and the "Final Solution"* (Cambridge, Mass.: Harvard University Press, 1992).
7. Sander L. Gilman, *Jewish Self-Hatred: Anti-Semitism and the Hidden Language of the Jews* (Baltimore: Johns Hopkins University Press, 1986), p. 127.
8. For the presentation of the Jews, see Linda Nochlin and Tamar Garb, *The Jew in the Text: Modernity and the Construction of Identity* (London: Thames and Hudson, 1995), p. 335.
9. Michael Ragussis, *Figures of Conversion: The "Jewish Question" & English National Identity* (Durham: Duke Unversity Press, Post-Contemporary Interventions, 1995), vi, p.340.
10. Sander L. Gilman, *The Jew's Body* (New York: Routledge, 1991), p. 128.
11. Raphael Patai, *The Jewish Mind* (New York: Charles Schribner's Sons, 1977).
12. Adolf Hitler, "Mein Kampf," in *Mein Kampf,* (Boston, 1943), pp. 301-303.
13. Michael Ragussis, "Anti-Semitism, Misogyny, and the Logic of Cultural Difference: Cesare Lombroso and Matilde Serao," *Victorian Studies*, (1997): p. 295.
14. László Németh, "Két nép: Hozzászólás Pap Károly, Zsidó sebek és bűnök című könyvéhez" [Two Peoples: Remarks on Károly Pap's

Book, Jewish Wounds and Vices], in *Életmű szilánkokban, I* [Life Work in Splinters, I] (1989), pp. 418-429.

15. Zsigmond Móricz, "Zsidó élet az irodalomban" [Jewish Life in Literature], *Nyugat*, (September 26, 1930), in *Irodalomról, művészetről, I* [On Literature and Art] (Budapest, 1959), pp. 113-115.
16. Zsigmond Móricz, "Zsidótörvény" [Jewish Law], *Pesti Napló*, (May 8, 1938), in *A tizenkettedik órában—Tanulmányok* [In the Twelfth Hour—Essays], Péter Nagy, ed., (Budapest: Szépirodalmi, 1984), pp. 451-456.
17. József Patai, "A modern zsidóság útja—Előadás a 'Nyugat' vitaestjén" [The Modern Jewry's Road—A Lecture at a "Nyugat" Debate], in *Harc a zsidó kultúráért* [A Fight for Jewish Culture] (Budapest: Múlt és Jövő, Jubilee Edition), p.12.
18. Gábor Gyáni-György Kövér, *Magyar Társadalomtörténet* [Hungarian Social History] (Budapest, 1998), p. 187.
19. László Németh, *Two Peoples*.
20. *Ibid.*
21. *Ibid.*
22. László Németh, "Ignotus," in *Készülődés: A tanú előtt* [Preparations: Before the Witness] (Budapest: Magyar Élet, 1941), pp. 354-355.
23. *Preparations,* p. 367.
24. Ágnes Heller, "Zsidótlanítás a magyar irodalomban" [De-Judaization in Hungarian Literature], in *A határ és határolt: Töprengések a magyar-zsidó irodalom létformáiról* [Limit and Limited: Pondering the Modes of Hungarian-Jewish Literature], Petra Török, ed., (Budapest: Országos Rabbiképző Intézet, 1997), pp. 349-363.
25. *Op. cit.* p. 105.
26. *Op. cit.* p.128.
27. *Op. cit.* p. 192.
28. See also Ferenc Katona, *Zsidó problémák a modern magyar irodalomban* [Jewish Problems in Modern Hungarian Literature], (Budapest: MIOK Annals, 1975), pp. 218-227.
29. András Komor, *Zsidó problémák a modern magyar irodalomban* [Jewish Problems in Modern Hungarian Literature] (Budapest: National Széchenyi Library, Manuscripts Archive, András Komor's Estate, Fond 29, 1935), p. 20, in print as an appendix of András Komor's novel, (Budapest: Múlt és Jövő, 1998).

Jewish Assimilation in Hungary and its Discontent

Anti-Semitism in Hungary survived the Holocaust and the decades of communism, though political Jew-baiting lost ground in the postwar period. Law prevents it from appearing openly, and it is suppressed also by the fact that no regime in the civilized world would support racism. There is, however, a wounded sensibility in the Jewish community and an overall uneasiness about the recurring efforts to establish a code for political anti-Semitism in public discourse. Potential targets of racism feel increasingly threatened by allusions to and allegations of "aliens among us." In a dialogue of an imagined Jew and a Christian one can read the following: "They call me a Jew, so they make a distinction to draw a line between me and the non-Jews. They make me put on the yellow badge, then discriminate, put me into a ghetto, to an internment camp or send me into exile, and finally exterminate me."[1]

Such reactions are usually branded as "Jewish oversensibility." Writers of Jewish extraction are not spared accusations of "hysterical reaction" in rightwing radical journals alongside with the allegation of being subservient to the orders of the "Tel Aviv-New York axis."

Current scholarship agrees on the fact that East-Central Europe has preserved specific forms of attitudinal and emotional anti-Semitism as a constant undercurrent.[2] Deeply ingrained in day-to-day beliefs and prejudices anti-Semitism is an accepted pattern of behavior sometimes tempered by such would be jovial excuses and hints as "the way of the world" or "as my father would have said it." This type of behavior serves as nothing more than the approval of continuity in history, a confirmation of unchanging "national character." The saving grace here is that it scarcely changes into political anti-Semitism, which is currently a marginal effort of a rightwing radical movements that used the transition-period of post-communism to revitalize the dated vocabulary of proto-fascism.[3]

There is, however, no innocent anti-Semitism in geographical regions where the Jewish population was decimated by the Holocaust. Its menace is enhanced rather than mitigated by the new language of racism and nationalism. This is a code language of substitution. Pretending innocence, the language of implications develops a new aura of double-speak. Working through constant emphasis and by reemphasis the concept of "alien" suggests "Jewish," whereas "native" means "non-Jewish" or "Magyar."

A peculiar warp happens to the word "Christian." Emulating Western European examples, some parties define themselves as "Christian." The resemblance to German or Italian Christian Democrats is mere surface. Western European Christian politics has no anti-Jewish edge or hidden nationalistic agenda.

Recently an active member of the Hungarian government declared that it is time to face the "Jewish question." An uproar followed in the press. The occasional surfacing of the "question," is of lesser importance compared to the coded language in the tainted spheres of communication, in the politics of language. There are some mainstream efforts to reinterpret national history in ethnocentric terms to obligate the troubled collective consciousness regarding the past and present of Hungarian Jews. Part of the problem is the overall sensitivity to past wounds in general. There is a consensus that Hungary lost the most in the two world wars. Truncatons of the country in the peace treaties were disproportionate to the supposed guilt. For long, during communism, it were the ruling classes which had dragged Hungary into calamities. In post-Communist years, however, the casting of perpetrators has become more diverse. A plethora of reasons are enumerated as causes for historical loss, and these include old accusations of the role of "non-native" social groups, rootless individualism, cosmopolitan stance etc. Anti-Judaism in East-Central Europe was interwoven with trends of anti-modernity. Due to the fact that the emancipation of the Jews was contemporaneous with an upward surge in capitalistic development and the broadening of market economies, the language of protest assumed camouflaged meanings of nationalistic doublespeak. In countries where the process of modernization was excruciatingly painful, where political fights for representation were suppressed by force, scapegoating became an almost natural reflex of rearguard action.

A not negligible role was played in this development by economic envy. The Jews were stereotyped as greedy, preserving their tribal qualities that emancipation was supposedly changing. Character-assassination was aggravated by the disease that often paralyzes small nations. "Hungarianness" according to these portrayal of the national self was residing not only in language but in inherited character. The "gentry" was typecast as a "seigneur," the peasant as the class that has a historic role of preserving fortitude, virtue and morals. The Jewish stereotype was a mirror image of self-aggrandizement of "Hungarians" or worse: the failures of the ruling elite were projected onto the Jewish community. As Raphael Patai puts it "A major part of Hungarian society treated assimilant Jews as a separate element, in which it could discover, and mock with a feeling of superiority, its own faults: conceit, snobbery, title mania, selfishness, the empty extroverted life, the bragging and bluster, the lack of manners—all features it either did nor recognize in itself or, if they were conspicuous, it excused as '*úri*' (seigneur-like) virtues."[4]

Would this state of affairs qualify Hungarians as a nation in which anti-Semitism became an element of national character, as Andrew Handler claims?[5]

Capitalism by proxy

Hungary, considering the social integration of her Jewish community differed in major aspect from their Western counterparts. The first difference was in numbers. The proportion of the Jewish population at the turn of the century was 6%, larger than in any Western European country, even more than in all of Western Europe. There was no Western capital that could compete with the number of Jews in Budapest.

The second difference, as Viktor Karady states, was the time-lag in assimilation.[6] Hungary became a target-country for immigration in the first half of the nineteenth century. Jews were latecomers in the complicated affairs of the fight against Austrian domination and in the modernization efforts of those noblemen who came to represent the efforts for independence and liberalism. There was a certain urgency and speed forced on the latecomers by assimilation. The Hungarian model has shown the emancipation of the largest numbers in the shortest span of time in the whole of Europe.

The third factor in the specificity of the Hungarian model was the difference in the structure of the host society into which the immigrant or recently accommodated Jews integrated. The pattern of Jewish "acculturation" was to a rich, politically dominant, economically weakened national elite.

The great number of the newcomers as well as the intensity of their assimilation evidently affected certain economic interests and aroused widespread social resentment. Parallel to the spectacular linguistic acculturation of large numbers of Jews, the vast layers of the ruling elite were losing ground in the restructuring of society due partly to the process of emancipation. The industrialization of agrarian production resulted in the emergence of the "gentry," a nobility that had lost its property and entered into state-administration and officialdom. It was this layer of the social fabric that gave some support to the overtly anti-Semitic parties of the end of the nineteenth century. This is clear from the fact that these political groups requested primarily the exclusion or curtailment of Jewish commerce and property ownership.

True enough, anti-Semitic parties were short-lived and were bypassed by traditional conservatives. They may not have been influential in the political arena, but they were much more so in setting a public agenda through pamphlets, journals and speeches. In a kind of self-fulfilling propaganda overt anti-Semitism injected the "Jewish question" into popular opinion. The accusations, that Jews are a separate entity, that their "acculturation" is not more than a tactical consideration, that the tribal solidarity of the Jews supersedes their allegiance to "magyardom," remained there as an element of national discourse.

Popular opinion in times of crises was prone to accept at least some bits of the anti-Semitic slanders arising from religious bias and calculated political maneuvers. It barred effectively the Jewish community from integration. Emancipation may have opened large fields of advancement, acculturation may have resulted in admitting the professional classes into every walk of life—social discrimination remained a fact no one disputed except official representatives of the Jewish community.

Zsigmond Móricz, a major fiction writer of the 20th century depicted this social barrier in one of his much-debated novels. A young Jewish man from the provinces tries to adjust to his environment by emulating gentry manners and attitudes, to no avail. When it came to a marriage, there was no bridge between the gentile society and the Jew. A functional cohabitation between two different traditions was possible.[7] It could even become amicable in term of social encounters. One could safely say that this *bonhomie*, the mixture of cynicism, acquiescence was itself an obstacle to a true blending.

Such social encumbrance was an accepted fact of assimilation, since the "acceptance pact" was loaded with inherent contradictions and negations. The first among these being a Hungarian proclivity for abrogating participation in the "capitalist" project. The specific "gentry" layer of society was justified in its anti-modernist ideology that thought it equitable to realize the advancement of the extended market economy through proxies. This development was aptly described by an eminent scholar of Eastern European affairs, Hugh Seton-Watson. "The Hungarian nobleman or minister or bureaucrat would not sully his hands with the kind of money-grubbing commercial activities which capitalists went in for. On the other hand, capitalists were needed for Hungary, so Capitalism must be encouraged. In so far as the Jewish element provided capitalist skills and the will to go ahead they should be given green light. The result was that the Jews responded very enthusiastically and became loyal Hungarian patriots."[8]

Needless to say, such "capitalism by proxy," that is via the Jews, raised and fueled anti-Semitic sentiments. A number of factors were at work to revive inherited Jewish stereotypes from diverse corners of society. The Catholic Church, as Hugh Seton-Watson continues his analysis, remained overall hostile to this development. Further, it aggravated the aversion of the peasants, natural losers to industrialized agriculture. Large estates were leased to Jewish entrepreneurs who were not initiated in the rituals of false bucolic as novels by Lajos Hatvany describe. Finally, the Jews were targeted by the animosity of the nationalities in the Dual Monarchy being exemplary Magyars against the Slovak or Romanian minorities.[9]

Sociological and historical elements, however, could not account for the full animus against the Jewish population. Anti-Semitism was not a simple sum of the perceived grievances. It took on a different quality from the sum of its parts, rather as a language of complaints. There were many reasons that tumbled over into the irrational. When the question was often raised what is it to be Hungarian, national character-definitions tended to draw a composite picture of traits that were markedly non-Jewish: leisure-prone attitudes, honesty against self-interest, a noble acceptance of doom. In contrast with this wishful dreaming the Jews were harsh reality itself, the drive, the push, the spirit of innovation, modernity, rootlessness and cosmopolitanism, the urban Diaspora, industrialization.

Social tension was breeding the mechanism of scapegoating; routines of false identification became the roots of stereotyping. This mentality-forming environment was to no small extent created by the contradictory historical and political situation of the Hungarian State. We could, to use shorthand, describe the situation of the "*Ausgleich*" as revolving around a central lie: namely that the compromise with the Austrian Monarchy was conceived not as a break with the insurrection against the oppressors of the nation but as a continuation of all the efforts of prior generations of reforms. There was a skeleton in the cupboard for the whole period between 1867 until the outbreak of the First World War. The ghost of 1848 was kept awake by a generation of émigrés who questioned the legitimacy of the new era—the era of industrialization, or capitalism in other terms.

The historical situation was to a certain extent comparable to the developments in Germany. At least there was a resemblance between the German and the Hungarian misery in the denial, through preservation of the lost cause of 1848, of a revolution betrayed, of doing business partly by proxies insofar as leaps to industrialization and financial restructuring were concerned.

In Hungary as in Germany a tendency towards romanticizing prevailed. The mirror image of the German "*völkisch*" upheaval was found in the "*Magyar*" mythology of the "*nép-nemzeti*" (national-popular) that had a distinct vision of proper discourse and mentality. The self-image stressed ancient roots as the basis for legitimating the Hungarians being elevated as equal partners in the Dual Monarchy while other minorities of the region had only subordinate roles. Hungarian nobility being "born to rule," the core of this romanticizing image, was self-serving and detrimental in the long run. It juxtaposed their uniqueness to the lesser others, including nationalities and—primarily—Jews.

One should not exaggerate the parallels of German and Hungarian romanticism. One common feature, however, should not be left unnoticed. At the heart of German romanticism was the self-flattering image of uniqueness by tradition and birth. It also added to the national image some integral and inherent traits that were claimed to be immutable and carved into the marble of memory. In any case it is immaterial that the Germanization of thinking in "*Blut und Boden*" of the centuries was rooted in Christian piety around the shores of the Elbe River whereas the Danube inspired different but equally glossy images of chosenness and notability.

In the sociopathology of weakness projecting strength are not uncommon. The Hungarian warrior and the Hungarian nobleman are just varieties of known blueprints for a national self-image. The problem with romanticized images is their associated demonology. They grow out of negative definitions, from parameters needed to construct delimiters for what we are not. As Werner Mosse observed, contrasting images poured out in abundance from popular literature in nineteenth century Germany, defining national character in opposition to whatever was thought to be alien. The most conspicuous alien was the Jew, not only because of religion but because of his having been identified with latecomers, not indigenous, different. A mutual exclusivity rendered this definition sharp and restricting. As George Mosse noticed, "New Romantic thought made the following assertions: the Jew was an alien in the land of the Germanic peoples, which was the native soil of the rooted Volk... The Jew was anathema to *völkisch* thought. In contrast to the German soul, which acted as a filter between man and cosmos, the soul of the Jew was insensitive, materialistic thing."[10]

The words of Hungarian Romanticism were of course not the same, but the message was. To define national character in juxtaposition to others, or sometimes THE Other, was not uncommon in the era of the second wave of nationalistic revival. Stereotyping the other was a major means of discourse in popular literature. Mosse cites Gustav Freytag's *Credit and Debit* as the archetypal novel exposing the rootless vileness of the Jewish merchant-character. Hungarian popular novels were preeminent in inspiring hatred. The historical novels of Baron Miklós Jósika, the earliest representative of pulp fiction such as Ignác Nagy or Lajos Kuthy could be accused of plagiarism since their Jewish characters were taken from the pool of ancient and recent stereotypes.

Home-grown Antisemitism

It took a long time and specific circumstances, for pulp fiction to be elevated to ideology. Here the German parallel is easily proven. In the 1870s the "true-born" Hungarian anti-Semitic political upheaval was undoubtedly inspired by the movement of the Prussian court preacher Adolf Stocker. In the Hungarian parliament Győző Istóczy voiced with venom an openly anti-Semitic policy to which impoverished smallholders rallied. Mainstream politician, representatives of the compromise between Austria and Hungary, embodying their personal reconciliation with their past, curbed the immediate political effects of the unbridled agitator. But they could not contain the poisoning and derailment of public discourse. The proof of how the atmosphere became contaminated by one of the harshest and most patent anti-Semitic attacks scarcely paralleled in its extremities in Europe—one of the most blatant blood-libel trials followed in Hungary. Liberals braced for the defense but the acquittal of the accused led to vicious anti-Jewish demonstration in Budapest.

Istóczy, mediocre journalist as he was, became one of the founding father of some of the most tenacious prejudices that took hold in the historically ongoing accusations against the Jewish community.

"Hungary Judaized" was his first dubious contribution. Like a virus this accusation was repeated throughout the years. We will see, how in various interpretations it resurfaced that Jews are disproportionately represented in the professional classes, that Jews occupied crucial posts in the world of banking and journalism. The "spiritualized" version (inoculated with residues of "*völkisch*" thought) refined the originally crude attack by asserting that indigenous culture was affected by the rapidly assimilating "*Jids*," whose basic inner disposition differed in its very nature from that of the Hungarian soul. "Judaized Hungary" was the trump card of the charges leveled against Jews.

The longevity of the Istóczy launched imputation is due to the elusiveness of the concept. It assigns a unique quality to national identity to which no community can assimilate. Or rather every attempt at assimilation would only reveal its futility, for it will always face an impassable barrier. As Istóczy put it in his journal, the object of the Jews was to exploit their country of residence, and their "filthy self-interest" is "directed at the final destruction of our homeland." From the text the anti-modernist tendency is transparent. The Jew "ruined our whole public life, forced our progress into a new, slanted direction." But the main negative contribution of Istóczy was his groundbreaking ideology of cultural anti-Semitism. "Intellectual activity has been almost totally monopolized by the Jew...," wrote Istóczy in the above quoted article and this dictum was repeated, without attribution of course, in all subsequent cultural theories striving to define the specificity of Hungarian letters, painting or music.

Istóczy was the first in Hungary to seriously suggest the emigration (or deportation) of the Jews to Palestine, thus devising, in the words of one researcher an early blueprint of Zionism.[11] This seems to me a dubious argument. If two parties reach similar conclusions that does not make them necessarily identical. The object of Istóczy was to rid Hungary of the Jews whereas even early

Zionism was trying to find a homeland for them. It is of course true, however, that both arguments meet at a central point of agreement; that anti-Semitism is incurable until there is one Jew left and he lives in the Diaspora. In spite of all the overlapping of these contentions, it does not eradicate the motive that underlies the propositions.

Overtly anti-Semitic parties were overwhelmed by mainstream conservatism and the liberal tradition. This was, however, a mixed blessing for the assimilation-driven Jewish community. First of all, as Rolf Fischer has observed, anti-Semitism—under the carpet—became embedded in a still more comprehensive ideology, namely, conservative anti-modernism.[12]

The defeat of the openly anti-Semitic parties was achieved at a high price. Conservative anti-Semitism extended the social basis of the chasm between the "*Magyar*" population and the Jewish "new-comers." It also heightened, as Rolf Fischer argues, the social standing of anti-Semitism. The shift from open to "embedded" types of discrimination became a decisive characteristic of the social discourse building up a "reserve pool" of convenient ideology that would serve as an integrating force of Hungarian conservatism that ruled politics for decades. There was a specific reason why anti-Semitism became "embedded" and held in reserve. In multi-ethnic Hungary, as Rolf Fischer observed, there was a limit to anti-Semitic trends. A final retreat to any ethnocentric clusters of ideology was rendered impossible by the existence of the Slav, German and Romanian minorities.

Liberal conservatism was eager to work out the conditions for the framework of a "political nation" where given rules of universal allegiance obliterated primary ethnic feelings and solidarities. Primary interest urged a cohabitation of the Jewish contingent with "*Magyar*" politics but in the background ressentiment was building ready to let the well-known genie out of the bottle.

Legally there was no discrimination against the Jewish community in the "Golden Age" of the last twenty-five years of dualism. The era of compromise functionally arbitrated between various layers of society: The Jewish lot being cast within the "useful" category. Underneath this "organic" model however, tension was building that in one stroke changed the outlook on the scope and depth of assimilation. Beneath the glitter—or "mortal splendor"—of the last decades of the Austro-Hungarian Monarchy—an unusual divide grew between rational political-economic conduct and instinctive behavior, a cleft between the rational and the affective spheres. Tribalism and ethnocentrism had no place in the forward-moving trends of modernization, nevertheless, as embers ready to be inflamed, prejudices and biases simmered under the surface.

In a convincing analysis Andrew C. Janos termed the unique situation the "politics of backwardness," meaning that at the peripheries of Europe the market penetration of society was limited, land and labor never became genuine commodities. "Here the images of the modern world were dispensed through an educational system, but they were not corroborated by actual social experience. The result was a lopsided process of rationalization and a fragmented view of reality."[13]

A decisive part of this fragmented view was a one-sided attack on any identity associated with the strategy of modernization. An almost universal condition of assimilation was to obliterate "getto mentality" of Jewish origin. The more a Jew of any prominence severed his ties with his community the better he fared. Conversion was one of the options though lineage or parentage was recorded in the press and in public opinion. At the beginning of the 20th century the ruling elite devised a strategy to co-opt into the state administration representatives of Jewish families with substantial financial means. Between 1905-1910 there were 84 deputies of Jewish extraction in the lower house of parliament.[14] A tendency of ennoblement of Jewish landowners and businessmen has clearly shown the tendency of the policy of assimilation. It was not only an adjustment to the ruling elite's feudal leniency, but rather an offer of political alliance. It also showed a shift in public opinion,[15] the way to acceptance in the political and business world.

Beneath the surface of the acknowledgement of the upward mobility of Jews there were isolated efforts to renew the debate of the place of the Jewish community in Hungary. Cultural anti-Semitism set new conditions for social admission. An exalted writer, always a maverick, a self-anointed prophet of cultural criticism opened up the controversy on the pages of the foremost liberal forum *Nyugat* with an innocuous remark on linguistics and dying languages. Dezső Szabó, the author in question argued that there are two roads open to the Jews. Either reinforcing their religious ties, preserving their cultural heritage, forge a nation or be the savior of modernity by "killing Jehovah, killing the Law, killing the Old Testament and the Jew of the Talmud..."[16]

In these lofty words, Dezső Szabó, an isolated, but trend-setting spokeman heralded a new chapter in dealing with the "Jewish Question." Finding a special vocation for the Jewish community in an assumed melting pot of the Dual Monarchy and seeing them as the bonding agent of nationalities was setting them apart as a special minority. Behind the flowery expressions a denial of assimilation—the creed of liberalism—came to the fore as its adversaries indicated in the ensuing debate. An opponent of Szabó discovered the "unconscious anti-Semitism" in his re-negotiating the organic place of the Jewish community.[17] The more official Jewish standpoint was, as usual, the denial of the "question" itself. In the Jewish cultural review *Múlt es Jövő* (Past and Future) József Patai argued that the Jewish question was already solved by political emancipation. The only problem remaining is economic which is part of a larger issue: that of the upward mobility of all social classes.[18]

The "official" Jewish reply to a renewed discussion over the social function of the Jewish community was in line with the special circumstances of assimilation in Hungary. Although in hindsight foremost liberal thinkers criticized the nature of this assimilation, there was a grain of truth in Oscar Jászi's evaluation of the fervent *Magyar* nationalism of the freshly assimilated Jewish elite.[19] They refused, in the analyses of Jászi to be what Szabó required, the ferment among the nationalities of the empire. The Hungarian Jews, as Jászi stated, took part in the forceful "magyarization" of the empire, creating the nation of "thirty million Hungarians."

A divided community, indeed!

Whereas intellectuals veered to the "left" in establishing centers of radicalism at the turn of the century, the mainstream or the official representatives of Hungarian Jewry were content with the result of assimilation. As Randolph Braham summed it up: "Since most of the Jews who were engaged in the magyarization drive were also the main representatives of the commercial-bourgeois class, in the agricultural communities inhabited by the national minorities they were looked upon as the vehicle of both exploitative capitalism and great Magyar chauvinism."[20]

The *Magyar*-Jewish symbiosis was part of national dream and a part of national reality,—a marriage of convenience that went sour when the reverie of expansion and domination ended after the first world war. While in the period from the "*Ausgleich*" and the outbreak of the war some three hundred Jewish families were ennobled by the crown to acknowledge their services, no social allowance was dealt to them in the postwar period. This view, however, needs a slight correction in retrospect. Jewish emancipation in Europe and especially in Hungary was based on a measure of political rights for individuals with a given religious background. It never emancipated Judaism itself as a viable option for faith or granted the institutions of this religion privileges on a par with other accepted religions.

The definition of Jews as a religious community was a paradox in itself because it acknowledged a community that in its upward mobility was already detaching itself from the very base of premodern orthodoxy that would make this definition conceivable as the ultimate common denominator.

The secular Jew, as Jacob Katz observed, was hard to place since neither his religious nor his social status was clear.[21] Emancipated Jews, continues Katz, remained an enigma that defied any simple formula.

Jews were, thus, less a religious community and more a minority tied together with family bonds, remnants of habits, dimming feelings of solidarity, an awareness of being different, but also trying to "resemble." The only denominator that could reduce this to "basics" was offered by those intending to disenfranchise the Jews. They proposed the idea of race. "Once the concept of race became infused with anti-Semitism, it became a most efficient instrument of political propaganda. If it did not actually create, it certainly deepened the alienation of the Gentile public from the Jews, and thus, in the fullness of time, it helped to set conditions for Nazism."—concludes Jacob Katz.

The Trianon Treaty only heralded this outcome, but it created the mental atmosphere for the complete disenfranchisement of the Jews in the fulness of time.

Notes

1. Letter, "Letter". *Szombat* [Saturday], the Journal of the Hungarian Jewish Association, nos. 1/2, (1991).
2. Randolph L. Braham, *Anti-semitism and the Treatment of the Holocaust in Post-Communist Eastern Europe*. East European Monographs, no. 405, (New York, N.Y., Boulder, Colo.: Rosenthal Institute for Holocaust Studies Graduate Center/The City University of New York; Social Science Monographs; distributed by Columbia University Press, 1994).
3. István Deák, "The Danger of Anti-Semitism in Hungary," in *The Danger of Anti-Semitism in Central and Eastern Europe in the Wake of 1989-1990*, Y. Bauer, ed., (Jerusalem: The Vidal Sassoon International Center for the Study of Anti-Semitism, 1991), pp. 53-61.
4. Raphael Patai, *The Jews of Hungary : History,Culture, Psychology*, (Detroit: Wayne State University Press, 1996), pp. 730 and 495.
5. Andrew Handler, *The Holocaust in Hungary : an Anthology of Jewish Response*. Judaic Studies series, (Alabama: University of Alabama Press, 1982), pp. xiii, 162.
6. Viktor Karády, "Asszimiláció és társadalmi krízis—A magyar-zsidó társadalomtörténet konjunkturális vizsgálatához" [Assimilation and Social Crisis—To the Conjuctural Analysis of the Hungarian-Jewish Social History], *Világosság*, vol. XXXIV, no. 3, (1993): pp. 33-60.
7. Zsigmond Móricz, : *Kivilágos kivirradtig...* [Until the Small Hours of Morning], Móricz Zsigmond elbeszélései és regényei [Zsigmond Móricz's Stories and Novels], vol. 4, (Budapest, 1963), p. 35.
8. Hugh Seton-Watson, "Government Policies Towards the Jews in Pre-Communist Eastern Europe," in *The Nazi Holocaust—Historical Articles on the Destruction of European Jews*, Michael R Marrus, ed., (Westport: Mekler, 1989), pp. 423-424.
9. Michael K.Silber, ed., *Jews in the Hungarian Economy: Studies Dedicated to Moshe Carmilly-Weinberger on his Eightieth Birthday*, (Jerusalem: Megnes Press, Hebrew University 1992).
10. George L. Mosse, *The Crisis of German Ideology; Intellectual Origins of the Third Reich*, 1st ed., (New York: Grosset & Dunlap, 1964), p. 373.

11. Andrew Handler, *An Early Blueprint for Zionism: Győző Istóczy's Anti-Semitism*, East European Monographs, vol. 261, (New York: Columbia University Press, 1989).
12. Rolf Fischer, "Anti-Semitism in Hungary 1882-1932," in *Hosteges of Modernization—Studies on Modern Anti-Semitism 1870-1933/39*, H.A. Strauss, ed., (1993), pp. 863-893.
13. Andrew C. Janos, A. C., *The Politics of Backwardness in Hungary 1825-1945*, (Princeton: Princeton University Press, 1982).
14. William O. McCagg Jr., *Jewish Nobles and Geniuses in Modern Hungary*, East European Monographs, vol. 3, (Boulder Colo.: East European Quarterly; distributed by Columbia University Press, New York, 1972), p. 254.
15. Andrew C. Janos, *op. cit.* p. 179.
16. Dezső Szabó, "A magyar zsidóság organikus elhelyezkedése—Nyílt levél a Múlt és Jövő szerkesztőinek" [The Organic Placement of Hungarian Jews—Open Letter to the Editors of Past and Future] *Huszadik Század*, vol. 15, nos. 1-7, (1914): p. 341.
17. Izsák Pfeiffer, "A zsidóság problémája" [The Jewish Question], *Huszadik Század*, (1914): pp. 561-565.
18. József Patai, "Nyílt válasz a 'Huszadik Század'-nak a 'Múlt és Jövő'-höz intézett nyílt levelére" [Open Reply to the 'Twentieth Century' to the their Open Letter to 'Past and Future'), *Múlt és Jövő*, (April, 1914): pp. 220-233.
19. Oscar Jászi, *The Dissolution of the Hapsburg Monarchy*, (Chicago: Chicago University Press, 1929).
20. Randolph L. Braham, *The Politics of Genocide : the Holocaust in Hungary*, (New York: Columbia University Press, 1981).
21. Jacob Katz, "Leaving the Ghetto," in *Commentary* (1996), p. 29.

The New Face of Cultural Anti-Semitism

The eminent social scientist and one time politician, Oscar Jászi described the segregation of Jews in the post-emancipation period. "We must not forget"—wrote Jászi in 1920, in the aftermath of the First Word War,—"that the contrast between Jewry and the Christian world is much greater in Eastern Europe than in the West. The Hungarian people is much more rural, conservative, and slow thinking than the Western peasant people. On the other hand, Hungarian Jewry is much less assimilated than Western Jews, it is much more an independent body within society, which does not have any real contact with the native soul of the country."[1]

Jászi, himself an émigré, was reiterating a stereotype that became the defining feature of the growing wave of interwar anti-Semitism, the leitmotiv of its Esperanto. The moment a nation is defined by the mythical quality of the "soul," when identity resides in the metaphysical nature of communal roots, the Jews are by definition excluded from the nation.

The putative social segregation of the Hungarian Jewish community may be explained by the special nature of their emancipation. In the nineteenth century Hungarian interest required the swelling of the "*Magyars*" in the Austro-Hungarian Dual Monarchy. The only substantial number of people without "another" homeland were the Jews whose eminent interest was to gain political rights. The price, as set in the "pact of assimilation" was ethnolinguistic one. The person speaking "*Magyar*" was considered Hungarian. After the so called Trianon Treaty ending the First World War Hungary became independent of Austria. There was no need to prove their linguistic or ethnic dominance. Hence the Jews lost their function and could be disenfranchised without hurting the immediate interests of the newly independent though truncated country. Hungary lost a substantial part of its territory to the so called successor states, like Yugoslavia, Czechoslovakia, Romania.[2] The Jews lost their temporary homeland.

Anti-Semitism *per Implicationem*

There is a historical heritage of anti-Semitism in Hungary, frozen during the years of communism and surfacing as a cultural divide in the contemporary public space. As the sociologist Sándor Révész has put it, in today's society there is a "strongly tainted sphere of communication," where a vulgar and at the same time refined, open or covert anti-Semitism is present once again. Officialdom, government-circles deny the charge heard mainly abroad that there is considerable anti-Semitism in Hungary today.[3] Some marginal groups of society, they maintain, may give voice to racist slogans, but they have no influence at all on political life.

Open anti-Semitism is absent in public life today, but there is a special and in certain aspects a new type of anti-Semitism. Let us call it a coded or cultural anti-Semitism. It is not expressed openly, but it burdens public life all the same. It is populist demagogy *per implicationem* that aims at winning the masses to a point of view.

It is of course more than tactics. It is the attempts at national self-identification prevalent in the unexpected democracy sweeping down on East-Central Europe, wanting to define the nature and the earmarks of power that we are talking about.[4]

The search for identity centers now around the intertwined concepts of "national" and "Christian." It is easier to define the latter which implies a kind of ethical standard and suggests a continuity with millennial Hungary that entered Europe by adopting it a thousand years ago. Christianity is not discriminative except perhaps in the sense of being non-Communist. Its less felicitous definitions include also the national aspect and define certain groups "more authentic," "more national," or "more Christian."

The concept "national" is far more ambiguous. In the spirit of Spinoza's *omnis determinatio est negatio*, let us first analyze what does not qualify as "national." Strong political factors come into violent collision and probably draw the lines between those in power and their opposition. The term "national" presumes here namely an ethnic consciousness that establishes its meaning just by being discriminative. There are loyal citizens in Hungary who are not ethnic Hungarians, and there are Hungarians living outside the borders as citizens of foreign states. So post-communist establishments did undertake themselves the task of creating democracy without a hierarchy in a political state but rather it wished to create a national state that was to shape its foreign and domestic policy, its legal system, its press, etc., in terms of a definite ethnic consciousness and its ideology.

This concept of the nation, just like that of Christianity, made clean of the rust of yesterday, became part of the dominant trend to express loyalty to the traditions of the nation, and to reject the colonial heritage of pseudo-internationalism by breaking with the supranational tendencies.

The only positive aspect of the concept "national" offered by today's right-radical ideology is a kind of cultural identity: common history, common fate, common experiences, common language. Should it refer only to these elements, it would remain within the boundaries of that mythicized romanticism from which it originates, and would not include the idea that everything is valid only in terms of ethnic consciousness. György V. Domokos was probably the first to emphasize that the Hungarian minority within its own country is as entitled to be defended as any other ethnic group. This age old slogan is charged with memories. "Let Hungary belong to the Hungarians"—the adage was formulated so that it truly meant the expulsion of Jews from the public sphere they occupied through cunning at the expense of the native Hungarians.[5]

Take the case of the former dramatist, self-confessed informer of the secret police after the 1956 revolution and currently an influential president of a right-wing party in parliament. The weekly columns of Csurka in his *Magyar Fórum* ventilates strong feelings of xenophobia, rambles about a secret conspiracy that allegedly prepares the space for immigrant Jews to be settled in Hungary to the detriment of the natives. Csurka, needless to say, vehemently denies being an anti-Semite. It is only in the interest of the country he raises his voice. Euphemisms and innuendoes cover up the message that is easy to decode. The Jews are our greatest misfortune as was said half a century earlier.

In August, 1992, being the vice-resident of the ruling party he published a pamphlet that caused quite a stir internationally.[6] It was not the content but the wording fueling the uproar. Attacking the prime minister of his own government Csurka wanted to steer his party to the radical right. A reformed government than should remain in power, gathering more strength to lead the country out of the abyss, and put an end to Bolshevism, to cosmopolitanism, to the foreign gangs dressed in liberal rags, to trampling the nation under foot, and to the rule of the left which has prevailed since 1945. After all, it will be the Christian middle classes that will create the Hungary that will finally belong to Europe, and then Hungary will belong to the Hungarians in the future, too. The borders will not be opened to all kinds of newcomers, and the Hungarian ethnic group will never be at the mercy of others.[7]

Csurka's party is currently in the Hungarian parliament. The protest of the press long abided to register his provocations. He is accepted as a fixture in Hungarian political life, getting airtime on state television. By his presence he lowered the overall sensibility to racial and ethnic matters.

The origins of his populist demagogy are well known. It was the virulent proto-fascist thinking of the mid-war period that identified Liberalism with Bolshevism, foreignness with the Left, and contrasted all this with the "national" and the "Christian."

The heritage of the past has, however, a new function today. In Adam Michnik's words, it expresses a kind of fear in Eastern

Europe, that is now realizing its backwardness. "Post-Communist nationalism... brands cosmopolitanism, which expresses an unadmitted fear of European tolerance, norms, and democracy."[8]

Csurka argued that threat induced preemptive aggression. The essence of this aggression is that this train of thought involves an unsaid but obvious conclusion, namely, that those who argue against all types of newcomers today, question also the reason for the existence of the settlers of yesterday. For them, all who do not belong to an imaginary tribal community are aliens. And the synonym of "alien" is "Jewish," as taught by the legacy of the populist tradition of the inter-war years.

This conclusion cannot be attributed to Csurka's shrewdness. It is a consequence of the tainted political force field, the logical consequence of a peculiar effort at legitimacy, of a tendency to distinguish between "us" and "them," "national" and "foreign," "patriotic" and "cosmopolitan." It was also Sándor Révész who noticed the conclusions left unsaid in this context. In the place of the final conclusions in Csurka's arguments there is a void or a vacuum where one can insert anything from the pool of associations preserved in subconscience of the followers of populist ideologies. There is a vocabulary of call-words easily set to motion to reveal their sub-context. This vacuum "exercises a suction force that can absorb in only what is present in the historical consciousness of the day. It is a matter of tactics and decency, whether the factors inherent in the statement will be identified or not."—so Révész.

By saying that there is and there is no anti-Semitism in Hungary today we mean that a strangely presentable but non the less dangerous form of anti-Semitism is spreading here in penetrable disguise. It is anti-Semitism *per implicationem*, the unsaid dimension that lies beneath certain efforts at self-identification.

Allusion and intimation in political newspeak serves special functions. Not naming the culprit of all the woes of a nation—as one analyst remarked—attributes demonic forces to the enemy very well in line with the satanic powers attributed to Jews in religious anti-Semitism. "The alien is in disguise, unveiling him would diminish the sense of danger, a consequence of his being abstract, and would make the association less believable. The hiding Jew is a real danger, who appears either as a liberal or a Marxist"[9]

There is another explanation to the "words-as-disguise" syndrome. A denial of existing anti-Semitic trends is also due to image-projection in post-totalitarian countries. Clandestine language is a veil for Western eyes. In Hungary "undercurrents of anti-Jewish attitudes are largely repressed—as Yehuda Bauer states—because of the self-image Hungarian society wants to project to the West."[10]

The Pitfalls of Dissimilation

The *cause celèbre* of cultural anti-Semitism raising its head again was to be found in the short diary notes of Sándor Csoóri. The noted poet was one of the founding fathers of the so called *Democratic Forum*, that was transformed later from a grass-root movement into the political party winning the first free elections in Hungary "after the wall came down." Csoóri in *Hitel* placed the question of Jewish assimilation on the agenda again in 1992.[11] The weight of his opinion is unquestionable. As Béla Bodor wrote, Csoóri had to understand "... that he was not a poet, a moralist and a publicist any more but the leading ideologist of the ruling party."[12]

In his note Csoóri spoke of new possibilities of cohesion between Hungarians and Jews. He said, it had only been natural for the Jews to assimilate to the Hungarians in the last century and share their fate. "However, the Hungarian Soviet Republic, the Horthy era and, above all, the Period of Disaster put an end to this mental and spiritual symbiosis."[13]

From this concise statement, there emerged a rewritten history of Hungary, and, as Péter Hanák suspected, it was outlined from the point of view of another image of the future.[14] Csoóri places the age of Jewish assimilation in the nineteenth century, though Hanák proves that it started much earlier than that. The Jews poured into Hungary not to reap the benefits of modernization, however ambiguous this process might have been, but to fight the battle of modernization hand in hand with the Hungarians even against the Habsburgs, proving thus the success of their assimilation.

As György Spiró says, "It is a historical fact that the great masses of Hungarian Jews were not assimilated aliens even hundred years ago but Hungarians who abandoned their religion, language, and traditions as early as the Reform Period, the war of independence, or in the Bach era at the latest, and assimilated to their environment with all their heart and soul."[15]

Assimilation is for Csoóri a process to be underrated probably because he suggests that first from 1920 then from the Period of Disaster onward the opposite and irreversible process of dissimilation began.

Employing aspects of several periods of Hungarian history (i.e., the Hungarian Soviet Republic, the Horthy era, and the Rákosi era) must have served to obscure the responsibility for the supposed process of dissimilation. At the time of the Republic of Councils, the union with the Hungarian nation was supposedly rejected by the Jewish revolutionary elite in "matrimony" with Communism, and this is what makes understandable the reaction of the Horthy era which punished the Jews for their role in the Communist takeover. The supposed thirst for revenge of the Jews during the Rákosi era is used to explain, in turn, their behavior in that period.

What a series of calculated misinterpretations in a single sentence! Its logic is not extended further and leaves the obvious consequences are left unsaid, blaming a whole group for certain allegedly historical crimes. The Jews are made responsible *in toto*, since this view of history defines them as an ethnic group, and a dissimilated social and spiritual community. They are blamed here even for their initiative of the strive for identity, and their assigned responsibility is mitigated at best by the assumption that their alienation is after all understandable if one takes into account the experiences in the "Period of Disaster."

When the "Period of Disaster" was over, Jews played a special role in Hungary, the argument goes. Jewry seemed to desire vengeance on a whole nation for its fate. To speak of dissimilation in connection with the Jews coming home from the concentration camps or just freed from the ghettos rakes up and accepts the legend of the vengeful Jewry. "Some Jews...were just as mean as the fascists,"—aserted István Benedek, a professor of psichiatry, novelist.[16] Some of the Jews realized their thirst for revenge as members of the new Communist secret police, the legend goes. Dilettante historians have come forward with hair-raising figures as to the number of the Jewish members of the Hungarian secret police after the Second World War.[17]

However, the ideology of the supposed revenge preceded the opportunity for its realization. It was first conjured up in the apocalyptic vision of László Németh at the *Szárszó Conference* in 1943. Németh, a prolific writer of essays, novels, and journalism was the spiritual leader of the so called populist writers of the inter-war period. Relentless in the pursuit of "true magyardom," he argued for a renewed contract with the Jews. By a strange logic, Németh criticized at the above mentioned conference the Hungarian decrees born in the wake of the Nuremberg laws for judging by the same standards the Jews and people who had long dissociated themselves from them. "And now we shall have a peace that will be dictated by them [the Jews—author]. A peace of which they will be the appointed redeemers. I have never made generalizations as to the Jewish question, as can be seen in my writings. However, it is but natural that vengeful Jews lacking self-criticism should have gathered strength in the last four or five years, and those who do not notice that Shylock wants hearts, have no ear for the sharpening of knives."[18]

The image of vengeful Jew, was thus taken from a text before the war. It was a myth, and there is nothing to prove that the Jewish members of Rákosi's secret police acted out of a thirst for revenge against the Hungarian people.[19] Another source of this alleged thirst for revenge was presented in a remark of the social historian László Lengyel. Rákosi exposed the trial following the arrest of Gábor Péter, former head of the secret police and a Jew by origin as a Zionist plot, so the atrocities committed by the secret police came to be ascribed deliberately to the Jews.[20] The motive of revenge in Rákosi, the communist dictator recurs in recent psychoanalitical analisys, stating that compensation for his Jewish origins must have played a role in devising his bloodthirsty acts.[21] The fact was, that Rákosi suspected clandestine and subversive conspiracies and one of his latest plans was to stage an anti-Zionist purge.[22]

It was not at all the thirst for revenge that characterized the Jews coming home at the end of the world war. They were rather hopeful that the new order, the new Hungarian democracy would grant them equal rights at last. The fact that certain Jewish intellectuals started to take part in political life is a proof of their share in these rights. The Jewish supporters of the Communist party were not more numerous than were those who joined other political trends. Analyzing the electoral statistics, Charles Gáti confirmed this fact.[23]

In addition the above statistics, the numerous discussions of the state of mind and attitude of those coming home from the concentration camps also deserve attention.[24] Speaking of the years after the "Period of Disaster," the writers maintain that assimilation seemed to be fulfilled at that time. As András Lányi, a distinguished author and filmmaker remarked, the Jews coming home "took it for granted or realized just then that they cannot possibly be anything else but Hungarians. Hungarians who had been discriminated, persecuted, outlawed, and deprived of everything. Still there was something that could not be taken away from them, and it was their being Hungarians. ... This spiritual and psychological interpenetration is the accomplished work of generations of Jewish and non-Jewish Hungarians that could not be changed even by the genocide. It was Hungarians who persecuted Hungarians. Those who did not perish, survived. It was the pursuers who are less Hungarian for that, not the pursued."[25]

Paradoxically, their experiences of the genocide made the Jews realize their Hungarian nationality. As Ákos Kertész, a fellow writer put it, it was just by their sufferings that the Jews paid for becoming real Hungarians. "Those who survived and returned from the death camps were convinced that there was no more Jewish question, and there was no difference between Hungarians and Hungarians any more. ... Assimilation would be complete from then on, discrimination and racism had been fascist inventions and had lost ground for good. The survivors felt that in suffering the horrors of persecution and genocide, they had really paid for being accepted as Hungarian, and nothing more could be demanded of them... ."[26]

In his reply, Csoóri rejected this analysis of the historical situation. His partners in the debate considered the years after World War II as the age of an accomplished assimilation, while Csoóri saw in them the period of uninterrupted dissimilation. "...According to my own personal experiences, assimilation in the years after the Period of Disaster had many other aspects than the one you can see. It could be flexible, uncertain, keeping its distance, convulsive, hiding, and pretending, and even had varieties that included also the possibility of emotional dissimilation."[27]

Emotional dissimilation? From what? Not necessarily from the nation, but only from those who let their fellow citizens be carried off by a foreign power. It is only the good shepherd who can expect loyalty from his flock.

Assimilation can, of course, never be a fully accomplished process.[28] It is the endless drama of acceptance and accommodation, a matter of a continuous political and social bargaining. Assimilation was attacked the most bitterly just where it developed to its fullest extent as, for example, in the Germany of Emperor William. On the other hand, any inclination to dissimilation should be considered justified and not at all "pretending" if it is a response to aggression and discrimination. The exemplary statement of Freud in this respect, made in 1926, many years prior to Hitler's takeover and Freud's involuntary emigration, reads as follows: "My mother tongue is German, and I am a German also culturally and as regards my tastes. I considered myself a German also intellectually until I had to realize that anti-Semitism was present and growing in Germany and in German-speaking Austria. From that time on, I prefer calling myself a Jew."[29]

It is interesting to observe the nuances of this statement. Freud did not deny being a German from an intellectual point of view even in a social crisis. However, he found a new identity in his community, with which he had been originally identified against his will. He did not become a worse German, but he did become a better Jew.[30]

The new Hungarian discussion on assimilation was not at all characterized by a sense for nuances. The debate was already an offense against decency when the opponents of Csoóri insisted upon their being flawless Hungarians, accepting by this the starting-points of the debate, however involuntarily. To put it even more simply, they accepted the dictate of assimilation.

What was actually the Csoóri debate? Was it another special way of raising the problems of modernization? Was it an effort to create a new image of the Hungarian nation? Was it just calling names and abusing the Jews, as Péter Esterházy[31] and Gyula Hegyi wrote,[32] or was it "a moving and honest confession?"[33]

Ferenc Fejtő, the doyen of Hungarian liberal radicalism, who lives in France, maintains that it is a new and unfortunate chapter in the debate over modernization: "It is really painful for the

Hungarians that although the Jews, pouring into Hungary on the invitation of the liberal Hungarian ruling class in the nineteenth century, actually contributed to the bourgeois development of the country, they took the places of the slower ethnic Hungarians, who were less ready to modernize their ways and thinking. As László Németh put it, they replaced the Hungarian minority."[34]

The idea of László Németh that the Hungarians, being natives in their own country, are ethnically defenseless must have been one of the sources of Csoóri's train of thought. His motive was actually something else. The Csoóri debate is much more than the revival of the question of modernization. It is the responsibility for the new Period of Disaster, i.e., the decades of Communism that it is all about. This is why the aliens and the Hungarians are counterpoised in his argument. The deteriorating Hungarian ethnic group is unimpaired only as regards its undisturbed national consciousness. It was the aliens who made compromises in the past decades. The true Hungarians went through the difficulties with undisturbed identity.

This is the real source of this "new" kind of anti-Semitism. As Rudolf Ungváry observed, this anti-Semitism really exists "and seems to have a new, a "historical" source of reference, namely, the interpenetration of the Jews (not only of the left-wing intellectuals of Jewish origin, but all Jews) and the Communist takeover after the war. Even those anti-Semites who have long made their political compromise with the ruling regime and entered the Communist Party are influenced by this argument"[35]

Mátyás Rákosi, the communist dictator after the war, elaborated the legend of the "guilty nation." Hungarians were responsible for participating in the war on the side of the Germans. Today the new myth spread by Csoóri speaks of an "innocent nation," saying that it was only the "lackeys of the Muscovites" who made compromises with the Communists. The true nation lived through oppression had hibernated until freedom arrived.

To speak of a union between Communism and the Jews amounts to acquitting the middle class, the possible social basis of Csurka's new order, of complicity and collaboration.

Freedom of Expression, Used and Abused

At festive and less festive occasions official statements speak of anti-Semitism as something outdated. At the same time, the public is poisoned by a latent and coded, still easily discernible racism that is given a special background and a social function by just such public denials.

At the moment, the structure of publicity in Hungary consists of two interdependent spheres conditional upon each other. On the one hand, there is the official side, the declarations flattering Europe, and including ecumenical ecclesiastical programs, as well as pathetic commemorations of the Holocaust. On the other hand, there are the attempts of the new Hungary at self-definition, saturated with arrogance and with the ideology of being chosen for a mission. All this has appeared again and again as a mere confusion about identity, in which the Jewish question now receives a new and important role.[36]

The revival of anti-Semitism must be interpreted only in terms of this schizophrenic social background. This background is evidence of a transitory stage where several different political trends try to find their purpose. The political trends in Hungary today do not always have a clear-cut purpose and program, and are not always legitimate socially, either.[37] Some tendencies even contain coded racism and related nationalism as their only essences.[38]

Anti-Semitism has obviously not slept through the Communist dictatorship just to wake up and infect society again as if it were temporarily neutralized virus. The anti-Semitism of today is not a symptom of the freedom of expression. On the contrary. While freedom of expression has actually expanded, coded anti-Semitism is seeking to narrow down this sphere by introducing double speak.[39] On the face of it, it is the anti-Semitism of the mid-war years that has been restored to life. However, the cultural racism of yesterday based on the characterology of nations provides only a means to support a new set of arguments attacking with new tactics and an almost new content.

The anti-Semitism of today is far from being merely emotional. This is why it is unjust to blame a whole country for its revival. The rude and vulgar type of anti-Semitism pops up occasionally in pubs and in private life and can be considered negligible.[40] It is not more than an error in communication under the conditions of an underdeveloped civil society. Those who use the names of genitals in each and every sentence in everyday dialogues, do not really think about what they are saying. When saying "Jew," they only use the ancient synonym for evil.

It is not worth while to fight directly against this kind of anti-Semitism; it is also impossible. Just as anti-Semitism exists even without Jews, abusing Jews also exists without anti-Semitism under the conditions of regressive rudeness that bring the *déclassé* elements away from a sensible social life. Social mobility today does not point to the creation of a new middle class. On the contrary, it lowers the social positions of the middle class and the classical intellectual occupations. There are only few who manage to rise successfully. It is mainly the new political elite, the upper layer of officials, and the thin layer of the new soldiers of financial fortune and other adventurers. The rest lag behind in this great transformation, whose direction is highly uncertain. It can lead equally to Europe and to the Third World.[41]

Anti-Semitism was given here a new function, drawing up from the pubs to the intellectual workshops. Occasionally and implicitly it became a component of the search for national identity.

Who Are the Jews and Who Are the Hungarians?

There are numerous definitions of who are the Jews, who could be considered Jewish. We confine here ourselves to historical interpretations widespread in Hungary.[42] The Jewish faith was accepted as religion at the end of the nineteenth century. Jews, however, were considered as a cultural sub-group of society. Euphemisms like "Hungarians of Moses's faith" were common some hundred years ago, hinting in disbelief to assimilation that left a recognizable body of society easily identified and often targeted as non-Hungarians. Nowadays even the apostates are defined as what they refuse to be. Being a Jew was a burden also for a number ill-fated literati who would have gladly sacrificed an arm to have been born in a detached farm in the countryside and to have used a language unmistakably from the provinces.[43] Today the former culture-czar of the Kádár-era, György Aczél is identified as Jew again and again, and his numerous misdeeds are credited to that fact.[44]

The fate of this man is a case in the point. As a former actor he performed minor parts in Jewish plays during the Second World War in the theater of the Jewish community. After the defeat of the Hungarian revolution he became a seminal figure in the hierarchy of the Communist Party and consented to the imprisonment of leading intellectuals who actively participated in the revolution.[45] Most of the writers and scholars who served a term of imprisonment after the revolution of 1956 were of Jewish origin. The pragmatic Kádár believed that nobody's heart would break for them.

The example of Aczél is very important. The figure of the Marrano or secret Jew is well-known in European history. They were the ones who practiced their religion secretly and seemed to be assimilated to Christian society. Aczél was, however, no Marrano, though he was often accused of being one. If his fate seems to be a Jewish fate, it belongs to the category of "Jewish self-hate."[46]

It is, however, noteworthy that the Jewish population of Eastern Europe today are mostly judged by its social position. Ironically, Jewry as an enemy can wear two contrasting masks: they can equally be Communists or capitalists. The personification of Scylla and Charybdis endangering "independent" national development goes back to such historically false identifications.

The above judgment expresses also the whole problem of assimilation in a concise form. It is illusory to consider assimilation as a completed process, as György Spiró does. To become part of a nation is, namely, only the first step towards assimilation. A Jew can easily want to become a Hungarian, a Moravian or an Austrian, but the Hungarians, the Moravians and the Austrians will immediately put obstacles in his way. Nowadays, little is said about the social limits of integration, as though it were just the social barriers and not the national ones that have been fought against in the long history of assimilation. The greatest concern of the wealthy Jewish bankers around the turn of the century was how they could be raised to the rank of a baron and not their becoming Hungarians.

Ludwig Börne, the anti-Semite descendent of a rabbi and the favorite poet of Karl Marx, wrote: "Some blame me for being a Jew, some praise me for it. Some forgive me for being one, but there are none who would neglect it."

There have been basically two types of assimilated Jews in modern Europe, the *pariah* and the *parvenu*.[47] The parvenu is the relative newcomer in the ruling classes and has overemphasized his assimilation. This type is the alibi of the recipient societies, by the way. The one-time Minister of Defense of the Austro-Hungarian Monarchy, Baron Samu Hazai was one of these alibi Jews. Just a small piece of Passover cake on top of the Hungarian pork cutlet will not readily change the opinion of the ruling class as to the place of the Jews in Hungarian society.

The opposite of the *parvenu* is the *pariah* awakened to self-consciousness. He is an assimilated person who stays outside the society of the *status quo* or even attacks it. All Jewish intellectuals are, so to say, like so many little Ignotuses, journalists supporting the government party in secret, public revolutionaries of art, aestheticians, and bureaucrats of literature. Ernő Osvát and Baron Lajos Hatvany nearly fought a duel, like members of the gentry would, to settle their differences over art as fully assimilated Hungarians.

The connecting link between these two prototypes was the fact that both could conform themselves to the requirements of society only through emphasizing their otherness, their prominence or through the frightening slavery of being a "domestic Jew."

As Horkheimer and Adorno put it, "They were allowed to own the means of production only with difficulty and very late in history. It is also true that Christianized Jews held high positions in administration and industry in the course of European history and even in the German empire, but they had to prove their fitness by renewed zeal and strict self-denial. They were allowed to fill these posts only if their behavior confirmed the general verdict pronounced over the rest of Jewry."[48] Whenever the Jews wished to integrate themselves into the society around them, they had to play a role to be admitted.

The figure of the *parvenu* and the self-conscious *pariah* reappears now as the target of modern anti-Semitism. The revival of their image is strangely topical, since it materializes the fears of Eastern Europe. The Eastern European societies, standing at crossroads, are still afraid of the "self-conscious" pariah who, by waving his Communist party card, tried to ward off the return of fascism, and they are already afraid of the parvenu who wants to convert his inherited mobility to economic life and to getting rich in the process. Eastern Europe makes demons of the Jewish Bolsheviks and the Jewish plutocrats by declaring all Bolsheviks and plutocrats Jews.[49]

The context in which the pariah and the parvenu play their parts is not valid, since not even the characters of the play are sure of what play they are performing.

The troubled identity of the small successor states of the Monarchy also forced people to play roles. From the point of view of the Hungarian people, the peace treaty following the First Wold War in Trianon can be seen as the vengeance or whim of the God of the Old Testament.[50] There is no reasonable explanation (though there may be some conjecture) for why just the territory of the Hungarian state should have been reduced most after the First World War. Trianon could not be digested without injury to Hungarian self-respect. Ideologies based on grievances are, however, prone to quick deterioration, and the resulting Hungarian sense of vocation is mistaken when it assumes the familiar condemned role of the "chosen people." Hungary's neighbors have a rather unfavorable opinion of this sense of vocation, while the great powers are usually not interested in the cultural aspect of Hungarian delusions of grandeur. Csurka, the populist reformulated the Hungarian vocation into palatable and mild terms. "A new Hungarian role can be substantiated which not only sets an example but, by its open economy and society, it can neutralize the nationalisms of the region and pull to Europe not only the Hungarians of the Carpathian Basin but also the peoples living with them." No need to textual analyses here. The dominant role of the Hungarians this time will be assured by the new magnetism of their advanced placement in the new world order, taking over the leadership of the region.[51]

Who are the Hungarians? A community far from being unified from a religious point of view with a very mixed ancestry, whose racial characteristics belong to the realm of mythology. Classical liberalism defines the Hungarians as inhabitants of a political nation state,[36] excluding the Hungarians living in minority status in the neighboring countries, compressed beyond its original frontiers by Trianon and Yalta. So the liberal definition is inevitably narrow, even if it is the best available definition. The political scientist Péter Kende in the wake of the new revisionist attempts wrote an article with a telling title: "Let us Break with the Idea of the Nation State." The article argues that: "The concept of the political nation is receptive, that of the cultural nation is discriminative, and that of the ethnically unified nation is impossible. An ethnic group based on a common tribal past or linguistic characteristics as a morphological unit should not be mistaken for a nation which is a political category."

The trend so many on the liberal side were fighting is called ethno-culturalism. This view projects vision of Hungarians united. There are historical ties between Hungarian minorities in the countries surrounding the legitimate state of Hungary. The Hungarian minorities are legally citizens of rump Yugoslavia, Slovakia and Romania. On a higher level, the problem can be dealt with only metaphorically, since it has no geopolitical solution. It still gave rise to such highly criticized and ridiculed claims as that of the late prime minister, elected democratically for the first time after the war, who declared that "in spirit" he wished to represent fifteen million Hungarians.

This prime minister defined himself as the leader of the sober right-center, whose populist wing fix the limits of the Hungarians as an ethnic unit. Recently reelected member of Parliament István Csurka is far from being a character in a comedy he himself might have written in his better days, but a conscientious politician. He is the epitome of the right-wing ideology of the populist bloc of the mid-war period. He is so saturated by this ideology that whenever he speaks in public, he uses the worst phrases of the populist tradition of the inter-war period without referring to the sources. However, Csurka takes care not to speak openly enough so that he can refute accusations of anti-Semitism. Still there is implied anti-Semitism in several of his statements. It is enough to consider his implications and it becomes immediately obvious against whom his "ethnic unit" needs to be defended.

The anti-Semitism of today has restricted itself to a legally unprovable sphere[37]: to populist ideology or to a covert *numerus clausus* that discriminates against former Communists, rewards ethnic identity, stresses the Christian character of the regime, and demands "moral" qualifications that are, by definition, not applicable to Jews, Gypsies, Slovaks, Serbs, or Croats.

In the communicative sphere of society, anti-Semitism is a context underlying all options and choices. In classical rhetoric, *epitropé* as a method for drawing conclusions is left to the public or to the opposition. It is also classical rhetoric that warns the speaker or writer that by applying it, he may put the public at a disadvantage, forcing them to give voice to thoughts they have thus far deliberately avoided.

The method implies an exchange of roles forced on one partner, while the argument maintains that it is the disturbed sense of identity of the Jews that is the issue, and that the Jews have to find a new identity and form of behavior.

However, the sense of identity of the surviving Hungarian Jewry does not seem to be in a crisis. On the one hand, the Hungarian Jews voted first when they decided which way to go after the war: to the Carpathian Basin or to Palestine. On the other hand, the conditions of assimilation or dissimilation are dictated not by those who wish to assimilate or to withdraw, but by the recipient community, its leaders, and its public opinion. The minority can only rely on defensive tactics and can never take the initiative.

It is naive to think that this problem can be discussed by certain experts first, and then taken before the public. Anti-Semitism is too serious a problem to be entrusted to self-anointed experts, especially since it belongs to the sphere of public mental health for the entire Hungarian society, and each and every "patient" must have a say in it.

There is, however, a sort of "cultural anti-Semitism" spreading both as an ideology and as public sentiment, resulting from the post-Trianon syndrome in Hungary, and from the defeat in the First World War. That peace treaty forced the successor states in Eastern Europe to find their new identity. At the core of their search for statehood was the remembrance of the Hungarian discrimination against minorities. As if in a mirror image, the Hungarians of the "mainland" had to find a virtual spiritual community to forget the mutilation of the country and the severance of so many Hungarians from it.[52]

The First World War was followed by a mental transformation of patriotism giving rise to mystic nationalism, a search for scapegoats, and all kinds of racist ideologies.[53] The race is an entity that cannot be confined within national borders. Each and every person belonging to it is part of the national spirit and can contribute to its development. Let us only think of the characters of Dezső Szabó's novels, pushed to the peripheries from a cultural point of view.

By racial theory I mean here not only its extreme national socialist version, but also its range from the debased ideas of Houston S. Chamberlain to the version glorified by Wagner and applied by pseudo-scientific anthropology, phrenology, the theory of destiny formulated by Leo Frobenius, and the sociology of Werner Sombart. The coexistence of racism and dying positivism was a nightmarish legacy of the nineteenth century. Racism is the bastard offspring of declining German irrationalism and the "objective" science having lost its inspiration.

Anti-Semitism is not merely implied in these racist theories, being their covert but logical presupposition in defining all communities or ethnic units as races. Racial theory speaks about mixed and pure races, hence of "bad" and "good." All racial theories are *eo ipso* hierarchical.

It is easy to demonstrate the social effect of racial theory from the 1920s in Hungary even in such seemingly innocent versions as the cultural concept of the nation. This concept is the sublimation of the former territorial supremacy, a kind of "intellectual imperialism" or the naive belief of school-teachers and others with a sense of mission that they can recover by force of cultural superiority what the armies have lost. In the inter-war period first it was Minister of Cult and Education Kunó Klebelsberg who tried to prove to the victorious peoples of Europe that the Hungarians were culturally superior than the people of the new successor states.[54] Then it was László Németh, who wished to convey the message of the cultural mission of the Hungarians in the successor states of the Carpathian Basin.

All versions of cultural supremacy were naturally based on an exaggerated ethnic characterization, and it followed from this that those who propagated them required the termination of the liberal pact of assimilation. In the Austro-Hungarian Monarchy, this pact of assimilation was in fact a giant with feet of clay. The central power and the court itself naturally supported assimilation as a prelude to the integration of the nationalities. Assimilation served the interests of the court also by weakening the national consciousness and surge of independence of the individual provinces. These territories yielded, in turn, to the pressure of modernization when they complied with assimilation, the milestone of liberalism.[55]

The problems inherent in assimilation appeared very early, as the example of Győző Istóczy reveals[38] or the anxiety of the agrarian party exaggerating the number of Jews immigrating from Galicia.[56]

Although based on a fragile compact, assimilation in Hungary was after all successful. In no other part of the world were there more middle-class Jews without earlocks, wearing short Hungarian coats with lacing, and imitating Emperor Franz Joseph, or more amiable members of the gentry laughing at Jewish jokes. Bourgeois development liberated the Jews of the ghettos, emancipated them economically and in part also politically, then, in the framework of another arrangement, let them influence public opinion. "Luckily or unluckily, a great number of Jews have come to our ill-fated Hungarian salt desert. There are many kinds of them, again to our luck or to our misfortune, and they number a million up to now. Most of them are corrupted, for the Jews have a special ability to master and even push to extremes all harmful characteristics of the race in whose territory they settle down," wrote the great national poet Ady, staunch advocate of the Hungarian-Jewish symbiosis in 1908.[57]

Ady's optimism as regards assimilation was difficult to explain away afterwards, especially since he was so enthusiastic about it that he often went too far. He maintained that in three generations the Jews would be just as Hungarians culturally as any other "true-born native."

This enthusiasm of Ady was too much both for historians and writers of the inter-war period. A trendsetting book of enormous influence was Gyula Szekfű's *Three Generations*. By the time of the appearance of this book the poet revered by the Hungarian reading public was dead. The appropriation of his legacy was one of the main goals of the generation of the twenties. In Ady the rare combination of the Hungarian genius was discovered, the visionary who predicted the downfall of his county. Just one feature of Ady had to explained away: his philo-Semitism. Szekfű failed to perform this almost impossible task. The poorest and nearly ridiculous passage of Szekfű's *Three Generations* was the comparison of the former Prime Minister of Hungary, István Tisza and Ady. For Szekfű both represented the virtues and shortcomings of the true Hungarians. The suggestion here was that the amalgam of their features would have produced a genuine leader of the nation.[58]

In the footsteps of Szekfű the writer László Németh struggled to explain away the relationship of Ady and Hungarian Jewry in desperate flowers of rhetoric: "The decade and a half when Ady produced the best of his poetry fell in the time of the Jewish breakthrough! ... His work is unthinkable without this break-through! ... He demanded adoration with the covetousness of beautiful women, and sought opportunities to enchant others. He needed a chorus behind him, and a brilliant one was fielded by the Jews, like in the ancient Greek tragedies. But this chorus never deceived him in the most essential points. There is no better visionary of the Hungarian fate than Ady. He is Tiresias, aware of the sin of the unsuspecting Oedipus, who is Oedipus himself at the same time. It is not only that he notices rottenness beneath the glamour of the millennium, but he is aware also of the earlier incest, committed innocently, that tears us away from the deepest instincts of our culture."[59]

The incest of course is the inter-marriage of Hungarians and Jews. These exaggerated metaphors take for granted what is still to be proved. László Németh distinguished between adaptable Jews who respected the values of society and "restricted themselves to their proper place," and those who "forged ahead" and "streamed" even around Tisza. It was only the gentile writers of the first decade of the century who "produced powerful antidote against the Jewish break-through."[60] Part of Jewry evidently seeks to become influential here, and if an antidote is needed against them, they are obviously virulent and dangerous.

After Trianon, nobody approached the Jews in the way Ady had done. Gyula Szekfű, and also Dezső Szabó, took over from him his symbolism of the "curse fallen on Hungary" and of the "destruction of the Hungarian race," but turned it upside down. Ady had hoped that assimilation would free the Hungarians from their "Asian backwardness and love of romance," in other words, that it would make them adopt bourgeois mentality. Szekfű, the talented propagandist of the after-war regime, maintained, however, that it was indeed the assimilated masses that caused stagnation for the Hungarians.

The idea that the assimilated might bend the recipient nation to their position and try to gain power appeared already in the writings of Gobineau and H.S. Chamberlain, but it could become a social force only in critical places like the Hungary of the 1920s.

Having his roots in Szekfű and debating with him during a life-time, it was László Németh who denounccd assimilation almost endlessly. While Szekfű attacked assimilation around the Compromise and the end of the nineteenth century, Németh daringly went much further and dedicated his life to a crusade of a retrospective mental cleansing of Hungarian history. He tried to separate Ady and his ilk from those who degraded their own Hungarian war of independence into the war for independence of art. "Hungarian art," Németh wrote, "can be nothing else but the recovery of the Hungarian racial character."

What does this "Hungarian racial character mean?" Németh does not give a definition. Race is for him the ultimate inspiration of art, the repository of the deepest character of the nation. He did not elaborate his specific idea of the race in detail, because he could have made up a definition only of what is not racial and Hungarian. Should the reader take the measure of the content of the race as a concept, he would find unutterable conclusions. He would get to dimensions that are difficult to put into words and extend the concept to a degree that not even the prophet Németh could undertake to express.

László Németh did not take the consequences of his train of thought: "These lines have nothing to do with anti-Semitism. Eight million people live on the territory of Smaller Hungary, herded together by fate, who cannot and must not be ousted from here. The state should see to it that they be melted into an effective unit beyond all racial and religious differences, with each group in its proper place, and that all of them should prosper under the hegemony of the strongest that can be nothing but the Hungarian peasantry and the new middle class deriving from it."[61]

The quotation comes from an article on Ignotus from 1927. At that time, Ignotus lived in exile, his name would soon be omitted from the cover of *Nyugat*, of which he was a co-founder and he remained the editor-in-chief even *in contumatiam*. The policy of the ruling classes by which they put the groups of society into their "proper place" was already under way. Let us only mention the *numerus clausus*. The purification of intellectual life was, however, still to be done. "Art is something else, it is the expression of race. The artist writes what is inherent in his character, and race is the common bond of characters. ... Art cannot be state-governed, i.e., expressive of all peoples living in a state. Art belongs to a people. Hungarian art means the Hungarian people. When Ignotus and his circle took up swords for the freedom of art, they wished—and they could not wish for anything else—to offer their own character in Hungarian, i.e., to make Jewish literature in Hungarian."

László Németh insisted that these statements were not anti-Semitic. It is the sensitivity of society and its threshold of response that determine the measure of pronouncements that qualify as anti-Semitic. When Jews can be beaten for being Jews and the offenders remain unpunished, as in inter-war Hungary at the beginning of the regime, this cultural variety of racism does really not qualify as anti-Semitism.

Space does not allow me to discuss here the debates of László Németh with his liberal contemporaries about his scattered remarks about the detrimental influence of Jews on Hungarian literature. Lajos Hatvany, a prominent Jewish writer and scholar protested with indignation: "Németh determined an intellectual ghetto for the Jews."[62]

Hatvany's indignation was not shared by some writers of Jewish origin. Pál Kardos and László Kardos from Debrecen, and later also Aladár Komlós turned against the hard core liberals. Pál Kardos repeated the arguments of Németh saying that Hatvany and his circle were defending against László Németh the monopoly of representing freedom, democracy and humanity.[63]

The debate recalls a frightening *déja vu*, the problem of liberalism as monopoly, the divided reaction of the Jews, and the designation of the Jews as "aliens." We are, however, interested here only in the shift of the threshold of sensitivity as regards anti-Semitism. This shift is the result of an entire period in history and is connected with the spread of populist ideas in the thirties.

The populist movements were not free from anti-Semitic features at all. As István Bibó, a remarkable political thinker (the State Secretary during the short-lived revolution of 1956, and political prisoner during the Kádár-era for almost a decade) has put it, "It should be worth clarifying the reasons for the accusation of anti-Semitism that resulted from the fact that nearly all leading members of the populist movement had made a statement that was very tinged and very specific, far from being anti-humanistic, but deviating from the expectations of both the Jews and philo-Semitic humanism."[64]

The clarification, demanded by Bibó, has not been done up to now. This much can, however, be established that, owing to certain historical reasons, the cultural discrimination against the Jews in Hungary became an established fact, which in civilized Western Europe or Northern America would qualify as anti-Semitism.[65]

The late László Németh is a useful guide to the transformation of today, as if it were his legacy that manages things now. It is not by chance that populism, claiming an official status nowadays, considers him its spiritual father. In the wake of his ideas, the gap between the civil and the cultural rights of the minorities and the various denominations is steadily growing. While the establishment guarantees the equality of civic rights for all citizens of the state, it wishes to maintain its hegemony as far as cultural rights are concerned. Arbitrary dismissals and assignments have created the praetorian guard of officials who serve, with the zeal of vassal, the institutional enforcement of an exaggerated ethnic consciousness.

It is up to you to choose if you are a Hungarian or not, Gyula Illyés said once. His remarks has, however, been often extended by the demand of accepting the "Hungarian fate" or the "tragic" feeling characteristic of Hungarians. As if it were not enough to undertake to be a Hungarian as a gesture of assimilation, full identification is demanded, empathy toward the vital questions of the Hungarian people, something that an alien race is by definition unable to do, as László Németh advocated. Ethnic consciousness, anxious for the race, cannot tolerate the double allegiance of someone's being a Gypsy and a Hungarian at the same time. Within the framework of cultural hegemony, the minorities can live only "restricted to their proper place."

The ideology of ethnic consciousness as a common fate or empathy for the nation was not an invention of László Németh, just like the supposition that the presence of assimilated races poisoned the Christian society. Németh was a man of immense reading. More important than his direct sources is the fact that[47] his work is fitting into the overall criticism of European Enlightenment, advocated from the 1920s by Marxists, Tolstoians, syndicalists, Christian legitimists, and proto-Fascists alike in the wake of the cultural philosophers of the first wave of romanticism, Herder and Friedrich Schlegel. Cultural anti-Semitism goes deeper than the efforts of the circles of *Action Française* in France, or the circle of *Die Tat* in Germany. The anti-Semitism of romanticism, illustrated by an unparalleled writing of the young Hannah Arendt, goes back to the Enlightenment itself.[66]

Roots of Cultural Anti-Semitism

Cultural anti-Semitism has grown into an international trend in the wake of European secularization. Ironically, Voltaire and Diderot condemned the Jews as the people that introduced Christianity and threatened the rule of reason, and one that shelters a religion alien to Europe.[67] Baron D'Holbach, the French *philosophe* proclaimed that "Christianity is nothing but reformed Judaism," and that the Jews are worse than the Christians, because they represent an alien and primitive horde in the heart of Europe.

There are numerous remarks against Jews in the early writings of Diderot who believed the Jews to be barbarians until he met Isaac de Pinto, an outstanding Jewish representative of the Enlightenment. Voltaire's stubborn anti-Jewish attitude remained, however, unshaken even in his debates with Pinto.

While some representatives of Enlightenment sought to open up vistas of assimilation by making the landless Jews—at home everywhere and, consequently, nowhere—Europeans under a new climate, Voltaire and D'Holbach considered the Jewish faith an incurable illness and a deadly peril to mankind.[68] Voltaire saw in the Jews oriental aliens, and the romantic criticism of the Enlightenment gave an ironic turn of this image considering them a nomadic European people. However, the Jews always remained outside the ethnic units accepting them. When the specific character of their language was discovered, the Hebrew came to be considered an oriental vernacular that cannot be adapted to the European way of thinking. This is how the slogan of romanticism came to be formulated by Heine: "A Jew can learn to read in German, to write in German, but he cannot learn to think in German."[69]

Romanticism saw a demon in Jewry, the embodiment cultural well-poisoning. This trend also had its role in the heritage of Europe, and in the search for cultural identity of the European nations. In Charles Maurras's words, the spirit of anti-Semitism set out to conquer the world, and it did not miss Hungary, either.

Hungarian Varieties

László Németh's *Kisebbségben* (In Minority) is not a hastily written pamphlet as the author himself used to call it, but an important and decisive stage in the belated criticism of the Enlightenment liberalism starting with Gyula Szekfű. They both blamed the Hungarian Enlightenment and the Compromise for Trianon—

Szekfű as a pro-Austrian legitimist, and Németh as a leading critic of Austro-Hungarian dualism flirting with populism. *Kisebbségben* is a search for the deepest levels of the national spirit, the innermost identity of the nation, and qualifies everything belonging to rational liberalism as cosmopolitan. It wishes to find a new identity with all its features exclusively characteristic of the Hungarian race.

It must be mentioned, however, that *Kisebbségben* was written in a country threatened by the great powers and for a people decreasing in number. Its train of thought was, however, not motivated exclusively by these factors, since its arguments in a strangely elitist spirit divided the Hungarians into "deep" and "shallow" spirits. Those who qualified for "deep" were marginalized through history, while shallow spirits ruled. Farfetched as these categories may seem to those not initiated into detail of ideological fight in inter-war Hungary, they had an unparalleled influence on younger generations. László Németh has a greater excuse for what he wrote in *Kisebbségben* than those who further his ideas on with minor modifications but still with a significant shifting of accent, on a socially dangerous level. This is the reason why we should return to the so-called Csoóri debate.

The debate had its roots in a few lines of an article by the poet-politician and dealt with matter that was actually extraneous: did the writer really meant it or not, did he hurt people or not, did he have the right to state what he did or not? Csoóri did nothing less than give notice to quit to the tenants who had been thrown out of the common home more than once before. He was even right in saying for the first time that Trianon put an end to the fragile process of assimilation. Csoóri is inclined to shift the responsibility to the historical process on the one hand, and on the "oversensitivity" of the Jews on the other.[13]

Csoóri did not take on this road a single step further than did Dezső Szabó, László Németh, and Géza Féja, populist writers of the inter-war period. Let us only quote Németh's article on Ignotus again: "The tragedy of Ignotus is not that he is not of Hungarian make-up, but that he is carried along by the current of a strong alien race that would produced nine similar characters out of ten children in a mixed marriage."[70]

So Csoóri did not have to go far to find justification for his anxiety about the Hungarian nation being spoilt by mixed marriages with the handful of Jews in the population. It was enough to believe László Németh, the official ideologist and spiritual father of today's populism that such a strong racial current existed.

It is interesting to note that the time when assimilation got out of shape and stopped short, i.e., when the intention of divorce became final, was pushed to an ever later date. Szekfű put it to the time of the Compromise, László Németh to the period of the beginning of the twentieth century, while Csoóri to the Republic of Councils: "Ady's time was probably the last when the problems of the nation, of the Hungarian race could really be grasped by the Jews as real existential and historical problems. They mastered not only the language but also the pain underneath. The Republic of Councils, the Horthy era, and especially the Period of Disaster put an end to spiritual and emotional unity."[71]

Let us now forget what the politician Csoóri thinks of the Jews. The real question is what he thinks of the Hungarians: "There are many people in this country who have had enough of the constant Hungarian jeremiad: Mohács, Nagymajtény, Világos, Trianon and thousands of other calamities. One can be tired of them, but they will always remain part of our insoluble problems."[11]

The key word is "insoluble" in this context. Just like Ady, Csoóri also keeps in view the unfortunate Hungarian fate and the losses the nation had to suffer in the course of its history. But while Ady believed the Hungarians were strong enough to attract millions with all their unfavorable characteristics, the poet of today sees only the weakness of the nation. In his paroxysm of anxiety for the Hungarian race, Csoóri specifies spiritual and existential preconditions for "true Hungarians" that are arbitrary and discriminating.

Csoóri's remark was, however, a revelation in a historical sense, since it shifted Hungarian self-recognition definitely and unequivocally to the sphere of unsolvable phenomena. This time, the politician was the prophet of depression and despair. At the same time, he did not notice that his tragic idea of the nation proves just the opposite of what it has been meant to prove, namely the fact that the Hungarian race can be determined only in terms of a political nation. The urge for modernization and liberalization reveals that the claim of becoming an empire of fifteen million Hungarians, however spiritually defined, had to be given up in the end.

The spiritual transformation of the modern concept of the nation is most probably a historical consequence. There are, however, alternatives that cannot be left out of consideration. Miklós Mészöly reacted, for example, very unfavorably on Csoóri's ideas.[72] He dealt with creating a new kind of national consciousness as early as the early 1980s. He believes that there are two ways of reviving the consciousness of the nation. One of them relies on the particular and the other on the universal aspect. "Long-term solutions can only be attained by methods reckoning with the transformation of the concept of the nation in the direction of becoming universal. ... A small nation can conclude from this that the traditional forms of self-preservation cannot be successful in the future. Its national existence can be assured only in a sublimated form that should not be mistaken for a mere material survival."[73]

One can easily connect the periods of anti-Semitic flare-up to the strengthening of the urge for modernization and liberalization. The contemporaries might think that modernization is accomplished by "aliens." The first step of modernization is, however, the establishment of the equality of the terms of competition. It is the neutrality of the market that enrages those who define themselves as privileged.[74]

However many their motives might have been, the voters at the first free election in Hungary voted for a slow change of regimes. The ruling elite understood the message and its response contained terms inherited from the one-time opponents of modernization, like "Christian morals," "our middle class," etc. Hungary in the early nineties was recreating capitalism with slogans inherited from romantic anti-capitalism, under the conditions of an ambiguous privatization and the political selection of a new middle class.

The background of all this is a latent anti-Semitism in various forms. Hidden anti-Semitism is creating a new version of history in retrospect. Retribution for Holocaust survivors was postponed indefinitely. Government-sources are hinting at a reexamination of the "Jewish Question" in 1999. Legal discriminations is not endangering the largest Jewish community in Europe. The hidden cultural discrimination, however, creates an atmosphere of despair. As there was a protracted struggle for cultural hegemony proliferating stereotypes about the over-representation of Jews in the media etc.

Legal evidence of discrimination is naturally not to be found in any of these cases, since the separation of cultural and political rights, advocated by László Németh, is perfect.

Anti-Semitism—Why and How Much Longer?

Anti-Semitism can be observed today within the context of a struggle for cultural hegemony. As the number of the Jews decreases, there is less rudeness and vulgarity in using abusive language about them, but the cultural aspect hidden in overtones is getting more and more cunning. The confusion of self-definition that assigned the half-hearted believers of modernization, the romantic supporters of Hungarian consciousness with the task of modernization, encouraged the policy of imposing cultural protective tariffs. Proofs for this statement are the cases when the problems were attributed to the uncertain self-consciousness of the other party. Jews are accused of "oversensitivity." As a recent article wittily remarked, the government prescribes to what measure Jews are allowed to fear, because any expression over concerns of their position may unfavorably effect the image of Hungary.[75]

It is a comforting feature of political anti-Semitism that, belonging to the sphere of tactics, it may disappear just as it appeared. Anti-Semitism is a concomitant of a crisis and not the crisis itself. It can be stopped or turned round by a comprehensive reform of the legal system, as the American struggle against racism and the success of the civil-rights movements there have proved. The suppression of racism can be, at the same time, the victory of social rationalism. Some dangerous ideologies in Eastern Europe serve their nations' interests only in their rhetoric. The truth is that the elite of the nations—though not without exceptions—sacrifice the interests of the peoples in their struggle to fill the vacuum of the post-Communist period.

The rational concept of representing national interests favors the suppression of political and cultural anti-Semitism under the current conditions of international politics. Such a turn would not be without precedents. It took place, for example, in the birthplace of cultural nationalism, in nineteenth-century France. The case of Captain Dreyfus, condemned on the strength of false accusations, threatened France with the boycott of the world exhibition to be staged at the turn of the century. When the new parliament came to power, it voted for the presidential reprieve for Dreyfus by a two-thirds majority.

At the same time, the compromise of the various interest groups of society put an end to the influence of the Catholic Church in public life, reformed the system of military intelligence, and the police. The French academy refused to grant membership to those otherwise outstanding poets and critics who had compromised themselves with giving voice by anti-Semitic views.

Notes

1. Oszkár Jászi, *Magyar Kálvária—magyar föltámadás* [Hungarian Calvary—Hungarian Resurrection], Reprint Magyar Hírlap könyvek, 1989 ed., (Bécs, 1920).
2. Cf. Béla K. Király, and László Veszprémy, *Trianon and East Central Europe : Antecedents and Repercussions*. War and Society in East Central Europe, vol. 32, (Boulder, Colo., Highland Lakes, N.J., New York: Social Science Monographs; Atlantic Research and Publications, distributed by Columbia University Press, 1995).
3. Deborah Lipstadt, "Anti-Semitism in Eastern Europe Rears its Ugly Head Again," in *USA Today* (Magazine), (1993), p. 50.
4. Robert Pearson, "Back to the Future or Forward to the Past (Viewpoints on the Political and Economic Future of Eastern Europe)," *History Today*, vol. 41, (January, 1991): p. 10-13.
5. György Varga-Domokos, "Kisebbség és zsarnokság" [Minority and Tyranny], *Népszabadság*, (April 29, 1990).
6. Judith Pataki, "István Csurka's Tract: Summary and Reactions," in *RFE-RL Research Report,* (1992), p. 15.
7. On I. Csurka see: Anna Husarska, His Kampf, in *New Republic*, (1992), p. 10.
8. Adam Michnik, "A kommunizmus utáni Európa avagy: bajok a demokrácia körül" [Europe After the Fall of Communism or Troubles around Democracy], *Beszélő*, (September 29, 1990).
9. János Zsolnay, "The Role of Press in Contemporary Anti-Semitism in Hungary," in *Anti-Semitism in Post-Totalitarian Europe*, (Prague: Franz Kafka Publishers, 1993), p. 281.
10. Yehuda Bauer, "On the Applicability of Definitions—Anti-Semitism in Present-Day Europe," in *Anti-Semitism in Post-Totalitarian Europe*, (Prague: Franz Kafka Publishers,1993), p. 57.
11. Sándor Csoóri, "Nappali hold" [Daylight Moon], *Hitel*, (September 5, 1990).
12. Béla Bodor, "Túl a mélyponton" [The Worst is over], *Élet és Irodalom*, (December 14, 1990): p. 8.
13. A detailed analysis: Ervin C. Brody, "Literature and Politics in Today's Hungary : Sándor Csoóri in the Populist-Urbanite Debate," *Literary Review*, vol. 38, no. 3 (Spring), (1995): pp. 426-449.

14. Péter Hanák, "Hagyomány és jövőkép" [Tradition and the Vision of Future], *Népszabadság*, (September 29, 1990).
15. György Spiró, "Különvélemény" [A Dissenting Opinion], *Népszabadság*, (October 21, 1990).
16. István Benedek, "Nemzetiség és kisebbség" [Nationality and Minority], *Hitel*, (September, 1990): p. 18.
17. Ferenc Kubinyi, "Bűnös nemzet—fasiszta nép?" [Sinful Nation—Fascist People?], *Kapu*, nos. 7-8, (1990).
18. László Németh, "Szárszói beszéd, 1943" [Lecture at Szárszó], in *Szárszó—Az 1943. évi balatonszárszói Magyar Élet-Tábor előadás- és megbeszéléssorozata* [The 1943 Balatonszárszó *Magyar Élet* Camp Lecture and Discussion Series] (Budapest: Magyar Élet, 1943).
19. János Pelle, "Rákosi Mátyás a zsidóságról és a cionizmusról" [Mátyás Rákosi on Hungarian Jews and Zionism], (Az MDP KB 1953. február 19-i ülésén tartott beszámolójából részletek), *Szombat*, no. 6, (1990).
20. László Lengyel, "Megjegyzés" [Note], *Századvég*, no. 2, (1990).
21. Gusztáv Lányi, "Rákosi Mátyás politikai antiszemitizmusa—Pszichohistóriai és történelmi szociálpszichológiai elemzés" [The Anti-Semitism of Mátyás Rákosi—Psycho-Historical and Social-Pycholigical Analysis), *Világosság*, vol. XXXV, no. 10, (1994): pp. 21-48.
22. Béla Fábián, "Rákosiék zsidóüldözése" [The Persecution of Jews under Rákosi], *Kommentár*, no. 5, (1992): pp. 45-49.
23. Charles Gáti, "Kommunisták és a zsidókérdés" [The Communists and the Jews], *Szombat*, no. 8, (1990).
24. Ferenc A. Szabó, "A zsidó származású lakosság helyzete a felszabadulás után" [The Condition of the Jewish Population after the Liberation], *Valóság*, no. 11, (1988).
25. András Lányi, "A zsidó áfium ellen való orvosság" [Antidote against the Jewish Opium], *Hitel*, no. 22, (1990).
26. Ákos Kertész, "Hagyjuk már abba!—Nyílt levél Csoóri Sándornak" [Stop it at Last!—Open Letter to Sándor Csoóri], *Magyar Nemzet*, (September 29, 1990).
27. Sándor Csoóri, *A mélypont. Válasz Kertész Ákos nyílt levelére* [Nadir. Reply to the Open Letter of Ákos Kertész] (October 6, 1990).
28. András Kovács, "Az asszimilációs dilemma" [The Dilemma of Assimilation], *Világosság*, nos. 8-9, (1988): p. 608.

29. Peter Gay, *Freud, Jews, and other Germans : Masters and Victims in Modernist Culture*, (New York: Oxford University Press, 1978), p. 289.
30. Jerry V. Diller, *Freud's Jewish Identity : a Case Study in the Impact of Ethnicity*, Sara F. Yoseloff memorial publications in Judaism and Jewish affairs, (Rutherford, NJ-London: Fairleigh Dickinson University Press, Associated University Presses, 1991).
31. Péter Esterházy, "Kedves Hitel-olvasó!" [Dear Readers of Hitel], *Hitel*, 1990.
32. Gyula Hegyi, "Stílus" [On Style], *Magyar Hírlap*, (October 6, 1990): p. 23.
33. Károly Vígh, "Balsikerű 'transzponáció'" [An Unsuccesful Transposition], *Élet és Irodalom*, (December, 1990): p. 24.
34. Ferenc Fejtő, "Néhány megjegyzés a pesti vitákhoz" [Some Remarks on the Debates in Budapest], *Népszabadság*, no. 8868, (September 26, 1990): p. 25.
35. Rudolf Ungváry, "Nem zsidónak lenni" [Not to be a Jew], *Múlt és Jövő*, no. 1, (1989).
36. Paul Hockenos, *Free to Hate : the Rise of the Right in Post-Communist Eastern Europe*, (New York: Routledge, 1993), p. 332.
37. Jason McDonald, "Transition to Utopia: a Reinterpretation of Economics, Ideas and Politics in Hungary, 1984 to 1990," in *East European Politics and Societies*, (1993), p. 203.
38. Koos Andre Postma, *Changing Prejudice in Hungary : a Study on the Collapse of State Socialism and its Impact on Prejudice against Gypsies and Jews*, (Amsterdam: Thesis Publishers, 1996), p. 200.
39. John Bierman, "New Openness, Old Hatred: Anti-Semitism Stalks Eastern Europe," in *Maclean's*, (1990), p. 26.
40. Ervin Gyertyán, "Hétköznapi antiszemitizmus" [Everday Anti-Semitism], *Élet és Irodalom*, (June 10, 1988).
41. V. Bunce, and M. Csanadi, "Uncertainty in the Transition—Post-Communism in Hungary," *East European Politics and Societies*, vol. 7, no. 2, (1993): p. 240-275.
42. Mihály Vajda, "Ki a zsidó Közép-Európában (Szekfű Gyula *Három nemzedéke* kapcsán)" [Who is a Jew in Central-Europe—Remarks on Gyula Szekfű's *Three Generations*], *Világosság*, nos. 8/9, (1989): pp. 648-656.
43. William O. McCagg Jr., "Jewish Conversion in Hungary in Modern Times," in *Jewish Apostasy in the Modern World*, T.M. Endelman,

ed., (New York/London: Holmes and Meier, 1987), pp. 142-165.

44. András Polgi, "Aczél György és a zsidóság" [György Aczél and the Jews], *Szombat*, no. 6, (1990): pp. 13-14.
45. "Aczél György és a zsidóság" [György Aczél and the Jews], (Az izraeli Al Hamishar 1989. évi cikke nyomán), *Szombat*, no. 6, (1990), p. 30.
46. Sander L. Gilman, *Jewish Self-Hatred : Anti-Semitism and the Hidden Language of the Jews*, (Baltimore: Johns Hopkins University Press, 1986), p. 461.
47. Hannah Arendt, *The Jew as Pariah:—Jewish Identity and Politics in the Modern Age*, ed. and intr. Ron H. Feldman, (New York: Grove Press, 1978).
48. Max Horkheimer, and Theodor W. Adorno, *Dialectic of Enlightenment*, (New York, 1995).
49. Michael Riff, *The Face of Survival: Jewish Life in Eastern Europe Past and Present*, (Vallentine Mitchell, 1992).
50. Béla K. Király, Peter Pastor, and Ivan Sanders, *Essays on World War I : Total War and Peacemaking, a Case Study on Trianon*, East European Monographs, no. 105, (New York: Social Science Monographs Brooklyn College Pres, distributed by Columbia University Press, 1982).
51. István Csurka, "Helyszíni közvetítés" [Report on Location], *Magyar Fórum*, (March, 1, 1991): p. 35.
52. Steven B.Vardy, "The Impact of Trianon: Hungary and the Hungarian Mind: The Nature of Inter-war Irredentism," *Hungarian Studies Review*, vol. 10, nos. 1/2, (1983): pp. 21-42.
53. Ezra Mendelsohn, "Trianon Hungary, Jews and Politics," in *Hostages of Modernization*, H.A. Strauss, ed., (Berlin-New York: de Gruyter, 1993), pp. 893-916.
54. Kuno Klebelsberg, *Ungarische Kulturpolitik nach dem Kriege.* Ungarische bibliothek ... ; 2. reihe 5, (Berlin, Leipzig: W. de Gruyter, 1925).
55. Jacob Katz, "The Identity of Post Emancipatory Jewry," in *A Social and Economic History of Central European Jewry*, Jehuda Don-Victor Karády, eds., (New Brunswick, 1990), pp. 13-33.
56. Andrew Handler, *An Early Blueprint for Zionism: Győző Istóczy's Anti-Semitism*, East European Monographs, vol. 261, (New York: Columbia University Press, 1989).
57. Endre Ady, "A zsidókról" [The Jews], *Vasárnapi Újság*, (September 27, 1908): p. 39.

58. Gyula Szekfű, *Három nemzedék és ami utána következik (1920)* [Three Generations and the Follow-up], (Budapest, 1935), pp. 335, 336, 360.
59. László Németh, "Magyarság és Európa" [The Hungarians and Europe] in *Sorskérdések.* 1989: Budapest. p. 308.
60. *Ibid.*
61. László Németh, "Ignotus" [On Ignotus], in *Készülődés. A tanú előtt*, (Budapest: Magyar Élet, 1941), pp. 354-355.
62. Lajos Hatvany, "Nyílt levél Németh Lászlóhoz" [Open Letter to László Németh], *Századunk*, no. 4, (May-June, 1934): pp. 179-182.
63. Pál Kardos, "Zsidó válasz" [The Jewish Response], *Válasz*, no. 2, (July, 1934): pp. 153-157.
64. István Bibó, "Levél Borbándi Gyulához" [Letter to Gyula Borbándi], in *Válogatott tanulmányok*, (Budapest: Magvető, 1986).
65. Ferenc Fehér, "István Bibó and the Jewish Question in Hungary: Notes on the Margin of a Classical Essay," *New German Critique*, no. 21, (Fall 1980): pp. 3-46.
66. Hannah Arendt, *Rahel Varnhagen: The Life of a Jewish Woman*, (New York: Harcourt, Brace, Jovanovich, 1974).
67. Paul A. Meyer, "The Attitude of Enlightenment toward the Jews," in *Studies on Voltaire and the Eighteenth Century*, (1963), pp. 1161-1205.
68. Marie Arouet Voltaire, *Oeuvres Complétes*, Garnier ed., ed., Louis Moland, vol. 28, (1887-95), pp. 439-440.
69. Richard Popkin, "Medicine, Racism, Antisemitism," in *The Languages of Psyche: Mind and Body in Enlightenment Thought*, Rousseau George S, ed., (Berkeley: University of California Press, 1990), p. 439.
70. In Ignotus *op. cit.*
71. István Deák, "The Danger of Anti-Semitism in Hungary," in *The Danger of Anti-Semitism in Central and Eastern Europe in the Wake of 1989-1990*, Yehuda Bauer, ed., (Jerusalem: The Vidal Sassoon International Center for the Study of Antisemitism, 1991), pp. 53-61.
72. Miklós Mészöly, "...Ott én nem vagyok otthon" [There I am not at Home], *Magyar Nemzet*, (September 29, 1990).
73. Miklós Mészöly, "Tudat és nemzettudat" [Conscience and National Conscience], *Valóság*, no. 7, (1982).
74. Tibor Tucker, "Political Transition and the 'Jewish Question' in Hungary," *Ethnic and Racial Studies*, vol. 19, no. 2, (April, 1996): pp. 290-316.

75. Miklós Szabó, "A fogadott prókátor üzeni: a zsidók ne merjenek félni" [The Hired Advocate's Message: Jews don't Dare to Fear], *Magyar Hírlap*, (September 1, 1999).

Biographies of Key Personalities

Aczél, György (1917-1991)
Politician, the leader of the Kádár regime's cultural and educational policy. Deputy Prime Minister between 1974-1982.

Ady, Endre (1877-1919)
Poet, journalist. Revolutionized modern Hungarian poetry in a symbolist vein. As noted radical in politics advocated Hungarian-Jewish symbiosis. Leading contributor to the periodical *Nyugat*.

Andrássy, Gyula, Count (1860-1929)
Minister of Foreign Affairs of the Austro-Hungarian Monarchy, 1918; Minister of the Royal Household, 1894-95; Minister of Interior, 1906-1910. After 1918 a monarchist politician in Hungary.

Apponyi, Albert, Count (1846-1933)
Hungarian politician and statesman. Minister of Education, 1906-1910, 1917-1918. Chairman of the Hungarian peace delegation, 1919-1920. Head of Hungarian delegation to the League of Nations, 1925-1933.

Arany, János (1817-1882)
Hungarian epic poet, author of the popular epic *Toldi*. Elevated his native language to represent the national literature of quality. In 1848 he participated in the revolution against Austria. He became secretary-general of the Hungarian Academy of Sciences in 1870.

Babits, Mihály (1883-1941)
Writer, literary historian, editor, literary translator. Outstanding member of the important Hungarian literary gen-

eration forming a group around the periodical *Nyugat*, and one of its editors.

Bajcsy-Zsilinszky, Endre (1886-1944)

Hungarian politician, Parliamentary Representative, journalist. Started as a right-wing politician, participated in extreme racist organizations, later joined the anti-Nazi democratic opposition, became a leader of the antifascist resistance, executed by the Government of the fascist Arrow-Cross in Sopronkőhida.

Balázs, Béla (1884-1949)

Playwright poet, *The Carved Prince* (1912) and *Bluebeard's Castle* (1912) served as librettos to Béla Bartók's music.

Bangha, Béla (1880-1940)

Jesuit priest, church speaker and writer. Participated in the foundation of the *Actio Catholica.*

Bartók, Béla (1881-1945)

Composer, pianist, ethnomusicologist, combining modernism and folk inspiration in his orchestral pieces and operas. Opposing Nazism he immigrated to the United States in 1940 where he was elected honorary doctor of Columbia University.

Bartucz, Lajos (1885-1966)

Anthropologist. His work *Racial Question—Racial Research* appeared in 1940.

Benedek, István (1915-1998)

Professor of psychiatry, writer, journalist raising again the "Jewish question" in the early nineties.

Benedek, Marcell (1885-1969)

Writer, literary historian, literary translator, son of the folk-tale collector Elek Benedek. He described the lonely and tragic heroes following the spirit of humanity in the modern society with sympathy. He wanted to help in bringing up readers in deeper understanding literature. Freemason provincial.

Bethlen, István, Count (1874-1946)

Member of the Hungarian Peace delegation, 1920; Prime Minister of Hungary, 1921-1931; Minister of Finance, 1921; Minister of Justice, 1924, 1929; Minister of Foreign Affairs, 1924; Minister of Agriculture, 1924.

Bibó, István (1911-1979)

Politician, historian. Member of the National Peasant Party. From 1946 lectured mainly on constitutional matters and public administration. In 1950 was removed from the university; became librarian. In 1956 became minister in the Imre Nagy government. After the suppression of the 1956 Revolution arrested and sentenced to life imprisonment. In 1963 pardoned. Continued to work as librarian. His essay on *The Jewish Question in Hungary* (1947) is considered a major historical and political contribution to the post-holocaust evaluation of the Hungarian-Jewish symbiosis.

Bíró, Lajos (1880-1948)

Writer, journalist. Under-secretary of state of the Ministry of Foreign Affairs at the time of the Károlyi government. Emigrated in 1919. Later wrote screenplays as well.

Blau, Lajos (1861-1936)

Bible- and Talmudic scholar, literary and cultural historian. Editor of the *Magyar Zsidó Szemle* between 1891-1930.

Bodor, Béla (1954)

Poet, writer, critic. Member of the editorial staff of the *Élet és Irodalom* since 1991.

Braun, Róbert (1879-1937)

Sociologist, librarian. His writings were the forerunners of the works of the rural sociologists.

Bródy, Sándor (1863-1924)

Novelist, playwright, journalist, an early representative of the naturalistic style. He openly identified himself as a Jewish-Hungarian author.

Chorin, Ferenc (?-1925)

Member of the Upper House in the Hungarian legislation. Member of the committee of the royal bank of issue in 1921.

Csiky, Gergely (1842-1891)

Writer, literary translator, dramatist.

Csokonai Vitéz, Mihály (1773-1805)

Poet, playwright, literary translator. Hungarian representative of Rococo style and the philosophy of the Enlightenment in his poetry.

Csoóri, Sándor (1930)

Poet, writer. One of the founders, later member of the presidency of the Hungarian Democratic Forum (MDF). President of the Hungarians' World Federation since 1990.

Csurka, István (1934)

Writer, right-radical politician. One of the initiators of the MDF. Member of the Presidium of the MDF. In 1993 expelled from the MDF (1988-93). Founder of the radical right-wing movement called Hungarian Road, from 1993 founder and leader of the Hungarian Life and Justice Party (MIÉP). MP (1990-94, 1998). Editor of the right-wing weekly magazine: *Magyar Fórum* since 1989.

Darányi, Kálmán (1886-1939)

Prime Minister of Hungary, 1936-1938; Minister of Agriculture, 1935-38; Minister of Interior, 1937.

Déry, Tibor (1894-1977)

Writer. Was born in an upper middle-class family. Joined the Communists' Party in Hungary in 1919. Emigrated in 1920, then after several journeys abroad returned home. His novels, short stories written after 1950 deviated from the requirements of the official socialist ideology. Member of the Revolutionary Committee of the Writers' Association in 1956. Sentenced to prison in 1957, got amnesty after three years because of the pressure of the international literary community.

Dohm, Christian Wilhelm von (1751-1820)
German scholar in constitutional law, befriended Moses Mendelssohn, served in the Prussian Government, author of the paper *Concerning the Amelioration of the Civil Status of the Jews* (Berlin, 1781).

Eckhardt, Tibor (1888-1917)
Hungarian politician, Parliamentary Representative, one of the founders and the leader of the extreme right-wing Association of Awakening Hungarians, Deputy President of the Hungarian Revisionist League in 1930, joined the independent Smallholders' Party, became its president (1932-1940), traveled to the USA as a government emissary to establish connections with the Anglo-Saxon powers to counter-balance German orientation, he did not return to Hungary.

Eötvös, József (1813-1871)
Minister of religious affairs and education (1848) and minister of religion and education (1867-1871). Among the first nineteenth century realist novelists in Hungary. Emigrated during the autumn of 1848. From 1861 once again member of Parliament, supporter of the Compromise. As minister of culture introduced universal and mandatory education; enshrined in law the religious emancipation of the Jews.

Eötvös, Károly (1842-1916)
Independent politician. Law graduate. In 1863 participated in a conspiracy against the Habsburgs and as a result was sentenced to imprisonment. Supported the Compromise. In 1872 governing party MP and an effective orator in Parliament. From 1877 professed opposition views. In 1883 undertook the defense of Jews accused of ritual murder in the politically motivated Tiszaeszlár court case and won.

Esterházy, Péter (1950)
Writer. The most important representative of the Hungarian post-modern with his novels. Member of the Széchényi Literary and Art Academy since 1993.

Falk, Miksa (1828-1908)
Publicist, political writer. Lived in Vienna between 1847-1867. The editor-in-chief of the *Pester Lloyd* in 1867.

Farkas, Gyula (1894-1958)
Literary historian, linguist. Leader of the Finno-Ugric seminary of the Göttingen University as a German citizen since 1947.

Fehér, Ferenc (1933-1994)
Philosopher, esthete, critic. Member of the Budapest school of philosophy following György Lukács. Went into exile after signing protest against the Soviet occupation of Czechoslovakia. Taught in Australia and the U. S.

Fejtő, Ferenc (1909)
Writer, critic, editor, publicist. Emigrated to Paris in the 1930s where he was the leader of the Hungarian press office. Director of the Soviet and East European seminar of the *Institut d'Ètudes Politiques* between 1972-1982.

Féja, Géza (1900-1978)
Writer, journalist, editor. Belonged to the inner circle of Endre Bajcsy-Zsilinszky until 1933. Member of the movement of "populist writers." Joined the March Front in 1937. He was discharged from his position as a teacher because of his sociography titled *Viharsarok* [Stormy Corner].

Fenyő, Miksa (1877-1972)
Critic, editor. Director of the National Association of the Factory Owners between 1917-1938. Emigrated in 1948. One of the founders and the editors of the periodical *Nyugat*.

Franz (Francis) Joseph I (1830-1916)
Emperor of Austria (1848-1916) and King of Hungary (1867-1916). Crushed the Hungarian Revolution of 1848, agreed to the *Ausgleich* (Compromise) in 1867, architect of the Austro-Hungarian Dual Monarchy, a strained coexistence of the two countries. From 1879 in alliance with Prussian-led Germany. His ultimatum to Serbia in 1914 led to World War I.

Frantz, Constantin (1817-1851)
German politician and publicist.

Freytag, Gustav (1816-1895)
German novelist and dramatist. The representative of the national liberalism of the aspiring bourgeoisie.

Frobenius, Leo (1873-1938)
German ethnologist, explorer, authority on prehistoric art, early representative of historical ethnology.

Fülep, Lajos (1885-1970)
Philosopher, art historian, influential on the ideology of the "populist writers."

Füst, Milán (1888-1967)
Poet, novelist, playwright, author of the novel *History of My Wife* translated into French and English. His esoteric poetry influenced generations of younger poets between the two world wars.

Gárdonyi, Géza (1863-1922)
Writer, editor. Author of novels on Hungarian history. Member of the Hungarian Academy of Sciences since 1910. His most important works: *Egri csillagok* [The Stars of Eger] (1901), A *láthatatlan ember* [The Invisible Man] (1902), *Az öreg tekintetes* [The Old Honorable Man] (1902), *Isten rabjai* [The Slaves of God] (1908).

Geiger, Abraham (1810-1874)
Rabbinic scholar, chief rabbi of Breslau, founding editor of the *Scientific Journal of Jewish Theology.*

Gellért, Oszkár (1882-1967)
Poet, journalist, editor. Co-editor of the periodical *Nyugat.*

Gobineau, Joseph-Arthur, comte de (1816-1882)
French diplomat, writer, social thinker, whose theory of racial determinism influenced programs of discrimination in the twentieth century. His main work, the *Dissertation on the Inequality of the Human Races* propagates the superiority of the Aryah race.

Gombos, Gyula (1913)
Writer, journalist, literary historian. Participated in the movement against the Nazis. Emigrated in 1948.

Gömbös, Gyula (1886-1936)
Hungarian politician of extreme right. Prime Minister, 1932-1936; Minister of Defense, 1929-1936. His reactionary and anti-Semitic views paved the way for alliance with Nazi Germany.

Gratz, Gusztáv (1875-1946)
Royalist politician, historian. Editor of the review *Huszadik Század*, 1899-1903. Minister of Foreign Affairs in 1921.

Grègoire, Henri-Baptiste, Abbot (1750-1831)
Jesuit priest, delegate to the French National Assembly, author of the pamphlet *Are there possibilities of Making the Jews more useful and happier in France?*

Hanák, Péter (1921-1998)
Historian. Authority on the Austro-Hungarian Monarchy, edited a book on the *Jewish Question in Hungary*.

Hatvany, Lajos, Baron (1880-1971)
Journalist, historian of literature, novelist. Son of a prominent Jewish-Hungarian magnate, founder of the review *Nyugat*. Participated in the 1918 revolution, exiled twice from Hungary. Returned to Budapest in 1947.

Hazai, Samu, Baron (1851-1942)
Hungarian Minister of Defense of Jewish origin in 1910-1917.

Heckenast, Gusztáv (1811-1878)
Bookseller, publisher. The *National Song* and the *Twelve Points* were printed in his printing house on March 15, 1848.

Hegyi, Gyula (1951)
Poet, journalist. Member of the presidium of the Hungarian organization of the Amnesty International since 1989. The spokesman of the Democratic Charta in 1991.

Heltai, Jenő (1871-1957)
Poet, novelist, journalist. Co-editor of the review *A Hét*, he

was a master of light verse and romantic comedies. President of the Hungarian PEN Club in 1945.

Herzl, Theodor (1860-1904)

Born in Hungary, moved with his family to Vienna. He became the editor of the *Neue Freie Presse*. Reporting on the Dreyfus-trial from Paris he became the advocate of a new Jewish homeland in Palestine. Founding father of modern political Zionist movement.

Horkheimer, Max (1895-1973)

German philosopher and sociologist. Leading theoretician of the Frankfurt School. Left Germany with his co-author Th. W. Adorno into U. S. exile.

Horthy, Miklós (1868-1957)

Naval commander in the First World War, admiral, Regent of Hungary, 1920-1944. His "crusade against Bolshevism" led to Hungary's participation on the Axis side. In 1944 October he first proclaimed to end the war, then yield power. By forced abdication and abduction prisoner of the Germans. Released by the Allied forces, he was allowed to go to Portugal. His memoirs, *Confidential Papers of Miklós Horthy* were published in 1965.

Horváth, János (1878-1961)

Literary historian. Founder of the Hungarian Literary Historic Society.

Ignotus (Veigelsberg), Hugó (1869-1949)

Journalist, poet, political commentator. Wrote under the simple pen-name "Ignotus" [the unknown]. First-generation of assimilated Jewish-Hungarian writers, founding editor of the review *Nyugat*, famous for his clashes with the conservative establishment. Exiled in the twenties, he returned to Hungary in 1948. Father of Pál Ignotus.

Ignotus, Pál (1901-1978)

Journalist, leading advocate of anti-Fascism in the so-called "urbanite" literary circle. Founding editor of the review *Szép*

Szó together with Attila József, the outstanding poet of the mid-war years in Hungary. Returned from exile in Britain to Hungary, he was arrested on trumped-up charges. Released in the early fifties, he fled Hungary after the 1956 Revolution, settled in London, worked for the BBC, published a noted book on *Hungarian History* in English.

Illyés, Gyula (1902-1983)

Poet and writer. Student during the time of the 1918-1919 revolutions. In 1920 emigrated to Austria, then to France. Lived in Paris until 1926, studied at Sorbonne. Prominent representative of the so-called *népi* or populist, as opposed to the urbanite or cosmopolitan trend in literary and academic circles. After 1945 Peasant Party MP.

Istóczy, Győző (1842-1915)

Politician. Law graduate. In 1872 became a Member of Parliament as a Deák supporter. In 1875 became a member of the Liberal Party. Founder of the Anti-Semitic Party. Sued for writings inciting racial hatred.

Jászi, Oszkár (1875-1957)

Sociologist, political writer, Minister of Nationalities in the Károlyi government. Head of the Council of Foreign Affairs, 1919. Left Hungary in May 1919, lived abroad (USA) until his death.

Joó, Tibor (1901-1945)

Philosopher, publicist, librarian.

Jósika, Miklós, Baron (1794-1865)

Writer. Novelist of popular historical fiction. Emigrated in 1849.

Kardos, László (1898-1987)

Literary historian, critic, translator. Chairman of the Department of World Literature at the Loránd Eötvös University since 1950.

Kardos, Pál (1900-1971)

Literary historian, translator. Associate Professor since 1947 then Chairman of the Debrecen University.

Kádár, János (1912–1989)

Hungarian communist party functionary. Participated in the resistance against Nazi rule. Minister of the Interior (1948-1950), imprisoned on trumped-up charges (1950-1954). First Secretary of the Hungarian Socialist Worker's Party during the 1956 Revolution, Secretary of State in the Imre Nagy Government. With Russian help formed a proxy-government against the legitimate Imre Nagy cabinet, and became Premier of Hungary (1956-58, 1961-65). First Secretary of the Hungarian Socialist Workers' Party (1956-1988), President of the Party (1988-1989).

Kertész, Ákos (1932)

Writer, novelist.

Keszi, Imre (1910-1974)

Writer, critic, scholar of musicology, literary translator. Author of the novel *Elysium.*

Kiss, József (1843-1921)

Poet, editor. Called the first assimilated Jewish poet of rank, wrote on Hungarian folk-heroes and novels in verse about his Jewish ancestry. Founding editor of the modernist review *A Hét.*

Klebelsberg, Kunó, Count (1875-1932)

Minister of Religion and Public Education, 1922-1931. Established Hungarian study centers (*Collegium Hungaricums*) in Europe.

Kóbor, Tamás (1867-1942)

Writer, journalist. Started his literary work in his father-in-law's, József Kiss' journal, *A Hét*. Described the life of the Budapest Jewry.

Kodály, Zoltán (1882-1967)
Composer, ethomusicologist, teacher of music. His pedagogical method is used in teaching of music all over the world.

Kohner, Adolf, Baron (1865-?)
Big landowner, President of the Hungarian National Fine Arts Association, the National Jewish Bureau, the National Hungarian Jewish Community; member of the board of the Francis Joseph Rabbinical Seminar.

Komlós, Aladár (1892-1980)
Writer, critic. Essayist of the periodical *Nyugat*. After the anti-Jewish laws he edited the yearbook *Ararát* publishing writers of Jewish origin who could not otherwise print their works. Deported to Bergen-Belsen at the end of World War II, in 1945 he returned to Budapest. His main work is a two volume history of Jewish-Hungarian literature.

Komor, András (1898-1944)
Novelist. His books were appreciated as realistic reflections of the Jewish middle-class in Hungary. Drafted to forced labor he committed suicide.

Kornfeld, Móric, Baron (1882-?)
Industrialist. Member of the Upper House of the Hungarian legislation since 1927.

Kossuth, Lajos (1802-1894)
Hungarian journalist, beacon of the Hungarian Enlightenment called "Reform-movement," staunch opponent of Austrian rule, advocate of independent Hungary, leader of the War of Independence of 1848. Finance Minister of the Batthyány Government (1848); President of the Hungarian Defense Committee, Governing President of Hungary (April 14, 1849). After the defeat of the War of Hungarian Independence he lived in exile.

Kovács, Alajos (1877-1963)
Statistician, contributed to the preparation of the so-called Vienna decree that gave back parts of Transylvania to

Hungary. His notorious work *The Spatial Occupation of Hungary by the Jews* appeared in 1922.

Kozma, Andor (1861-1933)

Poet, publicist. MP between 1910-1918, follower of István Tisza. In his satires he criticized social injustice, gentry idleness, anti-Semitic attitudes.

Kun, Béla (1886-1939)

Leader of the Hungarian Soviet Republic, 1919; Commissar of Foreign Affairs, Commissar of War, 1919.

Kuthy, Lajos (1813-1864)

Novelist. He was arrested by Austrian authorities between 1835 and 1837. Secretary of the first Hungarian Prime Minister, Lajos Batthyány. After a period of hiding he gave himself up to authorities. As a popular novelist he stereotyped with venom Jewish characters.

Lackó, Miklós (1921)

Historian. Speciality: intellectual movements of the mid-war years in Hungary.

Landerer, Lajos (1800-1854)

Printer. Entered into partnership with Gusztáv Heckenast in 1840. In 1848 he installed a banknote printery at Lajos Kossuth's request for printing the currency of independent Hungary, the Kossuth-bills. Went in exile, 1849.

Lendvai, István (1888-1945)

Journalist. Leading publicist of the extreme right in the twenties, propagator of racism, he opposed German influence. Arrested in 1944, he perished in captivity.

Lengyel, László (1950)

Economist, political scientist.

Lesznai, Anna (1885-1966)

Poet, novelist. Participated in early feminist movements. Emigrated twice, first to Vienna, then, during the World War II to the United States. Her novel *In the Beginning was the Garden* is a major work on Jewish assimilation.

Lőw, Immanuel (1854-1944)
Chief Rabbi of Szeged. Botanist, member of the Upper House of the Hungarian Parliament. His main work *Die Flora der Juden*, 1926-34.

Macaulay, Thomas Babbington (1800-1859)
English historian, essayist, poet, politician. His famous speeches had important role in the passage of the reform bills of 1831.

Maimonides, Moses (1138-1204)
Philosopher and medical writer. Doctor of Sultan Saladin.

Maurras, Charles (1868-1952)
French writer, journalist, politician. His "integral nationalism" anticipated the ideas of fascism.

Méhely, Lajos (1862-1953)
Zoologist, notorious for racist theories. Editor of *A Cél* [The Target].

Mészöly, Miklós (1921)
Writer. The founding president of the Széchényi Literary and Art Academy in 1992.

Mezei, Ernő (1851-1932)
Journalist. One of the leaders of the Jewish Community in Hungary. MP since 1881.

Mezei, Mór, (1836-1925)
Lawyer, editor of the *Magyar Izraelita* [Hungarian Izraelite] from 1862.

Mikszáth, Kálmán (1847-1910)
Novelist, journalist, Member of Parliament. Reported on the Blood-libel trial of Tiszaeszlár in 1882. Author of political sketches. Worked for liberal newspapers. His novels enjoyed great popularity in his time.

Móricz, Zsigmond (1879-1942)
Writer, editor, novelist. Leading member of the literary generation forming a group around the periodical *Nyugat*, and one of its editors.

Munkácsy, Mihály (1844-1900)
Painter, memoir-writer. Settled in Paris in 1872.

Nagy, Ignác (1810-1854)
Writer, dramatist. Chamber clerk since 1831, lost his office in 1848. Founder of the journal *Hölgyfutár*.

Négyesy, László (1861-1933)
Literary historian, esthete, linguist. Outstanding teacher of the literary generation of *Nyugat*.

Németh, László (1901-1975)
Writer, essayist, literary translator. Leading theoretician of his generation, a polymath in several languages. Advocated the group of populist-writers and the New Intellectual Front, was silenced in the 1950s. In 1958 he was awarded the Kossuth-price.

Nordau, Max (1849-1923)
Writer, physician. Hungarian by birth, wrote in German. Co-president of the Zionist Congress. Had important role in acceptance of the idea that Palestine should be the homeland of Jews.

Osvát, Ernő (1876-1929)
Editor, critic, writer. Established and edited the *Nyugat* since 1908.

Pap, Károly (1897-1945)
Novelist, short-story writer. Descendent of a family of rabbies. Joined the Red Army, was arrested in 1919. After a short emigration contributor of *Nyugat*. Inmate of forced labor camp in 1943, was taken to Buchenwald a concentration-camp and perished.

Patai, József (1882-1953)
Poet, writer, literary translator. Pursued Hebrew theological studies, emigrated to Palestine in 1940.

Pethő, Sándor (1885-1940)
Publicist, editor, historian. He took over the editorship of the

daily paper *Magyar Nemzet* in 1938, offered his columns to anti-Nazi views.

Petőfi, Sándor (1823-1849)

Poet. Published his first volume of poems in 1844. Leader of the so-called March Youth in 1848. Author of the hymn of the 1848 Revolution, the *National Song*. His radicalism prevented his election as a delegate for the Diet. Training officer as captain in the Hungarian army. Disappeared in the battle of Segesvár. His seven hundred poems have been translated into some fifty languages.

Péter, Gábor (1906-1993)

Communist functionary. Commander of the State Security Authorities during the Rákosi regim. Police lieutenant-general. Original profession, tailor.

Pope, Alexander (1688-1744)

English poet, critic. Representative of English classicism, best known for his poems "An Essay on Criticism," "An Essay on Man."

Radnóti, Miklós (1909-1944)

Poet, translator. Belonged to the circle of the *Nyugat*. Famous for his classicist poems. He was taken to forced labor camp in 1940. Wrote his masterpieces in the Serbian Lager Heidenau. He was taken on a long march to Austria, executed by one of the guards. His poems written into his note-book were found in the pocket of his windcheater when exhumated.

Rákosi, Mátyás (1892-1971)

Commissar of the Kun regime, 1919. Prime Minister of Hungary, 1952-1953. General Secretary of the Hungarian Communist Party, 1945-1956.

Saint Stephen (967-1038)

King of Hungary (1001-1038). Accepted Christianity as state religion, defeated pagan chieftains. Architect of Hungarian state, legislator laid down the foundations of medieval Hungary. Canonized in 1083.

Schlegel, Friedrich (1772-1829)
German esthete, philosopher. Leading theoretician of early German romanticism.

Schnitzler, Arthur (1862-1931)
Austrian writer, novelist, playwright.

Schöpflin, Aladár (1872-1950)
Writer, critic, literary historian, literary translator. Contributed to the *Nyugat*. Co-editor of the *Magyar Csillag* with Gyula Illyés till 1944.

Seton-Watson, Robert William (1879-1951)
English publicist, historian. From 1907 published essays describing nationality relations within the Austro-Hungarian Monarchy in English journals, and expressed sympathy towards Slav national ambitions.

Sombart, Werner (1863-1941)
German economist, university teacher in Berlin, co-editor of the *Archiv für Socialwissenschaft und Socialpolitik.*

Spinoza (Baruch) (1632-1677)
Dutch philosopher, wrote in Latin. Anathematized by the Jewish community because of his philosophic views in 1656. Noted work: *Ethics.*

Spiró, György (1946)
Writer, poet, literary historian.

Szabó, Dezső (1879-1945)
Writer, publicist. His novel, *Az elsodort falu* [The Swept away Village], a tableau of the disintegrating society of years of the World War I of Hungary, became an inspiration for the populist movement.

Széchenyi, István, Count (1791-1860)
Hungarian aristocrat, liberal politician, political writer, social philosopher. Minister of Transport and Public Works in the Batthyány Government in 1848, was called by Lajos Kossuth "the greatest Hungarian," entered the mental asylum in

Döbling (September 1848) at the news that the Habsburgs revoked the April Laws, committed suicide (1860).

Szekfű, Gyula (1883-1955)

Historian. Between the two world wars was a leading figure in historiography, and chief architect of the social philosophy of the mid-war period. A political loyalist, turned against Nazi influence instrumental in saying public opinion. After World War II ambassador to Moscow. From 1953 member of Parliament.

Szilágyi, Géza (1875-1958)

Poet, writer, journalist, lawyer.

Szomory, Dezső (1869-1944)

Writer, playwright.

Taine, Hippolyte Adolphe (1828-1893)

French philosopher, historian, literary- and art historian. Important representative of positivism, initiated the application of scientific methods into study of art.

Tábor, Béla (1907-1992)

Writer, literary translator, philosopher.

Tersánszky Józsi, Jenő (1888-1969)

Writer. Colleague of the *Nyugat*. Humorist, author of detective stories under pen-name. Was ousted from literary life between 1951-1954.

Tisza, István, Count (1861-1918)

Twice prime minister (1903-1905, 1913-1917). Son of Kálmán Tisza. After his first term as prime minister amended the house rules in order to curb the obstructionism of the parliamentary opposition. In his second term in office as prime minister opposed joining the war but consented to the dispatch of an ultimatum to Serbia. Murdered by soldiers after the end of war.

Turgot, Anne-Robert-Jacques, Baron (1727-1781)

French economist, statesman, writer, influential economist, contributor to the Encyclopedia.

Ungváry, Rudolf (1936)
Writer, critic. Participated in the 1956 Revolution, was interned.

Váradi, Antal (1854-1923)
Dramatist, lyric poet. Editor of the literary weekly, *Ország-Világ*.

Vázsonyi, Vilmos (1868-1926)
Minister of Justice (in 1917 and 1918). Law graduate. In 1894 founded the Democratic Circle. From 1901 Democratic Party MP. Obtained nationwide fame in connection with court cases involving trade union leaders and corruption. Drafted an electoral law. Exiled after the revolutions. From 1920 conducted legitimist politics and from 1924 organized the Democratic Bloc. Identified himself a Jewish, fought against discriminating legislation.

Veres, Péter (1897-1970)
Writer. One of the founders of the March Front in 1937. One of the leaders of the National Peasants' Party from 1939. Was taken to forced labor camp during World War II. President of the National Peasants' Party, 1945-1949. Member of the movement of the "populist" group of writers.

Vészi József (1858-1940)
Writer, journalist, editor. Founded the *Budapesti Napló* in 1896, which was the most important forum of Ady until the foundation of the *Nyugat*. Lived in Berlin between 1906-1911. Editor-in-chief of the *Pester Lloyd* since 1913.

Vörösmary, Mihály (1800-1885)
Poet and playwright. Law graduate. Wrote lyric and epic poems. Editor of literary magazines. Author of the second national anthem of Hungary, the *Szózat* [Proclamation]. In 1848 elected political representative. Went into hiding for fear of repression. Pardoned in 1850. Translator of Shakespeare.

Weber, Max (1864-1920)

German economist, social historian, known for his systematic approach to Western Civilization. Challenged Marxist theory of determinism. His method combined theoretical and historical methods.

Zilahy, Lajos (1891-1974)

Writer, editor. Turned against Nazism, propagated social reforms. Emigrated to the United States in 1947.

Zsolt, Béla (1898-1949)

Poet, novelist, playwright, survived forced-labor service in Russia and deportation to Nazi Germany. The story of his capture and escape is the basis of his novel *Nine Luggages* (1946).

Zweig, Arnold (1887-1968)

German-Jewish writer. Emigrated after Hitler's takeover.

Selected Bibliography

"A zsidókérdés Magyarországon" [The Jewish Question in Hungary]. In *Zsidókérdés, asszimiláció, antiszemitizmus*, ed. Péter Hanák. Budapest, 1984.

Abram, Léon. *The Jewish Question: A Marxist Interpretation*, 177. New York: Pathfinder Press, 1970.

Ágoston, Péter. "A zsidók útja" [The Path of Jews]. *A Jövő kérdései*, vol. 2. Nagyvárad: A Nagyváradi Társadalomtudományi Társaság, 1917.

Aldermann, Geoffrey. "English Jews or Jews of the English Persuasion? Reflections on the Emancipation of Anglo-Jewry." In *Paths of Emancipation—Jews, States, and Citizenship,* eds., Pierre Birnbaum and Ira Katznelson, 138-139. 1995.

Améry, Jean. *At the Mind's Limits: Contemplations by a Survivor on Auschwitz and Its Realities*, 95. Bloomington: Indiana University Press, 1980.

Arendt, Hannah. *Antisemitism—Part One of The Origins of Totalitarianism*, 11. New York: Harcourt, Brace and World, 1966.

————. *The Jew as Pariah:Jewish Identity and Politics in the Modern Age*, ed. and intr. Ron H. Feldman. New York: Grove Press, 1978.

Aschheim, Steven E. "'The Jew Within': The Myth of 'Judaization' in Germany." In *Culture and Catastrophe*, 45-69. New York: New York University Press, 1996.

Avineri, Shlomo. *Hegel's View of Jewish Emancipation*, 145-151. Jewish Social Studies, 1963.

Bányai, László, Anikó Kis. "Történelmi bevezetés" [Historical Introduction]. In *Hét évtized a hazai zsidóság életében*, eds. Ferenc L. Lendvai, et al., vol. 1. 104. Budapest, 1990.

Barta, István, ed. *Kossuth Lajos ifjúkori iratai* [Papers of the Young Lajos Kossuth], 179-180. Budapest, 1966.

Bauer, Bruno. *Die Judenfrage*, 224-245. Braunschweig, 1843.

————. *Einundzwanzig Bogen aus der Schweiz,* vol. 1. 71. Zürich, 1843.

Bauer, Yehuda. "On the Applicability of Definitions—Anti-Semitism in Present-Day Europe." In *Anti-Semitism in Post-Totalitarian Europe*, 57. Prague: Franz Kafka Publishers,1993.

Bein, Alex. *Die Judenfrage: Biogaphie eines Weltproblems,* vol. 2. Stuttgart: Deutsche Verlags-Anstalt, 1980.

Bernard, Paul P. *The Limits of Enlightenment: Joseph II and the Law*. Urbana: University of Illinois Press, 1979.

Bibó, István. "Zsidókérdés Magyarországon 1944 után" [Jewish Question in Hungary after 1944]. In *Válogatott tanulmányok*, 722-754. Budapest, 1986.

————. "Levél Borbándi Gyulához" [Letter to Gyula Borbándi]. In *Válogatott tanulmányok*. Budapest: Magvető, 1986.

————. "Zsidókérdés Magyarországon 1944 után" [The Jewish Question in Hungary after 1944]. In *Válogatott tanulmányok*, ed. Tibor Huszár, 701. Budapest: Magvető, 1986.

Botstein, Leon. *Essays zur Rolle der Juden in der deutschen und österreichischen Kultur, 1848-1938*. Wien: Böhlau, 1991.

Braham, Randolph L. *Anti-semitism and the Treatment of the Holocaust in Post-Communist Eastern Europe*. East European Monographs, no. 405. New York, N.Y., Boulder, Colo.: Rosenthal Institute for Holocaust Studies Graduate Center/The City University of New York; Social Science Monographs; distributed by Columbia University Press, 1994.

————. *The Politics of Genocide : the Holocaust in Hungary*. New York: Columbia University Press, 1981.

————. "The Uniqueness of the Holocaust in Hungary." In *The Holocaust in Hungary: Forty Years Later*, eds. Randolph L. Braham, Bela Vago, 186. New York, 1985.

Büchler, Sándor, *A zsidók története Budapesten a legrégibb időktől 1867-ig* [The History of the Jews in Budapest From Time

Immemorial to 1867]. Publications of the Hungarian Israelite Literary Society, vol. 14. 332-335. Budapest: Franklin Nyomda, 1901.

Cohen, Asher. "The Attitude of the Intelligentsia in Hungary toward Jewish Assimilation between the Two World Wars." In *Jewish Assimilation in Modern Times*, ed. Béla Vago, 57-74. Boulder (Co.), 1981

Conan, Eric and Henry Rousso. *Vichy : un passé qui ne passe pas*. Collection Folio/histoire. no. 71. Paris: Gallimard, 1996.

Deák, István. "The Danger of Anti-Semitism in Hungary." In *The Danger of Anti-Semitism in Central and Eastern Europe in the Wake of 1989-1990*, ed. Yehuda Bauer, 53-61. Jerusalem: The Vidal Sassoon International Center for the Study of Antisemitism, 1991.

Deutscher, Isaac. *The Non-Jewish Jew*, 38. Oxford, 1968.

Dohm, Christian W. v. and Franz Reuss. *Über die bürgerliche Verbesserung der Juden: 2 Teile in 1 Bd*, 200, 376, 105. Hildesheim, New York: Olms, 1973.

Don, Yehuda, Georg Magos. "A magyarországi zsidóság demográfiai fejlődése" [Demographic Development of the Hungarian Jews] *Történelmi Szemle*, no. 3 (1985): 436-469.

Endelman, Todd M. "The Englishness of Jewish Modernity in England." In *Toward Modernity: The European Jewish Model*, ed., Jacob Katz, 225-226. New Jersey, 1987.

————. *Comparing Jewish Societies*. Ann Arbor: University of Michigan Press: The Comparative Studies in Society and History Book Series, 1997.

————. *Radical Assimilation in English Jewish History, 1656-1945: The Modern Jewish Experience*. Bloomington: Indiana University Press, 1990.

Eötvös, József, Baron. *Költemények—tanulmányok* [Poems and Essays], 104. Budapest, 1934.

Erb, Rainer-Werner Bergman. *Die Nachseite der Judenemanzipation—der Widerstand gegen die Integration der Juden: Deutschland 1780-1860*. 51 Berlin: Metropol.

Ettinger, Shmuel. "The Modern Period." In *History of the Jewish People,* ed., Ben Sasson, 730-733. Cambridge, Mass, 1986.

Fackenheim, Emil E. *Encounters Between Judaism and Modern Philosophy*, 89-90. New York, 1980.

————. *To Mend the World-Foundations of Post-Holocaust Jewish Thought*, 103-147. Bloomington, 1989.

Fein, Helen. "Insiders, Outsiders, and Border-Crossers: Conceptions of Modern Jewry in Marx, Durkheim, Simmel and Weber." In *Antisemitismus und jüdische Geschichte: Studien zu Ehren von Herbert A. Strauss,* ed., Rainer Erb and Michael Schmidt, 479-494. Berlin: Wissentschaftlicher Autorenverlag,1987.

Fejtő, François. *Hongrois et Juifs—histoire millénaire d'un couple singulier*. Paris: Balland, 1997.

Fischer, Rolf. *Entwicklungsstufen des Antisemitismus in Ungarn 1867-1939. Die Zerstörung der magyarisch-jüdischen Symbiose*, 144. Munich, 1988.

————. "Anti-Semitism in Hungary 1882-1932." In *Hosteges of Modernization—Studies on Modern Anti-Semitism 1870-1933/39*, ed. H.A. Strauss, 863-893. 1993.

Friedländer, Saul. *Probing the Limits of Representation: Nazism and the "Final Solution."* Cambridge, Mass.: Harvard University Press, 1992.

Fritsch, T. and Werner Sombart. *Die Juden im Handel und das Geheimnis ihres Erfolges: Ausgleich eine Antwort und Ergänzung zu Sombarts Buch 'Die Juden und das Wirtschaftsleben,* 2, durchgesehene Aufl. Ed., 308. Steglitz: P. Hobbing, 1913.

Funkenstein, Amos. "The Political Theory of Jewish Emancipation." In *Deutsche Aufklärung und Judenemanzipation,* ed., Walter Grab, 17. Tel Aviv, 1980.

————. "Collective Memory and Historical Consciousness" *History and Memory*, vol. 1, no. 1 (1989): 5-26.

Gabel, Joseph. *Réflexions sur l'avenir des juifs—racism et aliénation*. Paris: Méridiens Klinksieck, 1987.

Gay, Peter. *Freud, Jews, and other Germans : Masters and Victims in Modernist Culture*, xx, 289. New York: Oxford University Press, 1978.

Gellner, Ernest. "Nationalism and Politics in Eastern Europe" *New Left Review* 9/10 (1991).

Gerő, András. "Liberálisok, antiszemiták és zsidók a modern Magyarország megszületésekor" [Liberals, Anti-Semites, and Jews at the Birth of Modern Hungary]. In *Zsidóság, identitás, történelem*, eds. Mária M. Kovács, Yitzhak M. Kashti, Ferenc Erős, 19. Budapest, 1992.

Gilman, Sander L. *Jewish Self-Hatred: Anti-Semitism and the Hidden Language of the Jews*, 127. Baltimore: Johns Hopkins University Press, 1986.

———. *The Jew's Body*, 128. New York: Routledge, 1991.

Girard, Patrick. *Les Juifs de France de 1789-1860: de l'émancipation et l'égalité.* Diaspora, 139. Paris: Calmann-Lévy, 1976.

Gogolák, Ludwig. *Zum Problem der Assimilation in Ungarn in der Zeit von 1790-1918*. Südostdeutsches Archiv, 1966.

Gonda, László. *A zsidóság Magyarországon, 1526-1945* [The Jews in Hungary 1526-1945], 115-116. Budapest, 1992.

Hanák, Péter. "A lezáratlan per" [The Undetermined Trial]. In *Zsidókérdés, asszimiláció, antiszemitizmus*, ed. Péter Hanák, 374. Budapest, 1984.

———. "Polgárosodás és asszimiláció Magyarországon a XIX. században" [Bourgeois Development and Assimilation in Hungary in the Nineteenth Century]. *Történelmi Szemle*, no. 4 (1974): 520.

Handler, Andrew. *An Early Blueprint for Zionism: Győző Istóczy's Anti-Semitism*. East European Monographs, vol. 261. New York: Columbia University Press, 1989.

———. *The Holocaust in Hungary : an Anthology of Jewish Response*, xiii, 162. Judaic Studies series. Alabama: University of Alabama Press, 1982.

Hertzberg, Arthur. *The French Enlightenment and the Jews: The Origins of Modern Anti-Semitism,* 360. New York: Schocken Books, 1970.

Herzl, Theodor. *Tagebücher*, vol. 1. 8. Berlin, 1922

Hockenos, Paul. *Free to Hate : the Rise of the Right in Post-Communist Eastern Europe*, x, 332. New York: Routledge, 1993.

Horkheimer, Max and Theodor W. Adorno. *Dialectic of Enlightenment*. New York, 1995.

Horváth, János. *Aranytól Adyig* [From Arany to Ady], 45. Budapest, 1921.

Ignotus. "Faj és művészet" [Race and Art]. *Nyugat* 22, no. 11 (1 June 1929): 717.

————. *Kísérletek* [Experiments], 82-83. Budapest, 1910.

Illyés, Gyula. "Zsidó sebek és bűnök. Pap Károly könyve" [Jewish Wounds—Jewish Vices. On Pap Károly's Book]. *Nyugat* 2 (1935): 37-41.

Istóczy, Győző. *Országgyűlési beszédei, indítványai és törvény-javaslatai* [Speeches in Parliament, Motions, and Bills], 16-18. Budapest, 1904.

Janos, Andrew C. *The Politics of Backwardness in Hungary 1825-1945*. Princeton: Princeton University Press, 1982.

Jászi, Oscar. *The Dissolution of the Hapsburg Monarchy*. Chicago: Chicago University Press, 1929.

Juhász, Gyula. "A magyar szellemi élet és a zsidókérdés a második világháború előtt és alatt (1938-1944)" [Intellectual Life in Hungary and the Jewish Question Before and During the Second World War, 1938-1944]. In *A háború és Magyarország 1938-1945*, 78-79. Budapest, 1986.

Kahler, Erich. "Forms and Features of Anti-Judaism." In *The Dynamics of Emancipation*, ed., N. L. Glatzer, 44. Boston, 1965.

Karády, Viktor-István Kemény. *Les juifs dans la structure des classes en Hongrie. Essai sur les antécédents historique des crises d'antisémitisme au XX. siècle.* Actes de la Recherche Sociale, 25-59. (1978. 21).

Karády, Viktor. "Asszimiláció és társadalmi krízis—A magyar-zsidó társadalomtörténet konjunkturális vizsgálatához" [Assimilation and Social Crisis—To the Conjuctural Analysis of the Hungarian-Jewish Social History]. *Világosság* 34, no. 3 (1993): 33-60.

———. "Zsidó identitás és asszimiláció Magyarországon" [Jewish Identity and Assimilation in Hungary]. *Mozgó Világ* 9 (1989): 47.

Katz, Jacob. "Anti-Semitism Through the Ages." In *The Persisting Question—Sociological and Social Contexts of Modern Antisemitism,* ed., Helen Fein, 52-53. Berlin-New York: Walter de Gruyter, 1987.

———. "The Term 'Jewish Emancipation': Its Origin and Historical Impact." In *Studies in Nineteenth-Century Jewish Intellectual History*, ed., Alexander Altmann, 5. Cambridge, Mass., 1964.

———. *A Social Background of Jewish Emancipation, 1770-1870*, Ch. XIII. Cambridge, Mass: Harvard University Press.

———. *Exclusiveness and Tolerance: Studies in Jewish-Gentile Relations in Medieval and Modern Times*. Westport, Conn: Greenwood Press, 1980.

———. *From Prejudice to Destruction. Anti-Semitism, 1700-1933*, 236. Cambridge, Mass., 1980.

———. *Jewish Emancipation and Self-Emancipation,* 1st ed., 12. Philadelphia: Jewish Publication Society, 1986.

———. *Zur Assimilation und Emanzipation der Juden: Ausgewählte Schriften*, 5. Darmstadt: Wissenschaftliche Buchgesellschaft.

———. "The Uniqeness of Hungarian Jewry." *Forum* 27, no. 2 (Jerusalem, 1977): 45-53.

Kaufmann, David. *A zsidók utolsó kiűzetése Bécsből* [The Jews' Last Ousting from Vienna]. Budapest, 1888.

Király, Béla K. and László Veszprémy. *Trianon and East Central Europe : Antecedents and Repercussions*. War and Society in East Central Europe, vol. 32. Boulder, Colo., Highland Lakes,

N.J., New York: Social Science Monographs; Atlantic Research and Publications, distributed by Columbia University Press, 1995.

———, Peter Pastor, and Ivan Sanders. *Essays on World War I: Total War and Peacemaking, a Case Study on Trianon*. East European Monographs 105. New York: Social Science Monographs Brooklyn College Press, distributed by Columbia University Press, 1982.

Klebelsberg, Kuno. *Ungarische Kulturpolitik nach dem Kriege*. Ungarische bibliothek... ; 2. reihe 5. Berlin, Leipzig: W. de Gruyter, 1925.

Komlós, Aladár. "Zsidó költők a magyar irodalomban" [Jewish Poets in Hungarian Literature]. In *Magyar-zsidó szellemtörténet a reformkortól a holocaustig. Bevezetés a magyar-zsidó irodalomba*, ed. János Kőbányai, 159. Budapest: Múlt és Jövő, 1997.

Kovács, András. "Az asszimilációs dilemma" [The Dilemma of Assimilation]. *Világosság*, nos. 8-9 (1988): 608.

Kracauer, Siegfried. "Ahasver oder das Rätsel der Zeit." In *Schriften (Aussenseiter)*, 148-149. Frankfurt am Main: Suhrkamp, 1975.

Kubinszky, Judit. *Politikai antiszemitizmus Magyarországon* [Political Anti-Semitism in Hungary]. Budapest, 1976.

Macaulay, Thomas B., ed.; G. T. Bettany. *Essays Historical and Literary from the 'Edinburgh Review' by Lord Macaulay*, 171-172.

Marx, Karl. "Zur Judenfrage." In *Deutsch-Französische Jahrbücher* (1844).

———. *Early Writings*, trans., and ed., Tom Bottomore, 40. New York: McGraw Hill, 1964.

Mayer, Hans. "Von Ahasver zu Shylock." In *Aussenseiter*, 312. Frankfurt am Main: Suhrkamp, 1975.

McCagg, William O., Jr. "The Jewish Position in Interwar Central Europe: A Structural Study of Jewry at Vienna, Budapest, and Prague." In *A Social and Economic History of Central*

European Jewry, Yehoda Don, Victor Karady, eds., 64. New Brunswick, 1990.

————. "Jewish Conversion in Hungary in Modern Times." In *Jewish Apostasy in the Modern World*, T.M. Endelman, ed., 142-165. New York/London: Holmes and Meier, 1987.

————. *Jewish Nobles and Geniuses in Modern Hungary*, 254. East European Monographs, vol. 3. Boulder Colo.: East European Quarterly; distributed by Columbia University Press, New York, 1972.

Mendelsohn, Ezra. "Jewish Reactions to Antisemitism in Interwar East Central Europe." In *Living with Antisemitism, Jewish Responses*, Jehuda Reinharz, ed., 269-313. London, 1987.

————. "Trianon Hungary, Jews and Politics." In *Hostages of Modernization*, H.A. Strauss, ed., 893-916. Berlin-New York: de Gruyter, 1993.

Meyer, Michael A. *The Origins of the Modern Jew: Jewish Identity and European Culture in Germany, 1749-1824*. Detroit: Wayne State University Press, Wayne Books; WB32, 1979.

Misrahi, Robert. *Marx et la question juive*. Paris: Gallimard, Collection Idées 259, 1972.

Momigliano, Arnaldo. "Le judaisme comme 'religion-paria' chez Max Weber." In *Mélanges Léon Poliakov*, ed., M. Olender, 201-207. Brussels: Complexe, 1981.

Móricz, Zsigmond. "A zsidó lélek az irodalomban" [The Jewish Spirit in Literature]. *Nyugat* 2 (1930): 421-422. Schöpflin, (1930), #9626.

Mosse, George L. *The Crisis of German Ideology; Intellectual Origins of the Third Reich*, 1st ed., vi, 373. New York: Grosset & Dunlap, 1964.

————. "Between Bildung and Respectability." In *The Jewish Responses to German Culture—From Enlightenment to The Second World War*, eds., Jehuda Reinharz-Walter Schatzberg, 1-17. Hanover-London: Clark University, 1985

Németh, László. "Két nép: Hozzászólás Pap Károly, Zsidó sebek és bűnök című könyvéhez" [Two Peoples: Remarks on Károly

Pap's Book, Jewish Wounds and Vices]. In *Életmű szilánkokban, I*, 418-429. 1989.

————. "Kisebbségben" [In Minority]. In *Twilight*, 628. Budapest: Magvető and Szépirodalmi, 1977.

Nipperdey, Thomas and Reinhart Rürup. "Semitismus und der sekuläre Begriff des Juden als Vorassetzungen." In *Geschichliche Grundbegriffen,* Werner O. C. Brunner and Reinhart Koselleck, eds., 131. Stuttgart, 1972.

Nordau, Max. *Bericht über den Zustand der Juden auf der ganzen Erde*. London: Gedruckt bei Wertheimer Lea & Co., 1900.

Patai, Raphael. *The Jews of Hungary: History, Culture, Psychology*, 730, 495. Detroit: Wayne State University Press, 1996.

Poliakov, Leon et al. *The History of Anti-Semitism*, vol. 3. 155. New York: Vanguard Press, 1975.

Poliakov, Leon. *The Aryan Myth: A History of Racist and Nationalist Ideas in Europe*. New York: New American Library, 1977.

Postma, Koos Andre. *Changing Prejudice in Hungary: a Study on the Collapse of State Socialism and its Impact on Prejudice against Gypsies and Jews*, Nugi; 652/664. 200. Amsterdam: Thesis Publishers, 1996.

Pulzer, Peter. *Jews and the German State—The Political History of a Minority, 1848-1933,* ed., David Sorkin. Oxford: Blackwell, Jewish Society and Culture,1992.

Ragussis, Michael. *Figures of Conversion: The "Jewish Question" & English National Identity*, vi, 340. Durham: Duke Unversity Press, Post-Contemporary Interventions, 1995.

Ranki, Vera. *The Politics of Inclusion and Exclusion. Jews and Nationalism in Hungary*. Sydney: Allen and Unwin, 1999.

Reich-Ranicki, Marcel. *Über Ruhestörer. Juden in der deutschen Literatur*, 21, 23. München, 1993.

Rose, Paul Lawrence. *German Question/Jewish Question—Revolutionary Antisemitism from Kant to Wagner*, 109. Princeton, New Jersey, 1990.

Rürup, Reinhart. "The European Revolution of 1848 and Jewish Emancipation." In *Revolution and Evolution—1848 in German-Jewish History*, E. Mosse et al., eds., 44. Tübingen: J. Mohr, 1981.

Schöpflin, George. "Jewish Assimilation in Hungary: A Moot Point." In *Jewish Assimilation in Modern Times*, B. Vago, ed., 75-89. Boulder, Colorado: Vestwiew Press, 1981.

Seton-Watson, Hugh. "Government Policies Towards the Jews in Pre-Communist Eastern Europe." In *The Nazi Holocaust—Historical Articles on the Destruction of European Jews*, Michael R Marrus, ed., 423-424. Westport: Mekler, 1989.

Silber, Michael K., ed. *Jews in the Hungarian Economy: Studies Dedicated to Moshe Carmilly-Weinberger on his Eightieth Birthday*. Jerusalem: Megnes Press, Hebrew University 1992.

Silberner, Edmund. *Kommunisten zur Judenfrage: zur Geschichte von Theorie und Praxis des Kommunismus.* Opladen: Westdeutscher Verlag, 1983.

Sombart, Werner and S. Z. Klausner. *The Jews and Modern Capitalism*, 30. Social Science Classics Series. New Brusnwick: Transaction Books, 1982.

Sombart, Werner. *A New Social Philosophy*, 177-179. New York, 1969.

————. *Deutscher Sozialismus*. 1934.

Sorkin, David J. *The Transformation of German Jewry, 1780-1840*, 15. New York: Oxford University Press, Studies in Jewish History, 1987.

Széchenyi, István. "A' Kelet népe" [The People of the East] (1841). In *A mai Széchenyi*, selected by Gyula Szekfű, 255. Budapest, 1935.

Szekfű, Gyula. *Három nemzedék és ami utána következik (1920)* [Three Generations and the Follow-up], 335-336, 360. Budapest, 1935.

Szinai, Miklós. "A magyar szélsőjobboldal történelmi helyéhez" [To the Historical Place of the Hungarian Extreme Right]. In *Jobboldali radikalizmusok tegnap és ma*, István Feitl, ed., 114-122. Budapest: Napvilág, 1998.

Talmon, Jacob. *The Unique and the Universal*, 151-152. New York: G. Braziller, 1966.

Toury, Jacob. "The Jewish Question: A Semantic Approach." *Leo Baeck Institute Yearbook* XI (London, 1966): 85-107.

Vágó, Béla, ed. *Jewish Assimilation in Modern Times* Boulder, Colorado, 1981.

Vardy, Steven B. "The Impact of Trianon: Hungary and the Hungarian Mind: The Nature of Inter-war Irredentism." *Hungarian Studies Review* 10, nos. 1/2 (1983): 21-42.

Venetiáner, Lajos. *A magyar zsidóság története—különös tekintettel gazdasági és művelődési fejlődésére a XIX. században* [The History of the Hungarian Jewry: With Special Emphasis on Its Economic and Cultural Development in the 19th Century], 34. Budapest: Könyvértékesítő Vállalat, 1986.

Volkov, Shulamit. "Juden und Judentum im Zeitalter der Emanzipation." In *Die Juden in der Europäische Geschichte,* ed. W. Beck, 86-108. München: Beck, 1992.

Weber, Max. *Economy and Society: an Outline of Interpretive Sociology*. New York: Bechminster Press, 1968.

————. *Gesammelte Aufsätze zur Religionssoziologie*. Tübingen: J.C.B. Mohr, 1988.

Weiner, Max, ed. *Abraham Geiger and Liberal Judaism: The Challenge of the Nineteenth Century*, 74. Philadelphia, 1962.

Yerushalmi, Yoseph H. *Zakhor—Jewish History and Jewish Memory*, 84. Seattle and London: University of Washington Press, 1982.

Yirmiahu, Yovel. *Dark Riddle: Hegel, Nietzsche, and the Jews*. Pennsylvania: Penn State University, 1998.

Name Index

Aczél, György 198, 201, 291
Adorno, Theodore 237, 293
Ady, Endre 75, 72, 85, 113-118, 157, 167, 169-170, 172, 174-175, 180, 185-186, 189, 192, 214, 248-250, 299-301, 307
Ágoston, Péter 91, 213
Améry, Jean 235, 237-238
Andrássy, Gyula 104-105
Angyal, Dávid 126
Apponyi, Albert 98-99
Arany, János 75, 153, 255
Arendt, Hannah 32, 34, 160, 232, 304
Árpád, Prince 190, 221
Aschner, Lipót 135
Avarffy, Elek 106
Avineri, Shlomo 36
Babits, Mihály 75-76, 78-79, 113-114, 116-117, 172-181, 185
Bach, Alexander 283
Bajcsy-Zsilinszky, Endre 108-109
Balassa, Ármin 103
Balázs, Béla 85
Ballagi, Ernő 106
Bangha, Béla 95, 105
Bartók, Béla 79, 85
Bartucz, Lajos 222
Bauer, Bruno 12, 20-22, 26, 29
Bauer, Yehuda 282
Békessy, Imre 190
Benedek, István 284
Benedek, Marcell 73
Berlin, Isaiah 28
Bethlen, István, Count 94, 127, 129-132, 134-136, 221
Bibó, István 83-84, 172-173, 176, 197,
Bíró, Lajos 102, 109
Blau, Lajos 214
Blum, Leon 126
Bodor, Béla 282
Börne, Ludwig 292
Braham, Randolph 6, 272
Braun, Róbert 80
Broch, Hermann 231
Bródy, Sándor 110, 176-177, 215-216, 222, 241
Buber, Martin 162
Budaváry, László 130
Celan, Paul 236, 238
Chamberlain, Houston S. 240, 297, 301
Cholnoky, László 173-174
Chorin family 214

Chorin, Ferenc, Baron 135
Cicero, Marcus Tullius 152
Clermont-Tonnerre, Stanislas de 13, 47
Cohen, Asher 219
Coleridge, Samuel Taylor 35
Csécsy, Imre 188
Csepeli, György 198
Csiky, Gergely 69
Csokonai Vitéz, Mihály 64
Csoóri, Sándor 282-283, 286-288, 306-308
Csurka, István 280-281, 289, 294-295
Dánér, Béla 130
Darányi, Kálmán 136
de Pinto, Isaac 305
Déry, Tibor 116, 201-202, 251, 253
Deutsch family 214
Deutscher, Isaac 17
Dickens, Charles 239
Diderot, Denis 304-305
Diner-Dénes, Rudolf 125-126
Disraeli, Benjamin 239
Dohm, Christian Wilhelm von 10-12, 31, 41, 210
Domokos, V. György 279
Dreyfus, Alfred 179, 310
Dubnow, Simon M. 15-17
Eckhardt, Tibor 134
Eötvös, József, Baron 66-67
Eötvös, Károly 69
Erdei, Ferenc 199-200
Erdélyi, József 187, 195
Esterházy, Péter 287
Ettinger, Shmuel 16
Falk, Miksa 109
Faludy, György 196
Fangler, Béla 122
Farkas, Gyula 75, 114
Fehér, Ferenc 83
Féja, Géza 79, 168, 195, 222, 306
Fejtő, Ferenc 186, 224, 287
Fényes, Adolf 158
Fenyő, Miksa 75, 104-105, 158, 187
Feuerbach, Ludwig 20, 22
Fichte, Johann Gottlieb 24, 39, 47
Fischer, Árpád 161
Fischer, József 100
Fischer, Rolf 98, 269
Földessy, Gyula 186-188
Frantz, Constantin 18
Franz Joseph I, Emperor 158
Freud, Sigmund 180, 232-234, 287
Freytag, Gustav 267
Frobenius, Leo 297
Fülep, Lajos 135
Funkenstein, Amos 238
Füst, Milán 85
Gábor, Gyula 130
Gárdonyi, Géza 215
Gáti, Charles 285
Geiger, Abraham, Rabbi 45, 47
Gellner, Ernest 45
Gelléri, Andor Endre 194

Gellért, Oszkár 241
Gerő, András 71
Gilman, Sander L. 239
Glagau, Otto 26
Gobineau, Joseph Arthur, Count 19, 301
Goethe, Johann Wolfgang von 40, 239
Goldberger, Arnold 135
Gombos, Gyula 84
Gömbös, Gyula 103, 127, 134-136, 148-149, 199
Grace, Divine 39
Gratz, Gusztáv 91-92
Grègoire, Henri-Baptiste, Abbot 28
Gutzkow, Karl (Ferdinand) 39
Habsburg family 156, 158, 283
Halász, Gábor 152
Hanák, Péter 65, 70, 282-283
Handler, Andrew 261
Harden, Maximilian 121, 231
Harrington, James 239
Hatvany, Lajos, Baron 75, 109-110, 113-114, 156, 178, 185-193, 196, 202-203, 223, 242, 249-250, 253, 264, 293, 302
Háy, Gyula 202
Hazai, Samu, Baron 214, 292
Heckenast, Gusztáv 62
Hegel, Georg Wilhelm Friedrich 20-22, 24
Hegyi, Gyula 287
Heine, Heinrich 19, 40, 46, 48, 170, 305
Heller, Ágnes 251-254
Heltai, Jenő 74, 214
Herder, Johann Gottfried 20, 22, 27, 64, 232, 304
Hermann, Lipót 156
Herzl, Theodor 70-71
Hevesi, Ferenc 161
Hevesi, Sándor 149, 159
Hevesi, Simon 161
Hitler, Adolf 198, 240, 287
Hoffmann, Sándor 159
Holbach, Paul-Henri Dietrich d', Baron 304-305
Horkheimer, Max 293
Horthy, Miklós 6, 94, 187, 194, 219, 282-283, 307
Horváth, Árpád 157
Horváth, János 75, 151, 167-169, 177, 213
Horváth, Márton 196, 198
Humboldt, Wilhelm von 31
Ibsen, Henrik (Johan) 159
Ignotus (Hugo Veigelsberg) 75, 77-78, 107, 110, 113-115, 118, 168-169, 171, 174, 177, 186, 190-192, 214-215, 222-224, 242, 248-250, 253, 301-302, 306-307
Ignotus, Pál 80, 204
Illyés, Gyula 79-82, 85, 135, 179, 188, 195-196, 201-202, 213, 217-218, 220-223, 255, 303
Istóczy, Győző 69-70, 267-268, 300

Iványi-Grünwald, Béla 157
Janos, Andrew C. 270
Jászai, Mari 158
Jászi-Jakobovits see Jászi
Jászi, Oscar see Jászi, Oszkár
Jászi, Oszkár 96, 109, 123-124, 186-188, 202, 253, 272, 275
Jókai, Mór 158
Joó, Tibor 221
Joseph II 11, 16
Jósika, Miklós, Baron 267
Judt, Tony 196
Juhász, Gyula 180
Juhász, Vilmos 194-195
Kádár, János 194, 201-202, 291, 303
Kahler, Erich 11
Kant, Immanuel 13, 20-21
Karácsony, Sándor 198
Karady, Victor see Karády
Karády, Viktor 62, 64, 68-69, 110, 127-128, 212, 262
Kardos, László 302
Kardos, Pál 302
Károlyi, Gyula, Count 91, 103
Károlyi, Mihály, Count 96, 134, 186
Katz, Jacob 12, 14, 23, 33, 46, 209, 273
Kecskeméti, György 121-122
Kecskeméti, Lipót 101
Kellér, Andor 156-158
Kende, Péter 295
Kéri, Pál 109
Kertész, Ákos 286
Keszi, Imre 225-226
Kiss, József 67, 69, 215, 241
Klebelsberg, Kunó 76-77, 126, 131-133, 191, 298
Kóbor, Tamás 106
Kodály, Zoltán 79
Kodolányi, János 153, 198
Kohner, Adolf, Baron 135
Komlós, Aladár (Álmos Korál) 65, 74, 80, 100, 107-108, 114-115, 117, 170, 215-216, 223-226, 302
Komor, András 214-217, 254-255
Könczöl, Csaba 201
Koppel, Reich 135
Kornfeld, Mór, Baron 135
Koselleck, Reinhart 27
Kossuth, Lajos 66
Kosztolányi, Dezső 114, 173, 175-176, 178, 180
Kovács, Alajos 123
Kovács, András 74, 84
Kovács, Imre 196, 202
Kovács, Mária M. 128
Kozma, Andor 72
Kozma, Miklós 135
Kracauer, Siegfried 19
Krúdy, Gyula 170
Kun, Béla 96-97, 135
Kunfi, Zsigmond 109, 186
Kuthy, Lajos 267
Lackó, Miklós 80
Landerer, Lajos 62
Lányi, András 285

Léderer, Sándor 104
Lendvai, István 76, 96, 107-108, 177
Lengyel, László 285
Lengyel, Menyhért 241
Lengyel, Péter 251
Leopold I 34
Lessing, Theodor 13, 121
Lesznai, Anna 111
Levi, Primo 237-238
Liszt, Ferenc 158, 160
Liszt, Franz see Liszt, Ferenc
Locke, John 12
Lombroso, Cesare 240
Louis Philippe 21
Lőw, Immánuel 103, 135
Lueger, Karl 97
Lukács, György 195-196, 198
Macaulay, Thomas Babbington 36-37
Maeterlink, Maurice 159
Mahler, Raphael 16
Maimonídes, Móses 255
Makai, Emil 176
Makkai, János 97, 115
Marczali, Henrik 126
Maria Theresa 34, 42
Marx, Karl 20-21, 24-26, 29, 36, 39, 42, 44, 96, 292
Maurras, Charles 305
Mayer, Hans 18
McCagg, William O., Jr. 65, 112
Méhely, Lajos 77
Mendelssohn, Moses 10, 13, 29, 49
Mészöly, Miklós 308
Mezei, Ernő 71
Mezei, Mór 109
Michnik, Adam 280
Mikszáth, Kálmán 68-69, 71, 77, 244
Milotay, István 93-95, 105, 150-152
Mirabeau, Honorè Gabriel de Riqueti, Count 13
Molnár, Ferenc 107, 156-157, 241, 251-253
Montesquieu, Charles-Louis de Secondat, Baron 47
Móricz, Zsigmond 65, 75, 79, 82-83, 115, 216-217, 225, 242-245, 249, 251, 255, 263
Moritz, Karl Philip 238-239
Mosse, George 266-267
Mosse, Werner 267
Munkácsy, Mihály 76
Nagy, Endre 175-176
Nagy, Ignác 267
Napoleon, Bonaparte 36
Négyesi, László 82
Németh, László 108, 119, 168, 185-188, 190-193, 195-203, 213, 220-223, 225-226, 240-250, 252, 284, 288, 298-307, 309
Nordau, Max 2, 210
Osvát, Ernő 75, 258, 293
Pálmai, Lajos 91-92 103
Pap, Károly 216, 218
Patai, József 245, 271
Patai, Raphael 240, 261

Paulus, H. E. G. 12
Péter, Gábor 285
Pethő, Sándor 221
Petőfi, Sándor 76
Pfordten, von der 14
Pirenne, Henri 41
Pope, Alexander 71
Radnóti, Miklós 194, 224-225
Ragussis, Michael 239
Rákosi, Jenő 172
Rákosi, Mátyás 196, 283, 285, 289
Rathenau, Walther 231
Reich-Ranicki, Marcel 231
Révai, József 195-196, 198
Révész, Sándor 198, 201, 278, 281
Réz, Pál 158
Rothermere, Harold Sidney Harmsworth, Wiscount 150
Rousseau, Jean-Jacques 64, 232
Rupert, Rezső 122
Sándor, Pál 130, 132
Sárközi, György 199-200
Sartre, Jean Paul 234
Schedel (Ferenc Toldy) 247
Scheiber, Sándor 170
Schlegel, Friedrich 304
Schleiermacher, Friedrich 24, 28
Schnitzler, Arthur 231
Schönfeld, József 101
Schöpflin, Aladár 75, 79-82, 149, 216-217
Schöpflin, George 218
Sértő, Kálmán 187-189
Seton-Watson, Hugh 264
Sinka, István 195
Sombart, Werner 38-39, 43-44, 212, 240, 297
Sorkin, David 30-31
Spinoza, Baruch (Benedictus) de 46, 49, 279
Spiró, György 283, 292
St. Augustine 43
St. Stephen, King of Hungary 63, 71, 221
Standeisky, Éva 202
Stocker, Adolf 267
Szabó, Dezső 77, 110, 115-116, 187, 198, 271-272, 297, 300, 306
Szabó, Lőrinc 152, 177
Szabó, Miklós 111
Szabolcsi, Lajos 103, 106, 134
Szálasi, Ferenc 198
Szász, Zoltán 118, 149
Széchenyi, István, Count 62-64, 66-67
Székely, Ferenc 103
Szekfű, Gyula 76, 119, 126, 168, 192, 220-221, 299-301, 305-307
Szende, Pál 123, 125
Szép, Ernő 107, 169-171, 177-181, 241
Szerb, Antal 152-153, 194
Szilágyi, Géza 74, 85, 214

Szimonyi-Szemedam, Sándor 98
Szomory, Dezső 75, 147, 149-162, 241
Tábor, Béla 216
Taine, Hippolyte Adolphe 213
Talmon, Jacob 41
Teleki, Pál 92-93, 99, 129-130, 191
Tersánszky Józsi, Jenő 79
Tharaud brothers 96
Tisza, István, Count 96, 125, 299-300
Toland, John 32
Tóth, Árpád 180
Tucholsky, Kurt 231-233
Turgot, Anne-Robert-Jacques, Baron 61
Ungváry, Rudolf 288
Vadász, Lipót 109
Vajda, Péter 32
Vámbéry, Rusztem 107
Váradi, Antal 72
Vázsonyi, Vilmos 133-134, 214
Venetiáner, Lajos 43
Veres, Péter 194, 224
Vida, Jenő, Baron 135
Voltaire, Francois-Marie Arouet 28, 46, 304-305
Vörösmarty, Mihály 68, 247
Wagner, Richard 19, 157-158, 297
Weber, Max 38, 41, 44, 213
Weininger, Otto 121
Weiss family 214
Weisz, Mór (Szomory Dezső) 160
Wertheimer, Max 34
Wilde, Oscar 153
William, Emperor 287
Wolf, Lucien 28, 131-132
Wolff, Károly 92
Yirmiahu, Yovel 49
Zákány, Gyula 92, 129
Zilahy, Lajos 75, 79, 136
Zola, Èmile 179
Zsilinszky, Endre 76
Zsolt, Béla 119-121, 135, 190, 195-196, 216
Zunz, Leopold 48
Zweig, Arnold 231

Geographical Index

Africa 14
Alsace-Lorraine 10
America 171, 303
Arad 91, 103
Auschwitz 235-237
Austria 2, 187, 267, 277, 287
Austrian Monarchy 265
Austro-Hungarian Monarchy 1, 4, 70, 71, 186, 264-265, 270-271, 277, 292, 298
Austro-Hungary 134
Baranya county 81
Beregszász 152
Berlin 75, 77
Bihar county 175-176
Breslau 45
Buda 42, 188
Budapest 3, 6-7, 80-81, 96-97, 110, 113, 124, 148, 176, 180, 186, 188, 196, 262, 267
Canary Islands 171
Carpathian Basin 126, 294, 296, 298
Carpathians 29
Chemnitz 70
Czechoslovakia 3, 278
Danube 97, 266
Debrecen 180, 302
Dresden 70
Dual Monarchy see Austro-Hungarian Monarchy
Elbe River 266
England 15, 23, 31-32, 35-36, 150, 174
Eperjes 100
Euphrates 159
Europe 1-2, 4-5, 10, 14, 17, 32, 34, 38, 40-41, 43, 147, 194, 210-211, 233, 243, 259, 261-262, 267, 270, 272, 277-278, 280-281, 289-290, 292-294, 297-298, 303-305, 309-310
France 19, 31, 150, 218, 236, 287, 304, 310
Frankfurt 40
Galicia 76, 97, 152, 298
Geneva 132-133
Germany 3-4, 18, 20, 27-29, 31, 35, 118, 135, 209, 236, 265-266, 287, 304
Grand Canal 171
Great Hungarian Plain 82
Hajdúszoboszló 180
Holland 38
Hungary 2-6, 42, 45, 63-65, 67, 71, 80, 82, 84, 91, 93-96, 98-99, 101-102, 110, 113-115, 117, 120-126, 129-134, 147,

149-151, 168, 174, 180, 186-187, 190, 193-194, 197, 199, 209, 211-212, 216, 218-220, 224-225, 245-248, 252, 259-260, 262, 264-265, 267-269, 271-272, 277-284, 288-289, 291, 294-295, 297-302, 305-306, 308-310
Israel 38, 45, 97, 160
Italy 134
Jerusalem 12, 45, 49, 96
Kassa 100-101
Kisvárda 152
Lemberg 152
Leopold Town see Lipótváros
Lipótváros 124, 196, 253
London 131, 171, 186
Mátészalka 152
Mohács 307
Monaco 155
Munkács 99, 101
Nagymajtény 307
Nagyvárad 101, 175
New York 6, 259
Nuremberg 210, 211, 284
Oberlin, Ohio 186
Ottoman Empire 14, 41
Palestine 36, 92, 268, 296
Paris 36, 91, 98, 125, 153, 157-159, 161, 171, 175, 236
Pest 42, 62, 81, 102, 153, 190
Poland 219
Pozsony/Bratislava 42, 101
Romania 3, 147, 278, 295
Rome 179
Russia 4, 42
Sianki 152
Slovakia 42, 82, 100, 295
Soviet Union 200
Szabadka 176, 180
Szeged 68, 103, 180
Székesfehérvár 161
Szekszárd 180
Tarnopol 96, 152
Tel Aviv 259
Temesvár 101
Tiszaeszlár 68-69, 187
Tolna county 81-82
Transdanubia 80
Transylvania 100
Trianon 75, 78, 82, 91-92, 96-97, 102, 107-108, 110-114, 118-122, 126, 128, 132-134, 190-191, 212, 216, 240-241, 245-246, 273, 277, 294-295, 297, 300, 305-307
Turkey 38
Újvidék 161
Ungvár 99, 101, 152
United States 174
Várad 175-176
Venice 170
Vichy 211
Vienna 3, 34, 65, 71, 93, 96, 124, 186, 190
Világos 307
Warsaw 36
Yalta 295
Yugoslavia 3, 278, 295

Volumes Published in "Atlantic Studies on Society in Change"

No. 1 *Tolerance and Movements of Religious Dissent in Eastern Europe.* Edited by Béla K. Király. 1977.

No. 2 *The Habsburg Empire in World War I.* Edited by R. A. Kann. 1978

No. 3 *The Mutual Effects of the Islamic and Judeo-Christian Worlds: The East European Pattern.* Edited by A. Ascher, T. Halasi-Kun, B. K. Király. 1979.

No. 4 *Before Watergate: Problems of Corruption in American Society.* Edited by A. S. Eisenstadt, A. Hoogenboom, H. L. Trefousse. 1979.

No. 5 *East Central European Perceptions of Early America.* Edited by B. K. Király and G. Barány. 1977.

No. 6 *The Hungarian Revolution of 1956 in Retrospect.* Edited by B. K. Király and Paul Jonas. 1978.

No. 7 *Brooklyn U.S.A.: Fourth Largest City in America.* Edited by Rita S. Miller. 1979.

No. 8 *Prime Minister Gyula Andrássy's Influence on Habsburg Foreign Policy.* János Decsy. 1979.

No. 9 *The Great Impeacher: A Political Biography of James M. Ashley.* Robert F. Horowitz. 1979.

No. 10 Vol. I* *Special Topics and Generalizations on the Eighteenth and Nineteenth Century.* Edited by Béla K. Király and Gunther E. Rothenberg. 1979.

No. 11 Vol. II *East Central European Society and War in the Pre-Revolutionary 18th Century.* Edited by Gunther E. Rothenberg, Béla K. Király, and Peter F. Sugar. 1982.

* Vols. no. I through XXXVI refer to the series *War and Society in East Central Europe*

No. 12 Vol. III	*From Hunyadi to Rákóczi: War and Society in Late Medieval and Early Modern Hungary.* Edited by János M. Bak and Béla K. Király. 1982.
No. 13 Vol. IV	*East Central European Society and War in the Era of Revolutions: 1775-1856.* Edited by B. K. Király. 1984.
No. 14 Vol. V	*Essays on World War I: Origins and Prisoners of War.* Edited by Samuel R. Williamson, Jr. and Peter Pastor. 1983.
No. 15 Vol. VI	*Essays on World War I: Total War and Peacemaking, A Case Study on Trianon.* Edited by B. K. Király, Peter Pastor, and Ivan Sanders. 1982.
No. 16 Vol. VII	*Army, Aristocracy, Monarchy: War, Society and Government in Austria, 1618-1780.* Edited by Thomas M. Barker. 1982.
No. 17 Vol. VIII	*The First Serbian Uprising 1804-1813.* Edited by Wayne S. Vucinich. 1982.
No. 18 Vol. IX	*Czechoslovak Policy and the Hungarian Minority 1945-1948.* Kálmán Janics. Edited by Stephen Borsody. 1982.
No. 19 Vol. X	*At the Brink of War and Peace: The Tito-Stalin Split in a Historic Perspective.* Edited by Wayne S. Vucinich. 1982.
No. 20	*Inflation Through the Ages: Economic, Social, Psychological and Historical Aspects.* Edited by Edward Marcus and Nathan Schmuckler. 1981.
No. 21	*Germany and America: Essays on Problems of International Relations and Immigration.* Edited by Hans L. Trefousse. 1980.
No. 22	*Brooklyn College: The First Half Century.* Murray M. Horowitz. 1981.
No. 23	*A New Deal for the World: Eleanor Roosevelt and American Foreign Policy.* Jason Berger. 1981.
No. 24	*The Legacy of Jewish Migration: 1881 and Its Impact.* Edited by David Berger. 1982.
No. 25	*The Road to Bellapais: Cypriot Exodus to Northern Cyprus.* Pierre Oberling. 1982.
No. 26	*New Hungarian Peasants: An East Central European Experience with Collectivization.* Edited by Marida Hollos and Béla C. Maday. 1983.

No. 27 *Germans in America: Aspects of German-American Relations in the Nineteenth Century.* Edited by Allen McCormick. 1983.

No. 28 *A Question of Empire: Leopold I and the War of Spanish Succession, 1701-1705.* Linda and Marsha Frey. 1983.

No. 29 *The Beginning of Cyrillic Printing — Cracow, 1491. From the Orthodox Past in Poland.* Szczepan K. Zimmer. Edited by Ludwik Krzyżanowski and Irene Nagurski. 1983.

No. 29a *A Grand Ecole for the Grand Corps: The Recruitment and Training of the French Administration.* Thomas R. Osborne. 1983.

No. 30 Vol. XI *The First War between Socialist States: The Hungarian Revolution of 1956 and Its Impact.* Edited by Béla K. Király, Barbara Lotze, Nandor Dreisziger. 1984.

No. 31 Vol. XII *The Effects of World War I, The Uprooted: Hungarian Refugees and Their Impact on Hungary's Domestic Politics.* István Mócsy. 1983.

No. 32 Vol. XIII *The Effects of World War I: The Class War after the Great War: The Rise Of Communist Parties in East Central Europe, 1918-1921.* Edited by Ivo Banac. 1983.

No. 33 Vol. XIV *The Crucial Decade: East Central European Society and National Defense, 1859-1870.* Edited by Béla K. Király. 1984.

No. 35 Vol. XVI *Effects of World War I: War Communism in Hungary, 1919.* György Péteri. 1984.

No. 36 Vol. XVII *Insurrections, Wars, and the Eastern Crisis in the 1870s.* Edited by B. K. Király and Gale Stokes. 1985.

No. 37 Vol. XVIII *East Central European Society and the Balkan Wars, 1912-1913.* Edited by B. K. Király and Dimitrije Djordjevic. 1986.

No. 38 Vol. XIX *East Central European Society in World War I.* Edited by B. K. Király and N. F. Dreisziger, Assistant Editor Albert A. Nofi. 1985.

No. 39 Vol. XX *Revolutions and Interventions in Hungary and Its Neighbor States, 1918-1919.* Edited by Peter Pastor. 1988.

No. 41 *Essays on East Central European Society and War, 1740-*

Vol. XXII *1920.* Edited by Stephen Fischer-Galati and Béla K. Király. 1988.

No. 42
Vol. XXIII *East Central European Maritime Commerce and Naval Policies, 1789-1913.* Edited by Apostolos E. Vacalopoulos, Constantinos D. Svolopoulos, and Béla K. Király. 1988.

No. 43
Vol. XXIV *Selections, Social Origins, Education and Training of East Central European Officers Corps.* Edited by Béla K. Király and Walter Scott Dillard. 1988.

No. 44
Vol. XXV *East Central European War Leaders: Civilian and Military.* Edited by Béla K. Király and Albert Nofi. 1988.

No. 46 *Germany's International Monetary Policy and the European Monetary System.* Hugo Kaufmann. 1985.

No. 47 *Iran Since the Revolution—Internal Dynamics, Regional Conflicts and the Superpowers.* Edited by Barry M. Rosen. 1985.

No. 48
Vol. XXVII *The Press During the Hungarian Revolution of 1848-1849.* Domokos Kosáry. 1986.

No. 49 *The Spanish Inquisition and the Inquisitional Mind.* Edited by Angel Alcala. 1987.

No. 50 *Catholics, the State and the European Radical Right, 1919-1945.* Edited by Richard Wolff and Jorg K. Hoensch. 1987.

No. 51
Vol.XXVIII *The Boer War and Military Reforms.* Jay Stone and Erwin A. Schmidl. 1987.

No. 52 *Baron Joseph Eötvös, A Literary Biography.* Steven B. Várdy. 1987.

No. 53 *Towards the Renaissance of Puerto Rican Studies: Ethnic and Area Studies in University Education.* Maria Sanchez and Antonio M. Stevens. 1987.

No. 54 *The Brazilian Diamonds in Contracts, Contraband and Capital.* Harry Bernstein. 1987.

No. 55 *Christians, Jews and Other Worlds: Patterns of Conflict and Accommodation.* Edited by Philip F. Gallagher. 1988.

No. 56
Vol. XXVI *The Fall of the Medieval Kingdom of Hungary: Mohács 1526, Buda 1541.* Géza Perjés. 1989.

No. 57 *The Lord Mayor of Lisbon: The Portuguese Tribune of the People and His 24 Guilds.* Harry Bernstein. 1989.

No. 58 *Hungarian Statesmen of Destiny: 1860-1960.* Edited by Paul Bödy. 1989.

No. 59 *For China: The Memoirs of T. G. Li, Former Major General in the Chinese Nationalist Army.* T. G. Li. Written in collaboration with Roman Rome. 1989.

No. 60 *Politics in Hungary: For A Democratic Alternative.* János Kis, with an Introduction by Timothy Garton Ash. 1989.

No. 61 *Hungarian Worker's Councils in 1956.* Edited by Bill Lomax. 1990.

No. 62 *Essays on the Structure and Reform of Centrally Planned Economic Systems.* Paul Jonas. A joint publication with Corvina Kiadó, Budapest. 1990.

No. 63 *Kossuth as a Journalist in England.* Éva H. Haraszti. A joint publication with Akadémiai Kiadó, Budapest. 1990.

No. 64 *From Padua to the Trianon, 1918-1920.* Mária Ormos. A joint publication with Akadémiai Kiadó, Budapest. 1990.

No. 65 *Towns in Medieval Hungary.* Edited by László Gerevich. A joint publication with Akadémiai Kiadó, Budapest. 1990.

No. 66 *The Nationalities Problem in Transylvania, 1867-1940.* Sándor Bíró. 1992.

No. 67 *Hungarian Exiles and the Romanian National Movement, 1849-1867.* Béla Borsi-Kálmán. 1991.

No. 68 *The Hungarian Minority's Situation in Ceausescu's Romania.* Edited by Rudolf Joó and Andrew Ludanyi. 1994.

No. 69 *Democracy, Revolution, Self-Determination. Selected Writings.* István Bibó. Edited by Károly Nagy. 1991.

No. 70 *Trianon and the Protection of Minorities.* József Galántai. A joint publication with Corvina Kiadó, Budapest. 1991.

No. 71 *King Saint Stephen of Hungary.* György Györffy. 1994.

No. 72 *Dynasty, Politics and Culture. Selected Essays.* Robert A. Kann. Edited by Stanley B. Winters. 1991.

No. 73 *Jadwiga of Anjou and the Rise of East Central Europe.* Oscar Halecki. Edited by Thaddeus V. Gromada. A joint publication with the Polish Institute of Arts and Sciences of America, New York. 1991.

No. 74 Vol. XXIX *Hungarian Economy and Society during World War Two.* Edited by György Lengyel. 1993.

No. 75 *The Life of a Communist Revolutionary, Béla Kun.* György Borsányi. 1993.

No. 76 *Yugoslavia: The Process of Disintegration.* Laslo Sekelj. 1993.

No. 77 Vol. XXX *Wartime American Plans for a New Hungary. Documents from the U.S. Department of State, 1942-1944.* Edited by Ignác Romsics. 1992.

No. 78 Vol. XXXI *Planning for War against Russia and Serbia. Austro-Hungarian and German Military Strategies, 1871-1914.* Graydon A. Tunstall, Jr. 1993.

No. 79 *American Effects on Hungarian Imagination and Political Thought, 1559-1848.* Géza Závodszky. 1995.

No. 80 Vol. XXXII *Trianon and East Central Europe: Antecedents and Repercussions.* Edited by Béla K. Király and László Veszprémy. 1995.

No. 81 *Hungarians and Their Neighbors in Modern Times, 1867-1950.* Edited by Ferenc Glatz. 1995.

No. 82 *István Bethlen: A Great Conservative Statesman of Hungary, 1874-1946.* Ignác Romsics. 1995.

No. 83 Vol. XXXIII *20th Century Hungary and the Great Powers.* Edited by Ignác Romsics. 1995.

No. 84 *Lawful Revolution in Hungary, 1989-1994.* Edited by Béla K. Király. András Bozóki Associate Editor. 1995.

No. 85 *The Demography of Contemporary Hungarian Society.* Edited by Pál Péter Tóth and Emil Valkovics. 1996.

No. 86 *Budapest, A History from Its Beginnings to 1996.* Edited By András Gerő and János Poór. 1996.

No. 87 *The Dominant Ideas of the Nineteenth Century and Their Impact on the State.* Volume 1. *Diagnosis.* József Eötvös. Translated, edited, annotated and indexed with an introductory essay by D. Mervyn Jones. 1997.

No. 88 *The Dominant Ideas of the Nineteenth Century and Their Impact on the State.* Volume 2. *Remedy.* József Eötvös.

Translated, edited, annotated and indexed with an introductory essay by D. Mervyn Jones. 1997.

No. 89 *The Social History of the Hungarian Intelligentsia in the "Long Nineteenth Century," 1825-1914.* János Mazsu. 1997.

No. 90 Vol.XXXIV *Pax Britannica: Wartime Foreign Office Documents Regarding Plans for a Post Bellum East Central Europe.* Edited by András D. Bán. 1997.

No. 91 *National Identity in Contemporary Hungary.* György Csepeli. 1997.

No. 92 *The Hungarian Parliament, 1867-1918: A Mirage of Power.* András Gerő. 1997.

No. 93 Vol. XXXV *The Hungarian Revolution and War of Independence, 1848-1849. A Military History.* Edited by Gábor Bona. 1999.

No. 94 *Academia and State Socialism: Essays on the Political History of Academic Life in Post-1945 Hungary and East Central Europe.* György Péteri. 1998.

No. 95 Vol.XXXVI *Through the Prism of the Habsburg Monarchy: Hungary in American Diplomacy and Public Opinion during World War I.* Tibor Glant. 1998.

No. 96 *Appeal of Sovereignity in Hungary, Austria and Russia.* Edited by Csaba Gombár, Elemér Hankiss, László Lengyel and Györgyi Várnai. 1997.

No. 97 *Geopolitics in the Danube Region. Hungarian Reconciliation Efforts, 1848-1998.* Edited by Ignác Romsics and Béla K. Király. 1998.

No. 98 *Hungarian Agrarian Society from the Emancipation of Serfs (1848) to Re-privatization of Land (1998).* Edited by Péter Gunst. 1999.

No. 99 *"The Jewish Question" in Europe. The Case of Hungary.* Tamás Ungvári. 2000.

No. 100 *Soviet Military Intervention in Hungary, 1956.* Edited by Jenő Györkei and Miklós Horváth. 1999.

No. 101 *Jewish Budapest.* Edited by Géza Komoróczy. 1999.